Authors
& Artists
for Young
Adults

ISSN 1040-5682

Authors
& Artists
for Young
Adults

VOLUME 50

THOMSON

Detroit • New York • San Diego   Maine • London • Munich

Authors and Artists for Young Adults, Volume 50

Project Editor
Scot Peacock

Editorial
Katy Balcer, Sara Constantakis, Anna Marie Dahn, Alana Joli Foster, Natalie Fulkerson, Arlene M. Johnson, Michelle Kazensky, Julie Keppen, Joshua Kondek, Thomas McMahon, Jenai A. Mynatt, Judith L. Pyko, Mary Ruby, Lemma Shomali, Susan Strickland, Maikue Vang, Tracey Watson, Denay L. Wilding, Thomas Wiloch, Emiene Shija Wright

Research
Michelle Campbell, Sarah Genik, Tamara C. Nott, Tracie Richardson

Permissions
Debra Freitas, Lori Hines

Imaging and Multimedia
Dean Dauphinais, Robert Duncan, Leitha Etheridge-Sims, Mary K. Grimes, Lezlie Light, Michael Logusz, Dan Newell, David G. Oblender, Christine O'Bryan, Kelly A. Quin, Luke Rademacher

Composition and Electronic Capture
Carolyn A. Roney

Manufacturing
Stacy L. Melson

LIBRARY OF CONGRESS CATALOG CARD NUMBER 89-641100

ISBN 0-7876-5179-6
ISSN 1040-5682

Contents

Introduction

Authors and Artists for Young Adults is a reference series designed to serve the needs of middle school, junior high, and high school students interested in creative artists. Originally inspired by the need to bridge the gap between Gale's *Something about the Author*, created for children, and *Contemporary Authors*, intended for older students and adults, *Authors and Artists for Young Adults* has been expanded to cover not only an international scope of authors, but also a wide variety of other artists.

Although the emphasis of the series remains on the writer for young adults, we recognize that these readers have diverse interests covering a wide range of reading levels. The series therefore contains not only those creative artists who are of high interest to young adults, including cartoonists, photographers, music composers, bestselling authors of adult novels, media directors, producers, and performers, but also literary and artistic figures studied in academic curricula, such as influential novelists, playwrights, poets, and painters. The goal of *Authors and Artists for Young Adults* is to present this great diversity of creative artists in a format that is entertaining, informative, and understandable to the young adult reader.

Entry Format

Each volume of *Authors and Artists for Young Adults* will furnish in-depth coverage of twenty to twenty-five authors and artists. The typical entry consists of:

—A detailed biographical section that includes date of birth, marriage, children, education, and addresses.

—A comprehensive bibliography or filmography including publishers, producers, and years.

—Adaptations into other media forms.

—Works in progress.

—A distinctive essay featuring comments on an artist's life, career, artistic intentions, world views, and controversies.

—References for further reading.

—Extensive illustrations, photographs, movie stills, cartoons, book covers, and other relevant visual material.

A cumulative index to featured authors and artists appears in each volume.

Compilation Methods

The editors of *Authors and Artists for Young Adults* make every effort to secure information directly from the authors and artists through personal correspondence and interviews. Sketches on living authors and artists are sent to the biographee for review prior to publication. Any sketches not personally reviewed by biographees or their representatives are marked with an asterisk (*).

Highlights of Forthcoming Volumes

Among the authors and artists planned for future volumes are:

Edward Albee	Hal Foster	Celia Rees
Woody Allen	Paul Gaugin	Louise Rennison
Bill Amend	Oscar Hammerstein	Richard Rodgers
Jean Auel	Hughes Brothers	Christina Rossetti
Natalie Babbitt	Chuck Jones	Dante Gabriel Rossetti
Margaret Bourke-White	Iain Lawrence	Alex Sanchez
Robert Burns	Julius Lester	Cynthia Leitich Smith
Ramsey Campbell	David Lubar	Sonya Sones
Tom Clancy	Alan Moore	Theodore Sturgeon
Max Allan Collins	Isamu Noguchi	Jill Thompson
Steve Ditko	Joyce Carol Oates	David Weber
Jeffrey Eugenides	Tillie Olsen	Lori Aurelia Williams

Contact the Editor

We encourage our readers to examine the entire *AAYA* series. Please write and tell us if we can make *AAYA* even more helpful to you. Give your comments and suggestions to the editor:

BY MAIL: The Editor, *Authors and Artists for Young Adults,* 27500 Drake Rd., Farmington Hills, MI 48331-3535.

BY TELEPHONE: (800) 347-GALE

Authors and Artists for Young Adults
Product Advisory Board

The editors of *Authors and Artists for Young Adults* are dedicated to maintaining a high standard of excellence by publishing comprehensive, accurate, and highly readable entries on writers, artists, and filmmakers of interest to middle and high school students. In addition to the quality of the entries, the editors take pride in the graphic design of the series, which is intended to be orderly yet appealing, allowing readers to utilize the pages of *AAYA* easily, enjoyably, and with efficiency. Despite the success of the *AAYA* print series, we are mindful that the vitality of a literary reference product is dependent on its ability to serve its readers over time. As critical attitudes about literature, art, and media constantly evolve, so do the reference needs of students and teachers. To be certain that we continue to keep pace with the expectations of our readers, the editors of *AAYA* listen carefully to their comments regarding the value, utility, and quality of the series. Librarians, who have firsthand knowledge of the needs of library users, are a valuable resource for us. The *Authors and Artists for Young Adults* Product Advisory Board, made up of school, public, and academic librarians, is a forum to promote focused feedback about *AAYA* on a regular basis, as well as to help steer our coverage of new authors and artists. The advisory board includes the following individuals, whom the editors wish to thank for sharing their expertise:

Acknowledgments

Grateful acknowledgment is made to the following publishers, authors, and artists for their kind permission to reproduce copyrighted material.

ARNOLD ADOFF. Adoff, Arnold, photograph by Virginia Hamilton Adoff. Reproduced by permission of Arnold Adoff./ Weaver, Michael, illustrator. From an illustration in *The Basket Counts,* by Arnold Adoff. Simon & Schuster Books for Young Readers, 2000. Illustrations © 2000 by Michael Weaver. Reproduced by permission of Simon & Schuster Books for Young Readers, an imprint of Simon & Schuster Children's Publishing Division./ Gutierrez, Rudy, illustrator. From an illustration in *Malcolm X,* by Arnold Adoff. HarperTrophy, 2000. Illustrations © 2000 by Rudy Gutierrez. Reproduced by permission of HarperCollins Publishers and the illustrator.

EDWARD BOND. Bond, Edward, photograph by Jerry Bauer. © Jerry Bauer. Reproduced by permission./ Detail from "Legacy: Bearing Witness," by Judy Chicago, photograph by Donald Woodman. From a cover of *Coffee,* by Edward Bond. Methuen Drama, 1995. Painting © 1992 Judy Chicago. Photograph © Donald Woodman. Reproduced by permission of The Random House Group Limited./ Clough, Stewart, illustrator. From a cover of *At the Inland Sea,* by Edward Bond. Methuen Drama, 1997. Reproduced by permission of The Random House Group Limited./ From a theatre production of Edward Bond's *Lear,* with Bob Peck as Lear, RSC, 1982, photograph. Donald Cooper, London. Reproduced by permission./ From a theatre production of *Saved,* by Edward Bond, Royal Court, London, December, 1984, photograph. © Donald Cooper/Photostage. Reproduced by permission.

MEG CABOT. Cabot, Meg, photograph. Reproduced by permission./ (Left to right) Anne Hathaway as Amelia Mignonette Thermopolis-Renaldi, Julie Andrews as Clarisse Renaldi, and Hector Elizondo as Joe, scene from the 2001 film *The Princess Diaries,* directed by Garry Marshall, based on the novel by Meg Cabot, movie still. The Kobal Collection/Batzdorff, Ron. Reproduced by permission.

MARK CRILLEY. Crilley, Mark, photograph by Mary Moylan. Reproduced by permission of Mark Crilley./ Crilley, Mark, illustrator. From an illustration in *Akiko and the Great Wall of Trudd,* by Mark Crilley. Delacorte Press, 2001. Copyright © 2001 by Mark Crilley. Reproduced by permission of Random House Children's Books, a division of Random House, Inc./ Crilley, Mark, illustrator. From an illustration in *Akiko in the Castle of Alia Rellapor,* by Mark Crilley. Delacorte Press, 2001. Copyright © 2001 by Mark Crilley. Used by permission of Random House Children's Books, a division of Random House, Inc./ Crilley, Mark, illustrator. From an illustration in *Akiko in the Sprubly Islands,* by Mark Crilley. Delacorte Press, 2000. Copyright © 2000 by Mark Crilley. Reproduced by permission of Random House Children's Books, a division of Random House, Inc./ Crilley, Mark, illustrator. From an illustration in *Akiko on the Planet Smoo,* by Mark Crilley. Delacorte Press, 2000. Copyright © 2000 by Mark Crilley. Reproduced by permission of Random House Children's Books, a division of Random House, Inc.

TERRY DAVIS. Matthew Modine as Louden Swain, scene from the 1985 film *Vision Quest,* directed by Harold Becker, based on a novel by Terry Davis, movie still. The Kobal Collection/Warner Bros. Reproduced by permission./ Cover of *Vision Quest: A Wrestling Story,* by Terry Davis. Eastern Washington University Press, 2002. Reproduced by permission.

JAMES DICKEY. Dickey, James, photograph. AP/Wide World Photos. Reproduced by permission./ Burt Reynolds as Lewis Medlock, scene from the 1972 film *Deliverance,* directed by John Boorman, based on the novel by James Dickey, movie still. The Kobal Collection/Warner Bros. Reproduced by permission./ Cover of *Buckdancer's Choice: Poems by James Dickey,* by James Dickey. Wesleyan University Press, 1965. Cover design by Joyce Kachergis. Copyright © 1964, 1965 by James Dickey. Reproduced by permission./ Taylor, Grant/Tony Stone Images, photographer. From a jacket cover of *Deliverance,* by James Dickey. Delta Trade Paperback, 1994. Cover design by Susan Koski Zucker. Copyright © 1970 by James Dickey. Reproduced by permission of Dell Publishing, a division of Random House, Inc./ Morrow, Mark, photographer. From a cover of *The James Dickey Reader,* by James Dickey, edited by Henry Hart. Touchstone Books, 1999. Copyright © 1999 by The Estate of James L. Dickey III. Reproduced by permission of the photographer.

ALEX FLINN. Flinn, Alex, photograph by J. Cabrera. Courtesy of Alex Flinn. Reproduced by permission.

KEN FOLLETT. Follett, Ken, photograph. AP/Wide World Photos. Reproduced by permission./ Bristol, Horace, photographer. From a jacket of *Jackdaws,* by Ken Follett. Dutton, 2001. Corbis. Photograph reproduced by permission of Corbis./ Donald Sutherland (left) as Faber, with Stephen Phillips, scene from the 1981 film *Eye of the Needle,* directed by Richard Marquand, based on a novel by Ken Follett, movie still. The Kobal Collection/United Artists. Reproduced by permission.

HEATHER GRAHAM. Cover of *Dark Stranger,* by Heather Graham. Harlequin, 1988. Copyright © 1988 by Heather Graham Pozzessere. Reproduced by permission./ Cover of *Night of the Blackbird,* by Heather Graham. Mira Books, 2001. Copyright © 2001 by Heather Graham Pozzessere. Reproduced by permission./ Jacket cover of *A Pirate's Pleasure,* by Heather Graham. Dell Books, 1989. Copyright © 1989 by Heather Graham Pozzessere. Reproduced by permission of Dell Publishing, a division of Random House, Inc./ Jacket cover of *Lord of the Wolves,* by Heather Graham. Dell Books, 1993. Copyright © 1993 by Heather Graham Pozzessere. Reproduced by permission of Dell Publishing, a division of Random House, Inc.

JENNY HOLZER. Holzer, Jenny, photograph. © Richard Schulman/Corbis. Reproduced by permission./ Holzer, Jenny, photographer. From a photograph in *Jenny Holzer,* by David Joselit and others. Phaidon Press, 1998. © 1998 Phaidon Press Limited. Photograph © 1998 by Jenny Holzer. Reproduced by permission of Artists Rights Society./ "What Scares Peasants Is . . ." from *Inflammatory Essays,* by Jenny Holzer, 1979-82. Poster. Copyright © 2003 Jenny Holzer/Artists Rights Society (ARS), New York. Copyright Tate Gallery, London/Art Resource. Tate Gallery, London, Great Britain. Reproduced by permission of ARS and Art Resource.

JOE R. LANSDALE. Lansdale, Joe, photograph. Courtesy of Joe Lansdale. Reproduced by permission./ Marquee for The Orbit Drive-In Theatre, featuring the name of author Joe R. Lansdale, photograph. Design by Meaty Design; courtesy of Lou Bank. Reproduced by permission./ Estevez, Herman, photographer. From a cover of *The Bottoms,* by Joe R. Lansdale. Warner Books, 2001. Cover design by Diane Luger. Copyright © 2000 by Joe R. Lansdale. Reproduced by permission./ Osycska, Dan, illustrator. From a cover of *Cold in July,* by Joe R. Lansdale. Warner Books, 1995. Cover design by Matt Tepper. Copyright © 1989 by Joe R. Lansdale. Reproduced by permission./ Pirtle, Woody, illustrator. From a cover of *Bad Chili,* by Joe R. Lansdale. Warner Books, 1998. Cover design and illustration by Woody Pirtle/Pentagram. Copyright © 1997 by Joe R. Lansdale. Reproduced by permission./ Tepper, Matt, illustrator. From a cover of *Mucho Mojo,* by Joe R. Lansdale. Warner, 1994. Copyright 1994 by Joe R. Lansdale. Reproduced by permission./ From the cover of *The Drive-In: A Double Feature Omnibus,* by Joe Lansdale. Carroll & Graf, 1997. Copyright © 1988 by Joe R. Lansdale. All rights reserved. Reproduced by permission.

JULIET MARILLIER. Marillier, Juliet, photograph by Design Images, Perth, Australia. Courtesy of Juliet Marillier. Reproduced by permission./ Palencar, John Jude, illustrator. From a cover of *Son of the Shadows,* by Juliet Marillier. Tor Books, 2002. Copyright © 2001 by Juliet Marillier. Reproduced by permission./ Palencar, John Jude, illustrator. From a jacket of *Child of the Prophecy,* by Juliet Marillier. Tor Books, 2002. Copyright © 2002 by Juliet Marillier. Reproduced by permission.

YUKIO MISHIMA. Yukio Mishima, in Tokyo, Japan, 1966, photograph by Nobuyuki Masaki. AP/Wide World Photos. Reproduced by permission./ Yukio Mishima, reviewing a parade of Tate No Kai (Shield Society), photograph. © Bettmann/Corbis. Reproduced by permission.

FARLEY MOWAT. Mowat, Farley, 1985, photograph. AP/Wide World Photos. Reproduced by permission./ Frankenberg, Robert, illustrator. From an illustration in *Owls in the Family,* by Farley Mowat. Yearling Books, 1996. Cover art copyright © 1981 by Bantam Books. Reproduced by permission./ Charles Martin Smith as Farley Mowat/Tyler, scene from the 1983 film *Never Cry Wolf,* directed by Carroll Ballard, based on the novel by Farley Mowat, movie still. The Kobal Collection/Walt Disney. Reproduced by permission./ (Left to right) Charles Martin Smith, Farley Mowat and Allan Lewis, standing together on the set of the film *Never Cry Wolf,* photograph. The Kobal Collection/Walt Disney. Reproduced by permission./ Geer, Charles, illustrator. From a jacket cover of *Lost in the Barrens,* by Farley Mowat. Bantam, 1982. Cover art © 1982 by Bantam Books. Reproduced by permission of Bantam Books, a division of Random House, Inc./ McDonald, Mary Ann, photographer. From a cover of *Never Cry Wolf,* by Farley Mowat. Little, Brown and Company, 2001. Cover design by Yoori Kim. Cover photograph by Mary Ann McDonald/Corbis. Copyright © 1963 by Farley Mowat. Reproduced by permission./ Mowat, Angus and Helen, photograph. From a photograph in *Born Naked,* by Farley Mowat. Houghton Mifflin, 1994. Copyright © 1993 by Farley Mowat. Reproduced by permission of Farley Mowat.

OCTAVIO PAZ. Paz, Octavio, photograph. AP/Wide World Photos. Reproduced by permission./ Cover of *Convergences: Essays on Art and Literature,* by Octavio Paz, translated by Helen Lane. Harvest/HBJ Books, 1991. Designed by Beth Tondreau. Copyright © 1973 by Editorial Joaquin Moritz, S.A., copyright © 1984, 1983, 1979 by Editorial Siex Barral, S.A., copyright © 1984, 1983, 1979 by Octavio Paz, English translation by Helen Lange copyright © 1987 by Harcourt, Inc., reprinted by permission of Harcourt, Inc. and Bloomsbury Publishing Ltd./ Cover of *The Labyrinth of Solitude,* by Octavio Paz, translated by Lysander Kemp, Yara Milos and Rachel Phillips Belash. Grove Press, 1985. © 1985 by The Grove Press, Inc. Reproduced by permission./ Juana Inez de la Cruz, painting. Philadelphia Museum of Art/Corbis-Bettmann. Reproduced by permission./ Gunther Gerzso, illustrator. From a cover of *Eagle or Sun?,* by Octavio Paz, translated by Eliot Weinberger. New Directions, 1976. Cover drawing by Gunther Gerzso from the collection of John and Barbara Duncan, design by Gertrude Huston. Courtesy of New Directions Publishing Corp. Reproduced by permission.

CHAIM POTOK. Photograph. © Jerry Bauer. Reproduced by permission.

REMBRANDT. Rembrandt, (self-portrait), photograph of the painting. AP/Wide World Photos. Reproduced by permission./ "The Anatomy Lesson of Dr. Tulp," by Harmensz van Rijn Rembrandt. Mauritshuis, The Hague, The Netherlands. Copyright Scala/Art Resource, NY. Reprinted by permission of Art Resource./ "The Apostle Bartholomew," attributed to Rembrandt Harmensz. van Rijn, photograph. © Burstein Collection/CORBIS. Reproduced by permission./ "The Raising of Lazarus," by Rembrandt Harmensz van Rijn, photograph. © Historical Picture Archive/CORBIS. Reproduced by permission./ "Faust in His Study," engraving by Rembrandt, 1652, photograph. © Historical Picture Archive/Corbis. Reproduced by permission.

HARRIETTE GILLEM ROBINET. Robinet, Harriette Gillem, photograph by McLouis Robinet. Reproduced by permission of Harriette Gillem Robinet./ Alder, Kelynn, illustrator. From the jacket of *If You Please, President Lincoln,* by Harriette Gillem Robinet. Atheneum Books for Young Readers, 1995. Jacket illustration copyright © 1995 by Kelynn Alder. Reproduced by permission./ Andreasen, Dan, illustrator. From a cover of *The Twins, The Pirates, and the Battle of New Orleans,* by Harriette Gillem Robinet. Aladdin Paperbacks, 2001. Copyright © 1997 by Harriette Gillem Robinet. Reproduced by permission./ Colon, Raul, illustrator. From a cover of *Walking to the Bus-Rider Blues,* by Harriette Gillem Robinet. Aladdin Paperbacks, 2002. Reproduced by permission of Raul Colon./ Nickens, Bessie, illustrator. From a jacket of *Forty Acres and Maybe a Mule,* by Harriet Gillem Robinet. Jean Karl Books, 1998. Jacket illustration copyright © 1998 by Bessie Nickens. Reproduced by permission of Bessie Nickens.

JERRY SIEGEL and JOE SHUSTER. Siegel, Jerry, seated with typewriter, photograph. AP/Wide World Photos. Reproduced by permission./ Shuster, Joe, on mats with weights, photograph. Corbis. Reproduced by permission./ Christopher Reeve as Superman, in scene from the 1978 film *Superman,* directed by Richard Donner, based on the comic strip created by Jerry Siegel and Joe Shuster, movie still. The Kobal Collection/Warner Bros./DC Comics/Hamshere, Keith. Reproduced by permission./ Poster advertising Superman, photograph. The Kobal Collection/Columbia. Reproduced by permission.

JOHN SINGLETON. Singleton, John, 1996, photograph. The Corbis Collection. Reproduced by permission./ Laurence Fishburne (left) as Professor Maurice Phipps, with arms wrapped around the neck of Malik Williams (Omar Epps), scene from the 1995 film *Higher Learning,* written and directed by John Singleton, movie still. The Kobal Collection/New Deal/Columbia/Reed, Eli. Reproduced by permission./ Samuel L. Jackson (right center) as John Shaft, arresting Peoples Hernandez (Jeffrey Wright), scene from the 2000 film *Shaft,* directed by John Singleton, based on the novel by Ernest Tidyman, movie still. The Kobal Collection/Paramount/Reed, Eli. Reproduced by permission./ Jon Voight (left) as John Wright and Ving Rhames (right) as Mann, in scene from the 1997 film *Rosewood,* directed by John Singleton, movie still. The Kobal Collection/New Deal/Peters Ent/Reed, Eli. Reproduced by permission./ Ice Cube in the 1991 movie *Boyz in the Hood,* directed by John Singleton, movie still. The Kobal Collection / Columbia. Reproduced by permission.

ZADIE SMITH. Smith, Zadie, photograph. © McPherson Colin/Corbis Sygma. Reproduced by permission.

ALFRED LORD TENNYSON. Lord Tennyson, Alfred, photograph. AP/Wide World Photos. Reproduced by permission./ Illustration of characters Merlin and Vivien from *Idylls of the King,* by Lord Alfred Tennyson, photograph. Fortean Picture Library. Reproduced by permission./ Title page from *The Death of Cenone, Akbar's Dream, and Other Poems,* by Alfred Lord Tennyson. Special Collections Library, University of Michigan. Reproduced by permission.

DAVID FOSTER WALLACE. Wallace, David Foster, photograph. Courtesy of Little, Brown and Company. Reproduced by permission./ Beard, Karen, photographer. From a cover of *Brief Interviews with Hideous Men,* by David Foster Wallace. Cover design by John Fulbrook III. Copyright © 1999 by David Foster Wallace. Little, Brown and Company, 2000. Reproduced by permission./ Cover of *Infinite Jest: A Novel,* by David Foster Wallace. Little, Brown and Company, 1995. Cover design by Elizabeth Van Itallie. Copyright © 1996 by David Foster Wallace. Reproduced by permission./ Mills, Joseph, illustrator. From a cover of *A Supposedly Fun Thing I'll Never Do Again: Essays and Arguments,* by David Foster Wallace. Little, Brown and Company, 1998. Cover design by Michael Ian Kaye. Copyright © 1997 by David Foster Wallace. Reproduced by permission.

JOSS WHEDON. Whedon, Joss, photograph. © PACHA/Corbis. Reproduced by permission./ Sigourney Weaver (right) as Lt. Ellen Ripley Clone #8 and Brad Dourif as Dr. Gediman, scene from the 1997 film *Alien: Resurrection,* directed by Jean-Pierre Jeunet, written by Joss Whedon, movie still. The Kobal Collection. Reproduced by permission./ Sarah Michelle Geller (left) as Buffy Summers, being choked by a creature, scene from the television series *Buffy the Vampire Slayer,* created, cowritten and directed by Joss Whedon, movie still. The Kobal Collection/20th Century Fox Television/Cartwright, Richard. Reproduced by permission./ Sale, Tim, illustrator. From an illustration in *Buffy the Vampire Slayer: Tales of the Slayer,* by Joss Whedon. Dark Horse Comics, 2001. *Buffy the Vampire Slayer* TM & © 2001, Twentieth Century Fox Film Corporation. All rights reserved. Reproduced by permission./ Movie still for the 2000 film *Titan A. E.,* directed by Don Bluth and Gary Goldman, cowritten by Joss Whedon. The Kobal Collection/20th Century Fox. Reproduced by permission.

BANANA YOSHIMOTO. Yoshimoto, Banana, photograph. Eiichiro Sakata and Kadokawa Shoten Publishing Co., Ltd. Reproduced by permission of Grove Press./ D'Innocenzo, Paul, illustrator. From a cover of *Asleep,* by Banana Yoshimoto, translated by Michael Emmerich. Grove Press, 2000. Cover design by Charles Rue Woods. Copyright © by Banana Yoshimoto. Translation copyright © 2000 by Michael Emmerich. Reproduced by permission./ Estrada, Sigrid, photographer. From a cover of *Kitchen,* by Banana Yoshimoto, translated by Megan Backus. Washington Square Press, 1994. Cover design by Adriane Stark. Cover photos © 1994 by Sigrid Estrada. Reproduced by permission of Sigrid Estrada./ Floyd, Rebecca, illustrator. From a jacket of *Goodbye Tsugumi: A Novel,* by Banana Yoshimoto, translated by Michael Emmerich. Grove Press, 2002. Design by Laura Hammond Hough. Copyright © 1989 by Banana Yoshimoto. Translation copyright © 2002 by Michael Emmerich. Reproduced by permission.

Arnold Adoff

■ Personal

Born July 16, 1935, in New York, NY; son of Aaron Jacob (a pharmacist) and Rebecca (Stein) Adoff; married Virginia Hamilton (a writer), March 19, 1960 (died, 2002); children: Leigh Hamilton (daughter), Jaime Levi (son). *Nationality:* American. *Education:* City College of New York (now City College of the City University of New York), B.A., 1956; graduate studies at Columbia University, 1956-58; attended New School for Social Research (now New School University), 1965-67. *Politics:* "Committed to change for full freedom for all Americans." *Religion:* "Freethinking pragmatist." *Hobbies and other interests:* History, music.

■ Addresses

Home—Yellow Springs, OH. *Office*—Arnold Adoff Agency, P.O. Box 293, Yellow Springs, OH 45387.

■ Career

Poet, writer of fiction and nonfiction, and anthologist. Teacher in New York City public schools, 1957-69; Arnold Adoff Agency, Yellow Springs, OH, literary agent, 1977—. Instructor in federal projects at New York University, Connecticut College, and other institutions; visiting professor, Queens College, 1986-87. Lecturer at colleges throughout the United States; consultant in children's literature, poetry, and creative writing. Member of planning commission, Yellow Springs. *Military service:* Served with New York National Guard.

■ Awards, Honors

Children's Books of the Year citation, Child Study Association of America, 1968, for *I Am the Darker Brother,* 1969, for *City in All Directions,* and 1986, for *Sports Pages;* Best Children's Books, *School Library Journal,* 1971, for *It Is the Poem Singing into Your Eyes,* and 1973, for *Black Is Brown Is Tan;* Notable Children's Trade Book citation, National Council for the Social Studies/Children's Book Council (NCSS/CBC), 1974, and Children's Choice citation, International Reading Association/Children's Book Council (IRA/CBC), 1985, both for *My Black Me: A Beginning Book of Black Poetry;* Art Books for Children Award for *MA nDA LA,* 1975; Books for the Teen Age citation, New York Public Library, 1980, 1981, and 1982, all for *It Is the Poem Singing into Your Eyes;* Jane Addams Children's Book Award special recognition, 1983, for *All the Colors of the Race;* Parents Choice Award (picture book) for *Flamboyan,* 1988; National Council of Teachers of English Award in Excellence in Poetry for Children, 1988.

■ Writings

POETRY; FOR CHILDREN

MA nDA LA, illustrated by Emily Arnold McCully, Harper (New York, NY), 1971.

Black Is Brown Is Tan, illustrated by Emily Arnold McCully, Harper (New York, NY), 1973, revised edition, 2002.

Make a Circle Keep Us In: Poems for a Good Day, illustrated by Ronald Himler, Delacorte (New York, NY), 1975.

Big Sister Tells Me That I'm Black, illustrated by Lorenzo Lynch, Holt (New York, NY), 1976.

Tornado!, illustrated by Ronald Himler, Delacorte (New York, NY), 1977.

Under the Early Morning Trees, illustrated by Ronald Himler, Dutton (New York, NY), 1978.

Where Wild Willie, illustrated by Emily Arnold McCully, Harper (New York, NY), 1978.

Eats, illustrated by Susan Russo, Lothrop (New York, NY), 1979.

I Am the Running Girl, illustrated by Ronald Himler, Harper (New York, NY), 1979.

Friend Dog, illustrated by Troy Howell, Lippincott (Philadelphia, PA), 1980.

OUTside/INside Poems, illustrated by John Steptoe, Lothrop (New York, NY), 1981.

Today We Are Brother and Sister, illustrated by Glo Coalson, Lothrop (New York, NY), 1981.

Birds, illustrated by Troy Howell, Lippincott (Philadelphia, PA), 1982.

All the Colors of the Race, illustrated by John Steptoe, Lothrop (New York, NY), 1982.

The Cabbages Are Chasing the Rabbits, illustrated by Janet Stevens, Harcourt (New York, NY), 1985.

Sports Pages, illustrated by Steven Kuzma, Lippincott (Philadelphia, PA), 1986.

Greens, illustrated by Betsy Lewin, Morrow (New York, NY), 1988.

Flamboyan, illustrated by Karen Barbour, Harcourt (New York, NY), 1988.

Chocolate Dreams, illustrated by Turi MacCombie, Lothrop (New York, NY), 1988.

Hard to Be Six, illustrated by Cheryl Hanna, Lothrop (New York, NY), 1990.

In for Winter, out for Spring, illustrated by Jerry Pinkney, Harcourt (New York, NY), 1991.

The Return of Rex and Ethel, illustrated by Catherine Deeter, Harcourt (New York, NY), 1993.

Street Music: City Poems, illustrated by Karen Barbour, HarperCollins (New York, NY), 1995.

Slow Dance Heart Break Blues, illustrated by William Cotton, Lothrop (New York, NY), 1995.

Touch the Poem, illustrated by Bill Creevy, Scholastic (New York, NY), 1996, new edition illustrated by Lisa Desimini, Blue Sky Press (New York, NY), 2000.

Love Letters, illustrated by Lisa Desimini, Scholastic (New York, NY), 1997.

The Basket Counts, illustrated by Michael Weaver, Simon & Schuster (New York, NY), 2000.

Daring Dog and Captain Cat, illustrated by Joe Cepada, Simon & Schuster (New York, NY), 2001.

EDITOR

I Am the Darker Brother: An Anthology of Modern Poems by Negro Americans, illustrated by Benny Andrews, Macmillan (New York, NY), 1968.

Black on Black: Commentaries by Negro Americans, Macmillan (New York, NY), 1968.

City in All Directions: An Anthology of Modern Poems, illustrated by Donald Carrick, Macmillan (New York, NY), 1969.

Black out Loud: An Anthology of Modern Poems by Black Americans, illustrated by Alvin Hollingsworth, Macmillan (New York, NY), 1970.

Brothers and Sisters: Modern Stories by Black Americans, Macmillan (New York, NY), 1970.

It Is the Poem Singing in Your Eyes: An Anthology of New Young Poets, Harper (New York, NY), 1971.

The Poetry of Black America: An Anthology of the Twentieth Century, introduction by Gwendolyn Brooks, Harper (New York, NY), 1973.

My Black Me: A Beginning Book of Black Poetry, Dutton (New York, NY), 1974.

Celebrations: A New Anthology of Black American Poetry, Follett (New York, NY), 1977.

OTHER

Malcolm X (nonfiction; for children), illustrated by John Wilson, Crowell (New York, NY), 1970, revised edition illustrated by Rudy Gutierrez, HarperTrophy (New York, NY), 2000.

Contributor of articles and reviews to periodicals.

■ Sidelights

An accomplished poet, biographer, and anthologist as well as a respected educator, Arnold Adoff is recognized as one of the first—and finest—champions of multiculturalism in U.S. literature for children and young adults. Described by Jeffrey S. Copeland in *Speaking of Poets* as "a writer on a mission," Adoff, whose works most often reflect the African-American experience, was among the first authors to consistently, accurately, and positively portray black subjects and concerns in a manner considered both specific and universal. Several of his books, most notably the anthologies *I Am the Darker Brother* and *City in All Directions,* the illustrated biography *Malcolm X,* and the picture book *Black Is Brown Is Tan,* are acknowledged as groundbreaking titles in their respective genres. Since the mid-1960s, noted Copeland, Adoff "has been influencing how young readers view such matters as equality of races, sex-role stereotyping, individual rights, and ageism. . . . [He] has spent his writing career expounding the strength of family, both in terms of the individual family structure and the family of humanity." Writing in the *St. James Guide to Children's Writers,* Marilyn Kaye stated that a "constant factor in Adoff's work is the imaginative expression of faith in people and their spirit. Each work, in its own way, salutes the human condition and its ability to triumph." *New York Times Book Review* contributor Ardis Kimzey called Adoff "one of the best anthologists in the world," and concluded, "With his taste and ear, it stands to reason that he should have turned to writing poetry himself, and done it well."

As a poet, Adoff characteristically utilizes free verse, vivid images, and unusual structures and sounds to express warm, affectionate family portraits; the intimate thoughts and feelings of children; and a variety of moods and tones. His poetry is noted for its invention and innovation as well as for its idiosyncratic use of capitalization and punctuation, elements Adoff believes have a strong effect on the movement and rhythm of a poem. Adoff seeks to visually represent the meaning of the words in his poetry by including variations of line length, type size, and letter arrangement. He uses punctuation and rhyme sparingly and sometimes incorporates black English into his verse. His collections of original poetry consist of books on a particular subject, such as eating, tornadoes, or birds; poems from the viewpoint of a particular character; and combinations of poetry and poetic prose that often focus on the duality of the fantastic and the realistic. He has also included some autobiographical material in his collections.

Praised for the depth and range of subjects of his poetry as well as for its sensitivity, insight, musicality, structure, and control, Adoff is perceived as a poet whose skill with language and unexpected variances of meaning and rhythm help to make his works especially distinctive. Writing in *Twentieth-Century Young Adult Writers,* Myra Cohn Livingston explained that Adoff "strives to present a poetry of

Arnold Adoff's highly praised 1970 biography *Malcolm X,* illustrated by John Wilson, introduces young readers to the life and convictions of a noted black leader of the civil rights era.

'shaped speech' that is colloquial, that is relevant, short, and exciting." She claimed that each of Adoff's books of poetry "promises and delivers something new, fresh, and challenging. . . . [Always] he fulfills his own code, the 'need of the poet to help mold a complete reality through control of technique and imagination . . . ,' in which he most assuredly excels." As an anthologist, Adoff is acknowledged for creating carefully selected poetry and prose collections that characteristically feature African-American writers and focus on themes of survival, transcendence, and hope. Directing these books to young adults, he includes works by such writers as Langston Hughes, Lucille Clifton, Paul Laurence Dunbar, Gwendolyn Brooks, Arna Bontemps, and Nikki Giovanni as well as the creations of talented but lesser-known contributors whose works were virtually unavailable before their publication in Adoff's collections.

Born in New York City

Adoff was born in New York City and grew up in a mixed-race, working-class neighborhood in the South Bronx. His father, who operated a pharmacy, immigrated to the United States from a town near the Polish/Russian border. "In our home, as in so many others, the emphasis was on being American with a keen sense of Jewish," Adoff once commented. Members of the Adoff family, especially the women, were deeply concerned with social justice. "There was a tradition of liberal, free-thinking females in the family," he recalled. "My mother was involved in Zionist and civil rights causes. I recall when a black Baptist congregation reclaimed a derelict church in our neighborhood, my mother playing her violin, welcoming the new congregation." The Adoff family was well read, and numerous magazines and newspapers could be found around the house—the exception being comics, which Adoff's grandmother strictly forbade as too lowbrow. Lively discussions on issues of the day were frequently exchanged. "Discussions were volatile, emotional as well as intellectual," Adoff once said. "In order to hold status within the family, you had to speak loudly . . . on such burning topics as economics, socialism, the Soviet Union, and how to be assimilated into the larger society without losing one's Jewishness."

Around the age of ten, Adoff attended a neighborhood Zionist school, where, as he once commented, he "studied the Old Testament and . . . Zionism as well as other aspects of Jewish history and culture." His childhood reading, Adoff related in an interview in *Top of the News*, "taught me, in sum, how to walk a cultural tightrope. *Little Women* and Sholem Aleichem; *The Five Little Peppers* and *The Story of the Chanukah*; Longfellow, Riley, and Peretz." As a teenager, Adoff read such authors as William Shakespeare, Honore Balzac, John Dos Passos, John Steinbeck, and Guy de Maupassant; in addition, he was exposed to the writings of Havelock Ellis and the works of psychologists such as Menninger, Steckel, and Horney as well as, he once told *Top of the News*, "Poets and poets and poets." Adoff's favorite poets, he noted, are the ones "who can sing and can control their word-songs with all-important craft"; among his most important influences he has counted Dylan Thomas, e. e. cummings, Rainer Maria Rilke, Marianne Moore, Gwendolyn Brooks, and Robert Hayden.

Adoff attended high school in Manhattan, initially with the goal of becoming a doctor; but, he once stated, "I felt like a fish out of water at that school because I was not a scientist in the depths of my soul." He developed an intense interest in jazz, an area in which his family had an influence. "Our house was filled with music," he noted. "My mother played the violin, my aunt sang, the radio played opera, gospel, and jazz." At sixteen Adoff began writing poetry; he also began sneaking into New York City jazz clubs and became familiar with such jazz legends as Dizzy Gillespie, Charlie Parker, and Sarah Vaughan. Jazz demonstrated to Adoff, as he remarked, that "what was called 'American culture' most often did not include black or Latino culture. . . . By the time I graduated high school, jazz was the only music I listened to. It pushed out the boundaries of my world."

Attends College and Turns to Writing

Adoff enrolled at the Columbia University School of Pharmacy, but withdrew to major in history and literature at New York's City College. He wrote for the college newspaper and literary magazine and was politically active, participating in protests for civil liberties. In college Adoff was introduced to writers such as James Joyce and Gertrude Stein who were especially gifted with language and wordplay. He was also greatly influenced by jazz artist Charles Mingus, who lectured before the jazz club of which Adoff was president. "Without a doubt, he was the most impressive person I had ever met," Adoff once commented, "From then on, I went to see him wherever he played, and we got to know each other. In time, he would become my spiritual father." Later, while Adoff was substitute teaching and living in Greenwich Village, he became Mingus's manager and maintained "running chronicles of the Village club scene." Through Mingus, Adoff also met his future wife, African-American novelist and children's writer Virginia Hamilton, in 1958; the couple were married in 1960.

Adoff attended graduate school at Columbia University, and although he finished the required course work for a Ph.D. in American history, he left before completing his dissertation. While at graduate school he began teaching seventh grade social studies at a yeshiva—a Jewish day school—in the Brownsville section of Brooklyn. This job, he once said, "gave me confidence knowing I could stay alive outside grad school. This was important, because after two years I wanted to leave. The desire to live independently and focus on my writing had become overpowering." Adoff moved to Greenwich Village and began substitute teaching in New York City public schools; he spent the remainder of his time writing and going to jazz clubs in the Village. As he described it, the Village scene was "a vibrant community of painters, writers, musicians who would meet in the coffeehouses and talk art. As a poet I have been more influenced by musicians and painters than by other writers. Man Ray was an important influence, as was Picasso, the Russian Constructivists, and other painters and sculptors influenced by technology and things industrial."

Shortly after Adoff and Virginia Hamilton were married, they moved to Spain and France to work on writing projects. During their stay in Europe, the civil rights movement was intensifying in the United States and they decided to return. "Virginia is black, our children brown—we felt somehow it would be wrong to stay," Adoff explained. "Besides, it all seemed very exciting and we didn't want to be removed from the action. So we returned to New York, where we threw ourselves into our work and as much political work as we could handle."

Back in New York, Adoff began teaching students in Harlem and on Manhattan's Upper West Side. In addition, he commented, "I resumed collecting black literature, which I had begun in the late 1950s and early 1960s. . . . I would dig up old magazines like *Dial* and look for specifically black periodicals. . . . I'd haunt bookshops all over town." Adoff also began to discover a paucity of appropriate and relevant materials available to his students that reflected their lives. In his preface to the anthology *The Poetry of Black America,* he describes the exchange that resulted: "As a teacher I had students who wanted life in those dusty classrooms. They wanted pictures of themselves inside themselves. . . . I was the dealer. The pusher of poems and stories. Plays and paintings. Jazz and blues. And my students began to push on me. To deal their sounds and write their poems. And I was made to become serious about myself. To get my head together and attempt to go beyond the classrooms and students and schools. To go beyond the racist textbooks and anthologies that were on the shelves and in the bookstores."

Compiles Poetry Anthology by Black Writers

Adoff began to assemble some of the poems he had been collecting and sharing with his students. Through an editor at Macmillan he received a positive response from the editor-in-chief of that publishing house. His first anthology, *I Am the Darker Brother: An Anthology of Modern Poems by Negro Americans,* was published in 1968, launching a number of subsequent anthologies of black poetry and prose. *The Poetry of Black America: An Anthology of the Twentieth Century* was one of the largest anthologies of black poetry ever published in the United States. Adoff once commented that the volume, which contains an introduction by one of the editor's favorite poets, Gwendolyn Brooks, "contains 600 poems, although my manuscript consisted of 3,000 poems that richly deserved to be included. The final choices were among the most agonizing selections I have ever had to make." Adoff faced another formidable selection task with the anthology *It Is the Poem Singing into Your Eyes,* for which he solicited work from young poets across the country and received over 6,000 submissions. "The tragedy . . . is that I was allowed to publish only one hundred poems," he reflected. "There were many, many, many poems that were absolutely superb. . . . The title of the volume was suggested by one of my young correspondents. I loved her statement—a poem truly does sing into your eyes and then on into your mind and soul." Among the young poets included in this collection was August Wilson, who would later become a Pulitzer Prize-winning playwright. In addition to his poetry anthologies, Adoff has compiled several collections of fiction and commentary by black writers.

In an interview with Lee Bennett Hopkins in *More Books by More People,* Adoff once commented that his objective in producing black literature anthologies is to portray a truer cultural picture of literary America. "I want my anthologies of Black American writing to make Black kids strong in their knowledge of themselves and their great literary heritage—give them facts and people and power. I also want these Black books of mine to give knowledge to White kids around the country, so that mutual respect and understanding will come from mutual learning. We *can* go beyond the murder and the muddles of the present. Children have to understand that the oversimplifications they get in classrooms, along with the token non-White artists represented, are not the true American literature. . . . But for those who want the truth, for themselves and for their students, using an anthology is the first step to discovery. The anthology then leads to individual works of the writers." Regarding his inclusion criteria, Adoff remarked in *Top of the News* that in all of his books "the material selected must be the finest in literary terms as well as in content/message/racial vision." He added: "If I can lay Malcolm and Du Bois on top of Sambo and Remus, will they finally die and disappear?"

During the time Adoff was focusing on his compilations, he continued to write poetry. "The negative aspect of doing so many anthologies," he once observed, "was that people came to think of me pri-

Adoff's 2000 poetry collection *The Basket Counts,* with illustrations by Michael Weaver, includes twenty-eight poems which focus on the game of basketball and the passion it inspires in many young players.

apart." Adoff decided to create poetry in which "form and physical shape . . . should serve to promote its message."

Begins Publishing Own Poetry

In 1971 Adoff published his first book of poetry for children, *MA nDA LA,* a story poem that uses only words containing the sound "ah." *MA nDA LA,* which features watercolor illustrations by Emily Arnold McCully, relates the cycle of African family life in a small village. "Logically, the poem makes no sense and is not supposed to," Adoff once commented. Writing in the *St. James Guide to Children's Writers,* Marilyn Kaye described Adoff's "sing-song verse" in *MA nDA LA* as "a simple compilation of sounds which evoke a sense of celebration." The book demonstrates Adoff's poetic principles: "I use the image of invisible rubber bands pulling the reader's eye from the last letter of the last word in the first line down to the first letter of the first word in the last line. . . . The music of language greatly affects meaning. . . . Ideally, each poem should be read three times: for meaning; for rhythm; for technical tricks. My poems demand active participation."

Throughout the 1970s and 1980s Adoff published several volumes of poetry for young people that display his characteristic use of free verse, vivid sensory images, striking word pictures, and lively rhythms while offering sensitive portrayals of family life and interior emotions. *Black Is Brown Is Tan*—modeled after Adoff's own family—is one of the few children's books to depict interracial families; according to Kaye, it "extends the focus beyond color to encompass a family's delight in each other." In *All The Colors of the Race* Adoff explores the feelings of a girl with a black mother and a white father; "contemplative, jubilant, and questioning, the upbeat verses stress the young person's humanity in terms of gifts received from her forebears," wrote Ruth M. Stein in *Language Arts.* In *Where Wild Willie,* which Stein called "Adoff's paean to independence" in another review in *Language Arts,* the poet describes a child who temporarily leaves her family to go on her own adventure of learning. The poem recounts the girl's journey and is interspersed with the encouraging words of her parents. Zena Sutherland wrote in *Bulletin of the Center for Children's Books* that *Where Wild Willie* "describes with lilting fluency Willie's rambles and then the voices from home speak for themselves, an antiphonal arrangement in which the two draw closer until Willie comes

marily as an anthologizer. . . . I, however, have always thought of myself as a poet first." Shortly after returning from Europe in 1965 he enrolled in a class at the New School of Social Research taught by Filipino-American poet José Garcia Villa which had a profound effect on Adoff's own poetry. "José became my second spiritual father," Adoff related. "He talked about creating a poetry that was as pure as music. . . . His extremism based on an exhaustive knowledge of the art and craft of poetry set him home." In an essay for *Something about the Author Autobiography Series,* Adoff admitted that his favorite self-authored book is *OUTside/INside Poems,* a poem cycle that recreates a day in the life of a small boy and expresses his range of feelings. He called this work "a great vehicle for teaching young readers to write poetry. Also, this is the one that really has the greatest element of reality/fantasy."

Adoff considers *Sports Pages,* a book of poetry for middle graders, to be "a breakthrough" because, as he noted, he "worked in a longer form of a combination of poetic prose and poetry and dealt with some autobiographical material using individual voice in the midst of organized activity." A reviewer for *Bulletin of the Center for Children's Books* acknowledged the work as "one of his best collections," while a critic in *Kirkus Reviews* suggested that *Sports Pages* might "easily lure the adolescent" who will enjoy Adoff's "sensitivity and acuity."

With *Flamboyan,* Adoff again uses poetic prose in a picture book fantasy about a Puerto Rican girl who longs to fly with the birds who circle above her yard. Called "a magical story of a girl's yearning to be outside her own life" by a reviewer in *Publishers Weekly, Flamboyan* will "appeal to all who long to go beyond the ordinary." Illustrated by Karen Barbour, the book contains an unusual typographic device: a red leaf that appears in the text to provide directions for reading aloud. Ruth K. MacDonald of *School Library Journal* called *Flamboyan* a "dazzling combination of both text and illustration." Adoff's next book, *Chocolate Dreams,* collects original poems on one of his—and many children's—favorite subjects: food. Described by Betsy Hearne in *Bulletin of the Center for Children's Books* as a "rich confection of wordplay, rhythms, and unexpected twists of rhyme and meaning from a poet in his element," the poems, contended Hearne, reveal Adoff's ability to combine "invention and control, depth and delight."

Pens Poetry about City Life

In 1995 Adoff published both *Street Music: City Poems,* a collection of jazzy poems in free verse that celebrates the vibrancy of city life, and *Slow Dance Heart Break Blues,* a volume of poems about the thoughts and experiences of adolescence that he directs to readers in their early teens. Written "in a gritty, hip-hop style," according to Susan Dove Lempke in *Booklist,* Adoff's poems for urban youth are, a critic in *Kirkus Reviews* stated, "laden with empathy." Sharon Korbeck of *School Library Journal* concluded that "there is a great deal of depth here," challenging readers to question what poetry is and

to reexamine "who and where they are in light of today's fast-moving issues and society." Writing in *Horn Book,* Robert D. Hale stated, "If the word gets out, *Slow Dance Heart Break Blues* will become a best seller. Arnold Adoff knows what teenagers are thinking and feeling, which is evident in this collection of on-target poems."

In *The Basket Counts* Adoff writes about young people playing basketball in the streets, backyards, and neighborhood parks of a big city. Gillian Engberg in *Booklist* explained that "these poems talk about what it actually feels like to play the game." The shapes of Adoff's poems even mimic the bounce of a dribbling basketball and the arc that a thrown ball makes when it is in the air. The accompanying illustrations by Michael Weaver, a critic for *Publishers Weekly* claimed, "feature careening angles, skewed perspectives, a multicultural cast of characters and hip teens." Engberg concluded that young people who enjoy playing basketball "will find themselves within these innovative high-energy poems."

Adoff has also collaborated with photographer Lisa Desimini. In *Love Letters,* a volume of poetry illustrated by Desimini, Adoff presents primary graders with twenty valentines written as anonymous notes. Dulcy Brainard of *Publishers Weekly* claimed that "much of the pleasure" comes from the author's and illustrator's "abilities to evoke not only . . . everyday feelings but the more complicated sense of privacy and mystery they summon." Writing in *Bulletin of the Center for Children's Books,* Elizabeth Bush suggested, "When it's got to be sweet, but it can't be saccharine, drop one of these on a desktop or into a booktalk and wait for the sparks to fly." In *Touch the Poem,* Adoff writes poems about the sense of touch. The book's photographs by Desimini depict such varied sensations as walking on a sandy beach, touching peach fuzz, or rubbing dad's unshaved, stubbly cheek. A reviewer in *Publishers Weekly* admitted that "the accumulation of detail evokes the sensation of the described activity," while Ilene Cooper of *Booklist* believed that "the solid imagery of Adoff's poetry takes on a visual dimension when paired with Desimini's bold photographs."

Adoff lives and works out of Yellow Springs, Ohio, in a house he and his wife built on land behind her parents' farm. He continues to write for young people, seeing a link with his concerns for social justice. "I began writing for kids," Adoff once commented, "because I wanted to effect a change in American society. I continue in that spirit. By the time we reach adulthood, we are closed and set in our attitudes. The chances of a poet reaching us are very slim. But I can open a child's imagination, develop his appetite for poetry, and most importantly, show him that poetry is a natural part of everyday life. We all need someone to point out that the emperor is wearing no clothes. That is the poet's job."

If you enjoy the works of Arnold Adoff, you might want to check out the following books:

Nikki Giovanni, *Ego-Tripping and Other Poems for Young People,* 1973.
Paul B. Janeczko, *Preposterous: Poems of Youth,* 1991.
Naomi Shihab Nye, *The Space between Our Footsteps,* 1998.

Speaking of Adoff's varied career as a writer, Kaye concluded that the writer "has distinguished himself as a poet, anthologist, and biographer. His poetry is notable for its pungent musical quality, best appreciated when read aloud. Unusual word, phrase, and sentence configurations, which may appear arbitrary on the page, take on a rhythmic logic when spoken. His poems range in tone and mood from the festive to the meditative, but a common element is a sense of gentle warmth." In an interview with Jeffrey S. Copeland in *Speaking of Poets,* Adoff added another perspective: "I'm still attempting to influence kids one way or another, whether it is the way they view the color of skin or reality and fantasy. I hope always to be considered perhaps controversial, perhaps dangerous, to the status quo. . . . It is a struggle to create something you hope is art. I work long and hard at my craft. I like to feel I have good instincts when it comes to language. All in all, I am very proud of what I've done."

■ **Biographical and Critical Sources**

BOOKS

Adoff, Arnold, *The Poetry of Black America: An Anthology of the Twentieth Century,* Harper (New York, NY), 1973.
Authors in the News, Volume 1, Gale (Detroit, MI), 1976.

Children's Literature Review, Volume 7, Gale (Detroit, MI), 1984.
Hopkins, Lee Bennett, *More Books by More People: Interviews with Sixty-five Authors of Books for Children,* Citation Press, 1974.
St. James Guide to Children's Writers, 5th edition, St. James Press (Detroit, MI), 1989.
Something about the Author Autobiography Series, Volume 15, Gale (Detroit, MI), 1993.
Speaking of Poets: Interviews with Poets Who Write for Children and Young Adults, National Council of Teachers of English, 1993.
Twentieth-Century Young Adult Writers, St. James Press (Detroit, MI), 1994.

PERIODICALS

Booklist, December 15, 1995, Susan Dove Lempke, review of *Slow Dance Heart Break Blues,* p. 694; February 1, 2000, Gillian Engberg, review of *The Basket Counts,* p. 1017; February 15, 2000, Hazel Rochman, review of *Malcolm X;* March 15, 2000, Ilene Cooper, review of *Touch the Poem,* p. 1378; October 1, 2001, Annie Ayres, review of *Daring Dog and Captain Cat,* p. 322; April 15, 2002, Hazel Rochman, review of *Black Is Brown Is Tan,* p. 1405.
Bulletin of the Center for Children's Books, March, 1979, Zena Sutherland, review of *Where Wild Willie,* p. 109; June, 1986, review of *Sports Pages,* p. 181; November, 1989, Betsy Hearne, review of *Chocolate Dreams,* p. 49; March, 1997, Elizabeth Bush, review of *Love Letters,* p. 239.
Horn Book, May-June, 1995, Nancy Vasilakis, review of *Street Music: City Poems,* p. 337; November-December, 1995, Robert D. Hale, review of *Slow Dance Heart Break Blues,* p. 770.
Kirkus Reviews, May 1, 1986, review of *Sports Pages,* p. 721; July 1, 1995, review of *Slow Dance Heart Break Blues,* p. 942; August 15, 2001, review of *Daring Dog and Captain Cat,* p. 1206; March 15, 2002, review of *Black Is Brown Is Tan,* p. 404.
Language Arts, September, 1979, Ruth M. Stein, review of *Where Wild Willie,* pp. 690-691; April, 1983, Ruth M. Stein, review of *All the Colors of the Race,* pp. 483-484.
New York Times Book Review, April 25, 1982, Ardis Kimzey, "Verse First, Poetry Next," p. 37.
Publishers Weekly, August 26, 1988, review of *Flamboyan,* p. 88; December 2, 1997, Dulcy Brainard, review of *Love Letters;* January 10, 2000, review of *The Basket Counts,* p. 68; April 17, 2000, review of *Touch the Poem,* p. 80; May 15, 2000, review of *The Return of Rex and Ethel,* p. 118; September 24, 2001, review of *Daring Dog and Captain Cat,* p. 93.
School Library Journal, October, 1988, Ruth K. MacDonald, review of *Flamboyan,* p. 114; September, 1995, Sharon Korbeck, review of *Slow Dance Heart Break Blues,* p. 221.
Top of the News, January, 1972, interview with Arnold Adoff, pp. 153-155.*

Edward Bond

■ Personal

Born July 18, 1934, in London, England; married Elizabeth Pable, 1971. *Nationality:* British; English. *Education:* Attended state schools in England. *Politics:* Socialist. *Religion:* "Atheist."

■ Addresses

Agent—c/o Casarotto Ramsay Ltd., 60-66 Walton St., London W1V 3HP, England.

■ Career

Writer. Worked previously in factories and offices; member of Royal Court Theater writers group; University of Essex, resident theatre writer, 1982-83. *Military service:* British Army Infantry; served two years.

■ Awards, Honors

Oscar nomination for best screenplay (with Michelangelo Antonioni and Tonino Guerra), 1967, for *Blowup;* George Devine Award, English Stage Society, 1968, for *Early Morning;* John Whiting Playwrights Award (with Peter Barnes), Arts Council, 1969, for *Narrow Road to the Deep North;* Best New Play award, *Plays and Players,* 1976, for *The Fool,* and 1985, for *The War Plays;* Northern Arts Literary fellow, 1977-79; D.Litt., Yale University, 1977.

■ Writings

PLAYS

The Pope's Wedding and Other Plays (includes *The Pope's Wedding,* produced in the West End, 1962; *Mr. Dog; The King with Golden Eyes;* and *Sharpeville Sequence*), Methuen (London, England), 1971.

Saved (produced in the West End, 1965; produced Off-Broadway, 1970), Hill & Wang (New York, NY), 1966, reprinted, Heinemann (London, England), 1984.

The Three Sisters (adapted from the play by Anton Chekhov), produced in London, England, 1967.

Early Morning (produced in the West End, 1968; produced Off-Broadway, 1970), Calder & Boyars (London, England), 1968, Hill & Wang (New York, NY), 1969.

Narrow Road to the Deep North (produced in Coventry, England, 1968; produced in the West End, 1969; produced on Broadway, 1972), Methuen (London, England), 1968, Hill & Wang (New York, NY), 1969.

Black Mass, produced in Sheffield, England, 1970.

Lear (produced in the West End, 1971; produced at Yale Repertory Theater, 1973), Hill & Wang (New York, NY), 1972.

Bingo: Scenes of Money and Death [and] *Passion* (*Passion* produced in the West End, 1971, then at Yale Repertory Theater, 1972; *Bingo,* produced in the West End, 1974; also see below), Eyre Methuen (London, England), 1974.

The Sea (comedy; produced in the West End, 1973; also see below), Hill & Wang (New York, NY), 1973.

Bingo [and] *The Sea: Two Plays,* Hill & Wang (New York, NY), 1973.

The Fool (produced in London, England, 1975), Dramatic Club Publications (Chicago, IL), 1978.

(Author of libretto) *We Come to the River* (opera; produced at Covent Garden, 1976), music by Hans Werner Henze, published as *We Come to the River: Actions for Music,* Schott (New York, NY), 1976.

A-A-America! [and] *Stone,* Eyre Methuen (London, England), 1976, revised edition, 1981.

The Fool [and] *We Come to the River,* Eyre Methuen (London, England), 1976.

Plays, Methuen (London, England), 1977, published as *Plays One: Saved, Early Morning, The Pope's Wedding,* 1983.

Plays Two (includes *Lear, The Sea, Narrow Road to the Deep North, Black Mass,* and *Passion*), Methuen (London, England), 1978.

The Woman: Scenes of War and Freedom (produced in London, England, 1978), Hill & Wang (New York, NY), 1979.

The Bundle; or, New Narrow Road to the Deep North (produced by Royal Shakespearean Company, 1978; produced at Yale Repertory Theater, 1979), Eyre Methuen (London, England), 1978, Dramatic Publishing (Chicago, IL), 1981.

The Worlds [and] *The Activists Papers* (*The Worlds* produced by Newcastle University Theater Society, 1979), Eyre Methuen (London, England), 1980.

(Translator) Frank Wedekind, *Spring Awakening,* Methuen (London, England), 1980.

Restoration: A Pastoral [and] *The Cat* [includes *Restoration* (musical), music by Nick Bicat, produced at the Royal Court Theater, 1981, then Washington, DC, 1986; and *The Cat* (libretto for opera), music by Hans Werner Henze, produced by Stuttgart Opera, 1983, produced as *The English Cat,* Santa Fe, NM, 1985, then New York, 1986], Eyre Methuen (London, England), 1982, 2nd edition, Methuen (London, England), 1982, published as *The English Cat: A Story for Singers and Instrumentalists,* Schott (New York, NY), 1983.

Summer (produced in London, England, 1982; produced at Manhattan Theater Club, 1983), Methuen (London, England), 1982.

Summer [and] *Fables,* Methuen (London, England), 1983.

Derek [and] *Choruses from after the Assassinations,* Methuen (London, England), 1984.

The War Plays; Part 1: Red, Black, and Ignorant, Part 2: The Tin Can People, Part 3: Great Peace (produced by Royal Shakespeare Company, 1985), two volumes, Methuen (New York, NY), 1985, in one volume, 1991.

Human Cannon (produced in Edinburgh, Scotland), Methuen (New York, NY), 1985.

Jackets 2 (produced in London, England, 1990), Methuen (London, England), 1990.

Two Post-Modern Plays (contains *Jackets 1, Jackets 2, In the Company of Men, September,* and "Notes on Post-Modernism"), Methuen (London, England), 1990.

At the Inland Sea: A Play for Young People (produced in Birmingham, England, 1995), Methuen (London, England), 1997.

Coffee (produced in London, England, 1997), Methuen (London, England), 1995.

Eleven Vests (also see below; produced in Birmingham, England, 1997), Methuen (London, England), 1997.

The Children [and] *Have I None,* Methuen (London, England), 2000.

The Crime of the Twenty-first Century, produced in Paris, France, then London, England, and Bochum, Germany, 2000.

Existence (produced in London, England, 2002), Methuen (London, England), 2002.

SCREENPLAYS

Blow-Up (based on a short story by Julio Cortazar), Premier Productions, 1969.

(With Clement Biddle-Wood and Schlondorff) *Michael Kohlhaas* (based on the novella by Heinrich Von Kleist), Columbia, 1969.

Laughter in the Dark (based on the novel by Vladimir Nabokov), Lopert, 1969.

Walkabout (based on a novel by James Vance Marshall), Twentieth Century-Fox, 1971.

(Author of additional dialogue) James Goldman, *Nicholas and Alexandra* (based on the book by Robert K. Massie), Columbia, 1971.

Fury, 1973.

OTHER

The Swing Poems, Inter-Action (London, England), 1976.

First produced in 1965 and published the following year, Edward Bond's play *Saved* was reprised on the London stage at the Royal Court Theatre in December of 1984.

Theater Poems and Songs, edited by Malcolm Hay and Philip Roberts, Eyre Methuen (London, England), 1978.

Orpheus: A Story in Six Scenes (ballet scenario; produced in Stuttgart, Germany, then New York, NY, 1979), Schott (New York, NY), 1986.

Poems, 1978-1985, Methuen (New York, NY), 1987.

Olly's Prison (television play), Heinemann (London, England), 1993.

Tuesday (television play), Methuen (London, England), 1993, published in *Eleven Vests* [and] *Tuesday,* Methuen (London, England), 1997.

Edward Bond Letters, selected and edited by Ian Stuart, Harwood (Philadelphia, PA), Volume 1, 1994, Volume 2, 1995, Volume 3, 1996, Volume 4, 1998, Volume 5, 2001.

Selections from the Notebooks of Edward Bond, two volumes, Methuen (London, England), 2000.

The Hidden Plot: Notes on Theatre and the State, Methuen (London, England), 2000.

Bond's plays have been translated into twenty-five languages.

■ Sidelights

British playwright and author Edward Bond has created over thirty plays, including his groundbreaking *Saved,* a metaphorical tale of an infanticide that aroused violent controversy in his native England and abroad when it was first produced in 1965. *Saved* was banned in England for its violence, but the ensuing furor ultimately led to the abolition of censorship in that country. Dubbed everything from a Marxist playwright to a realist and lyric dramatist, Bond writes plays intended to make people think rather than simply be entertained. "Bond does not write about violence," observed Simon Trussler in *British Writers.* Instead, Trussler contended, "he writes about the effects upon the human spirit of a violent environment." Bond's work includes drama, comedies, screenplays, poetry, and criticism, but his focus is on the political use of the theater. "Drama is quite useful at helping us to understand what our position is and, conversely, we might then understand why our theatre is being destroyed," he told director Michael Bogdanov in an interview published in *New Statesman.* "The theatre, our theatre, comes from the Greeks. They created democracy: they needed a theatre; the two go hand in hand."

Bond "is distinguished by his historical perspective and his social awareness," Mel Gussow observed in the *New York Times.* The playwright's scrutiny of the past enables his audience to comprehend injustice

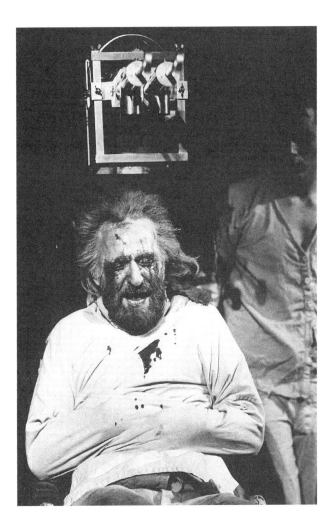

As in this 1982 production by the Royal Shakespeare Company, *Lear* presents audiences with an updated version of the Shakespearian drama in which unrestrained violence takes center stage.

in the present—and vice versa. In the 1970 play *Black Mass,* written to commemorate the tenth anniversary of the Sharpeville, South Africa, massacre, Bond's Christ gives the South African prime minister poison at the communion table during the Eucharist. *Restoration* also addresses issues of freedom and interracial justice as they affect the lives of a wealthy murderer's valet and his black wife. *The Woman,* set against the backdrop of the Trojan War, is an allegory about a state's abuses of power. Bond's adaptation of *King Lear* and *In the Company of Men* have also reached international audiences with their messages of alienation and hope. Ruby Cohn, an essayist for *Contemporary Dramatists,* noted the rich language to be found in Bond's plays: "Bond writes the most lapidary language of today's English theatre, absorbing dialects, pastiches, metaphors, and questions into a rich mineral vein. Pithy phrases, swift scenes, and vivid characters are his building-blocks for what he calls Rational Theatre, dedicated to the creation of a rational society. . . . His plays range through history and legend, as well as the contemporary scene." For Trussler, Bond's plays "probe cause and display effects," yet despite, or perhaps because of such explorations, he has found more popularity abroad, particularly in France, than he has in his native England. Writing in the *International Dictionary of Theatre,* essayist John Bull dubbed Bond "something of a paradox, a playwright with a world-wide reputation dealing with political debate on a global scale, but one with far less than the honour due him in his own country."

Working-Class Background

Born in 1934 to working-class parents in the North London suburb of Holloway, Bond was one of four children. As Trussler noted in *British Writers,* "He might never have left [Holloway's] drab, slum-pocked streets had it not been for the war." Bond and his siblings were evacuated to the countryside twice during World War II. At the start of the war he was sent to Cornwall; during the blitz he was again sent out of London, this time to his grandparents in the East Anglian Fens. These experiences added to Bond's ability to analyze as an outsider and ultimately encouraged him to become a writer. As he noted in an interview for *Theater Quarterly,* "If I had lived all my life in London, I would have sensed what the feel about certain things when they happened; one would have been taught the responses. Being put into a strange environment created a division between feeling and the experience of things. If there is any one reason, I dare say it's because of that that I'm a writer."

After the war Bond attended secondary school in Holloway. In *Theatre Quarterly* he disparaged the education he received, and once remarked that he was glad his education was so "deplorable." "It was marvelous for me. [Schools make] children . . . competitive, aggressive. People are not born violent by nature. Society . . . makes men animals in order to control them. I write because I want to change the structure of society. I think that society as it exists is primitive, dangerous and corrupt—that it destroys people. . . . I've no Utopia, no image of the society I want to see emerge. It would simply be people being themselves, happy in their own way—what could be more natural?"

One positive result of Bond's formal education was a school trip he took to a stage production of Shakespeare's *Macbeth.* As he recalled in *Theatre Quarterly,* from this production he took away a "sense of dignity about people," but at the same time felt "real surprise . . . that other people had seen this [play], so how was it that their lives could just go on in the same way." This revelation from a single visit to the theater was, for Bond, the sum total of his received education. He quit school as soon as legally possible and worked at various menial jobs before serving in the army for two years.

Bond began writing around age twenty-one. At first he turned his hand to verse, which he has since characterized as very bad, but soon was trying his skill at plays. This was in part a result of the influential performance of *Macbeth* he had seen, but was also inspired by the movement in the 1950s to revitalize English theater. Writers such as John Osborne and Harold Pinter stood theatrical and dramatic conventions on their head with their socially realistic dramas.

Plays Evoke Outraged Reactions

Bond wrote several unproduced plays before his debut drama, *The Pope's Wedding,* was staged in 1962 in London's West End. While the play did not receive much critical attention, it did pave the way for further productions of Bond's work in London. Bond made his breakthrough as an original playwright in 1965 with *Saved,* a play in which a street gang stones an infant to death. Conceived in a casual affair between two working-class youths, the child has failed to elicit affection from its grandparents, who share their home with the couple. The child's father makes an attempt to establish meaningful communication with others in the household, but the young mother finds a gang leader less boring. The infanticide has little effect on the family, who have been numbed by years of repressed aggression and exploitation. "Although the stoning is meant to shock, and certainly succeeds, it is very

clearly part of the fabric of life of these people," noted Frances A. Shirley in *Reference Guide to English Literature.* And in a *New Criterion* review of the play's 2001 New York revival, Mark Steyn observed that "time passes and events occur but no matter how dramatic or life-changing they ought to be everything stays the same, as if the characters are unable to do anything but dig themselves deeper into their own decay."

With *Saved,* Bond's name quickly became associated with disturbing depictions of violence. His next play, *Early Morning,* is a farce in which Queen Victoria, a lesbian Florence Nightingale, Prince Albert, and British prime minister Benjamin Disraeli destroy each other and continue to attack each other in the afterlife. The violence in *Saved* and *Early Morning* resulted in both plays being banned by British censors; it was not until the fall of 1968, when official censorship of the English stage was ended, that Bond could even hope to produce his plays without difficulty.

Bond was outraged by the reception to *Saved.* During an interview with Ronald Bryden published in the London *Observer Review,* the playwright remarked, "It didn't knock me out exactly, it surprised me. I was a very simple person. I'd spent a long time learning to write, and do it well. I knew I'd finally done it—written just what I intended; got it right. And suddenly all these people who set themselves up as custodians of art, of artistic opinion, were sounding off in every direction except that. They weren't involved with art at all. . . . But it didn't affect me as a writer. Art is the most private of all activities, and the theatre is the most private of all arts." In a letter published in the *Guardian,* Bond explained, "I chose to show violence in an inarticulate, working-class group because this brings out clearly our general social position vis-a-vis violence. Socially we are as confused about our own larger use of violence as my characters are about theirs."

In Bond's preface to the published version of *Saved* he explains that he believes people have been dehumanized by cultural institutions so that individuals try to reclaim some sense of personal power by acts of violence, which require energy and passion to execute. He also notes the acts of mass destruction perpetrated in wartime and the neglected state in which many children live, and asks the audience to compare such instances to the baby's death in *Saved.* Furthermore, he believes audiences desensitized by daily exposure to violence should be shocked awake by representations of violence on the stage; he reasons that feelings of outrage or disgust are better than no feeling at all. Indeed, some critics and view-

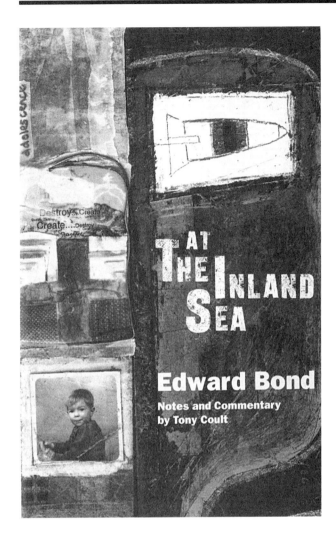

First produced in England, this drama for young audiences about the interaction between a boy and a stranger he encounters on the way to school was produced as a touring production in British schools during 1995.

ers were appalled by the violence in his plays and denounced the playwright for portraying murder on stage.

In *Plays and Players,* John Russell Taylor observed that in Bond's preface to *Saved* Bond "offers what may well be the key to most of the difficulties people . . . have often found in his work. 'Like most people,' he says, 'I am a pessimist by experience, but an optimist by nature, and I have no doubt that I shall go on being true to my nature. Experience is depressing, and it would be a mistake to be willing to learn from it.'" Taylor maintained that in Bond's early plays "some sort of hope gleams through, if only because some sort of basic goodness survives indestructibly the horrors of experience and steadfastly refuses to learn from them."

Commenting on Bond's career, Bryden stated: "Serious critics generally agree that he is the foremost of the new wave of dramatists who followed Osborne and his contemporaries in the 1960s. When his play *Saved* was staged at the Court in 1965, it was more or less howled down for its violence. . . . But when it was revived in 1969, in repertory with Bond's subsequent plays *Early Morning* and *Narrow Road to the Deep North,* recantations poured in and the consensus was that a formidable talent had been savagely misjudged. The conversion of the critics was completed by the arrival of Bond's *Lear* in 1971."

A Social Critic

In his adaptation of Shakespeare's *King Lear,* set in the Britain of 3100, the evil that the aged Lear suffers is more horrifying than that of his Shakespearean antecedent because it stems not from individual greed but from a society's collective renunciation of all natural human compassion. Writing in the *Dictionary of Literary Biography,* Max le Blond noted that in the play's action, "one ruling clique replaces another only to be replaced in its turn." In le Blond's estimation, "It is arguable that Bond was offering *Lear* as a parable of political violence in the twentieth century." *Library Journal* reviewer J. H. Crouch related that Bond's skill "transmutes the stuff of classic tragedy into horrifying, yet splendid melodrama." A *Variety* reviewer, on the other hand, felt that "the play's psychopathy of stupidity and violence is repeated and repeated. There is apostrophized humor, but it's an otherwise unremittingly downbeat piece, a longish (almost three hours) and grueling evening of allegorical drama." Writing in the *New York Times,* Walter Kerr expressed a similar view. "There had been no controlling principle to account for the deeds being done, nothing intimately human or narratively necessary to engage us," wrote the critic. "We were only being invited to watch violence as violence, to accept it as the occasion's *sole* activity. . . . Bond, whose earlier *Saved* was a relatively realistic play . . . has here become so obsessed with the idea of violence that he has neglected to give it plausible, or even theatrically coherent, organization."

Shakespeare appears as a character in Bond's 1971 production *Bingo.* Clive Barnes, in the *Times Literary Supplement,* wrote: "Bond's new play is about the death of Shakespeare. It is his most direct play since *Saved,* avoiding both absurdism and symbolism, and dealing with a man at the point of death, literally a man at point of accounting. The man happens to be William Shakespeare, and Mr. Bond is artistically honest with the basic facts known of the poet's life and character. But it could almost be any man of feeling, nervously aware of love and hate, and significance and insignificance of worldly goods, coming naked and fearful to that final summing up that is the only thing certain after birth." Bond further explores the lives of real and fictional historical personages in *The Fool,* about the poet John Clare, and *Restoration,* about yet another sort of fool, the servant, Bob, of a Restoration-age rake, Lord Are. Bob ultimately takes the blame for a murder committed by his master and is hanged for it.

Though Bond's plays received largely negative reviews when first produced because of misunderstandings about their representations of violence, they won the respect of critics and audiences in the 1970s and 1980s. Because of different approaches to character, Bond's working relationships with actors also came under strain during the late 1970s, culminating in his 1985 withdrawal from the Royal Shakespeare Company production of *The War Plays,* a "postatomic epic with impassioned pleas for social responsibility," according to Cohn in *Contemporary Dramatists.* Thereafter, Bond took a long sabbatical from the London stage, producing his play about the Spanish Civil War, *Human Cannon,* with a group of amateur actors in South Wales. London *Times* reviewer Jim Hiley said of the play with which Bond returned to the London stage in 1990, "*Jackets 2* seems unlikely to diminish the combative aura that surrounds [Bond]. But his return to the London theatre is surely to be welcomed. However abrasive his character and elusive his vision, Edward Bond's talent is too rare to be left in the wilderness."

Throughout the 1990s Bond continued to write and produce biting satirical and realistic plays, such as *In the Company of Men,* but found more respect in Europe than he did in England. As Marvin Carlson wrote in *Theatre Journal,* "Bond has not always been pleased by his English productions, and has found on the continent not only a growing interest in his work but several young directors who bring to it a deep dedication and sensitivity." By the year 2000, for example, Moliere was the only dramatist staged more often than Bond in France. French television also made a ninety-minute film about his international work in 2002.

Bond gained renewed attention in 2001 with the New York revival of *Saved.* "The play's clear-eyed observation of the interplay between need and neglect, and how people are warped by them, is as pertinent and powerful today as it was in 1965," commented Charles Isherwood in *Variety. New Criterion*'s Steyn thought that the play's "power is immediate, from the moment the curtain rises," while the production led *New Republic* critic Robert Brust-

ein to call *Saved* "an extraordinary work that is possibly Bond's masterpiece, and that is certainly among the most potent English dramas of the century."

Speaking of his mission as a dramatist to a *Twentieth-Century Literature* interviewer, Bond said, "It seems to me to be the job of rational people, of writers, of dramatists to plead for a just society, in their plays to rationally argue for a just society, to state clearly the conditions under which we live and try to make everybody understand that they must bear the consequences of the sort of life they lead. To show that our society is irrational and therefore dangerous—and that it maintains itself by denegating and corrupting human beings—that is what *Bingo* is about." Bond continued, "If you are an unjust person it doesn't matter how cultured you are, how civilized

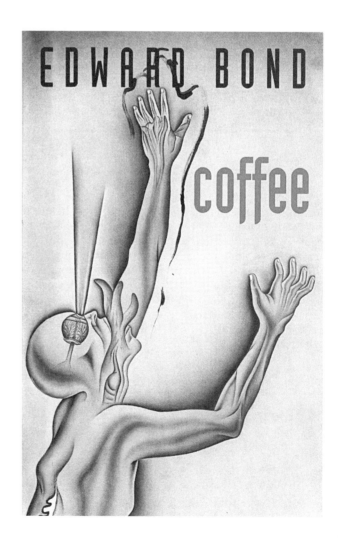

Bond continues his focus on the intersection between acts of violence and the reaction of polite society in this 1995 play.

you are, how capable you are of producing wonderful sayings, wonderful characters, wonderful jokes, you will still destroy yourself. And so a writer, nowadays, has to, as it were, put the cards on the table for the public and say: 'These are the consequences of your life; they are inescapable. If you want to escape violence you don't say "violence is wrong," you alter the conditions that create violence.' If you don't do that, then you are like somebody who says 'Well, the children in our village are dying of diphtheria, but we will not do anything about the drains!'"

If you enjoy the works of Edward Bond, you might want to check out the following:

Look Back in Anger, a play by John Osbourne, first produced in 1956.
The Caretaker, a play by Harold Pinter, first produced in 1960.
Blasted, a play by Sarah Kane, first produced in 1995.

Bond concluded to Bogdanov that what he tries to do in his work "is put a problem on stage, head-on, without evasion. At the end, some people will go out worse people, some people better. . . . But . . . both sets of people will have to redefine themselves; I will have put a certain amount of pressure on them. . . . If it then matters to you, you will have to seek a solution. To ask the dramatist to provide an answer is like asking the sea to invent a fish. All you can do is present a sea: if somebody wants to swim, there it is."

■ Biographical and Critical Sources

BOOKS

British Writers, Supplement 1, Charles Scribner's Sons (New York, NY), 1987, pp. 421-436.
Contemporary Dramatists, 6th edition, St. James Press (Detroit, MI), 1999.
Contemporary Literary Criticism, Gale (Detroit, MI), Volume 4, 1975, Volume 6, 1976, Volume 13, 1980, Volume 23, 1983.

Coult, Tony, *The Plays of Edward Bond: A Study,* Eyre Methuen (London, England), 1977, revised edition, 1979.
Dictionary of Literary Biography, Volume 13: *British Dramatists since World War II,* Gale (Detroit, MI), 1982.
Donahue, Delia, *Edward Bond: A Study of His Plays,* Bulzoni (Rome, Italy), 1979.
Drama for Students, Gale (Detroit, MI), 1998.
Hay, Malcolm, and Philip Roberts, *Edward Bond: A Companion to the Plays,* TQ Publications (London, England), 1978.
Hay, Malcolm, and Philip Roberts, *Bond: A Study of His Plays,* Methuen (London, England), 1980.
Hirst, David L., *Edward Bond,* Macmillan (London, England), 1985, Grove Press (New York, NY), 1986.
International Dictionary of Theatre, Volume 2: *Playwrights,* St. James Press (Detroit, MI), 1993.
Lappin, Lou, *The Art and Politics of Edward Bond,* Peter Lang (New York, NY), 1987.
Reference Guide to English Literature, 2nd edition, St. James Press (Chicago, IL), 1991.
Roberts, Philip, editor, *Bond on File,* Methuen (London, England), 1985.
Scharine, Richard, *The Plays of Edward Bond,* Bucknell University Press (Cranbury, NJ), 1976.
Stuart, Ian, *Politics in Performance: The Production Work of Edward Bond, 1978-1990,* Peter Lang (New York, NY), 1996.
Trussler, Simon, *Edward Bond,* Longman (Harlow, Essex, England), 1976.

PERIODICALS

Choice, September, 1967.
Christian Science Monitor, July 6, 1968.
Contemporary Review, August, 2001, Tom Phillips, "All the World's a Stage," p. 113.
Cue, December 14, 1968.
Guardian (London, England), November 12, 1965; January, 1978; October 15, 1992, Claire Armistead, "Flight of the Sparrow," p. 2.
Independent, May 21, 1997, p. S4.
Library Journal, December 1, 1972, J. H. Crouch, review of *Lear.*
Listener, April 18, 1968; August 8, 1968; June 18, 1970.
Los Angeles Times, April 9, 1983.
Nation, November 16, 1970.
National Review, November 24, 1989.
New Criterion, April, 2001, Mark Steyn, "Policy Paper Plays," p. 38.
New Republic, February 17, 1992; April 9, 2001, Robert Brustein, "The Aesthetics of Violence," p. 32.

New Statesman, October 18, 1996, Michael Bogdanov, "Theatre Has Only One Subject: Justice," pp. 34-36.

New Statesman & Society, November 6, 1992; January 26, 1996, p. 32.

Newsweek, November 9, 1970.

New York, November 9, 1970.

New York Times, November 26, 1970; October 24, 1971; January 7, 1972; April 29, 1973; May 13, 1973; August 19, 1974; August 25, 1974; March 11, 1979; June 3, 1979; February 11, 1983; February 20, 1983; February 2, 1986, Mel Gussow, review of *Restoration,* p. L54; May 8, 1996, p. C14; February 18, 2001, Benedict Nightingale, "An English Playwright with Very Mixed Notices," p. AR5.

Observer (London, England), October 18, 1992, Michael Coveney, "A Prophet Sees Little of His Own Land," p. 57.

Observer Review, November 9, 1969, Ronald Bryden, "Society Makes Men Animals," p. 27.

Opera News, March 12, 1988.

Plays and Players, August, 1970, John Russell Taylor, "British Dramatists," pp. 16-18.

Prompt, Number 13, 1969.

Show Business, January 4, 1969.

Stage, October 7, 1971; May 31, 1973.

Stand, summer, 1989.

Theatre Journal, May, 1993, Marvin Carlson, review of *In the Company of Men,* pp. 240-241.

Theatre Quarterly, Volume 2, 1972, "Drama and the Dialectics of Violence."

Time, November 9, 1970; January 17, 1972.

Times (London, England), July 27, 1985; February 23, 1987; February 28, 1990; March 5, 1990; June 29, 1995, Alan Franks, "'Despair Time' at the State of Our Theatres," p. 37.

Times Literary Supplement, January 3, 1992, p. 16; July 29, 1995, p. 19; December 22, 2000, Oliver Reynolds, review of *The Hidden Plot,* pp. 16-17.

Transatlantic Review, autumn, 1966, Giles Gordon, "Edward Bond: An Interview," pp. 7-15.

Twentieth-Century Literature, February 28, 1990; March 5, 1990.

Variety, December 18, 1968; January 29, 1969; March 12, 1969; November 18, 1970; October 20, 1971; March 1, 1972, review of *Lear;* July 4, 1973; March 5, 2001, Charles Isherwood, review of *Saved,* p. 52.

Washington Post, May 18, 1984; January 24, 1986.*

Meg Cabot

Personal

Born February 1, 1967, in Bloomington, IN; daughter of A. Victor (a college professor) and Barbara Cabot; married B. D. Egnatz (a financial writer), April 1, 1993. *Education:* Indiana University, B.A., 1991.

Addresses

Office—532 La Guardia Place, No. 359, New York, NY 10012. *Agent*—Laura Langlie, 275 President St., #3, Brooklyn, NY 11231. *E-mail*—megcabot@ earthlink.net.

Career

Writer. New York University, New York, NY, assistant manager of an undergraduate dormitory for ten years.

Member

Authors Guild, Society for Children's Book Authors and Illustrators, Romance Writers of America.

Awards, Honors

Romantic Times Reviewers Choice Award for Best British Isles Historical Romance, 1999, for *An Improper Proposal;* Top Ten Quick Picks for Reluctant Readers selection, Best Book selection, American Library Association, and New York Public Library Teen Book for the New Millennium citation, all 2001, all for *The Princess Diaries.*

Writings

The Princess Diaries, HarperCollins (New York, NY), 2000.
The Princess Diaries Volume II: Princess in the Spotlight, HarperCollins (New York, NY), 2001.
The Princess Diaries Volume III: Princess in Love, HarperCollins (New York, NY), 2002.
All American Girl, HarperCollins (New York, NY), 2002.

Contributor of short story to *Seventeen.*

UNDER PSEUDONYM JENNY CARROLL; "MEDIATOR" SERIES

Shadowlands, Pocket Pulse (New York, NY), 2000.
Ninth Key, Pocket Pulse (New York, NY), 2001.
Reunion, Pocket Pulse (New York, NY), 2001.
Darkest Hour, Pocket Pulse (New York, NY), 2001.
(Under name Meg Cabot) *Haunted: A Tale of the Mediator,* HarperCollins (New York, NY), 2003.

UNDER PSEUDONYM JENNY CARROLL; "1-800-WHERE-R-YOU" SERIES

When Lightning Strikes . . . , Pocket Pulse (New York, NY), 2001.
Code Name Cassandra, Pocket Pulse (New York, NY), 2001.
Safe House, Pocket Pulse (New York, NY), 2002.
Sanctuary, Pocket Pulse (New York, NY), 2002.

UNDER PSEUDONYM PATRICIA CABOT

Where Roses Grow Wild, St. Martin's Press (New York, NY), 1998.
Portrait of My Heart, St. Martin's Press (New York, NY), 1998.
An Improper Proposal, St. Martin's Press (New York, NY), 1999.
A Little Scandal, St. Martin's Press (New York, NY), 2000.
A Season in the Highlands (anthology), Pocket Books (New York, NY), 2000.
Lady of Skye, Pocket Books (New York, NY), 2001.
Educating Caroline, Pocket Books (New York, NY), 2001.
Kiss the Bride, Sonnet (New York, NY), 2002.

OTHER

(As Meggin Cabot) *The Boy Next Door* (adult novel), Avon (New York, NY), 2002.

■ Work in Progress

Nicola and the Viscount and *Victoria and the Rogue,* romance novels for young adult readers.

■ Adaptations

The Princess Diaries, starring Anne Hathaway and Julie Andrews, was filmed by Disney; the "1-800-WHERE-R-YOU" series was optioned by Lions Gate Films.

■ Sidelights

Meg Cabot has written novels for young adults, mysteries, and historical romances. Cabot is best known as the author of *The Princess Diaries,* the story of a teenage girl whose rather ordinary life changes the day she learns she has been born into royalty. That popular work has been followed by a pair of sequels: *The Princess Diaries Volume II: Princess in the Spotlight* and *The Princess Diaries Volume III: Princess in Love.*

Speaking of her childhood, Cabot told Cathy Sova of the *Romance Reader:* "I was born in Bloomington, Indiana. My childhood was spent in pursuit of air conditioning. A primary source proved to be the Monroe County Public Library, where I whiled away many hours, reading the complete works of Jane Austen, Judy Blume, and Barbara Cartland." After graduating from Indiana University with a fine arts degree, Cabot moved to New York City with the intention of becoming a professional illustrator. When that plan did not work out, she got a job as the assistant manager of a dormitory at New York University. It was then that she began writing short stories and novels in her spare time. In an interview posted at the *All about Romance* Web site, she remarked that "I have thousands (literally) of rejections to show for my efforts." Eventually her efforts paid off: in 1998 the first of Cabot's historical romance novels was accepted for publication. Two years later her young adult novel *The Princess Diaries* appeared on bookstore shelves.

The Princess Diaries

In her young adult novels, Cabot quickly earned a reputation for capturing the essence of the way adolescents think and talk. Her use of the novel-as-diary genre showcases this talent. *The Princess Diaries* concerns Mia, a fourteen-year-old New Yorker whose ordinary troubles with such things as a crush on the most popular boy in school, her flat chest, and the fact that her mother is dating her algebra teacher are magnified the day her father returns to reveal that he is a prince of a small European country. Much of the subsequent diary entries are consumed by Mia's revelations concerning life as a princess, including taking lessons in how to act like royalty from her imperious grandmother and being followed around by nosy reporters. Speaking to Sova, Cabot revealed the source of her teenaged characters: "I think my years working in a freshman dorm definitely helped shape my teen characters. And I do believe my natural inner voice is about 14 and a half."

"Readers will relate to Mia's bubbly, chatty voice and enjoy the humor of this unlikely fairy tale," contended Debbie Stewart in her review of *The Princess Diaries* for *School Library Journal.* While a reviewer for *Publishers Weekly* thought that Cabot's humor descends into "slapstick" on occasion, Chris Sherman wrote in *Booklist* that reading *The Princess Diaries* "is like reading a note from your best friend." Sherman went on to praise Cabot's accurate rendition of contemporary adolescent slang and her demonstrated ability to create well-rounded, lovable characters, arguing that teens will "be lining up for this hilarious story."

The character of Mia rejoins readers in the novels *The Princess Diaries Volume II: Princess in the Spotlight* and *The Princess Diaries Volume III: Princess in Love.* These stories continue the adventures of the awkward but spirited teen, and both are told in the diary style of the first volume. According to a reviewer for *Kirkus Reviews, Princess in Love* "has the best ending yet, which proves that princesses—even tall, flat-chested, algebraically challenged ones— always find true love." Chris Sherman in *Booklist* maintained that with the three "Princess" novels "Cabot has secured Mia's position as teen readers'

new best friend." Foreign rights to all three of the "Princess Diaries" books were sold to thirteen countries, including England, Japan, and Germany.

In an interview posted at the *ReadersRead* Web site, Cabot explained: "The voice of Mia, of course, is taken directly from my own diaries that I kept when I was in high school. . . . I still have them, though I am the only one who will ever be allowed to read them. I was pretty much a huge geek in high school—although I was pretty involved with the school's drama group. Most of what's in my journals from those days is about boys, boys, boys, and that's why I am the only one who is allowed to look at them! It is too embarrassing!"

Speaking to an interviewer for *TeenReads* online, Cabot explained: "There will probably be more than four books about Mia. I hope to write about her for as long as people want to keep reading about her. And I think the reason people want to read about Mia is that she is a genuinely nice person, who al-

Anne Hathaway (left), Julie Andrews, and Hector Elizondo star in the 2001 film adaptation of Cabot's *The Princess Diaries*, directed by Garry Marshall.

ways tries to do the right thing, except that sometimes she messes up—which is very human and appealing. In spite of her best efforts, Mia really can't help being a princess—someone who strives to right wrongs and make the world a better place. You have to admire that. . . . I know I do. I wish I could be more like her!"

Turns to Mystery Novels

Cabot also writes mysteries with a supernatural element under the pseudonym Jenny Carroll. In the inaugural works in the "1-800-WHERE-R-YOU" and the "Mediator" series, she exhibits some of the same winning characteristics as a writer who earned praise from young adult reviewers of *The Princess Diaries.* In *When Lightning Strikes,* the first book in the "1-800-WHERE-R-YOU" series, sixteen-year-old Jessica has been struck by lightning and now has the ability to find missing children. Unfortunately, the government wants her to use her ability to find criminals, and Jessica turns to a handsome biker for help in eluding the authorities. "Jessica's thrilling first-person account of her adventure is enhanced by raucously funny teen observations," remarked Roger Leslie in *Booklist.* Jessica returns in *Code Name Cassandra,* where she has taken a job at a summer camp for kids with musical abilities only to find herself drawn into using her psychic powers once again. Frances Bradburn in *Booklist* found that Cabot "paces the story well, smoothly moving from typical teen and camp conversations and situations to the tense and mysterious stalking of Jess by both police and kidnappers."

The idea for the "1-800-WHERE-R-YOU" series came about after Cabot and a friend were nearly struck by lightning. She told the interviewer for the *All about Romance* Web site: "A friend and I went for a walk in lower Manhattan, and got caught in a huge storm. The scaffolding we took refuge under was struck by lightning. We both got very excited, thinking we'd be getting psychic powers soon, . . . but alas, it did not happen, so I wrote a story about a girl who did get special powers."

Cabot as Carroll again employs a first-person teenage narrator in *Shadowlands,* the first book in the "Mediator" series. Like the protagonist of *When Lightning Strikes,* narrator Suze of *Shadowlands* has the mixed blessing of a sixth sense. Her special ability is as a mediator, which means putting ghosts in contact with the living world in order to resolve the conflicts between them. Though a reviewer for *Publishers Weekly* found Suze to be a less-than-credible narrator, the reviewer also noted that "the intriguing premise of a 16-year-old with a sixth sense may stand more than a ghost of a chance at snaring teen readers."

Writes Romances as Patricia Cabot

In addition to her "Princess Diaries" books and her mysteries, Cabot has written several romances under the name Patricia Cabot. In works such as *Lady of Skye, Portrait of My Heart,* and *An Improper Proposal,* Cabot earned praise for effectively injecting elements of mystery into her fiery romances, and for creating characters whose humor and humanity earn readers' empathy. A critic for *Publishers Weekly,* reviewing *Kiss the Bride,* found that "this witty, well-crafted romance is written with panache and peopled by unique secondary characters." Cabot has also written an adult contemporary novel, *The Boy Next Door,* under her full name of Meggin Cabot. Set in New York City, the novel follows gossip columnist Melissa Fuller as she tries to sort out her love life while helping out the elderly neighbor who has been attacked by a mysterious intruder. Told entirely through a series of e-mails between the primary characters, *The Boy Next Door* is full of "tongue-in-cheek humor," wrote a critic for *Publishers Weekly.*

If you enjoy the works of Meg Cabot, you might want to check out the following books:

Ellen Conford, *A Royal Pain,* 1986.
Francess Lantz, *A Royal Kiss,* 2000.
Ella Thorp Ellis, *The Year of My Indian Prince,* 2001.

Cabot explained in her *Romance Reader* interview: "I was drawn to the romance genre because it offered an escape from my real life problems, which at times have been very serious. One thing I don't think there's enough of in real life is humor, so I try to instill as much of that as possible into my work, as well as the rest of my life. Some readers don't like humor in their romances—or their life. I am not one of those people."

■ Biographical and Critical Sources

PERIODICALS

Booklist, September 15, 2000, Chris Sherman, review of *The Princess Diaries,* p. 233; May 1, 2001, Roger Leslie, review of *When Lightning Strikes,* p. 1744;

January 1, 2002, Frances Bradburn, review of *Code Name Cassandra*, p. 841; July, 2002, Chris Sherman, review of *Princess in Love*, p. 1837.

Kirkus Reviews, April 1, 2002, review of *Princess in Love*, p. 488.

Publishers Weekly, November 30, 1998, review of *Portrait of My Heart*, p. 69; October 18, 1999, review of *An Improper Proposal*, p. 78; October 9, 2000, review of *The Princess Diaries*, p. 88; November 6, 2000, review of *Shadowlands*, p. 92; December 11, 2000, review of *Lady of Skye*, p. 68; July 9, 2001, review of *The Princess Diaries*, p. 21; October 29, 2001, review of *Educating Caroline;* February 11, 2002, "And Then What Happened?," p. 188; April 22, 2002, review of *Princess in Love*, p. 56; June 24, 2002, review of *All American Girl*, p. 59; October 7, 2002, review of *The Boy Next Door*, p. 54.

School Library Journal, October, 2000, Debbie Stewart, review of *The Princess Diaries*, p. 155.

OTHER

All about Romance, http://www.likesbooks.com (July 23, 2001), "Patricia Cabot: Cross-Genre Phenomenon."

Meg Cabot's Web site, http://www.megcabot.com (August 23, 2002).

ReadersRead, http://www.readersread.com (August 23, 2002), "Interview with Meg Cabot."

Romance Reader, http://www.theromancereader.com (May 16, 2001), Cathy Sova, "Meet Author Patricia Cabot."

TeenReads, http://www.teenreads.com (April 23, 2002), "Interview with Meg Cabot."*

Mark Crilley

■ Personal

Born May 21, 1966, in Hartford City, IN; son of Robert H. (a Presbyterian minister) and Virginia A. (a secretary; maiden name, Ruffin) Crilley; married Miki Hirabayashi (a teacher), May 2, 1998; children: Matthew. *Nationality:* American. *Education:* Kalamazoo College, B.A., 1988. *Religion:* Presbyterian. *Hobbies and other interests:* Foreign languages, especially Japanese and Chinese, and collecting books from the 1920s and 1930s.

■ Addresses

Office—P.O. Box 71564, Madison Heights, MI 48071. *Agent*—Robb Horan, Sirius Entertainment, 264 East Blackwell, Dover, NJ 07801. *E-mail*—mcrilley@twmi. rr.com.

■ Career

Author and illustrator. English teacher at Young Men's Christian Association, Changhua, Taiwan, 1988-90 and 1993-94 and Morioka English Academy, Iwate, Japan, 1991-93; Sirius Entertainment, Dover, NJ, staff illustrator of comic book series "Akiko," 1995—.

■ Awards, Honors

Twelve nominations for Eisner Award, for "Akiko" comic books.

■ Writings

SELF-ILLUSTRATED JUVENILE NOVELS

Akiko on the Planet Smoo, Delacorte (New York, NY), 2000.

Akiko in the Sprubly Islands, Delacorte (New York, NY), 2000.

Akiko and the Great Wall of Trudd, Delacorte (New York, NY), 2001.

Akiko in the Castle of Alia Rellapor, Delacorte (New York, NY), 2001.

Akiko and the Intergalactic Zoo, Delacorte (New York, NY), 2002.

Akiko and the Alpha Centauri 5000, Delacorte (New York, NY), 2003.

OTHER

Author/illustrator of "Akiko" comic books, including *Akiko on the Planet Smoo.* Also creator of *32 Pages* (anthology); contributor of short story to *Trilogy Tour II Book.*

■ Work in Progress

More "Akiko" novels, to be published by Delacorte; further "Akiko" comic books for Sirius Comics.

■ Sidelights

Artist and writer Mark Crilley creates comic books and children's books that are "all about the possibility of the impossible," according to Jeff Dancer and David T. van Sweden, writing in *LuxEsto.* "The stories follow trails blazed by Alice through Wonderland and Dorothy through Oz. And they do so without violence or graphic scenes of gore. No muscular super-heroes in tights prowl these pages." Crilley instead opts for a fourth-grade girl named Akiko and her bizarre adventures on the mythical planet Smoo with her assortment of eccentric friends, including Mr. Beeba, Spuckler, Poog, and Gax. "The stories are intelligent, humorous, and written to appeal to adults as well as kids," according to Dancer and van Sweden. Crilley, in an interview with *Authors and Artists for Young Adults* (*AAYA*), reaffirmed that assessment: "I think of my audience as a true 'all ages' audience. I'm trying to entertain in the same way that [the comic strip] "Calvin and Hobbes" entertains; there is nothing in my work to offend the very young, but plenty in it (I hope) to amuse adults."

Crilley began his comic-book career in 1995 while teaching English in Japan, and his first published work was the comic book *Akiko on the Planet Smoo.* Nominated for an impressive dozen Eisner Awards, his "Akiko" series reached over fifty volumes in its first seven years. Crilley once commented: "I entered the world of children's books after having created the 'Akiko' comic book series. Luckily one of my comics found its way into the hands of Lawrence David, an editor at Random House Children's Books. Though I had no experience in writing (apart from my own comic books), Lawrence felt confident that I would be able to create a series of four novels based on the first eighteen issues of my 'Akiko' comics."

Crilley's judgement proved correct, and the initial series of four graphic novels for middle-grade readers was extended to ten, the early tales covering much of the same story line employed in the *Akiko* comic books.

From Kalamazoo to Japan

Born in 1966 in Hartford City, Indiana, Crilley was brought up in Detroit, Michigan, and began doing artwork at an early age. "Crilley family legend has

Author/illustrator Mark Crilley introduces readers to his humorous, off-beat, and out-of-this-world adventure in the 2000 fantasy *Akiko on the Planet Smoo.*

it that my older brothers, Bob and Jeff, taught me everything I know about drawing," Crilley told *AAYA.* "I do recall watching them draw and imitating them, but soon it became clear that I was the one getting a bit obsessed with it. Mom says I chose friends according to whether or not they were willing to sit and draw with me. My parents were the ideal artist's parents: always encouraging, never pressuring. They gave me all the paper and pencils I needed and just let me do my thing." Reading and the enjoyment of books were also early achievements for Crilley. "My favorite book as a child was an oversized, lavishly illustrated edition of *Pinocchio.* I suspect it was the illustrations that were grabbing me more than the story. Looking back, I can't say that I had any particular favorite author as a child, though I did have a favorite artist: M. C. Escher."

In school Crilley recalled he was a "fairly good student." Up until the fourth or fifth grade, however, he was also shy. A breakthrough came during a student production. "I took part in a talent show and wound up standing up on a stage doing a mock news report that was nothing more than a string of one liners," Crilley told *AAYA*. "One that seemed hilarious back then but now strikes me as rather ominous: 'The world will blow up at ten o' clock tonight; details at eleven.' From that time on I became a bit of a class clown (though a well-behaved one; I have a highly exaggerated respect for authority figures) and to this day I see myself more as an entertainer than a true artist." Soon he began to channel this creative energy. "I continued to draw and was regarded as the best of my class, which resulted in me being rather smug by the time I went off to college. I was also a regular in the high school drama club and for a time thought I might just as soon be an actor as an artist. (You will note, no doubt, that being a writer didn't even come into the mix; that was not to come until much, much later.)"

Crilley attended Michigan's Kalamazoo College. "I enjoyed my college years, though they were a real roller coaster ride for me emotionally, more so than my high school years, oddly enough," Crilley told *AAYA*. "I was lucky to study under David Small, who was then in his final years as a teacher at Kalamazoo College. I was there at what I now realize was a very trying time in his life—making the transition from teacher to full-time writer/illustrator—but all I recall from those days was how he took me under his wing and got me to work harder, to learn from the masters, to always strive for excellence as an artist. Another important figure for me was Conrad Hilberry, with whom I took a creative writing poetry class; Looking back, I see that he was my first writing teacher, and that whatever modest writing skills I've developed over the years can be traced directly back to him."

A year of study abroad in Senegal during his junior year added to Crilley's artistic equipment, developing his sense of wonder and love of adventure. "In my comic books, you'll see a lot of architecture and scenes which attempt to convey the awe-inspiring wonder of stepping into a foreign environment," he told Dancer and van Sweden.

Graduating from college in 1988, Crilley initially gave no thought to making a living as an artist or a writer, instead spending the next five years as an English teacher in Taiwan and in Japan. During these years, however, he began to put his twin loves of drawing and writing together; partly at the encouragement of some of his Japanese students he created the thirty-three-page story that would eventually be published in comic book form as *Akiko on the Planet Smoo*.

In *Akiko in the Sprubly Islands,* Crilley's young heroine and a team of friends set out to seek the help of a lonely queen in rescuing the kidnaped Prince Froptoppit from an intergalactic menace.

Partly influenced by American classics such as Winsor McCay's "Little Nemo" and the more contemporary "Calvin and Hobbes," *Akiko on the Planet Smoo* introduces a ten-year-old Japanese-American girl with distinctive braids and round eyes. This fourth grader is taken to the planet Smoo, where she has, according to Crilley in a *Worlds of Westfield* interview with Roger Ash, "a series of adventures with amazing and silly characters." Crilley further typified the story in that same interview as "*Wizard of Oz* meets *Star Trek.*" There are four main supporting characters populating this initial story, as well as in all subsequent comic books and graphic novels. Spuckler is a swashbuckler hero, part Han Solo of *Star Wars,* and part Indiana Jones. Mr. Beeba is the opposite of Spuckler, an "intellectual librarian type character," according to Crilley in his interview with Ash. Gax is Spuckler's rather beat-up robot, a butler who is smarter than his master. Lastly there is Poog, a floating head who speaks his own language. The first "Akiko" comic-book creation remained in Crilley's writer's trunk until his return to the United States, when it was picked up by Sirius Comics.

Comics Adapted into Book Format

After their publication, the "Akiko" comics quickly became underground favorites, and by 1998 they had surfaced to reach a mainstream comic readership. Now with several years of comic-book creation under his belt, Crilley was that year honored by *Entertainment Weekly* as a young artist to watch, and soon after made the cross-over into graphic novels. The first of these novels follows the arc of an eighteen-issue series in the "Akiko" comic book series titled "The Menace of Alia Rellapor." Crilley's debut book, *Akiko on the Planet Smoo,* has young Akiko being whisked away from her seventeenth-story apartment to find a kidnaped prince on the planet of Smoo. The humanoid ruler of Smoo, King Froptoppit, has insisted that Akiko, despite her lack of experience in such matters, is the perfect candidate to search for his missing son, indeed to rescue him from the clutches of the evil Alia Rellapor. Froptoppit's commands force Akiko and her companions, Spuckler, Gax, Poog, and Mr. Beeba to battle a dangerous group of sky pirates, among other incidents, and readers are left waiting for the sequels to see if the heroine will get her man or not.

Crilley's first middle-grade graphic novel, with black and white illustrations, was warmly received by critics. Diane Roback and Jennifer M. Brown, writing in *Publishers Weekly,* dubbed *Akiko on the Planet Smoo* a "stylish debut" and called Akiko an appealing character with "a conversational voice and global flair" who looks like a "cross between an anime character and a Raggedy Ann doll." Chris Sherman, writing in *Booklist,* also praised Crilley's work, mentioning the "fast-paced" action, the "easy-reading, conversational style [which] is appealing," and the "broadly drawn characters." David Lininger, reviewing the same title in *Library Talk,* felt that during each adventure of her rescue mission Akiko "learns a little bit more about her leadership abilities," and Lisa Prolman in *School Library Journal* also commented on the leadership theme, which she felt was "occasionally overdone." However, Prolman felt that such concerns did not "detract from the story's humor," which Crilley himself elsewhere characterized as containing "a dash of Monty Python." Sherman concluded that "in true comic-book serial fashion" readers are left "wondering what will come next."

Illustrated with Crilley's imaginative pen-and-ink drawings, *Akiko and the Great Wall of Trudd* find the pigtailed fourth grader and her allies still on their rescue mission, with their biggest obstacle yet to overcome.

Next up was *Akiko in the Sprubly Islands,* in which the intrepid ten year old and her buddies log some new and even more amazing adventures on their way to Alia Rellapor's castle to save Prince Froptoppit, surviving a skugbits storm and crashing into the Moonguzzit Sea. Lost, they figure they need to find Queen Pwip, a clairvoyant who will thus be able to guide them to the castle. However, when both Spuckler and Mr. Beeba go missing one night, the mantle of leadership falls directly on Akiko's shoulders and she must decide how to survive in this strange world.

Again, Crilley's efforts met with praise from reviewers. *Booklist* contributor Shelle Rosenfeld recommended *Akiko in the Sprubly Islands* "for reluctant readers or children making a transition from comics to novels," while *School Library Journal* reviewer Prolman concluded that by using "short chapters, a quick pace, and lots of cliff-hangers, Crilley keeps readers wondering what will happen next." Prolman also felt that the characters "play off [Akiko] and one another nicely." Similarly, a reviewer for *Family Life* contended that part of Akiko's appeal "is her Pokemon-ish appearance—that cute, Japanese anime look."

In their third outing, *Akiko and the Great Wall of Trudd,* Akiko, Spuckler, Gax, Mr. Beeba, and Poog continue their search for the prince, nearing the castle of Alia Rellapor, but first they must scale the Great Wall of Trudd. This wall is similar to the Great Wall of China, but much bigger, so long, in fact, that the team cannot go around it; they must go over it. But the wall is only one of the challenges the team meets. Others include an encounter with the gruesome Throck, and a Smud Burger snack on the bridge over the Moonguzzit Sea. Elaine E. Knight, writing in *School Library Journal,* felt the sequel "will be confusing to readers unfamiliar with the previous books," but also noted that Akiko "is a

Akiko in the Castle of Alia Rellapor recounts the end of the mission as Akiko and her crew—Mr. Beeba, Gax, Poog, and Spuckler Boach—finally reach the prince and his sinister captor.

strong female character whose leadership holds her strange band together." A contributor for *Publishers Weekly* wondered if the band would ever get to the castle of Alia Rellapor, and then answered the question: "Read the next installment to find out."

Akiko in the Castle of Alia Rellapor concludes the first adventure of Akiko and her fearsome foursome of friends. Here they finally arrive at the castle where the prince is being held prisoner, only to find it filled with "weird monsters and dangerous traps," according to Knight in *School Library Journal.* The team must deal with these unexpected obstacles before even getting to Alia Rellapor. When they finally do, they discover that Alia is actually the prince's mother and, under mind control of the monster Throck, she comes close to having the group put to death. However, combining their talents in one last valiant effort, Akiko and her friends manage to defeat Throck and make their escape from the castle with both the prince and his mother in tow. Knight praised the "bickering dialogue among the adventurers [which] is amusing," but again questioned if new readers unfamiliar with previous installments would be able to follow the story. *Booklist* contributor Francisca Goldsmith also felt that this "mostly text version" of the story was "less substantial than Crilley's full-out graphic novel" as presented in the eighteen issues of the comic-book version. However, Goldsmith also noted that "youngsters unfamiliar with sf may find that being led into space by Akiko is a fun introduction to the genre."

Perils of Akiko Continue

With book number five in the "Akiko" series, *Akiko and the Intergalactic Zoo,* Crilley created a stand-alone novel, and it was decided that all future books in the series would also be complete in one volume. In this novel, Akiko has been back on her own planet for some time, has just started the fifth grade, and has been chosen leader of the safety patrol at school. Her adventurous spirit is rekindled after the grateful King of Smoo sends her and her band of adventurers on an expense-paid vacation to the planet Quilk and its Intergalactic Zoo. The king's thank-you gift goes bad, however, when the zookeeper decides to add Akiko to his personal zoo collection. This volume in the series also adds three new characters to the ongoing adventures. Book number six in the graphic novel series, *Akiko and the Alpha Centauri 5000,* "is certainly the most action-packed story I've ever written," Crilley commented on his author Web site. The book recounts the adventures of an exciting rocket ship race from one side of the universe to the other. Further tales will have Akiko experiencing adventures on planet Earth, crash-landing in Japan, and dealing with a new culture closer to home. Meanwhile, Crilley also continues work on his "Akiko" comic books.

"The process of writing juvenile fiction has certainly been challenging for me," Crilley once commented. "I think of myself as a storyteller really, and I simply do my best to entertain. I try to provide a quiet message in my books about the value of friendship and the great things a child can achieve when people really believe in her. I am fortunate to have both my "Akiko" comics and novels embraced by a small band of dedicated fans, without whom I'd never have made it to where I am today."

Crilley writes at a desk in his home, "though sometimes I'll get a bit of writing done at a coffee shop or some such place," as he told AAYA. "When I'm at work on a particular book I write nearly every morning; on a good day I'll get three or four pages." Speaking with Ash, Crilley noted that he generally works from an outline of a story arc, but leaves room for new developments as the story progresses. "Even when you sketch [the story] down in advance, I find that I have to really get down to the final artwork before I realize what's going to work best." Crilley also scans his line art into a computer to help develop the distinctive gray tones in his work.

If you enjoy the works of Mark Crilley, you might want to check out the following:

The "Bone" series of graphic novels by Jeff Smith.
Naoko Takeuchi's work in the "Sailor Moon" series.
The "Usagi Yojimbo" series by Stan Sakai.

Speaking with Christine Broda in the Canton Observer, Crilley indicated the direction in which his career has progressed since he first began "Akiko": "I thought of myself mainly as an illustrator who got into writing so I would have something to illustrate. Now I think of myself as a writer who is able to illustrate my own books."

■ Biographical and Critical Sources

PERIODICALS

Booklist, March 1, 2000, Chris Sherman, review of Akiko on the Planet Smoo, p. 1243; January 1, 2001, Shelle Rosenfeld, review of Akiko in the Sprubly Islands, p. 958; January 1, 2002, Francisca Goldsmith, review of Akiko in the Castle of Alia Rellapor, p. 856.
Canton Observer (Canton, MI), August 4, 2002, Christine Broda, "Quick on the Draw," pp. A1-A9.
Entertainment Weekly, June 26, 1998, "Mark Crilley: Cult Cartoonist," p. 90.
Family Life, March 1, 2001, review of Akiko in the Sprubly Islands, p. 87.
Library Talk, September-October, 2000, David Linger, review of Akiko on the Planet Smoo, p. 41.
LuxEsto, winter, 2002, Jeff Dancer and David T. van Sweden, "From Kalamazoo to Smoo: The Journeys of Mark Crilley," pp. 5-7.
Publishers Weekly, January 17, 2000, Diane Roback and Jennifer M. Brown, review of Akiko on the Planet Smoo, p. 57; January 8, 2001, review of Akiko and the Great Wall of Trudd, p. 68; June 18, 2001, review of Akiko on the Planet Smoo and Akiko in the Sprubly Islands, p. 83; August 27, 2001, review of Akiko in the Castle of Alia Rellapor, p. 86.
School Library Journal, February, 2000, Lisa Prolman, review of Akiko on the Planet Smoo, p. 92; November, 2000, Lisa Prolman, review of Akiko in the Sprubly Islands, p. 113; April, 2001, Elaine E. Knight, review of Akiko and the Great Wall of Trudd, p. 105; November, 2001, Elaine E. Knight, review of Akiko in the Castle of Alia Rellapor, pp. 113-114.

OTHER

Akiko Homepage, http://www.randomhouse.com (August 30, 2002).
Crilley, Mark, interview with J. Sydney Jones for Authors and Artists for Young Adults, August 30, 2002.
Mark Crilley Web site, http://www/geocities.com/Athens/Olympus/6912/ (August 30, 2002).
Worlds of Westfield, http://westfieldcomics.com (August 30, 2002), Roger Ash, "Mark Crilley Interview."*

—Sketch by J. Sydney Jones

Terry Davis

■ Personal

Born 1947, in Spokane, WA; son of Roy (in the car business) and Lucille Bernice (Thomson) Davis; children: Pascal, Anissa. *Nationality:* American. *Education:* Eastern Washington State University, B.A., 1969; University of Iowa Writer's Workshop. M.F.A., 1973; attended Stanford University, 1974-75.

■ Addresses

Home—103 James Ave., Mankato, MN 56001. *Office*—c/o English Department, Mankato State University, Mankato, MN 56002-8400. *E-mail*—VQDavis@aol.com.

■ Career

Writer and educator. Monroe High School, Monroe, WA, English teacher, 1969-70; Escola Americana do Rio de Janeiro, Rio de Janeiro, Brazil, English teacher, 1970-71, 1973-74; Association Culturelle Franco-Americaine, 1975-76; Eastern Carolina University, English instructor, 1976-80; University of Idaho, English instructor, 1981; Eastern Washington State University, English instructor, 1981-82; Gonzaga University, English instructor, 1984-86; Shadle Park High School, Spokane, WA, instructor, 1985-86; Mankato State University, Mankato, MN, English instructor, 1986—.

■ Awards, Honors

Wallace Stegner literary fellowship, Stanford University; Washington State Governor's Award for the Arts, 1980; American Book Award nomination and American Library Association (ALA) Best Books for Young Adults designation, both 1980, and ALA Best Books for Young Adults in the Last Quarter Century designation, 1995, all for *Vision Quest*; Distinguished Alumni Award, Eastern Washington University, 1984; ALA Best Books for Young Adults designation, 1993, Best Books for Young Adults, Association for Library Service, 1993, and Books for the Teen Age designation, New York Public Library, 1994, all for *If Rock and Roll Were a Machine*; Edwin M. Hopkins *English Journal* Award, 1996.

■ Writings

Vision Quest, Viking (New York, NY), 1979, reprinted, Eastern Washington University Press (Spokane, WA), 2002.

Mysterious Ways, Viking (New York, NY), 1984.

If Rock and Roll Were a Machine, Delacorte (New York, NY), 1992.

Presenting Chris Crutcher (criticism), Twayne (New York, NY), 1997.

The History of the Houston Comets (sports history), Creative Education (Mankato, MN), 1999.

Roll Tide!: The Alabama Crimson Tide Story, Creative Education (Mankato, MN), 1999.

Contributor to books, including short-story anthology *On the Edge: Stories at the Brink*, edited by Lois Duncan, and to *Children's Writers and Illustrators Market*, 2002. Contributor to periodicals, including *ALAN Review, Sports Illustrated, Library Journal, English Journal*, and *Northfield Magazine*.

■ **Adaptations**

Vision Quest was adapted for a movie by Warner Bros., 1985.

■ **Work in Progress**

Two novels, *The Silk Ball*, about a Hmong high school senior applying to the screenwriting program at USC, and *Six Dogs Long*, a novel in three acts.

■ **Sidelights**

Terry Davis "burst onto the literary scene with a celebrated piece of literature that remains to this day a bible for many high school wrestling coaches and their charges," wrote young adult novelist Chris Crutcher in the introduction to the 2002 edition of Davis's *Vision Quest*. That novel, adapted for a film in 1985, has had a long shelf life, reaching out to young readers over the span of more than two decades to talk about what it means to take life on your own terms, and to create, as Crutcher wrote, your own "challenges."

"My goal when I write is to create a reality on the page that pulls the reader in so deeply that his own reality evaporates and there is only the story we are living through together," commented Davis in an interview with *Authors and Artists for Young Adults* (*AAYA*). With his first novels, Davis did exactly that, carving out a definite niche in the field of young adult literature with works that "explore the lives of young men who confront seemingly insurmountable challenges and obstacles successfully," as an essayist in the *St. James Guide to Young Adult Writers* commented. "His protagonists are not perfect young men," the contributor further noted. "They are adolescents who have seen their share of grief and failure. Yet, somehow, they manage to rise above what is lacking in their lives." Davis—in his novels

Vision Quest, Mysterious Ways, and *If Rock and Roll Were a Machine*—uses school athletics or the saving grace of an interest in motorcycles to center his protagonists, drawing strongly out of personal experience for each of these titles.

A Precocious Kid

Davis described himself in his interview with *AAYA* as a physically and intellectually precocious child." Born in Spokane, Washington in 1947, Terence Albert Davis was an only child. "My mom and my dad and my mom's folks read to me constantly when I was little, and I learned to read early and then read constantly to myself." One book Davis remembers best as a very young reader was *The Little Engine That Could*. Soon he graduated to sports stories and tales of the outdoors. With no brothers or sisters, a mother who was ill much of the time, and a father who was selling on the road, Davis began to build his own worlds. "I had plenty of friends in the neighborhood," the author noted in his interview, "but I sought more friends in books, and I found plenty. I still remember George and Lenny from *Of Mice and Men*. I was so, so sad at Lenny's death. I suppose because I sought the world of literature to supplant my real world, I probably read things that were generally for older readers."

Davis remembered school up to the fourth grade as "heaven" for him. "There were all those kids to play with, all that stuff to learn, and all that attention to get." However, in the fifth grade this all changed when he had his first male teacher. This teacher felt that the precocious Davis—who was always first to answer the teacher's questions—needed changing; for two years he made Davis's life a "nightmare," as the author related in his interview, humiliating the boy at every chance. "By the seventh grade I was a basket case. I stuttered, and I sure as hell didn't want to answer any questions."

"I was diagnosed with bi-polar disorder a few years ago," Davis noted, "and I can look back and see those symptoms in me as a child. I was hyperactive. I was a handful. But I was good-hearted." Luckily, Davis's mother and her parents supplied a loving home, a refuge from the humiliations being served up in school daily. Yet his schoolwork suffered. From being an "A" student, he slipped to "C" student status. "High school was more fun because of sports and social life," Davis commented in his interview, "but I kept on the 'C' track and graduated with a 2.5 GPA."

In addition to new teachers and coaches who brightened things for Davis, in high school he discovered wrestling and baseball and was undefeated for two

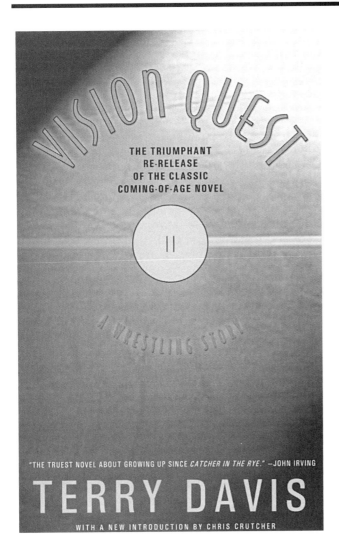

THE TRIUMPHANT
RE-RELEASE
OF THE CLASSIC
COMING-OF-AGE NOVEL

"THE TRUEST NOVEL ABOUT GROWING UP SINCE *CATCHER IN THE RYE*." —JOHN IRVING

TERRY DAVIS

WITH A NEW INTRODUCTION BY CHRIS CRUTCHER

First published in 1979, Terry Davis's award-winning novel about a young athlete's use of self-discipline to succeed in both his personal life and his sport was re-released for a new generation of readers in 2002.

years as a wrestler. These experiences stuck with Davis: as a kid he thought he would be a teacher and a coach, and in his first novel he focuses on the character of the high school wrestler.

College was a revelation for Davis, who finally "fell in love with learning again." Attending Eastern Washington State College, he had strong and supportive writing instructors who helped to turn his life around. He also has fond memories of friends at the fraternity he pledged, Lambda Chi Alpha. After graduation, he taught high school English in Washington, and then went to Rio de Janeiro for a year, also teaching English. More and more, however, he was beginning to think of himself as a

writer; he applied to the Iowa Writer's Workshop and was accepted.

Returning to the United States, Davis spent two years at the Writer's Workshop, a "horrible experience for me while I was there, but [one that] evolved into a great learning experience as the years went by." At the workshop he learned the tools of the writer's trade, but the downside was that he was trying so hard to write literary stories that he ignored the real material he should have been dealing with all along. "On the last day there, cleaning out my desk in the graduate assistant's office, I sat down and wrote the first and last sentences of *Vision Quest*." He had finally found, or rediscovered, his own voice. "Out of desperation I turned to a subject matter and a narrative style that came from my heart. I wrote about a high school wrestler who was in many ways—except for the superior athletic gifts—me. And I wrote about a place I loved."

Vision Quest

After leaving Iowa, Davis returned for another year of teaching at the American School in Rio de Janeiro, all the while continuing to work on his novel. With half of it finished, Davis sent the manuscript to Stanford University in application for a Wallace Stegner literary fellowship. He won and spent the next year at Stanford finishing his novel. After thirty rejections, the book was picked up by Bantam and the magazine *Sports Illustrated* also published excerpts.

Vision Quest tells the story of Louden Swain, a wrestler attempting to drop two weight classes so that he can challenge the reportedly unbeatable Gordon Shute in their last year of high school competition. To do this requires tremendous physical discipline, part of which is mental discipline or a "vision quest," in which Louden attempts to find his balance. "Balance in life is a recurring theme in *Vision Quest*," wrote the *St. James Guide to Young Adult Writers* essayist. "Davis's characters must achieve the proper balance in their lives in order to find happiness and fulfillment." Thus, Louden cannot simply obsess about his sport. His personal life requires his attention as well. Such personal issues include his relationship with his father, his teammates and friends, and with Carla, an older girl he is beginning to fall in love with. All of these people have their place in Louden's life and in his quest for his personal best. The novel ends with Louden and Shute about to begin their first wrestling match.

Critical reception to *Vision Quest* at the time of its 1979 publication was overwhelmingly positive, with comparisons to *Catcher in the Rye* and the "Rocky" movies. One of a handful of important young adult titles of the late 1970s, it paved the way for much of the hard-hitting fiction in that genre to follow. As Dan Webster noted in the *Spokesman-Review.com, Vision Quest* "was a pioneer in the field." In 1985 it was filmed for a movie by Warner Bros., and in 2002 the novel was reprinted, with some stylistic editing from Davis. Reviewing the 2002 edition, *Library Journal* contributor Michael Rogers noted that Davis uses high school wrestling as a "metaphor for growing up." Jim Naughton, reviewing the updated edition in the *Washington Post,* commented that the "book is still fresh and true to life," and that the publisher, Eastern Washington University Press, "has done a service to a new generation of young readers."

Reputation for High-Quality Fiction

Davis's more recent novels have generally been categorized as young adult. In *Mysterious Ways* he deals with his college years and the teaching posi-

tion in Brazil. In the tale, Karl Russel, orphaned at sixteen, keeps a journal of his innermost thoughts. These entries deal with the 1960s in the United States and with political terrorism in Rio de Janeiro and that city's almost invisible population of disfigured people. This novel, Davis's personal favorite, won critical acclaim when published in 1984. Almost a decade later, in an assessment of current young adult fiction in *Horn Book,* Patty Campbell grouped *Mysterious Ways* together with Robert Cormier's *I Am the Cheese* as "rare treasures," books that take "hardened young-adult reviewers by surprise, . . . so unlike what has gone before, so rich in levels of meaning, so daring in complexity of symbol and metaphor, so challenging in the ambiguity of its conclusion, that we are left with all our neat little everyday categories and judgments hanging useless."

Eight years passed before Davis published his next novel. For this one, he again mined personal experience. Bert Bowden, the protagonist of *If Rock and Roll Were a Machine,* is sixteen and in high school. He is a shy and conflicted kid as a result of

Matthew Modine stars as protagonist Louden Swain in the 1985 film adaptation of Davis's novel *Vision Quest.*

the humiliation he suffered at the hands of his fifth and sixth grade teacher, Mr. Lawler, a sadistic man who felt he needed to get the youngster into shape. As a result, Bert's self-esteem is non-existent. He fantasizes himself as the star of the football team, but actually he is too small for the sport. Sports are important in Bert's high school, the same high school attended by Louden Swain, protagonist of *Vision Quest*, some twenty years earlier. Bert begins to find salvation through the intercession of both machine and man. The purchase of a motorcycle signals the teen's separation from his childhood and the painful memories it holds for him. He not only discovers a freedom on the bike but also the acceptance by other bikers. Adults also figure into Bert's slow transformation and recovery. The motorcycle dealer becomes a friend and confidante, and his English teacher encourages Bert to continue writing. Bert's essays and other writings provide insight into his thoughts and feelings. In the pages of *If Rock and Roll Were a Machine* fans of Davis's earlier books learn what ultimately became of Louden Swain: he went on to become an Olympic wrestler and an astronaut who was killed in a space shuttle explosion. Ultimately, Bert confronts his old teacher Mr. Lawler and is able to regain confidence by the incident.

Gail Richmond, reviewing *If Rock and Roll Were a Machine* in *School Library Journal*, felt that Bert's writings are "nicely integrated into the text and include some of the book's strongest images." Richmond also noted that Bert's "teen psyche is fully developed through his anger, impatience, and words," and that teen readers would recognize "his questions and feelings as their own."

Balancing Teaching and Writing

"I write about young people," Davis noted in his *AAYA* interview, "because the feelings are with me every day. Those pains and joys and uncertainties are with me every single day. And the people who were good to me then are with me still, too. I write about those days because I am expert in those passions."

When working on a project, Davis writes every morning and then revises later in the afternoon. In addition to his fiction-writing, he is also the author of the critical study *Presenting Chris Crutcher*, an "honest and sharply accurate analysis," according to Phyllis Graves in *School Library Journal*. Additionally, Davis has penned two sports books, *The History of the Houston Comets* and *Roll Tide!: The Alabama Crimson Tide Story*. However, his writing has always shared space with his university instruction.

He teaches in a Master of Fine Arts writing program at Minnesota State University, Mankato. "I love my work," he noted in his interview. "I have a lot of reading to do, of course, but it doesn't detract from my life as a writer. It enhances my writing life." Davis has also battled manic depression for many years, a condition that has limited the amount he could write. In 2001 his condition was diagnosed as partly due to a chemical imbalance; taking mineral supplements has helped Davis, like his popular protagonist Louden Swain, find an inner balance again.

If you enjoy the works of Terry Davis, you might want to check out the following books:

J. D. Salinger, *The Catcher in the Rye*, 1951.
Chris Crutcher, *Running Loose*, 1983.
Rich Wallace, *Wrestling Sturbridge*, 1996.

"When I write," Davis concluded in his interview, "I have an ageless audience in mind, The readers I envision are thoughtful and good hearted. They are not cynical. Cynicism is the cheapest of intellectual poses. Cynicism masquerades as wisdom, but it is not wisdom. It's a sophisticated form of cowardice. . . . What led me to become a writer was the desire to people a tiny room of the house of literature with voices I know and love. Aside from being a father, I write better than I do anything else, and writing gives me a chance to give something beautiful to the world, or at least to be of use in the world."

■ Biographical and Critical Sources

BOOKS

Davis, Terry, *Vision Quest*, foreword by Chris Crutcher, Eastern Washington University Press (Spokane, WA), 2002.
St. James Guide to Young Adult Writers, 2nd edition, St. James Press (Detroit, MI), 1999.

PERIODICALS

ALAN Review, spring, 1997, Terry Davis, "On the Question of Integrating."

Booklist, November 1, 1992, p. 510.

Book Report, March-April, 1993, Elaine Patterson, review of *If Rock and Roll Were a Machine,* p. 38.

English Journal, May, 1980, pp. 92-93; September, 1980, p. 88; November, 1980 p. 87; November, 1991, pp. 87-88.

Horn Book, November-December, 1993, Patty Campbell, "The Sand in the Oyster," pp. 717-721.

Library Journal, May 1, 2002, Michael Rogers, review of *Vision Quest,* p. 140.

Mankato Free Press, October 10, 2001, Rachel Hanel, "Out of the Pit."

Publishers Weekly, June 8, 1984, p. 57; November 30, 1992, review of *If Rock and Roll Were a Machine,* p. 56.

San Angelo Standard-Times (San Angelo, TX), November 20, 1997, Todd Martin, "Parent Questions Book Selection at Middle School."

School Library Journal, November, 1992, Gail Richmond, review of *If Rock and Roll Were a Machine,*

p. 119; June, 1998, Phyllis Graves, review of *Presenting Chris Crutcher,* p. 156.

Voice of Youth Advocates, June, 2002, Joel Shoemaker, "Crutch, Davis & Will," pp. 94-99.

Washington Post, June 2, 2002, Jim Naughton, review of *Vision Quest.*

Wilson Library Bulletin, January, 1985, p. 341.

OTHER

Davis, Terry, interview with J. Sydney Jones for *Authors and Artists for Young Adults,* September 15, 2002.

Spokesman-Review (Spokane, WA), http://www.spokesmanreview.com/ (March 7, 2002), Dan Webster, "Double Vision."

Terry Davis Web site, http://www.terrydavis.net (September 7, 2002).*

—*Sketch by J. Sydney Jones*

James Dickey

■ Personal

Born February 2, 1923, in Buckhead, GA; died of complications from lung disease, January 19, 1997, in Columbia, SC; son of Eugene (a lawyer) and Maibelle (Swift) Dickey; married Maxine Syerson, November 4, 1948 (died, October 28, 1976); married Deborah Dodson, December 30, 1976; children: (first marriage) Christopher Swift, Kevin Webster; (second marriage) Bronwen Elaine. *Nationality:* American. *Education:* Attended Clemson College (now University), 1942; Vanderbilt University, B.A. (magna cum laude), 1949, M.A., 1950.

■ Career

Poet, novelist, and essayist. Instructor in English at Rice Institute (now Rice University), Houston, TX, 1950, 1952-54, and University of Florida, Gainesville, 1955-56; worked in advertising, 1956-60, first as copywriter for McCann-Erickson, New York, NY, then as an official for Liller, Neal, Battle & Lindsey and Burke Dowling Adams, both in Atlanta, GA; poet-in-residence at Reed College, Portland, OR, 1963-64, San Fernando Valley State College (now California State University, Northridge), Northridge,

CA, 1964-65, University of Wisconsin—Madison, 1966, University of Wisconsin—Milwaukee, 1967, and Washington University, St. Louis, MO, 1968; Georgia Institute of Technology, Atlanta, Franklin Distinguished Professor of English, 1968; University of South Carolina, Columbia, professor of English and poet-in-residence, 1969-97. Library of Congress, consultant in poetry, 1966-68, honorary consultant in American Letters, 1968-71; Yale Younger Poets contest, judge, 1989-94. *Military service:* U.S. Army Air Corps; served in World War II; flew 100 combat missions in 418th Night Fighter Squadron. U.S. Air Force; served in Korean War; awarded Air Medal.

■ Member

American Academy of Arts and Sciences, American Academy of Arts and Letters, National Advisory Council on the Arts, National Institute of Arts and Letters, Fellowship of Southern Writers, South Carolina Academy of Authors, Writer's Guild of America, Phi Beta Kappa.

■ Awards, Honors

Sewanee Review poetry fellowship, 1954-55; *Poetry* magazine, Union League Civic and Arts Foundation Prize, 1958, Vachel Lindsay Prize, 1959, and Levinson Prize, 1982; Guggenheim fellowship, 1961-

62; National Book Award for poetry and Melville
Cane Award of Poetry Society of America, both
1966, both for *Buckdancer's Choice;* National Institute
of Arts and Letters grant, 1966; Medicis prize for
best foreign book of the year (France), 1971, for *Deliverance;* read poem "The Strength of Fields" at In-
auguration of U.S. President Jimmy Carter, 1977;
New York Quarterly Poetry Day Award, 1977; read
poem "For a Time and Place" at second inaugura-
tion of South Carolina Governor Richard Riley, 1983;
Order of the Palmetto, South Carolina, 1983.

■ Writings

POETRY

Into the Stone, and Other Poems, Scribner (New York,
NY), 1960.
Drowning with Others (also see below), Wesleyan
University Press (Middletown, CT), 1962.
Helmets (also see below), Wesleyan University Press
(Middletown, CT), 1964.
Two Poems of the Air, Centicore Press (Portland, OR),
1964.
Buckdancer's Choice, Wesleyan University Press
(Middletown, CT), 1965.
Poems, 1957-1967 (selections originally issued in
miniature edition), Wesleyan University Press
(Middletown, CT), 1968.
*The Eye-Beaters, Blood, Victory, Madness, Buckhead,
and Mercy,* Doubleday (Garden City, NY), 1970.
Exchanges, Bruccoli Clark (Columbia, SC), 1971.
The Zodiac (long poem; based on Hendrik Mars-
man's poem of the same title), Doubleday (Garden
City, NY), 1976.
The Strength of Fields (poem; also see below), Bruc-
coli Clark (Columbia, SC), 1977.
Tucky the Hunter (for children), Crown (New York,
NY), 1978.
The Strength of Fields (collection; title poem previ-
ously published separately), Doubleday (Garden
City, NY), 1979.
*Head Deep in Strange Sounds: Improvisations from the
UnEnglish,* Palaemon Press (Winston-Salem, NC),
1979.
Scion, Deerfield Press (Deerfield, MA), 1980.
*The Early Motion: "Drowning with Others" and "Hel-
mets,"* Wesleyan University Press (Middletown,
CT), 1981.
Falling, May Day Sermon, and Other Poems, Wesleyan
University Press (Middletown, CT), 1981.
The Eagle's Mile (also see below), Bruccoli Clark
(Columbia, SC), 1981.

Puella, Doubleday (Garden City, NY), 1982.
Vaermland: Poems Based on Poems, Palaemon Press
(Winston-Salem, NC), 1982.
False Youth: Four Seasons, Pressworks (Dallas, TX),
1983.
The Central Motion, Wesleyan University Press
(Middletown, CT), 1983.
(With Sharon Anglin Kuhne) *Intervisions: Poems and
Photographs,* Visualternatives, 1983.
Veteran Birth: The Gadfly Poems, 1947-1949, Palaemon
Press (Winston-Salem, NC), 1983.
*Bronwen, the Traw, and the Shape Shifter: A Poem in
Four Parts* (for children), illustrations by Richard
Jesse Watson, Harcourt (New York, NY), 1986.
Of Prisons and Ideas, Harcourt (New York, NY), 1987.
Summons, Bruccoli Clark (Columbia, SC), 1988.
The Eagle's Mile (collection), Wesleyan University
Press (Middletown, CT), 1990.
The Whole Motion: Collected Poems, 1945-1992, Wes-
leyan University Press (Middletown, CT), 1992.
James Dickey: The Selected Poems, edited and with an
introduction by Robert Kirschten, University
Press of New England (Hanover, NH), 1998.

Poetry represented in anthologies, including *Contemporary American Poetry,* edited by Donald Hall,
Penguin, 1962; *Where Is Viet Nam? American Poets
Respond,* edited by Walter Lowenfels, Doubleday,
1967; *The Norton Anthology of Poetry,* revised shorter
edition, edited by Alexander W. Allison, Herbert
Barrows, Caesar R. Blake, Arthur J. Carr, Arthur M.
Eastman, and Hubert M. English, Jr., Norton, 1975;
and *The Norton Anthology of American Literature,* Vol-
ume 2, edited by Ronald Gottesman, Laurence B.
Holland, William H. Pritchard, and David Kalstone,
Norton, 1979.

PROSE

The Suspect in Poetry (criticism), Sixties Press
(Madison, MN), 1964.
A Private Brinksmanship (lecture), Castle Press
(Pasadena, CA), 1965.
*Spinning the Crystal Ball: Some Guesses at the Future
of American Poetry* (lecture), Library of Congress
(Washington, DC), 1967.
Metaphor as Pure Adventure (lecture), Library of Con-
gress (Washington, DC), 1968.
Babel to Byzantium: Poets and Poetry Now (criticism),
Farrar, Straus (New York, NY), 1968.
Deliverance (novel; excerpt originally published in
Atlantic Monthly; also see below), Houghton Miff-
lin (Boston, MA), 1970.
Self-Interviews (informal monologues), recorded and
edited by Barbara Reiss and James Reiss, Double-
day (Garden City, NY), 1970.

Sorties: Journals and New Essays, Doubleday (Garden City, NY), 1971.

(With Hubert Shuptrine) *Jericho: The South Beheld,* Oxmoor (Birmingham, AL), 1974.

(With Marvin Hayes) *God's Images: The Bible, a New Vision,* Oxmoor (Birmingham, AL), 1977.

The Enemy from Eden, Lord John Press (Northridge, CA), 1978.

In Pursuit of the Grey Soul, Bruccoli Clark (Columbia, SC), 1978.

The Water Bug's Mittens (Ezra Pound Lecture at University of Idaho), Bruccoli Clark (Columbia, SC), 1980.

The Starry Place between the Antlers: Why I Live in South Carolina, Bruccoli Clark (Columbia, SC), 1981.

Night Hurdling: Poems, Essays, Conversations, Commencements, and Afterwords, Bruccoli Clark (Columbia, SC), 1983.

Alnilam (novel), Doubleday (Garden City, NY), 1987.

Wayfarer: A Voice from the Southern Mountains, Oxmoor House (Birmingham, AL), 1988.

Southern Light, photography by James Valentine, Oxmoor House (Birmingham, AL), 1991.

To the White Sea (novel), Houghton Mifflin (Boston, MA), 1993.

The James Dickey Reader, edited by Henry Hart, Simon & Schuster (New York, NY), 1999.

Contributor to books, including *Modern Southern Literature in Its Cultural Setting,* edited by Louis D. Rubin, Jr., and Robert D. Jacobs, Doubleday, 1961; *Poets on Poetry,* edited by Howard Nemerov, Basic Books, 1966; *Pages: The World of Books, Writers, and Writing,* Volume 1, Gale, 1976; *Conversations with Writers,* Volume 1, Gale, 1977; and *From the Green Horseshoe: Poems by James Dickey's Students,* University of South Carolina Press, 1987.

OTHER

(Adapter, with others, of English version) Evgenii Evtushenko, *Stolen Apples: Poetry,* Doubleday (Garden City, NY), 1971.

Deliverance (screenplay; based on Dickey's novel of the same title; produced by Warner Bros., 1972), Southern Illinois University Press (Carbondale, IL), 1982.

(With Charles Fries) *Call of the Wild* (screenplay; based on the novel by Jack London), produced by National Broadcasting Co. (NBC-TV), 1976.

Striking In: The Early Notebooks of James Dickey, edited by Gordon Van Ness, University of Missouri Press (Columbia, MO), 1996.

Crux: The Letters of James Dickey, edited by Matthew J. Bruccoli and Judith S. Baughman, Knopf (New York, NY), 1999.

Also author of screenplays *To Gene Bullard* and *The Sentence.* Contributor of poems, essays, articles, and reviews to more than thirty periodicals, including *Atlantic Monthly, Harper's, Hudson Review, Nation, New Yorker, Paris Review, Poetry, Sewanee Review, Times Literary Supplement,* and *Virginia Quarterly Review.*

■ Adaptations

Deliverance was filmed in 1972, directed by John Boorman; *To the White Sea* was filmed by the Coen brothers, starring Brad Pitt, for a 2003 release.

■ Sidelights

Writer James Dickey led a remarkable life as poet, novelist, critic, and screenwriter. Winner of the National Book Award for his verse collection *Buckdancer's Choice,* Dickey attained national and international fame for his 1970 novel of survival, *Deliverance,* which also became a popular movie with Dickey himself cast in one of the roles. This advertising man who turned writer was a relentless self-promoter, as well, and created a macho image of himself with his numerous interviews and public statements. This self-image translated to the printed page; he was widely regarded as a major American poet because of what critics and readers identified as his unique vision and style. "It is clear," said Joyce Carol Oates in her *New Heaven, New Earth: The Visionary Experience in Literature,* "that Dickey desires to take on 'his' own personal history as an analogue to or a microscopic exploration of twentieth-century American history, which is one of the reasons he is so important a poet." Dickey was called an expansional poet, not only because the voices in his work loomed large enough to address or represent facets of the American experience, but also because his violent imagery and eccentric style exceeded the bounds of more traditional norms, often producing a quality he described as "country surrealism."

One of Dickey's principal themes, usually expressed through a direct confrontation between or a surreal juxtaposition of the world of nature and the world of civilized man, was the need to intensify life by

POEMS BY
JAMES DICKEY
BUCKDANCER'S
CHOICE
WINNER OF NATIONAL BOOK AWARD

James Dickey's award-winning volume of poetry, first published in 1965, included a number of poems originally published in such noted periodicals as *Hudson Review* and the *New Yorker*.

maintaining contact with the primitive impulses, sensations, and ways of seeing suppressed by modern society. It was a theme made explicit in his internationally bestselling novel, *Deliverance,* and was one given much attention in critical reviews. Through his poetry and prose Dickey came to be known as a shaman of contemporary culture; as Joan Bobbitt wrote in *Concerning Poetry,* he "sees civilization as so far removed from nature, its primal antecedent, that only [grotesque] aberrations can aptly depict their relationship and, as he implies, possibly restore them to harmony and order."

Urban Southern Upbringing

Born in 1923 in Buckhead, Georgia, Dickey grew up the privileged son of a lawyer. As Richard J. Calhoun and Robert W. Hill noted in their critical study *James Dickey,* Dickey's "roots are in the South, but not the agrarian South," for he was reared in

Atlanta. His father introduced him to written and oral literature, as well as the pleasures of hunting in the Appalachian Mountains. Dickey noted in his *Self-Interviews* that his father would read to him from famous court cases "from the trial of Jesus Christ up to the trial of Fatty Arbuckle." As Calhoun and Hill noted, Dickey "makes it clear that great lawyers, not great poets, were the heroes of his family." Special in this legion of heroes was Clarence Darrow, famous for the Scopes 'monkey trial' of 1924. He was also introduced to the poetry of Longfellow through his mother, and to Lord Byron because of a biography he once read of that poet. However, Dickey's interests in youth were not literary. Athletics, hunting, and carpentry were his obsessions. At North Fulton High School in Atlanta he became a star football player, and after graduation spent a year at Clemson University, where, as a freshman, he was a distinguished wingback on the varsity team.

As a college student in 1942, Dickey knew that it was only a matter of time before he was called up for the military: his academic standing in no way rivaled his output on the football field and when he enlisted in the Army Air Force that year, the only class he had passing grades in was English. One of his teachers at Clemson later noted that Dickey, of all the pupils he had ever taught, seemed the least likely to ever become a poet.

As a member of the 418th Night Fighter Squadron, Dickey flew more than 100 combat missions in the Pacific Theater: over the Philippines, Okinawa, and Japanese cities. It was during this time that Dickey began to read poetry he found in the various post libraries where he was stationed. "I read whatever I laid my hands on," Dickey told Paul O'Neill in *Life* magazine. "Novels. Prose. But I sensed immediately that writers like [William] Faulkner or [Thomas] Wolfe had a different orientation with language than, say, [Somerset] Maugham. I responded to this quality. I kept looking for writers who had this thing. [Herman] Melville. James Agee. I felt writers like this were sort of failed poets who were trying to use prose for higher things; if those fellows were aspiring for something higher, I thought that was the direction to go." And so Dickey began to experiment with writing poetry.

After the war he attended Vanderbilt University, where he became a track star. There, as an English major, he fell under the influence of Southern writers such as Allen Tate, Robert Penn Warren, and Cleanth Brooks. In 1948 he married Maxine Syerson, and graduated the following June magna cum laude with a graduate fellowship and having had a poem accepted by the prestigious *Sewanee Review.*

Completing his master's degree in 1950, he took a teaching position at Rice University that was interrupted when Dickey was called up again for the U.S. Air Force during the Korean War. After this second tour in the military, Dickey returned to Rice, but it was clear that without a Ph.D. he would not get a tenured position. A *Sewanee Review* fellowship bought Dickey a year in Europe, and when he returned to the United States, he took a position at the University of Florida teaching freshman composition. Reading one of his poems, "The Father's Body," to an audience of faculty wives, Dickey managed to shock one of the women with the outspoken sensual nature of the material. Asked to apologize to the woman, Dickey decided he would rather give up teaching than bow to such puritanical thinking. "I thought if my chosen profession, teaching, was going to fall out to be that sort of situation," he once explained in *Conversations with Writers*, "I'd rather go for the buck and make some damn dough in the market place. I had the confidence of Lucifer in myself by that time, and I was beginning to appear all over the place in the *Hudson Review, Partisan* [*Review*], *Sewanee* [*Review*], *Kenyon* [*Review*], and so on. I figured that the kind of thing that an advertising writer would be able to write, I could do with the little finger of the left hand, and they were getting paid good dough for it. I happened to have been right."

From Advertising to Versifying

Dickey got a job with McCann-Erickson, the biggest ad agency in New York at the time, and wrote jingles for its Coca-Cola account. Later, he went to Liller, Neal, Battle & Lindsey in Atlanta, Georgia, for twice the salary, working on potato chips and fertilizer accounts, and then jumped agencies again for still another increase, becoming an executive with Burke Dowling Adams, where his primary concern was the Delta Airlines account. Robert W. Hill reported in the *Dictionary of Literary Biography* that by the late 1950s Dickey was earning enough to have a secure future in the business. However, after his first book, *Into the Stone, and Other Poems*, was published in 1960 and he was awarded a Guggenheim fellowship, Dickey left advertising to devote all his time to poetry. "There could have been no more unpromising enterprise or means of earning a livelihood than that of being an American poet," he later admitted in *Conversations with Writers*. "It's different now. They're still having a relatively rocky road, but it ain't like it was when I used to give readings sometimes for maybe ten or fifteen dollars, where there would be five people in the audiences, three of them relatives."

Dickey's emotional attachment to his craft—obviously great enough to lead him to abandon a lucrative career in advertising—surfaced early in his writing career. "I came to poetry with no particular qualifications," he recounted in Howard Nemerov's *Poets on Poetry*. "I had begun to suspect, however, that there is a poet—or a kind of poet—buried in every human being like Ariel in his tree, and that the people whom we are pleased to call poets are only those who have felt the need and contrived the means to release this spirit from its prison."

In seeking the means to liberate his poetic spirit, Dickey concentrated at first on rhythms, on anapests and iambs. "Although I didn't care for rhyme and the 'packaged' quality which it gives even the best poems," he said in *Poets on Poetry*, "I did care very much for meter, or at least rhythm."

In Italy as a result of the Guggenheim money, Dickey finished his third book of poems, *Helmets*, and then returned to the United States, where he served as poet-in-residence at several colleges in the early 1960s. With his prize-winning collection *Buckdancer's Choice* in 1965, he began using the split line and free verse forms that came to be associated with his work. Perhaps the most recognizable feature of his stylistic development was his ambitious experimentation with language and form: inverted or odd syntax, horizontal spaces within lines, spread-eagled and ode-like shaped poems. Dickey's poems, wrote Paul Zweig in the *New York Times Book Review*, "are like richly modulated hollers; a sort of rough, American-style bel canto advertising its freedom from the constraints of ordinary language. Dickey's style is so personal, his rhythms so willfully eccentric, that the poems seem to swell up and overflow like that oldest of American art forms, the boast."

According to David Kalstone in another *New York Times Book Review* article, Dickey's "achievement has been to press the limit of language and, in his criticism, to point up the strengths of other writers who do: Hart Crane, [D. H.] Lawrence, [Theodore] Roethke." L. M. Rosenberg expressed a similar sentiment in the *Chicago Tribune Book World*. Claiming that for "sheer beauty and passion we have no greater spokesman, nor do we have any poet more powerfully, naturally musical [than Dickey]," Rosenberg maintained that Dickey's "experiments with language and form are the experiments of a man who understands that one of the strangest things about poetry is the way it looks on the page: It just isn't normal. The question of how to move the reader's eye along the page, particularly as it makes an unnatural jump from line to line . . . how to slow the reader down or speed him up, how to give words back their original, almost totemic power—that's something any poet thinks a lot about, and it's something Dickey works with almost obsessively."

Dickey's stylistic endeavors, however, only partially explain why he was, in the minds of several critics, the most frequently discussed American poet of his generation. As noted in *Poets on Poetry,* Dickey admitted that he considered style subordinate to the spirit of poetry, the "individually imaginative" vision of the poet, and, according to William Meredith in the *New York Times Book Review,* he consequently looked "for shapes and rhythms that correspond exactly to the kind of testimony his poems have always been. When he is testifying to an experience that declares its shape and meaning eloquently—'The Shark's Parlor' and 'Falling' are examples of this—the poems have form in [Ezra] Pound's phrase, as a tree has form." But, observed William Heyen in *Southern Review,* in addition to the unity of form and content, there is in Dickey's poetry and criticism "an emphasis on the humanism, or the morality or larger concerns of poetry. There's the idea that what the poet has to reach for is not necessarily affirmation, but, yes, a kind of affirming of values."

A primary thematic concern of Dickey's, one well served by his vigorous style, was the need "to get back wholeness of being, to respond full-heartedly and full-bodiedly to experience," observed Anatole Broyard in the *New York Times.* In *Poets on Poetry,* Dickey once recalled that the subject matter of his early poems came from the principal incidents of his life, "those times when I felt most strongly and was most aware of the intense reality of the objects and people I moved among. If I were to arrange my own poems in some such scheme, chronologizing them, they would form a sort of story of this kind."

Despite the many allusions to his own life which he included in his poetry, Dickey was "able to assimilate and report the experiences of others and himself, coming to that kind of peculiarly Dickeyesque fusion of selves so powerfully worked in 'Drinking from a Helmet,' 'Slave Quarters,' and 'The Firebombing,'" claimed Hill. "This aesthetic viewpoint, with the speaker self-consciously observing, knowing that he has a perspective that is momentary and unique, that the time and the place are special, that the voice of the visionary observer is the only one to deal with the striking matter before him, emphasizes Dickey's dedication to art, to the exploration of the creative process, especially with regard to the use of narrative voice under special, extreme conditions." Extreme conditions permeated Dickey's work. "To make a radical simplification," wrote Monroe K. Spears in *Dionysus and the City: Modernism in Twentieth-Century Poetry,* "the central impulse of Dickey's poetry may be said to be that of identifying with human or other creatures in moments of ultimate confrontation, of violence and truth. A good example is [the poem] 'Falling,' which

imagines the thoughts and feelings of an airline stewardess, accidentally swept through an emergency door, as she falls thousands of feet to her death" in a field in Kansas. Alive as she hurtles through space, she strips and imagines making love "in a furious, death-defying motion toward fertile farms and sensuous people who must in their blood understand even such a strange, naked ritual," explained Robert W. Hill. "Hers is a dance all the way to death; she makes a poem of her last life and a fertility prayer of her last breath: 'AH, GOD—.'"

Many of Dickey's poems explore moments of being as known by horses, dogs, deer, bees, boars, and other inhabitants of non-human worlds. In "The Sheep Child," for example, a creature half child and half sheep—the result of boys coupling with sheep—

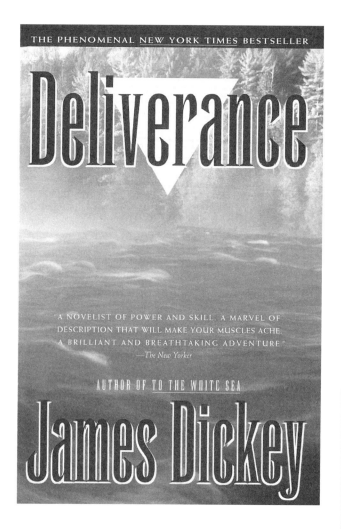

Dickey's 1970 novel about four men whose canoeing trek turns into a nightmare caused the poet to gain a new audience among fiction readers after it climbed to bestseller status.

speaks out from a jar of formaldehyde. The poem "attains very nearly the power of mythic utterance," maintained Hill, for the sheep child "shows its magnified view of the truth of two worlds," the fusion of man and nature, with an "eternal, unyielding vision." In Hill's opinion, "The Sheep Child" is "the most radical expression of Dickey's sense of transcendence in fusing man and nature to achieve 'imperishable vision,'" but it is not the only such expression.

"Everywhere in [Dickey's] body of writing, intouchness with 'the other forms of life' stands forth as a primary value," asserted Benjamin DeMott in *Saturday Review.* "The strength of this body of poetry lies in its feeling for the generative power at the core of existence. A first-rate Dickey poem breathes the energy of the world, and testifies to the poet's capacity for rising out of tranced dailiness—habitual, half-lived life—into a more intense physicality, a burly appetitive wanting-ness of being. To read him is, for an instant, to share that capacity." Richard Tillinghast, writing in *Southern Review,* agreed: "Alone among his contemporaries, Dickey has a quality of exuberance that one must go back to [Walt] Whitman to see equaled. . . . This exuberance has hurt Dickey among critics, just as it has hurt Whitman; with Randall Jarrell in his praising mood a notable exception, a critic almost by nature dislikes exuberance and rejects it when he sees it."

In Touch with Nature

Along with DeMott, critics generally agreed that by pressing "the neglected natural nerve in humanness" through shockingly bizarre or surreal images, Dickey sought to depict man's proper relationship with nature. "It is rarely or never so simple as this," cautioned Nemerov in *Reflexions on Poetry and Poetics,* "yet the intention seems often enough this, a feeling one's way down the chain of being, a becoming the voice which shall make dumb things respond, sometimes to their hurt or deaths, a sensing of alien modes of experience, mostly in darkness or in an unfamiliar light; reason accepting its animality; a poetry whose transcendences come of its reconciliations. Salvation is this: apprehending the continuousness of forms, the flowing of one energy through everything." "Dickey makes it clear," suggested Bobbitt, "that what seems to be unnatural is only so because of its context in a civilized world, and that these deviations actually possess a vitality which modern man has lost."

In an interview with William Heyen in *Southern Review,* Dickey once commented on the necessity for man to make some sort of connection with animal life: "I remember a quotation from D. H. Lawrence to the effect that we are in the process of losing the cosmos. We dominate it, but in a sense we've lost it or we're losing it. It's the sense of being part of what Lovejoy called 'the great chain of being.' Randall Jarrell, one of my favorite critics and poets, was a great punster, and he said that we have substituted for the great chain of being 'the great chain of buying,' which is, maybe, something that's diametrically opposed, and will be the ruination of everything." Dickey was widely praised for having what Herbert Leibowitz in the *New York Times Book Review* called "a shrewd and troubled knowledge of the 'primal powers'" of nature, as well as "a dramatic skill in presenting the endless beauty of instinct, the feel of icy undertows and warm shallows, the bloodlettings which are a regular part of nature's law." But because a Dickey poem centers on "moments of ultimate confrontation," as Spears said, and because that confrontation often seems to involve a conflict with the norms of civilized society, Dickey was criticized for what some saw as an inherent preoccupation with violence that led to a castigation of modern society. Zweig, for example, maintained that Dickey's "imagination rides the edge of violence," and James Aronson claimed in the *Antioch Review* that this characteristic gave Dickey a reputation as "a kind of primitive savage" who extolled the virtues of uncivilized life.

Although Dickey's images were often primitive, many reviewers considered it a mistake to see him as a spokesman for a return to savagery. Oates wrote that Dickey, "so disturbing to many of us, must be seen in a larger context, as a kind of 'shaman,' a man necessarily at war with his civilization because that civilization will not, cannot, understand what he is saying." A writer in the *Virginia Quarterly Review* observed that at the heart of Dickey's work lay a "desperate insistence that every human experience, however painful or ugly, be viewed as a possible occasion for the renewal of life, [and] with Dickey any renewal inevitably requires struggle."

According to Hill and Aronson, a typical case of misinterpretation involves "The Firebombing," the first poem in *Buckdancer's Choice.* In part a result of Dickey's own experiences in the air force as a fighter-pilot, the poem presents a speaker who, in a momentary flashback, recalls that twenty years earlier he was dropping 300-gallon tanks filled with napalm and gasoline on neighborhoods much like his own. Aronson reported that some readers believe the poem portrays the "joy of destroying" experienced by men at war, or even suggests that destruction itself is natural, when actually the poem expresses the complex emotion of "guilt at the inability to feel guilt." Hill noted that "the moral in-

Burt Reynolds stars in the John Boorman-directed 1972 film based on Dickey's screenplay adaptation of his classic novel *Deliverance* alongside actors Ned Beatty, Ronny Cox, and Jon Voight.

dignation that might flood so readily for artists and thinkers flows less surely and less fleetingly for one whose life has depended upon a certain screening out of moral subtleties in times of actual combat. The 'luxury' of moral pangs seems to come upon the fighter-pilot in 'The Firebombing' only after his war is over, his safety and his family's restored, to allow the contemplation of distant and not-to-be-altered acts of horrible proportion."

Noting the characteristic power of Dickey's vision and the intensity of his language, Oates called "The

Firebombing" the central poem of his work. "It is," she wrote, "unforgettable, and seems to me an important achievement in our contemporary literature, a masterpiece that could only have been written by an American, and only by Dickey. Having shown us so convincingly in his poetry how natural, how inevitable, is man's love for all things, Dickey now shows us what happens when man is forced to destroy, forced to step down into history and be an American ('and proud of it'). In so doing he enters a tragic dimension in which few poets indeed have operated."

Turns to Prose with *Deliverance*

In *Deliverance,* critics generally saw a thematic continuity with Dickey's poetry. A novel about how decent men kill, it is also about the bringing forth, through confrontation, of those qualities in a man that usually lie buried. Simply put, *Deliverance* is the story of four Atlanta suburbanites on a back-to-nature canoe trip which turns into a terrifying test of survival. Dickey, who made a number of canoe and bow-hunting trips in the wilds of northern Georgia, told Walter Clemons in the *New York Times Book Review* that much of the story was suggested by incidents that had happened to him or that he had heard about through friends. All those experiences, according to Dickey, shared the feeling of excitement and fear that "comes from being in an unprotected situation where the safeties of law and what we call civilization don't apply, they just don't. A snake can bite you and you can die before you could get treatment. There are men in those remote parts that'd just as soon kill you as look at you. And you could turn into a counter-monster yourself, doing whatever you felt compelled to do to survive."

"In writing *Deliverance,*" said *New York Times* columnist Christopher Lehmann-Haupt, "Dickey obviously made up his mind to tell a story, and on the theory that a story is an entertaining lie, he has produced a double-clutching whopper." Three ill-prepared businessmen join Lewis Medlock, an avid sportsman who constantly lectures about the purity of nature and the corruption of civilization, on a weekend escape from the banality of suburban living. Canoeing down a wild and difficult stretch of the Cahulawassee River, the men experience only the natural hazards of the river on the first day. Their idyllic sense of community with nature and of masculine camaraderie is shattered on the second day, however, when two members of the party, resting from the unaccustomed strain, are surprised by a pair of malicious strangers coming out of the woods. Ed Gentry, the novel's narrator, is tied to a

tree while Bobby Trippe is held at gunpoint and sexually assaulted by one of the mountain men. Before the attack can go much further, Lewis catches up, kills one of the assailants by shooting an arrow into his back—thereby partially avenging the homosexual rape—and scares off the other. Fearing a trial conducted by city-hating hicks, the canoeists decide to bury the body and continue down the river. However, after Drew, the sole member of the party to advocate informing the authorities, accidentally drowns and Lewis suffers a broken leg, Ed must kill the other assailant who is firing upon them from the cliffs above the Cahulawassee.

Critical reactions to *Deliverance* helped explain its popular success. "The story is absorbing," wrote Evan S. Connell, Jr., in the *New York Times Book Review,* "even when you are not quite persuaded Dickey has told the truth. He is effective and he is deft, with the fine hand of an archer." Lehmann-Haupt gave the book similar praise, stating that Dickey "has succeeded in hammering out a comparatively lean prose style (for a man in the habit of loading words with meaning) and built the elements of his yarn into its structure. And except for one blind lead and an irritating logical discrepancy, he has built well. Best of all, he has made a monument to tall stories."

Though Christopher Ricks, critiquing the novel in the *New York Review of Books,* believed *Deliverance* was "too patently the concoction of a situation in which it will be morally permissible—nay, essential—to kill men with a bow and arrow," Charles Thomas Samuels pointed out in the *New Republic* that Dickey "himself seems aware of the harshness of his substructure and the absurdity of some of his details," and overcomes these deficiencies through his stylistic maneuvers. Samuels continued, "Such is Dickey's linguistic virtuosity that he totally realizes an improbable plot. How a man acts when shot by an arrow, what it feels like to scale a cliff or to capsize, the ironic psychology of fear: these things are conveyed with remarkable descriptive writing. His publishers are right to call *Deliverance* a *tour de force.*"

Much more than a violent adventure tale, *Deliverance* is a novel of initiation that, according to William Stephenson in the *Georgia Review,* "has the potential of becoming a classic." As a result of their experience, Lewis and Ed come to a realization of the natural savagery of man in nature; noted C. Hines Edwards in *Critique,* "In three days they have retraced the course of human development and have found in the natural state not the romantic ideal of beauty in nature coupled with brotherhood among men but beauty in nature coupled with the necessity to kill men, coolly and in the course of things." In line with this view, several critics have noted Dickey's allusions to Joseph Conrad's novel *Heart of Darkness.*

In *American Visionary Fiction: Mad Metaphysics as Salvation Psychology,* Richard Finholt suggested that there are other literary allusions: "Ed Gentry, the quintessential contemporary American, a soft and overweight suburbanite, finds himself nonetheless [among the chosen] of Lewis. If this is not exactly the honor of being chosen by Odysseus to man the voyage to Ithaca, it is at least as good as being asked by [Ernest Hemingway] himself to join him on the 'tragic adventure' of fishing the swamp on the big two-hearted river. And since Lewis's river happens to flow through just such a dreaded underworld, his weekend canoe trip takes on an epical significance demanding an American-bred heroism that is at least Hemingwayesque, if not Homeric." Finholt considered the novel a return to a time when "the final difference between meaning and meaninglessness was the hero's ability, versus his inability, to act when the necessary time came. This is the nature of Ed's discovery after undergoing an initiation rite into heroism on the death climb up the cliff."

Consistent with this interpretation of *Deliverance* as epic, a *Times Literary Supplement* reviewer claimed Lewis and Ed "are not horrified by what has happened, they are renewed by it; it was, once it became inevitable, indispensable to them. This shockingly credible insight is the central point of the book, and James Dickey reveals it with an appropriate and rewarding subtlety."

Donald W. Markos, discussing the novel in the *Southern Review,* observed that while the book "is in an obvious sense a celebration of an anachronistic concept of manhood," it is more complex than that. "It does not propose that all men embark on canoe trips or undergo a regimen of weight lifting and archery in order to salvage their manhood. An interesting conversation between Medlock and the narrator prior to the outing reveals that masculine prowess is not the primary norm of the book." Oates echoed this sentiment, noting that *Deliverance* is "about our deep, instinctive needs to get back to nature, to establish some kind of rapport with primitive energies; but it is also about the need of some men to do violence, to be delivered out of their banal lives by a violence so irreparable that it can never be confessed." Oates called the book "a fantasy of a highly civilized and affluent society, which imagines physical violence to be transforming in a mystical—and therefore permanent—sense, a society in which rites of initiation no longer exist. . . . Dickey's work is significant in its expression of the savagery that always threatens to become an ideal, when faith in human values is difficult to come by or when a culture cannot accommodate man's most basic instincts."

Edward Doughtie concluded in *Southwest Review* that through *Deliverance* "Dickey shows art to be a necessary mediator between nature—both the exterior nature of woods and rivers and the interior nature of man's drives and dreams—and modern urban 'civilized' life. . . . The positive elements of nature can be stifled by civilization; but without civilization the darker, destructive natural forces may get out of hand. Art is a product of civilization, and a civilizing force, yet for Dickey genuine art never loses touch with the primitive: in short, art embraces both Dionysus and Apollo."

Other Ventures into Prose

Deliverance represented only one of Dickey's ventures outside the realm of poetry. He not only adapted the novel for the screen but also appeared in the box-office smash as the "redneck" Sheriff Bullard, whom the canoeists face at the end of their journey. In addition to criticism, Dickey published a retelling of several biblical stories, *God's Images: The Bible, a New Vision,* as well as *Jericho: The South Beheld,* an exploration of "the rich prose language and sensual impressions of the American South, which Dickey has publicly championed," wrote Hill. "Like Whitman or [Mark] Twain," said Michael Dirda in the *Washington Post Book World,* "Dickey seems in a characteristic American tradition, ever ready to light out for new territories."

Dickey told *Publishers Weekly* that he spent thirty-six years working on his lengthy World War II novel *Alnilam.* Named for the central star in the belt of the constellation Orion, *Alnilam* concerns recently blinded Frank Cahill's search for his son, Joel, whom he has never met. Cahill slowly discovers that his son, an extraordinary pilot thought to have been killed in an aircraft-training accident, had been the leader of a mysterious, dictatorial military training cult known as Alnilam. By interviewing those who knew Joel, Cahill forms an impressionistic and sometimes contradictory portrait of this unusual young man. Describing the novel to R. Z. Sheppard in *Time* magazine, Dickey once explained, "I've tried to do for the air what [Herman] Melville did for water." Sheppard elaborated: "Flying, in the mechanical as well as transcendental sense, is basic to the action, which is surprisingly abundant for a book that is shaped by poetic impulses rather than plot."

Alnilam received mixed reviews, with most critics comparing it unfavorably to *Deliverance.* As Erling Friis-Baastad put it in the Toronto *Globe and Mail, Alnilam* "is an awkward and overworked book, but the touch of a master poet can still be experienced periodically throughout . . . at least by those who can endure the uphill read." Robert Towers, writing in the *New York Times Book Review,* said that *Alnilam* "is, for better and worse, very much a poet's novel, Mr. Dickey's extended hymn to air, light, wind and the ecstasies of flight." Although he found Cahill an engaging character, Towers faulted Dickey for the "inordinately slow pacing" of the novel. He noted that one of Dickey's innovative devices interrupts the flow of the already slow-moving narrative. Wrote Towers, "On many of its pages, the symbolic contrasts between blindness and sight, between darkness and light, are typographically rendered. The page is split down the middle into two columns. The left, which represents Cahill's internal sensations and thoughts, is printed in dark type; the right, which contains the objective narration of speech and events, is printed in ordinary type. Such a device has, of course, the effect not only of dividing one's attention, but also of modifying the degree of one's involvement in what is taking place."

Although the situations in *Alnilam* sometimes seemed implausible to critics, Henry Taylor believed that Dickey was able to write so convincingly that he overcame many of these problems. In the *Los Angeles Times Book Review,* Taylor commented, "One of Dickey's great strengths as a poet has been his extraordinary ability to give plausibility to nearly incredible situations and events." Taylor concluded by saying, "There are a few brief passages in which the style becomes self-conscious, or where the intensity seems too laboriously worked up. But Dickey's ear for Southern talk, his understanding of the sensations involved in flying, and his interest in a wide array of minor characters, make the novel rich and rewarding reading. *Alnilam* is a solid achievement."

In his final novel, *To the White Sea,* published in 1993, Dickey returned to the themes of his earlier novels. The book's one character, Muldrow, is an Air Force tail gunner whose plane is shot down over Tokyo during World War II. During the early stages of the novel, Muldrow endures supremely difficult circumstances as he struggles for survival. Fleeing Tokyo and heading north to the island of Hokkaido, whose cold and wintry climate appeals to his own childhood experiences growing up in Alaska, Muldrow kills several people while in search of food and clothing. "Initially one identifies with . . . [Muldrow's] unbelievable courage and control in the face of almost hopeless odds," noted Steve Brzezinski in *Antioch Review.* However, as the novel progresses,

the JAMES DICKEY reader

EDITED BY HENRY HART

This 1999 collection of Dickey's poetry and prose, published two years after the author's death, includes portions from his unfinished novel among its selections.

Muldrow's actions grow increasingly violent and shocking, as he enjoys his murderous actions. "His 'heart of ice' proves to be another heart of darkness," commented John Melmoth in the *Times Literary Supplement.* "Things take an apocalyptic turn and end in a welter of blood and feathers." During his journey, Muldrow comes to identify with the animals he encounters in the wilderness and seeks to transform himself into a facet of the harsh landscape around him.

As with *Alnilam,* critical reaction to *To the White Sea* was mixed, with critics praising Dickey's prose style but recoiling at the novel's disturbing plot. "Dickey takes language as far as it will go and sometimes overdoes it," remarked Melmoth, who added that "some of the writing has an eerie brilliance." While commending Dickey's "haunting" imagery and stylistic achievement, Brzezinski averred that *To the White Sea* "is a bleak and unsettling book." In the end, concluded Ronald Curran in a *World Literature Today* review, "however the reader conceives of Muldrow's musings about his adaptive identifications with animals or his eventual transcendence into weather itself, the success of *To the White Sea* depends upon whether or not empathetic identification can be fostered" among readers.

Dickey died of a lung ailment early in 1997. Two posthumous works have since been released: *Crux: The Letters of James Dickey* and *The James Dickey Reader.* The latter is a compilation of Dickey's best poetry and prose, while *Crux* is a collection of an estimated twenty percent of his correspondence. According to J. D. McClatchy in the *New York Times Book Review,* Dickey's work has not stood the test of time admirably. "By the time Dickey died in 1997, at the age of 73, his public had thinned out," the critic wrote. "Some years earlier, the critics had begun to narrow their eyes. His swagger only seemed to undermine the seriousness of his ambition. His reputation as a performer turned sour. His writing, with its lust for excess, its fascination with guts and grit, blood and soul, had long since grown bloated and undisciplined." McClatchy further commented: "A few years ago, the publication of Philip Larkin's letters dented his reputation by revealing the poet's vicious streak. Dickey's letters expose something worse: under all that chest hair, he was a hollow man."

Bronwen Dickey, the poet's daughter by a second marriage, offered a countering view of Dickey in *Newsweek.* She noted that his was "not the greatness of the writer but the greatness of the father and the teacher. One time in the class he taught, my father was reading his poem, 'Good-bye to Big Daddy,' about the death of football player Big Daddy Lipscomb, and this big, ox-headed football player in the class started bawling in the middle of the reading. The class was dismissed and my dad just went over to this guy and held him while he wept like a child, saying, 'It's all right, Big Boy; it's gonna be OK.' That is the kind of teacher James Dickey was. There are no words for the kind of father he was."

Other reviewers also joined in the reassessment. A contributor for *Publishers Weekly,* reviewing *The James Dickey Reader,* felt that Dickey's best poems, such as "Buckdancer's Choice," "Power and Light," and "The Sheep-Child," make his "frustrations and his mythographic ambitions, sources of memorably tormented potency." Noting the damage to Dickey's reputation that some of the letters and his son's memoir, *Summer of Deliverance,* had caused, this same reviewer concluded that "this generous compilation does much to bolster [Dickey's] literary prominence." And John Mort, reviewing *Crux,* felt that Dickey's letters "are beautifully reasoned meditations on poetics, poets, and critics that reveal the politics of a literary genius."

Despite his excursions into other genres, Dickey's main concern was always poetry, as he once admitted in the *New York Times.* "In poetry you have the utmost concentration of meaning in the shortest space." In 1992 a major collection of Dickey's poems was published as *The Whole Motion: Collected Poems, 1945-1992.*

If you enjoy the works of James Dickey, you might want to check out the following:

The poetry of Gerard Manley Hopkins (1844-1889), whose work served as a model for Dickey.

The works of Randall Jarrell (1914-1965), one of Dickey's favorite poets and critics.

John Hersey's novel *The War Lover,* 1959.

Dickey once commented: "I'm the same way about novels as I am about anything I write. I build them very slowly. I work on the principle that the first fifty ways I try to write a novel or a critical piece or a poem or a movie are going to be wrong. But you get a direction in some way or other. Keep drafting and redrafting and something emerges eventually. If the subject is intense, if you are intense about it, something will come. In my case, at least, the final work is nothing like what I started out with; generally I don't have a very good idea at first. But something begins to form in some unforeseen, perhaps unforeseeable, shape. It's like creating something out of nothing—creation ex nihilo, which is said to be impossible. God must have done it, I guess, but nobody else can—except poets."

■ Biographical and Critical Sources

BOOKS

Authors in the News, Gale (Detroit, MI), Volume 1, 1976, Volume 2, 1976.

Baughman, Ronald, editor, *The Voiced Connections of James Dickey: Interviews and Conversations,* University of South Carolina Press (Columbia, SC), 1989.

Boyars, Robert, editor, *Contemporary Poetry in America,* Schocken (New York, NY), 1974.

Bruccoli, Matthew J., and Judith S. Baughman, *James Dickey: A Descriptive Bibliography,* University of Pittsburgh Press (Pittsburgh, PA), 1990.

Calhoun, Richard J., editor, *James Dickey: The Expansive Imagination,* Everett/Edwards (DeLand, FL), 1973.

Calhoun, Richard J., and Robert Hill, *James Dickey,* Twayne (Boston, MA), 1983.

Carroll, Paul, *The Poem in Its Skin,* Follett (New York, NY), 1968.

Contemporary Authors Bibliographical Series, Volume 2: *American Poets,* Gale (Detroit, MI), 1986.

Contemporary Literary Criticism, Gale (Detroit, MI), Volume 1, 1973, Volume 2, 1974, Volume 4, 1975, Volume 7, 1977, Volume 10, 1979, Volume 15, 1980, Volume 47, 1988.

Contemporary Poets, 6th edition, St. James Press (Detroit, MI), 1996.

Contemporary Popular Writers, St. James Press (Detroit, MI), 1997.

Contemporary Southern Writers, St. James Press (Detroit, MI), 1999.

Conversations with Writers, Volume 1, Gale (Detroit, MI), 1977.

De la Fuente, Patricia, editor, *James Dickey: Splintered Sunlight,* School of Humanities, Pan American University, 1979.

Dickey, Christopher, *Summer of Deliverance: A Memoir of Father and Son,* Simon & Schuster (New York, NY), 1998.

Dickey, James, *Self-Interviews,* recorded and edited by Barbara Reiss and James Reiss, Doubleday (Garden City, NY), 1970.

Dictionary of Literary Biography, Volume 5: *American Poets since World War II,* Gale (Detroit, MI), 1980.

Dictionary of Literary Biography Documentary Series, Volume 7, Gale (Detroit, MI), 1989.

Dictionary of Literary Biography Yearbook, Gale (Detroit, MI), 1982, 1983, 1993, 1994.

Elledge, J., *James Dickey: A Bibliography, 1947-1974,* Scarecrow Press (Metuchen, NJ), 1979.

Encyclopedia of World Biography Supplement, Volume 19, Gale (Detroit, MI), 1999.

Finholt, Richard, *American Visionary Fiction: Mad Metaphysics as Salvation Psychology,* Kennikat (Port Washington, NY), 1978.

Garrett, George, editor, *The Writer's Voice: Conversations with Contemporary Writers,* Morrow (New York, NY), 1973.

Glancy, Eileen, *James Dickey: The Critic as Poet,* Whitston Publishing (Troy, NY), 1971.

Howard, Richard, *Alone with America: Essays on the Art of Poetry in the United States since 1950,* Atheneum (New York, NY), 1969.

Kirschten, Robert, *Critical Essays on James Dickey,* G. K. Hall (New York, NY), 1994.

Kirschten, Robert, editor, *Struggling for Wings: The Art of James Dickey,* University of South Carolina Press (Columbia, SC), 1997.

Kirschten, Robert, *Approaching Prayer: Ritual and the Shape of Myth in A. R. Ammons and James Dickey,* Louisiana State University Press (Baton Rouge, LA), 1998.

Lieberman, Laurence, editor, *The Achievement of James Dickey,* Scott, Foresman (Glenview, IL), 1968.

Lieberman, Laurence, *Unassigned Frequencies: American Poetry in Review, 1964-77,* University of Illinois Press (Champaign, IL), 1978.

Nemerov, Howard, editor, *Poets on Poetry,* Basic Books (New York, NY), 1966.

Nemerov, Howard, *Reflexions on Poetry and Poetics,* Rutgers University Press (New Brunswick, NJ), 1972.

Newsmakers 1998, issue 2, Gale (Detroit, MI), 1998.

Oates, Joyce Carol, *New Heaven, New Earth: The Visionary Experience in Literature,* Vanguard (New York, NY), 1974.

Pages: The World of Books, Writers, and Writing, Volume 1, Gale (Detroit, MI), 1976.

Rosenthal, M. L., *The New Poets: American and British Poetry since World War II,* Oxford University Press (Oxford, England), 1967.

Shaw, Robert B., editor, *American Poetry since 1960: Some Critical Perspectives,* Carcanet (Manchester, England), 1973.

Spears, Monroe K., *Dionysus and the City: Modernism in Twentieth-Century Poetry,* Oxford University Press (Oxford, England), 1970.

Stepanchev, Stephen, *American Poetry since 1945,* Harper (New York, NY), 1965.

Vernon, John, *The Garden and the Map: Schizophrenia in Twentieth-Century Literature and Culture,* University of Illinois Press (Champaign, IL), 1973.

Walsh, Chad, *Today's Poets,* Scribner (New York, NY), 1964.

Weigl, Bruce, and Terry Hummer, editors, *James Dickey: The Imagination of Glory,* University of Illinois Press (Champaign, IL), 1984.

PERIODICALS

Agenda, winter-spring, 1977.

Alaska, February, 1994, p. 75.

American Literature, June, 1990, p. 370.

Antioch Review, fall-winter, 1970-71; spring, 1994, Steve Brzezinski, review of *To the White Sea,* p. 358.

Atlantic Monthly, October, 1967; November, 1968; December, 1974; February, 1980.

Best Sellers, April 1, 1970.

Booklist, July 15, 1971; November 15, 1999, John Mort, review of *The Letters of James Dickey,* p. 593.

Bulletin of Bibliography, April-June, 1981, pp. 92-100; July-September, 1981, pp. 150-155.

Chicago Review, November 1, 1966.

Chicago Tribune, May 10, 1987.

Chicago Tribune Book World, January 27, 1980.

Christian Science Monitor, December 3, 1964; November 12, 1970; February 20, 1980.

Commonweal, December 1, 1967; February 19, 1971; September 29, 1972; December 3, 1976.

Concerning Poetry, spring, 1978.

Contemporary Literature, summer, 1975.

Critic, May, 1970.

Critique, Volume 15, number 2, 1973.

English Journal, November, 1990, p. 84; January, 1992, p. 27.

Esquire, December, 1970.

Georgia Review, spring, 1968; summer, 1969; spring, 1974; summer, 1978; fall, 1993, p. 603.

Globe and Mail (Toronto, Ontario, Canada), August 15, 1987, Erling Friis-Baastad, review of *Alnilam.*

Hudson Review, spring, 1966; autumn, 1967; autumn, 1968; spring, 1993, David Mason, review of *The Whole Motion,* p. ?23; spring, 1994, p. 133; summer, 1999, review of *James Dickey: The Selected Poems,* p. 323.

James Dickey Newsletter, 1984—.

Kirkus Reviews, September 15, 1999, review of *The Letters of James Dickey,* p. 1460.

Library Journal, October 15, 1999, Henry L. Carrigan, review of *Crux: The Letters of James Dickey,* p. 70.

Life, July 22, 1966, Paul O'Neill, "The Unlikeliest Poet," pp. 68-70; July, 1987, p. 35.

Literary News, May-June, 1967.

Los Angeles Times, May 19, 1968; February 26, 1980; July 9, 1987; December 8, 1987.

Los Angeles Times Book Review, June 27, 1982; January 18, 1987, p. 8; June 7, 1987, Henry Taylor, review of *Alnilam,* p. 1.

Mademoiselle, September, 1970; August, 1972.

Milwaukee Journal, March 20, 1966.

Modern Fiction Studies, summer, 1975.

Mother Earth News, March-April, 1990.

Nation, June 20, 1966; April 24, 1967; March 23, 1970; April 6, 1970; February 5, 1983.

National Review, November 15, 1993, p. 64.

New Leader, May 22, 1967; May 20, 1968.

New Republic, September 9, 1967; June 29, 1968; April 18, 1970; December 5, 1970; August 5, 1972; November 30, 1974; November 20, 1976; January 5, 1980; January 12, 1980.

New Statesman, September 11, 1970.

Newsweek, March 30, 1970; August 7, 1972; December 6, 1976; January 31, 1977; August 30, 1993, Malcolm Jones, Jr., review of *To the White Sea,* p. 54; March 24, 1997, Bronwen Dickey, "He Caught the Dream," p. 19.

New Yorker, May 2, 1970; August 5, 1972; September 27, 1993, Brad Leithauser, review of *To the White Sea,* p. 101.

New York Review of Books, April 23, 1970; November 18, 1999, reviews of *James Dickey: The Selected Poems, The James Dickey Reader,* and *The Letters of James Dickey,* p. 55.

New York Times, March 16, 1966; September 10, 1966; March 27, 1970; December 17, 1971; July 31, 1972; August 20, 1972; January 22, 1977; June 1, 1987; May 19, 1988; October 27, 1990, p. 16; March 23, 1997; December 10, 1999, review of *The Letters of James Dickey,* p. E61.

New York Times Book Review, January 3, 1965; February 6, 1966; April 23, 1967; March 22, 1970; June 7, 1970; November 8, 1970; December 6, 1970; January 23, 1972; February 9, 1975; November 14, 1976; December 18, 1977; July 15, 1979; January 6, 1980; June 3, 1984, p. 23; February 15, 1987; March 8, 1987, p. 31; June 21, 1987, p. 7; September 19, 1993; December 19, 1999, J. D. McClatchy, "A Poet Turns Pitchman," p. 18.

Paris Review, spring, 1976.

Partisan Review, summer, 1966.

People, July 6, 1987, p. 16; October 11, 1993, J. D. Reed, review of *To the White Sea,* p. 29; January 31, 1994, p. 80.

Playboy, May, 1971; September, 1993, p. 78.

Poetry, October, 1966; March, 1968; July, 1971.

Publishers Weekly, May 29, 1987, p. 62; October 19, 1990, p. 52; June 8, 1992, review of *The Whole Motion,* p. 57; June 7, 1993, p. 65; June 21, 1993, p. 82; August 31, 1998, review of *James Dickey: The Selected Poems,* p. 72; June 14, 1999, review of *The James Dickey Reader,* p. 59; October 25, 1999, review of *Crux: The Letters of James Dickey,* p. 65.

Rapport, Volume 17, number 5, 1993, p. 31.

Salmagundi, spring-summer, 1973.

Saturday Review, May 6, 1967; March 11, 1970; March 28, 1970; March 11, 1972.

Saturday Review of Science, August 5, 1972.

Sewanee Review, winter, 1963; summer, 1966; spring, 1969; summer, 1971.

Sixties, winter, 1964; spring, 1967.

Southern Review, winter, 1971; summer, 1971; winter, 1973; spring, 1973; spring, 1981; autumn, 1992, Richard Tillinghast, review of *The Whole Motion,* p. 971; autumn, 1994, Monroe K. Spears, "James Dickey's Poetry," pp. 751-760; winter, 1997, pp. 164-180; spring, 2000, Henry Hart, "James Dickey: Journey to War," p. 348.

Southwest Review, spring, 1979.

Time, December 13, 1968; April 20, 1970; August 7, 1972; June 29, 1987; October 11, 1993, John Skow, review of *To the White Sea,* p. 88.

Times (London, England), February 3, 1990.

Times Literary Supplement, October 29, 1964; May 18, 1967; September 11, 1970; May 21, 1971; December 2, 1983, p. 1342; January 24, 1986, p. 95; May 10, 1991, p. 22; February 11, 1994, John Melmoth, review of *To the White Sea,* p. 21.

Tribune Books (Chicago, IL), November 16, 1986, p. 4; May 24, 1987, p. 3.

Triquarterly, winter, 1968.

Village Voice, February 4, 1980.

Virginia Quarterly Review, autumn, 1967; autumn, 1968; winter, 1971; spring, 1990, p. 66; summer, 1991, p. 100; winter, 1994, p. 23; spring, 1999, review of *James Dickey: The Selected Poems,* p. 66.

Washington Post, March 31, 1987; May 24, 1987; December 8, 1987.

Washington Post Book World, June 30, 1968; March 15, 1970; December 6, 1970; April 25, 1971; November 21, 1976; December 30, 1979; May 24, 1987, p. 1; November 22, 1992, p. 8.

World Literature Today, summer, 1991, p. 489; spring, 1993, p. 384; autumn, 1994, Ronald Curran, review of *To the White Sea,* p. 809; summer, 2000, Ashley Brown, review of *Crux: The Letters of James Dickey,* p. 605.

Yale Review, October, 1962; December, 1967; winter, 1968; October, 1970.

OTHER

James Dickey Newsletter & James Dickey Society, http://www.jamesdickey.org/ (April 8, 2001).

James Dickey Page, http://www.james.dickey.com/ (April 8, 2001).

■ **Obituaries**

PERIODICALS

Newsweek, February 3, 1997, p. 53.

New York Times, January 21, 1997, p. C27.

Time, February 3, 1997, p. 75.*

Alex Flinn

■ Member

Society of Children's Book Writers and Illustrators.

■ Personal

Born October 23, 1966, in Glen Cove, NY; daughter of Nicholas (a ship chandler), and Manya (a homemaker; maiden name, Ellert) Kissanis; married Eugene Flinn, Jr. (an attorney), May 23, 1992; children: Katherine, Meredith. *Nationality:* American. *Education:* University of Miami, bachelor of music, 1988; Nova Southeastern University Law School, law degree, 1992. *Religion:* Greek Orthodox. *Hobbies and other interests:* Volunteer work, theater, opera.

■ Addresses

Home—7860 Southwest 157 Terrace, Miami, FL 33157. *Agent*—c/o Author Mail, HarperCollins Children's Books, 1350 Avenue of the Americas, New York, NY 10019. *E-mail*—Alixwrites@aol.com.

■ Career

Writer and lawyer. Miami-Dade State Attorney's Office, Miami, FL, intern; Martinez & Gutierrez, Miami, FL, lawyer, 2001.

■ Awards, Honors

American Library Association (ALA) Best Book for Young Adults and Quick Picks for Reluctant Young Adult Readers, both 2001, American Booksellers Association Pick of the Lists, *Book Sense* 76 list, New York Public Library Books for the Teen Age designation, Tayshas (TX) State List, Iowa Educational Media Association High School Book Award Master List, Rhode Island Teen Book Award Master List, Popular Paperbacks for Young Adults List nomination, and Children's Literature Choices List, all 2002, and Oklahoma Sequoya Young Adult Master List, 2003-04, all for *Breathing Underwater*; American Library Association Quick Picks, 2002, and Young Adults Books nomination, 2002, both for *Breaking Point*.

■ Writings

Breathing Underwater, HarperCollins (New York, NY), 2001.
Breaking Point, HarperCollins (New York, NY), 2002.

Flinn's works have been translated into Spanish, Catalan, and Slovenian.

■ Adaptations

Both *Breathing Underwater* and *Breaking Point* have been adapted for audiocassette by Listening Library, 2002.

■ Work in Progress

Nothing to Lose, a novel, for HarperCollins, due 2004; *Fading to Black* (working title), HarperCollins, for 2005.

■ Sidelights

"I write for teens because I never finished being one," commented author Alex Flinn in an interview with a contributor for *Embracing the Child.* Flinn also noted on her author Web site, "In my mind, I am still thirteen-years-old, running laps on the athletic field, wearing this really baggy white gymsuit. I'm continually amazed at the idea that I have a checking account and a mortgage." Despite their author's outlook, Flinn's young adult titles are anything but nostalgic looks back at childhood. Instead, she has produced two highly praised and edgy novels for young adults. *Breathing Underwater* is about an abusive relationship and dating violence and the other, *Breaking Point,* focuses on school violence and peer pressure. Interestingly, both books are told from the point of view of a young male. As Flinn told *Embracing the Child,* "I mostly just listen to the voices in my head and see who is talking. That is the only way I know how to write."

Flinn was destined to be a writer from the age of five, when her mother suggested that she should be an author. "I guess I must have nodded or something," Flinn commented on her Web site, "because from that point on, every poem I ever wrote in school was submitted to *Highlights* or *Cricket* magazine. I was collecting rejection slips at age seven." Born in New York state, Flinn grew up in both Syosset, New York, and in Miami, Florida. Reading was an early habit for her, with her list of favorite authors including Astrid Lindgren, Beverly Cleary, Judy Blume, Marilyn Sachs, and Laura Ingalls Wilder. Flinn also noted that she has read Frances Hodgson Burnett's *A Little Princess* fifty times.

Despite her love of reading, when it came to reading her school work, Flinn was always behind, prompting one teacher to comment to her mother

that young Alexandra marched to her own drum. By the time she was in high school, Flinn's artistic aspirations had expanded to include performing arts. In college at the University of Miami, she studied opera, singing as a coloratura, "the really loud, high-pitched soprano," as Flinn described her voice on her Web site.

Following graduation from the University of Miami, Flinn attended law school and then interned with the Miami-Dade State Attorney's Office in a misdemeanor court and volunteering with battered women. As an intern, she pled out or tried numerous domestic violence cases, usually sending batterers to programs similar to the one later portrayed in *Breathing Underwater.* She thereafter went into private practice for a time and married a fellow attorney. Slowly, however, she began coming back to her first love, writing. On sabbatical leave for a pregnancy, she decided to devote full time to writing.

Breathing Underwater

Flinn's legal work and volunteer work with battered women strongly influenced her choice of topic for her first novel, as did a startling statistic she read: about twenty-six percent of high school and college women report having been in an abusive relationship. Additionally, one of the clients in the shelter for battered women where she volunteered was murdered by her husband in front of the woman's children. This tragedy convinced Flinn that the subject of abuse needed wider understanding. Researching the subject, she read books on counseling and on abuse, and interviewed several women who worked in a domestic violence program. Additionally, she began reading young adult novels, for she saw her tale as one dealing with teenagers. "I knew that I wanted to write Y.A.," she told Sue Corbett in an interview for *Knight-Ridder/Tribune News Service,* "and I saw little out there about this subject. I had a daughter and thought there should be something out there so that girls would recognize the warning signs of such a relationship."

The work of Richard Peck particularly impressed her. "I was self-taught," Flinn commented on her author Web site. "Reading [Peck's] books is like listening to Mozart—you learn the right way to write a novel. Then you fill in your own style." She subsequently attended a workshop given by Peck, and in another writing workshop, given by Joyce Sweeney, was steered toward literary agent George Nicholson.

Initially, Flinn began her tale by using two characters she had employed in a young adult fantasy she partially wrote while still in college. For *Breathing Underwater,* she took the same Caitlin and Nick, and began telling of the abusive relationship from the girl's point of view. Soon, however, the inner voice told her it was Nick she wanted to use as her point of view character. As Flinn discovered in her research, it is the troubled home life of the abuser that sets the cycle of abuse in action, and she wanted to get at the root of the problem. Writing during her breaks and lunchtime once she returned to work, Flinn finally finished her manuscript and it was accepted.

Told through the journal entries of Nick Andreas, *Breathing Underwater* is an examination of an abusive relationship told from the viewpoint of the abuser. At sixteen, Nick has long been considered one of the cool kids in school. He is wealthy, good looking, popular, intelligent, a charmer, a football player, and drives a classic Mustang. That is his public face, however. Peeling the onion, the reader finds a different Nick, one tainted by the abuse of his father who continually tells his son he is a loser. He and his father live alone, and he has not seen his mother since he was five. Angry, frustrated, and confused, the inner Nick is like a bomb waiting to go off.

"When I close my eyes, I am still thirteen years old. I remember everything about that time in sharp focus, the pain of not really fitting in at school, struggles with schoolwork (Math!), wondering if I'd ever meet the guy of my dreams, and wanting so bad to grow up because I felt it was the light at the end of the tunnel. I write my books for that girl, what she would want to read."

—Alex Flinn

One day soon after school starts, he sees his dream girl, Caitlin McCourt, who was once overweight and still has little self-confidence as a result. With the help of his best friend, Tom, Nick is able to meet Caitlin and starts dating her. However, soon Nick is replaying the only relationship tapes he knows, turning a controlling relationship with Caitlin into a verbally abusive and ultimately physically abusive one.

Breathing Underwater opens with Nick in court, facing a restraining order from Caitlin, whom he admits he has slapped. The court finds him guilty and sentences him to six months of counseling. He must also keep a weekly journal that explains his relationship with Caitlin from the first time he met her up to the present. The book is told in a dual narrative, both from Nick's journal entries, and also in the present with him returning to the affluent Key Biscayne High School where everybody now knows of the secret, abusive Nick. At first Nick resists taking responsibility for what he has done. In his counseling program, however, he begins to see the ugliness of his actions when another member of the program, Leo, manages to get his girlfriend to drop her charges. Leo subsequently kills the girl and then commits suicide, providing a powerful wake-up call for Nick.

Critical response to *Breathing Underwater* was overwhelmingly positive. "The voice of Nick," Corbett wrote, "the most unsympathetic creep a reader will ever find herself feeling sorry for, is pitch-perfect." In reality, though, this cool exterior hides a kid who himself has been a victim of abuse and is desperate to find love. A reviewer for *Publishers Weekly* felt that the "correlation between Nick's controlling behavior and his father's abuse is subtle but effective." The same contributor concluded that Nick ultimately takes responsibility for his actions, an action which carries "heavy emotional weight in this gripping tale." Joel Shoemaker, writing in *School Library Journal,* felt that Flinn's narrative was an "open and honest portrayal of an all-too-common problem," while a critic for *Booklist* found the elements of the tale provided "a quick and absorbing read." And reviewing the novel in *Voice of Youth Advocates,* Beth Anderson wrote that the book was "almost too painful to read," but that it also provided a "road map to warning signs" of abuse.

Flinn has stated that she purposely set her novel in the midst of an affluent community and amid high-achieving teenagers so as to bring her message home: abuse can happen anywhere and is not simply an inner-city problem. The universality of her message has seemed to reach a broad spectrum of readers. In her interview with *Embracing the Child,* the author noted that she hears not only from victims of abuse, but also from young boys. One such letter came from two boys in a juvenile detention system. According to Flinn, "They said the book really related to their lives and their anger. Both of them said they didn't like to read, but they liked *Breathing.*"

Breaking Point

Flinn tackles another serious juvenile problem—school violence—in her second novel, *Breaking Point,* which appeared in 2002. Fifteen-year-old Paul, the narrator, is at a breaking point in his young life. His parents have recently divorced: his father, who is in the military, wants no part of him now, while his mother uses Paul as an emotional crutch. Home-schooled until the divorce, nerdish Paul now enters an exclusive private school in Miami where his mother works so that her son can pay lower tuition. Paul and his mother also live in reduced circumstances in a small, rent-controlled apartment. Thus the new kid is an easy target for harassment by all the rich, popular students at Gate-Brickell Christian School. He is at best ignored by many, at worst made the subject of practical jokes, until, miraculously, he is befriended by one of the most popular kids at school, Charlie Good. But Charlie seems to have his own plans for Paul. He tests him by telling him to destroy mailboxes, steal, and drink. Paul, desperate to fit in, follows these suggestions from his new friend. Charlie even manipulates Paul into gaining access to the school computer to change one of his grades. Finally the angry and malevolent Charlie talks Paul into planting a bomb in the school.

Critical reaction to Flinn's second novel included Kimberly L. Paone, writing in *Voice of Youth Advocates,* who welcomed the book, commenting that not since Robert Cormier's *The Chocolate War* "have characters been drawn to be so brilliantly twisted." Francisca Goldsmith in *Booklist* found the novel to be "grim and emotional, this is cathartic reading for teens." However, a critic for *Kirkus Reviews* felt that the novel was "just one more variation on the familiar theme of paying a high price for popularity." Janet Hilburn, writing in *School Library Journal,* saw Flinn's novel as more noteworthy, concluding that the author "has succeeded in her goal" of understanding what can make teens angry and isolated. Hilburn further noted, "Despite his actions, Paul comes across as a likable, although misguided, teen in a book that is well worth reading." Paone concluded, "This timely, engaging book is certain to grab the interest of teens."

Breaking Point was a difficult book for Flinn to write; in the process she had to relive her own school experiences of feeling like an outsider and trying hard to fit in. "The whole time I was writing [*Breaking Point*]," the author noted on her Web site, "I felt like I was back at that school I hated. But I know a lot of people have had that experience and will relate to Paul, if not his actions. I think it's especially important because of all the violence in schools in re-

cent years. There is an increased awareness of kids who don't fit in. And, unfortunately, there have been kids who have been allowed these feelings of isolation—which are, in the end, temporary—to cause them to commit actions with permanent effects."

With two books to her credit, Flinn was soon busy with another young adult novel, *Nothing to Lose,* about a teen who joins the carnival after his mother has been charged with the murder of her abusive husband. Despite dealing with serious themes, Flinn feels that she is first and foremost a storyteller. "The story has to come first," she commented in her interview with *Embracing the Child.* "Writing, especially for teenagers, can't just be like a P[ublic] S[ervice] A[nnouncement]. . . . It has to be a good story with characters they really care about, and the 'S' word: Suspense." Flinn also finds the whole business of writing and publishing thrilling and fun. As she told Kathie Bergquist in a *Publishers Weekly* interview, "Sometimes I feel like I should be the one paying [my publishers]. It's just been so exciting!"

If you enjoy the works of Alex Flinn, you might want to check out the following books:

Robert Cormier, *The Chocolate War,* 1974.
Chris Crutcher, *Ironman,* 1995.
Sarah Dessen, *Dreamland,* 2000.

"When I close my eyes," Flinn concluded, "I am still thirteen years old. I remember everything about that time in sharp focus, the pain of not really fitting in at school, struggles with schoolwork (Math!), wondering if I'd ever meet the guy of my dreams, and wanting so bad to grow up because I felt it was the light at the end of the tunnel. I write my books for *that* girl, what she would want to read. When I've met with teenagers (and I've spoken to all types—from gifted magnet schools to last-chance alternative programs), I've been pleased to find that the students there have almost universally related to what I write. That's what is most important to me."

■ Biographical and Critical Sources

PERIODICALS

Booklist, August, 2001, review of *Breathing Underwater,* p. 2106; June 1, 2002, Lolly Gepson, review of *Breathing Underwater* (audio version), p. 1753; September 1, 2002, Francisca Goldsmith, review of *Breaking Point,* p. 16.

Kirkus Reviews, April 1, 2002, review of *Breaking Point,* pp. 490-491.

Knight-Ridder/Tribune News Service, April 25, 2001, Sue Corbett, "New Novels for Teens Tackle Domestic Violence, Other Mature Subjects," p. K2283.

Long Beach Press-Telegram, August 10, 2002, Heatehr Wood, review of *Breaking Point,* p. U5.

Publishers Weekly, April 23, 2001, review of *Breathing Underwater,* p. 79; June 25, 2001, Kathie Bergquist, "Alex Flinn," p. 26; May 20, 2002, review of *Breaking Point,* p. 68.

School Library Journal, May, 2001, Joel Shoemaker, review of *Breathing Underwater,* p. 149; May, 2002, Janet Hilburn, review of *Breaking Point,* p. 152; June, 2002, Tina Hudak, review of *Breathing Underwater* (audio version), p. 72; October, 2002, Barbara S. Wysocki, review of *Breaking Point* (audio version), p. 84.

Voice of Youth Advocates, June, 2001, Beth Anderson, review of *Breathing Underwater;* June, 2002, Kimberly L. Paone, review of *Breaking Point,* pp. 117-118.

OTHER

Alex Flinn Web site, http://www.alexflinn.com/ (August 20, 2002).

Cynthia Leitich Smith Children's Literature Resources Web site, http://www.cynthialeitichsmith.com/storyflinn.html/ (November 7, 2002), "The Story Behind The Story: Alex Flinn on *Breaking Point.*"

Embracing the Child, http://www.eyeontomorrow.com/embracingthechild/ (August 27, 2002), "Interview with Alex Flinn."*

—Sketch by J. Sydney Jones

Ken Follett

don, England, editorial director, 1974-76, deputy managing director, 1976-77; full-time writer, 1977—. Bass guitarist and singer for group Damn Right I Got the Blues, 1994—.

■ Personal

Born June 5, 1949, in Cardiff, Wales; son of Martin D. (a tax inspector) and Lavinia C. (Evans) Follett; married Mary Emma Ruth Elson, January 5, 1968 (divorced, September 20, 1985); married Barbara Broer, November 8, 1985; children (first marriage): Emanuele, Marie-Claire. *Nationality:* British; Welsh. *Education:* University College London, B A., 1970. *Religion:* Atheist. *Hobbies and other interests:* Music.

■ Addresses

Home—P.O. Box 4, Knebworth, Hertfordshire SG3 6UT, England. *Agent*—Writers House, Inc., 21 West 26th St., New York, NY 10010. *E-mail*—ken@ken-follett.com.

■ Career

Trainee journalist and rock music columnist at *South Wales Echo,* 1970-73; *Evening News,* London, England, reporter, 1973-74; Everest Books Ltd., Lon-

■ Member

National Literacy Trust.

■ Awards, Honors

Edgar Allan Poe Award, Mystery Writers of America, 1978, for *Eye of the Needle.*

■ Writings

NOVELS

The Shakeout, Harwood-Smart (London, England), 1975.
The Bear Raid, Harwood-Smart (London, England), 1976.
The Secret of Kellerman's Studio (juvenile), Abelard, 1976, illustrated by Stephen Marchesi as *Mystery Hideout,* Morrow (New York, NY), 1990.

Eye of the Needle, Arbor House (New York, NY), 1978, published as *Storm Island,* Macdonald & Jane's (London, England), 1978.

Triple, Arbor House (New York, NY), 1979.

The Key to Rebecca, Morrow (New York, NY), 1980.

The Man from St. Petersburg, Morrow (New York, NY), 1982.

Lie down with Lions, Hamilton (London, England), 1985, Morrow (New York, NY), 1986.

The Pillars of the Earth, Morrow (New York, NY), 1989, portions published as *Pillars of the Almighty,* 1994.

Night over Water, Morrow (New York, NY), 1991.

A Dangerous Fortune, Delacorte (New York, NY), 1993.

A Place Called Freedom, Crown (New York, NY), 1995.

The Third Twin, Crown (New York, NY), 1996.

The Hammer of Eden, Crown (New York, NY), 1998.

Code to Zero, Dutton (New York, NY), 2000.

Jackdaws, Dutton (New York, NY), 2001.

Hornet Flight, Dutton (New York, NY), 2002.

UNDER PSEUDONYM SYMON MYLES

The Big Needle, Everest Books (London, England), 1974, published as *The Big Apple,* Kensington (San Diego, CA), 1975, published under name Ken Follett, Zebra (New York, NY), 1986.

The Big Black, Everest Books (London, England), 1974.

The Big Hit, Everest Books (London, England), 1975.

OTHER

(Under pseudonym Martin Martinsen) *The Power Twins and the Worm Puzzle: A Science Fantasy for Young People,* Abelard, 1976, published under name Ken Follett as *Power Twins,* Scholastic (New York, NY), 1991.

(Under pseudonym Bernard L. Ross) *Amok: King of Legend,* Futura (London, England), 1976.

(Under pseudonym Zachary Stone) *The Modigliani Scandal,* Collins (London, England), 1976, published under name Ken Follett, Morrow (New York, NY), 1985.

(Under pseudonym Zachary Stone) *Paper Money,* Collins (London, England), 1977, published under name Ken Follett, Morrow (New York, NY), 1987.

(Under pseudonym Bernard L. Ross) *Capricorn One,* Futura (London, England), 1978.

(With Rene Louis Maurice) *The Heist of the Century* (nonfiction), Fontana Books (London, England), 1978, published as *The Gentlemen of 16 July,* Arbor House (New York, NY), 1980, revised edition published as *Under the Streets of Nice: The Bank Heist of the Century,* National Press Books, 1986.

On Wings of Eagles (nonfiction), Morrow (New York, NY), 1983.

Also author of film scripts *Fringe Banking,* for British Broadcasting Corp., 1978, *A Football Star,* with John Sealey, 1979, and *Lie down with Lions,* for Scott Reeve Enterprises, 1988. Contributor to *New Statesman* and *Writer.* Author of "Hoochie Coochie Man" (song), on the CD *Stranger than Fiction,* Don't Quit Your Day Job Records.

■ Adaptations

Eye of the Needle, directed by Richard Marquand and starring Donald Sutherland and Kate Nelligan, was adapted for the screen by Stanley Mann, United Artists, 1981. *The Key to Rebecca* was adapted as an Operation Prime Time television miniseries, 1985. *On Wings of Eagles* was filmed by Edgar Schenick Productions as a television miniseries, 1985. *The Third Twin* was adapted as a 1997 television feature starring Kelly McGillis and Jason Gedrick. *Under the Streets of Nice* was adapted as a sound recording, Dove Audio (Beverly Hills, CA), 1991. Film rights to *Jackdaws* were sold to Dino De Laurentiis.

■ Sidelights

Ken Follett, author of best-selling thrillers such as *Eye of the Needle, Triple, The Key to Rebecca, The Man from St. Petersburg, The Third Twin, The Hammer of Eden, Code to Zero,* and the 2001 title, *Jackdaws,* has created a winning blend of historical events and action-adventure fiction. Many of his books are set during war time, World War II being a favorite motif. Follett has, however, never ventured onto a battlefield or dangerous situation, a la Ernest Hemingway, in pursuit of a story. "I don't think I would have found any battle or wartime situation congenial," Follett told David Bowman in a *Salon.com* interview. "I've always been fond of creature comforts. Hot baths. I never liked danger."

Follett's fictional creations, however, are often weaned on danger; their creator has the knack of making his bad guys understandable if not almost likable, and his female characters strong movers and shakers rather than decorative bystanders. "Most of my stories have some basis in fact," Follett explained to an interviewer for *Bookreporter.com.* "I like to create imaginary characters and events around a real historical situation. I want readers to feel: 'Okay, this probably didn't happen, but it might have.'"

The author's breakout novel, *Eye of the Needle,* propelled him into international prominence, and his subsequent novels have proved as popular in the United States as in his native Great Britain. With *Pillars of the Earth,* a sprawling medieval tale about the construction of a great cathedral, Follett surprised fans and critics alike, penning a non-thriller every bit as much a page-turner as his novels of espionage and intrigue. However, after a couple more forays into mainstream fiction, Follett returned to the territory for which he is best known: thrillers. *Washington Post* correspondent Paul Hendrickson claimed that Follett has earned a reputation as an "international thriller writer with a genius for threading the eye of the literary needle."

Welsh Background

Born in Cardiff, Wales, in 1949, Follett grew up in a household where radio and television were forbidden. His father, Martin Follett, was a tax inspector whose salary did not allow for many luxuries in the Follett household. Additionally, Martin and his wife, Veenie, were devout born-again Christians who felt that watching television or going to the cinema was sinful behavior. "With no TV or radio, and no Saturday morning pictures which all the other kids used to go to, reading was my entertainment," Follett wrote on his Web site. "I didn't have many books of my own and I've always been grateful for the public library. Without free books I would not have become a voracious reader, and if you are not a reader you are not a writer." Follett credits this early love of reading with enabling him to build a creative world of the imagination. "I was a great liver in fantasy worlds from an early age," he once told a contributor for the *Washington Post.*

When he was ten, Follett and his family moved from Wales to London. As he noted on his Web site, he was bored and badly behaved in school for the next several years. "When I got interested in girls, school suddenly became much more fun," he commented. This interest manifested itself in better grades. During these years he also began playing guitar, purchasing his first instrument second hand for four pounds and learning a standard repertoire of pop songs from artists such as Bob Dylan and the Beatles. Graduating from secondary school, the eighteen-year-old Follett attended University College, London, where he studied philosophy in search of answers to his religious doubts. A student during the 1960s, Follett was caught up in the political atmosphere of the time, which included rallies against the Vietnam War as well as in opposition to the apartheid regime in South Africa.

Toward the end of Follett's first year in college his high school girlfriend, Mary Elson, became pregnant. Follett's first child, a son named Emanuele, was born while his father and mother were not yet out of their teens. "I felt doubly rich," Follett noted on his Web site, "because I was having a great time at university and it was also tremendously exciting to have a little baby and take care of him."

From Journalism to Novels

After graduating with a degree in philosophy in 1970, Follett became a newspaper reporter, first in Cardiff, on the *South Wales Echo,* where he worked as a general reporter and also covered the pop music beat, interviewing stars such as Stevie Wonder and Led Zeppelin. In 1973 he went back to London, where he worked as a journalist on the *Evening News,* writing a regular column about the River Thames and also covering Scotland Yard and the crime beat. That same year he and his wife had a baby daughter, Marie-Claire. Follett did not feel a great deal of satisfaction from his journalism work. "I wanted to be a hot shot investigative reporter, but I never made the grade."

Frustrated with his work, he began writing fiction on the side when he needed extra money for car repairs. "It was a hobby for me," he said in a *Chicago Tribune* interview. "You know, some men go home and grow vegetables. I used to go home and write novels. A lucrative hobby. I sold them for far more than you could sell vegetables for." Follett did not, however, quit his day job for several years, even after he began publishing novels.

Follett's early novels were published under various pseudonyms. Most of these were murder mysteries or crime fiction based loosely on cases he covered as a reporter for the London *Evening News.* The author admitted in the *Los Angeles Times* that he learned how to write good books "by writing mediocre ones and wondering what was wrong with them." In order to further his knowledge of the book business, Follett joined the staff of Everest Books in 1974. Remembering his decision to move to the publishing house, Follett told the *Chicago Tribune:* "A good deal of it was curiosity to know what made books sell. Some books sell and others don't. All the books I had written up to that point fell into the category of those that did not."

In the mid-1970s, Follett met U.S. literary agent Al Zuckerman, who had a major effect on changing this mid-list writer into a best-selling author. From the beginning, the two worked collaboratively, Follett sending Zuckerman outlines for books, and the agent telling him why these would not make it in the U.S. market. "I would send him an outline or a draft," Follett explained in his introduction to Zuckerman's *Writing the Blockbuster Novel,* "and back would come a little homily. It invariably began: 'I cannot sell this book in the U.S. because—.' What followed purported to be a comment on the American publishing business, but in reality it was a little lesson in what it takes to write a best-seller." From Zuckerman, Follett learned the tricks of the trade,

the techniques for turning a novel from mid-list into best-seller: a main character with a past with whom readers could closely identify; an appealing setting for the novel; and a "big dramatic question" that would keep the readers turning pages.

Follett finally got the formula right with his eleventh book, *Eye of the Needle.* He told readers in a *Barnesandnoble.com* interview that he concentrated on doing three things differently with this book: planning it with care, researching his subject thoroughly, and slowing the book's pace. The result was a popular sensation that catapulted to the top of best seller lists across the globe. The World War II thriller about a ruthless Nazi spy and a crippled pilot's wife received critical raves as well. In the *Washington Post Book World,* reviewer Roderick MacLeish called *Eye of the Needle* "quite simply the best spy novel to come out of England in years," and *News-*

Donald Sutherland and Stephen Phillips star in the screen adaptation of Ken Follett's *Eye of the Needle,* directed by Richard Marquand and released in 1981.

week correspondent Peter Prescott described the work as "rubbish of the very best sort . . . a triumph of invention over convention." Still in print more than twenty years after its initial publication, *Eye of the Needle,* which won the Edgar Allan Poe Award from the Mystery Writers of America, has since sold more than ten million copies worldwide and been translated into more than twenty-five languages.

Internationally Bestselling Author

With *Eye of the Needle,* Follett established himself as a new sort of thriller writer—one who found a compromise between the serious and the popular. Follett's works have been cited for their special sensitivity to female characters as well as for an overall psychological complexity not often found in adventure stories. As Andrew F. Macdonald and Gina Macdonald noted in the *Dictionary of Literary Biography,* a positive feature of Follett's novels "is his humanizing of his villains. All are well rounded and complete, with credible motives and understandable passions—if anything, they are sometimes so sympathetic that they jeopardize the reader's relationship with the hero." His heroines are equally appealing, though Follett does not set out to make them different from other lead characters in the books. "When I'm writing a woman character," he told *Salon's* Bowman, "I don't think, 'What would a woman do?' I just think, 'What would this character do in this situation?' I've never made a big distinction between the way that women react and the way that men react. . . . I don't think there's any great mystery about writing female characters, so long as you talk to them." Follett also noted that most thriller writers do female characters very poorly. "So just doing it OK gets a lot of credit." By creating such sympathetic heroines, Follett has been able to lure female readers to novels that traditionally appeal primarily to men.

Follett's forte—in fiction and nonfiction—is the variation upon history. Every human relationship is somehow blighted or molded by the complexities of world politics, and all emotional and sexual entanglements are played out against a backdrop of historical events. Andrew and Gina Macdonald wrote: "Each of [Follett's] best works grows out of news stories and historical events. Cinematic in conception, they follow a hunter-hunted pattern that leads to exciting chase scenes and games of wit and brinkmanship."

In quick succession, Follett turned out several bestselling thrillers. His second success was *Triple,* in which he presents two sides of the Arab-Israeli conflict, humanized by characters in the Mossad, Israel's espionage organization, and terrorists in the Palestine Liberation Organization. This novel uses the actual theft, in 1968, of a shipload of raw uranium, as its historical backdrop. *The Key to Rebecca* came next, set in wartime Cairo and based on the historical events of the German spy John Eppler during General Erwin Rommel's push toward Alexandria. This novel is, according to a contributor for *Contemporary Popular Writers,* "one of Follett's most carefully written books," with a psychopathic spy going up against a well-realized and sympathetic military intelligence officer. *The Man from St. Petersburg* is the story of a World War I anarchist who is determined to stop Russian support for England in its war with Germany. *On the Wings of Eagles* is an account of Ross Perot's actual rescue of two of his corporate executives in Iran, while Follett's novel *Lie down with Lions* offers an ambiguous portrait of the factional strife in Afghanistan. *Time* contributor Michael Demarest claimed that the author's strength remains "an acute sense of geographical place, and the age-old knowledge that character is action. . . . He brilliantly reproduces a distant terrain, complete with sounds and smells and tribal rites."

Michael Adams, writing in *Dictionary of Literary Biography Yearbook 1981,* related some of the reasons for Follett's extraordinary success as a novelist, explaining that in his "exciting, intelligent, generally well-written . . . thrillers, not only are the major characters well developed, but the minor characters are given attention as well. The reader is always able to understand all the characters' political, social, economic, and sexual motives. Follett makes certain that even his villains have sympathetic sides. . . . He also reveals a thorough understanding not only of the history and techniques of espionage but of the intertwining complexities of twentieth-century world politics. Equally important is the skill of his plotting. While spy fiction is frequently complex and bewildering to the reader, Follett's work is consistently clear and easy to follow."

Vacation from Thriller Fiction

In 1985 Follett divorced his first wife and married Barbara Broer, a British civil servant and Member of Parliament. He also began working on a new novel which was several years in the writing. In 1989, with publication of *The Pillars of the Earth,* Follett made a break with thriller fiction. Set in twelfth-century England, *The Pillars of the Earth* recounts the four-decades-long construction of a cathedral and the efforts of Prior Philip and his master mason, Tom Builder, to complete the building and keep it

In the 2001 sequel to *Code to Zero*, Follett spins the story of a British undercover agent who, with her husband, must help lay the groundwork for D-Day.

The historical novel genre has proved compatible with Follett's skills. His subsequent works, which include *A Dangerous Fortune* and *A Place Called Freedom*, weave complicated stories of intrigue in England and the Americas. In *A Dangerous Fortune*, an English schoolboy's drowning sets off a chain of events that leads to national crisis, as rival bankers seek to undermine each others' positions. "*A Dangerous Fortune* leaves us feeling as though we've visited an age very different from our own, and understand it far better than we did," wrote a *Rapport* correspondent. "Follett's . . . tour through privileged Victorian society . . . won't be easily forgotten." In the *Los Angeles Times Book Review*, Thomas Hines cited *A Dangerous Fortune* for its "eye for the telling historical detail and a fair sense that people from the past weren't like us—and that's precisely what makes them so interesting." *A Place Called Freedom* tells the story of Malachi McAsh, a Scottish miner who rebels against a lifetime of servitude to the brutal local laird. McAsh's quest for freedom leads him to trouble in London and indentured servitude in America, at a time when the very ideals of human liberty are being debated there. A *Publishers Weekly* reviewer noted that in the novel, Follett "adroitly escalates the suspense by mixing intrigue and danger, tinged with ironic complications." The critic concluded that *A Place Called Freedom* is redeemed "by Follett's vigorous narrative drive and keen eye for character."

Between these various historical sagas, Follett completed yet another thriller, *Night over Water*. Set in the last dark days of 1939, the novel recounts the last transatlantic voyage of the opulent Pan American Clipper, its passengers all bent upon various deadly intrigues. According to *Spectator* reviewer Christopher Hawtree, *Night over Water* "marks a return to World War II and top form" for Follett. Hawtree added that the novel provides "a smoothly-controlled bumpy landing. There is no reverse-thrust to this narrative which sedulously leads one into the dark and all that is revealed therein."

from falling into the hands of a rival bishop. Critical reaction to that novel was mixed, perhaps because it was such an unexpected departure for Follett. Gary Jennings in the *Washington Post Book World*, for example, found that "the legions of fanciers of Ken Follett's spy novels will likely be dismayed by his having turned now to historical fiction." Margaret Flanagan in *Booklist* called *The Pillars of the Earth* "a towering triumph of romance, rivalry, and spectacle from a major talent." Margaret Cannon in the Toronto *Globe and Mail*, while acknowledging the book's tendency toward overwriting, admitted that "the period is so good and the cathedrals so marvelous that one keeps reading anyway." Despite some skepticism from critics, *The Pillars of the Earth* became Follett's most popular book.

Comes Back to Thrillers

Follett chose more up-to-the-minute topics for his next two thrillers. *The Third Twin* spins a dark plot of violence and intrigue around genetic research and human cloning. Deemed "great plane reading" by a reviewer in *Entertainment Weekly*, the book was adapted as a TV miniseries. Also pertinent to themes in late-twentieth-century American culture is *The Hammer of Eden*, in which a charismatic cult leader in California threatens violence when the state plans to build a new power plant on the site of his secret commune. The leader, named Priest, steals a seismic vibrator from a local oil-drilling operation and vows to flatten the entire state with a super earthquake if his demands are not met. "Taut plotting, tense action, skillful writing, and myriad unexpected twists make this one utterly unputdownable," wrote Emily Melton in *Booklist*. *Library Journal* reviewer V. Louise Saylor, however, cited the novel's reliance on coincidence and its sympathetic portrayal of Priest as flaws that keep *The Hammer of Eden* below the level of Follett's best work.

Code to Zero marked a return to classic espionage for Follett. Set in 1958, the novel concerns the U.S. Army's attempt to launch the *Explorer 1*, which would have been the country's first rocket in space, during the height of the Cold War with the Soviet Union. Though some critics objected to Follett's use of amnesia as a major plot device in the novel, others hailed *Code to Zero* as a welcome return to form. A reviewer in *Publishers Weekly* considered it an "absorbing" and "tightly plotted" tale, and *Booklist* contributor Bill Ott praised it as "a classic page-turner on a classic theme." However, Tom LeClair in *Book* found the novel filled with improbabilities and dull writing. Though he also noted Follett's lack of stylistic flair, *New York Times Book Review* contributor John W. Dean suggested that "For most readers, *Code to Zero* will be gripping."

With the 2001 title *Jackdaws* Follett returned to the familiar terrain of World War II. Likened to the fast-paced *The Dirty Dozen* "recast as The Dirty Half-Dozen, Girl Version" by *Booklist* contributor Bill Ott, the novel posits a formulaic thriller incident: a small team of special forces is inserted behind the lines to take out an enemy position before it is too late. In Follett's take on the premise, a misfit team of six women is chosen for the mission. Their goal: to destroy the German telephone exchange in Reims, France, just before D-Day. This team, picked from the rejects of Special Operations branch, includes "outsiders for the twenty-first century," according to Ott, such as a safe-cracker, a couple of lesbians, a gypsy, and a transvestite from Germany. Ott further noted that this may all sound melodramatic and full of cliches, "but when Follett starts the clock and slips the narrative gearshift into syncromesh, one's literary misgivings are abandoned in the wake of the plot's forward thrust." "Bullets fly and blood flows while the fate of D-Day hangs, obligatorily, in the balance," wrote a critic for *Kirkus Reviews*. Cynthia Sanz, writing in *People*, felt that Follett had trouble with the romance sections of his novel. According to Sanz, "Follett's love scenes feel clunky." But for Sanz, there were other rewards to the novel, such as the action scenes during which the story

"speeds along at breakneck pace." A *Publishers Weekly* contributor noted that Follett "delivers a very entertaining, very cinematic thriller about a ragtag, all-female band of British agents." The same reviewer concluded that *Jackdaws* "promises to be one of Follett's most popular novels ever." Bruce Fretts in *Entertainment Weekly* commented that, with *Jackdaws*, "Follett once again puts his cross-gender gift to good use by telling the story of an all-female World War II espionage team." Fretts further declared, "*Jackdaws* aims to please as a suspense thriller . . . and as a soap opera. . . . On both accounts, Follett delivers plenty of bang for your buck."

If you enjoy the works of Ken Follett, you might want to check out the following books:

Frederick Forsyth, *The Day of the Jackal,* 1971.
Jack Higgins, *The Eagle Has Landed,* 1975.
W. J. Weatherby, *Coronation,* 1990.

Unlike many of his contemporaries, Follett positively relishes the label "popular writer." He once commented in *Dictionary of Literary Biography:* "I'm not under the illusion that the world is waiting for my thoughts to appear in print. People want to be told a story, and that's what I'm up to. I think of myself as a craftsman more than an artist." Although he likes to read such noted English writers as Thomas Hardy, Jane Austen, and George Eliot, Follett remains satisfied with his own aims and accomplishments. "What I enjoy," he told the *Chicago Tribune*, "is writing a book and then having *millions* of people read it and love it. I wouldn't want to write something that ten people loved; so I'm constrained by what I think are the preferences of my readers. If I'm careful, I'll take them along with me."

■ Biographical and Critical Sources

BOOKS

Contemporary Popular Writers, St. James Press (Detroit, MI), 1997.
Dictionary of Literary Biography, Volume 87: *British Mystery Writers since 1940,* Gale (Detroit, MI), 1989.

Dictionary of Literary Biography Yearbook 1981, Gale (Detroit, MI), 1982.

McCormick, Donald, *Who's Who in Spy Fiction,* Elm Tree Books (London, England), 1977.

St. James Guide to Crime and Mystery Writers, 4th edition, St. James Press (Detroit, MI), 1996.

Zuckerman, Al, *Writing the Blockbuster Novel,* introduction by Ken Follett, Writer's Digest Books (Cincinnati, OH), 1994.

PERIODICALS

Book, January, 2001, Tom LeClair, review of *Code to Zero,* p. 78.

Booklist, June 15, 1989, Margaret Flanagan, review of *Pillars of the Earth;* September 1, 1998, Emily Melton, review of *The Hammer of Eden,* p. 5; October 15, 2000, Bill Ott, review of *Code to Zero,* p. 390; September 15, 2001, Bill Ott, review of *Jackdaws,* p. 164.

Chicago Tribune, October 14, 1983; October 25, 1987; September 10, 1989.

Chicago Tribune Book World, October 5, 1980.

Detroit Free Press, September 10, 1989.

Entertainment Weekly, October 24, 1997, review of *The Third Twin,* p. 59; December 14, 2001, Bruce Fretts, "Spy Dames," p. 73.

Globe and Mail (Toronto, Ontario, Canada), September 2, 1989, Margaret Cannon, review of *Pillars of the Earth.*

Guardian (London, England), October 29, 2000, "The Great Entertainer."

Kirkus Reviews, October 21, 2001, review of *Jackdaws,* p. 1382.

Library Journal, July, 1989; January, 1997, Gordon Cheatham, review of audio recording of *The Third Twin,* p. 173; October 1, 1998, V. Louise Saylor, review of *The Hammer of Eden,* p. 132; February 1, 1999, Mark Pumphrey, review of *The Hammer of Eden,* p. 136; August, 2000, p. 72; November 1, 2000, Robert Conroy, review of *Code to Zero,* p 133; October 15, 2001, Robert Conroy, review of *Jackdaws,* p. 106.

London Review of Books, August 19, 1982, p. 18.

Los Angeles Times, October 1, 1980; June 3, 1990.

Los Angeles Times Book Review, October 7, 1979; September 28, 1980; May 30, 1982; September 11, 1983; February 16, 1986; October 4, 1987, p. 6; December 12, 1993, Thomas Hines, review of *A Dangerous Fortune,* p. 8.

Nation, April 26, 1980, pp. 504-505.

New Statesman, April 10, 1987.

Newsweek, August 7, 1978; September 29, 1980.

New Yorker, August 21, 1978; August 16, 1982.

New York Times, May 12, 1978; October 3, 1979.

New York Times Book Review, July 16, 1978; September 21, 1980; May 9, 1982; October 23, 1983, pp. 20, 22; January 26, 1986; September 10, 1989; September 29, 1991, p. 22; January 9, 1994, p. 19; January 14, 2001, John W. Dean, review of *Code to Zero.*

People, December 10, 2001, Cynthia Sanz, review of *Jackdaws,* p. 49.

Publishers Weekly, January 17, 1986; June 30, 1989; July 21, 1989; April 13, 1990, p. 66; July 19, 1991, pp. 44-45; June 5, 1995, review of *A Place Called Freedom,* pp. 48-49; December 18, 2000, review of *Code to Zero,* p. 20; October 15, 2001, review of *Jackdaws,* p. 44.

Rapport, January, 1994, review of *A Dangerous Fortune,* p. 21; November 9, 1998, J. D. Reed, review of *The Hammer of Eden,* p. 45.

Saturday Review, August, 1978.

Spectator, November 16, 1991, Christopher Hawtree, review of *Night over Water,* p. 46.

Time, October 30, 1978; November 5, 1979; September 29, 1980; May 3, 1982.

Times Literary Supplement, December 26, 1980; June 4, 1982.

Tribune Books (Chicago, IL), September 10, 1989, p. 7; August 30, 1992, p. 8.

Washington Post, October 11, 1979; September 15, 1980; September 7, 1983; September 21, 1983; June 1, 1985.

Washington Post Book World, April 25, 1982; February 2, 1986, p. 9; August 20, 1989, Gary Jennings, review of *Pillars of the Earth;* November 21, 1993, p. 4.

Writer, June, 1979.

OTHER

Barnesandnoble.com, http://www.barnesandnoble.com/ (November 2, 2000), interview with Ken Follett.

Bookreporter.com, http://www.bookreporter.com/ (September 11, 2002), "Interview with Ken Follett, Author."

Ken Follett Official Web site, http://www.ken-follett.com/ (November 15, 2000).

Salon.com, http://www.salon.com/ (December 2, 1998), David Bowman, "The Salon Interview: Ken Follett."

Tuttle Books Web site, http://www.tuttlebook.co.jp/ (September 11, 2002), "Ken Follett: Special Interview."*

Heather Graham

■ Personal

Born in Dublin, Ireland; immigrated to the United States; married Dennis Pozzessere (a writer); children: Jason, Shayne, Derek, Bryee-Annon, Chynna. *Nationality:* Irish; American. *Education:* Attended University of South Florida.

■ Addresses

Home—Coral Gables, FL. *Agent*—c/o Author Mail, Zebra Books, 850 Third Ave., 16th Floor, New York, NY 10022-6222. *E-mail*--hgraham@booktalk.com.

■ Career

Writer. Worked variously in dinner theatre, as a model, bartender, and actress.

■ Awards, Honors

Best Silhouette "Ecstasy" novel award nomination, 1987, for *The Maverick and the Lady;* best Silhouette "Intimate Moments" novel award nomination, 1987, for *A Matter of Circumstance,* and 1988, for *King of the Castle;* award for best sensual romance set during the U.S. Civil War, 1988, for *Dark Stranger;* best series writer award nomination; numerous trade awards from *Romantic Times* and *Affaire de Coeur;* bestseller awards from B. Dalton, Walden Books, and BookRak; numerous Reviewer's Choice and People's Choice awards.

■ Writings

ROMANCE AND HISTORICAL NOVELS; AS HEATHER GRAHAM POZZESSERE

Night Moves, Silhouette (New York, NY), 1985.
Double Entendre, Silhouette (New York, NY), 1986.
The DiMedici Bride, Silhouette (New York, NY), 1986.
The Game of Love, Silhouette (New York, NY), 1986.
A Matter of Circumstance, Silhouette (New York, NY), 1987.
Bride of the Tiger, Silhouette (New York, NY), 1987.
King of the Castle, Silhouette (New York, NY), 1987.
Strangers in Paradise, Silhouette (New York, NY), 1988.
Angel of Mercy, Silhouette (New York, NY), 1988.
Lucia in Love, Silhouette (New York, NY), 1988.
This Rough Magic, Silhouette (New York, NY), 1988.
Dark Stranger, Harlequin (Toronto, Ontario, Canada), 1988, as Heather Graham, Severn House (London, England), 1993.

Apache Summer, Harlequin (Toronto, Ontario, Canada), 1989.

A Perilous Eden, Silhouette (New York, NY), 1991.

Wedding Bell Blues, Silhouette (New York, NY), 1991.

Forbidden Fire, Harlequin (Toronto, Ontario, Canada), 1991.

Mistress of Magic, Silhouette (New York, NY), 1992.

Borrowed Angel, Silhouette (New York, NY), 1992.

Hatfield and McCoy, Silhouette (New York, NY), 1992.

The Last Cavalier, Silhouette (New York, NY), 1993.

The Trouble with Andrew, Silhouette (New York, NY), 1993.

Between Roc and a Hard Place, Silhouette (New York, NY), 1993.

Snowfire, Silhouette (New York, NY), 1993.

NOVELS; UNDER NAME HEATHER GRAHAM

A Season for Love, Dell (New York, NY), 1983.

Forbidden Fruit, Dell (New York, NY), 1983.

Quiet Walks the Tiger, Dell (New York, NY), 1983.

Tempestuous Eden, Dell (New York, NY), 1983.

Tender Taming, Dell (New York, NY), 1983.

When Next We Love, Dell (New York, NY), 1983.

Night, Sea, and Stars, Dell (New York, NY), 1983.

Arabian Nights, Dell (New York, NY), 1984.

Hours to Cherish, Dell (New York, NY), 1984.

Red Midnight, Dell (New York, NY), 1984.

Serena's Magic, Dell (New York, NY), 1984.

Tender Deception, Dell (New York, NY), 1984.

Hold Close the Memory, Dell (New York, NY), 1985.

Sensuous Angel, Dell (New York, NY), 1985.

An Angel's Share, Dell (New York, NY), 1985.

Queen of Hearts, Dell (New York, NY), 1985.

Golden Surrender, Dell (New York, NY), 1985.

Dante's Daughter, Dell (New York, NY), 1986.

Eden's Spell, Dell (New York, NY), 1986.

Devil's Mistress, Dell (New York, NY), 1986.

Handful of Dreams, Dell (New York, NY), 1986.

The Maverick and the Lady, Dell (New York, NY), 1986.

Every Time I Love You, Dell (New York, NY), 1987.

Liar's Moon, Dell (New York, NY), 1987.

Siren from the Sea, Dell (New York, NY), 1987.

Love Not a Rebel, Dell (New York, NY), 1987.

All in the Family, Silhouette (New York, NY), 1987.

Sweet, Savage Eden, Dell (New York, NY), 1989.

Pirate's Pleasure, Dell (New York, NY), 1989.

Rides a Hero, Silhouette (New York, NY), 1989.

Viking's Woman, Dell (New York, NY), 1990.

One Wore Blue, Dell (New York, NY), 1991.

One Wore Gray, Dell (New York, NY), 1992.

And One Rode West, Dell (New York, NY), 1992.

Lord of the Wolves, Dell (New York, NY), 1993.

Three Complete Novels, Wings Books (New York, NY), 1994.

Runaway, Delacorte (New York, NY), 1994.

Three Complete Civil War Novels, Wings Books (New York, NY), 1995.

Captive, Topaz (New York, NY), 1995.

A Magical Christmas, Topaz (New York, NY), 1996.

Rebel, Topaz (New York, NY), 1997.

Surrender, Topaz (New York, NY), 1998.

Drop Dead Gorgeous, Onyx (New York, NY), 1998.

Tall, Dark, and Deadly, Onyx (New York, NY), 1999.

Glory, Topaz (New York, NY), 1999.

Triumph, Signet (New York, NY), 2000.

Long, Lean, and Lethal, Onyx (New York, NY), 2000.

Dying to Have Her, Onyx Books (New York, NY), 2001.

Night Heat, Mira (Toronto, Ontario, Canada), 2001.

Night of the Blackbird, Mira (Toronto, Ontario, Canada), 2001.

A Season of Miracles, Mira (Toronto, Ontario, Canada), 2001.

Hurricane Bay, Mira (Toronto, Ontario, Canada), 2002.

NOVELS; UNDER PSEUDONYM SHANNON DRAKE

Tomorrow the Glory, Pinnacle (New York, NY), 1985.

Blue Heaven, Black Night, Berkley (New York, NY), 1986.

Lie down in Roses, Charter (New York, NY), 1988.

Ondine, Charter (New York, NY), 1988.

Princess of Fire, Berkley (New York, NY), 1988.

Emerald Embrace, Berkley (New York, NY), 1991.

A Damsel in Distress, Avon (New York, NY), 1992.

Knight of Fire, Avon (New York, NY), 1993.

Tomorrow the Glory, Pinnacle (New York, NY), 1994.

Branded Hearts, Avon (New York, NY), 1995.

No Other Man, Avon (New York, NY), 1995.

No Other Woman, Avon (New York, NY), 1996.

No Other Love, Avon (New York, NY), 1997.

The King's Pleasure, Kensington (New York, NY), 1998.

Come the Morning, Kensington (New York, NY), 1999.

Beneath a Blood Red Moon, Zebra Books (New York, NY), 1999.

When Darkness Falls, Zebra Books (New York, NY), 2000.

Conquer the Night, Zebra Books (New York, NY), 2000.

Deep Midnight, Zebra Books (New York, NY), 2001.

Seize the Dawn, Zebra Books (New York, NY), 2001.

Knight Triumphant, Zebra Books (New York, NY), 2002.

Realm of Shadows, Zebra Books (New York, NY), 2002.

OTHER

Christmas Stories, Harlequin (Toronto, Ontario, Canada), 1989.

The Spirit of the Game, Delacorte (New York, NY), 1993.

Slow Burn (mystery-romance novel) Mira (Toronto, Ontario, Canada), 1994.

For All of Her Life (mystery-romance novel), Zebra (New York, NY), 1995.

Eyes of Fire (mystery-romance novel), Mira (Toronto, Ontario, Canada), 1995.

An Angel's Touch (fantasy novel), Kensington (New York, NY), 1995.

Down in New Orleans, Kensington (New York, NY), 1996.

Forever My Love, Harlequin (Toronto, Ontario, Canada), 1996.

If Looks Could Kill (mystery novel), Mira (Toronto, Ontario, Canada), 1997.

Never Sleep with a Stranger (mystery-romance novel), Mira (Toronto, Ontario, Canada), 1998.

Contributor, under pseudonym Shannon Drake, to *Haunting Romance,* Avon (New York, NY), 1991; contributor, as Heather Graham, to *With a Southern Touch,* Mira (Toronto, Ontario, Canada), 2002. Work represented in anthologies, including (under name Heather Graham) *The Ultimate Dracula,* 1991.

■ Sidelights

Heather Graham is the author of over one hundred books in genres including romance, history, mystery, suspense, and horror. Publishing her work under three names, Graham has sold over twenty million copies in a score of languages, and has been honored for her efforts with trade awards and bestseller awards from magazines and booksellers. Graham's fiction encompasses a wide range of temporal and geographic settings, ranging from the Vikings to English history to the U.S. Civil War, from a Scottish castle to New York City to the Florida Everglades. The author seems equally at home in any milieu and has also proven adept at incorporating elements of mystery and fantasy into a number of her works. According to Barbara E. Kemp in *Twentieth-Century Romance and Historical*

Writers, regardless of their setting or whatever elements are introduced from other genres, Graham's novels deal mainly with a "spirited, spicy romance between the hero and heroine." Kemp describes Graham's characters as "engaging and vividly drawn," her dialogue as "witty, sharp," and her books as "solid, well-written love stories with lots of sizzle."

Born in Dublin, Ireland, Graham noted in an interview with *Authors and Artists for Young Adults* (*AAYA*) that "some of the Irish influence has followed me throughout my life." Born to parents who loved books, Graham was encouraged to read at an early age. "I had no idea what a wonderful world

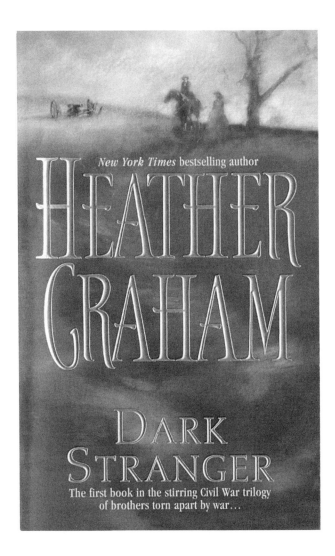

Heather Graham's 1988 romance finds Kristin McCahy joined in her efforts to save her home after a stranger on horseback enters her life, captures her heart, and helps her defend the McCahy family ranch from marauders.

they were opening for me," she told *AAYA*. The author grew up in Dade County, Florida, and went to the University of South Florida in Tampa, where she majored in theater arts. This led to a career in dinner theater and bartending. "I loved it," Graham commented in her interview, "loved college, mime classes, some martial arts, dance, performance, language, and so on." Marriage and a family of five children, however, altered her life's course. "After having children, I wasn't making enough to warrant the time away from home. To this day I am the world's worst housekeeper, so once at home, I began writing, and I was desperate to publish because I loved books so much, and because I couldn't do

anything else. Actually, my first real sales were short horror stories." Graham managed to sell her first novel, *When Next We Love,* to Dell in 1983, and has been publishing steadily ever since. For the first decade of her career, Graham concentrated on romances, both historical and contemporary, then in the 1990s she branched out into other genres, publishing under her married name of Heather Graham Pozzessere, her maiden name of Heather Graham, and the pseudonym Shannon Drake.

Historical Novels and Family Sagas

Graham's "Civil War" trilogy spans the lives of characters of that era. Talking about the books in *Romantic Times,* Graham said that she became interested in the U.S. Civil War after her first trip to Gettysburg, Pennsylvania. She contended that "no other period in our history was so achingly sad" as the Civil War. It was while visiting Gettysburg that she read the story of two brothers who went to war, fighting on opposing sides. This tale was the basis of the first two books of the trilogy, *One Wore Blue* and *One Wore Gray.* Each of the books is devoted to the story of one brother. *One Wore Blue* concerns Jesse, a doctor who joins the Union forces, while *One Wore Gray* relates the adventures of Jesse's younger brother, Daniel, who fights for the Confederacy. Reviewing this second novel in the trilogy, a critic for *Publishers Weekly* noted that the "South comes out battered but smelling like a rose" in this Civil War romance. The concluding volume in the series, *And One Rode West,* features Christa, the sister of Jesse and Daniel, as she attempts to save the family home from the conquering Northerners in post-war Virginia. A *Publishers Weekly* reviewer praised the "11th-hour twist that makes this tale a bit more exciting and its ending less certain." Writing about the brothers in *Romantic Times,* Graham declared: "I've come to know them well. I have told their stories with a great deal of love and respect."

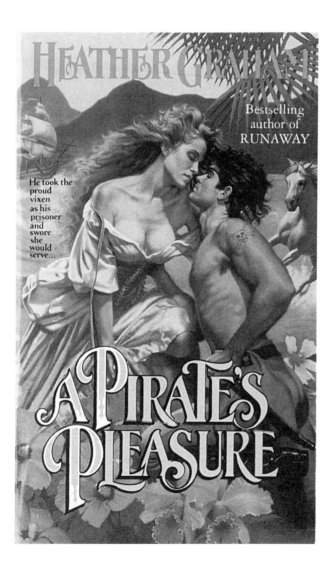

Part of Dell's "North American Woman" series, Graham's 1989 bodice-ripper finds beautiful Skye Kinsdale forced into captivity after her ship is waylaid by pirates on its way to the New World.

The author has also penned a multi-volume series set in nineteenth-century Florida. The initial volume, *Runaway,* features the love between Jarrett McKenzie and Tara Brent, whom he wins for a night of love in a poker game but who eventually becomes his wife and partner in the Florida wilderness. Tara ultimately learns to love Jarrett and to accept the Seminole natives who live nearby. A *Publishers Weekly* reviewer noted that while Graham is "an indifferent stylist," she knows how to deliver "tempestuous protagonists, titillation and just enough history to ground the plot." The same reviewer felt Graham produces these elements "with panache" in this "entertaining . . . swift historical drama."

Graham continues the McKenzie family saga with *Captive* and *Rebel,* the latter set during the Civil War and featuring Union Major Ian McKenzie and a beautiful Southern spy known as the Moccasin. A critic for *Publishers Weekly* praised the author's "deftly sexy and convincing pen," and *Rebel*'s "easy-to-digest Civil War history." The fourth novel in the series, *Surrender,* has a rebel captain, Jerome McKenzie, at the center of action, with his female opposite, Risa Magee, the daughter of a Union general who tends to the wounded. "It's a classic formula historical romance," according to a critic for *Publishers Weekly,* "but Graham does it better than anyone." In the fifth installment, *Glory,* more Civil War action is served up, this time with Dr. Julian McKenzie, a Southern soldier, taking center stage. McKenzie kidnaps a Union sympathizer, Rhiannon Tremaine, a widow with the power to heal. Critics were less positive about this work. *Booklist*'s Melanie Duncan felt that this title did not "live up to its potential," and a reviewer for *Publishers Weekly* also found problems with the tale, noting that plot summaries of earlier stories in the series "slow the momentum."

Another multi-volume family saga from Graham, writing as Shannon Drake, features members of the Graham clan. The action begins with *Come the Morning,* a "swashbuckling tale of warring factions in 12th-century Scotland," according to a *Publishers Weekly* reviewer. Young Waryk de Graham proves his mettle on the battlefield as a thirteen-year-old boy, and subsequently becomes the most respected knight in the land. Given the Blue Isle as a reward, he must marry Mellyora MacAdin, heiress of the Isle, as part of the arrangement. While Waryk is eager to have the estates, Mellyora, a Viking's daughter, is incensed that her marriage has been arranged for her. "Amid a tangle of lies, treachery, and obvious villainy, these two strong-willed people must come to terms so that there can be peace throughout the land," wrote *Booklist*'s Duncan of this first volume in the series.

The series continues with *Conquer the Night, Seize the Dawn,* and the 2002 title *Knight Triumphant.* In *Knight Triumphant* the action progresses to the war between King Edward I and Robert the Bruce, an "epic story of love, war and conviction," as one *Publishers Weekly* contributor described the tale. In this "well-researched and thoroughly entertaining read," as the same reviewer wrote, Eric Graham captures Igrainia, an Englishwoman, in hopes that she can help get his own wife and child out of an English prison. In the event, both Eric's wife and daughter die of the plague, and when he also falls

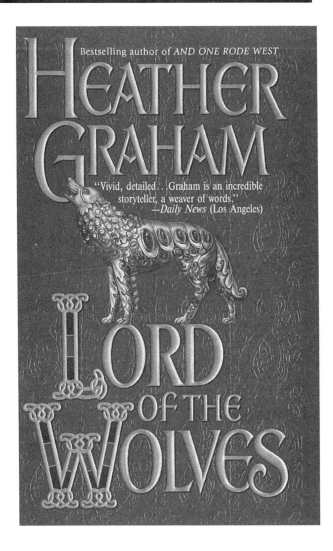

A violet-eyed countess has waited for years for the return of her warrior husband, but upon his return she fears her independence may be lost in Graham's 1993 offering.

ill of the disease, Igrainia helps nurse him back to health, then flees back to England. However, Eric once again recaptures her, this time forcing her to marry him.

"I truly love history," Graham told *AAYA,* "and writing historicals has given me some of the best times—we've attended dozens of battle reenactments, scoured museums, and done much of it on family vacations. My favorite was a time at Culpeper, Virginia, when the battle was fought on the same day, same place, same temperature, as truly happened in history. It was also the same temperature—106. One volley of fire went off, and the fellows on the field were all so hot that they all decided to 'die.' They then realized that they were all flat, and valiantly became wounded, slightly, rising again to finish out the scene. One of my favorite moments was finding one of my Civil War novels in the Abe Lincoln museum in Gettysburg. One of my sons had found the series and told me. I was holding the book when the saleslady asked if she could help me. I said, 'This is my book!' She shook her head and said, 'Oh, no, dear, it's not your book until you pay for it!' I explained what I meant, and she was wonderful, very sweet, making it a great day for me."

Spotlights Mystery, Suspense, Fantasy

Graham has also added a string of mysteries and occult novels to her list of bestsellers. *Slow Burn* is a contemporary romance novel that is also a mystery. After the murder of Miami police officer Danny Huntington, his wife, Spencer, and his former partner, David Delgado, must track down the killer. A romance between Spencer and Delgado, former high school sweethearts, inevitably follows. Finding the book to be "fast-paced" and "an enjoyable read," a *Publishers Weekly* reviewer credited Graham with "some nice local detail" and for showing "what it was like [for Delgado] to grow up as a Cuban refugee in Miami." However, the same reviewer found the romance elements of the novel "more satisfying than the mystery, as the murderer turns out to be incidental."

Mystery and mayhem again unite with romance in novels published under both the Pozzessere and Graham names. A serial killer is stalking young Madison Adair in *If Looks Could Kill,* while *Drop Dead Gorgeous* features sportswear designer Lori, who comes back to her hometown to care for her father. There she sets out to discover who killed her best friend fifteen years earlier, aided in her searches by Sean Black, who was once tried and acquitted for the murder and who is now a forensic archaeologist and bestselling thriller writer. A *Publishers Weekly* reviewer noted that the author "leaves behind the cliches of her reliably titillating bodice rippers for the cliches of romantic suspense" in this novel. *Never Sleep with a Stranger* posits a classic mystery formula with a gathering of mystery writers at an old castle. The owner of the castle, Jon Stuart, holds the conference annually. The year before at the same event, Jon's wife fell to her death, and there are still those who think this accident may have been a murder. In attendance this year is Sabrina Holloway, who, between bed-hopping and avoiding her ex-husband, finds time for some real-life detection in this "exceptionally dexterous mystery-cum-romance," according to a writer for *Publishers Weekly.*

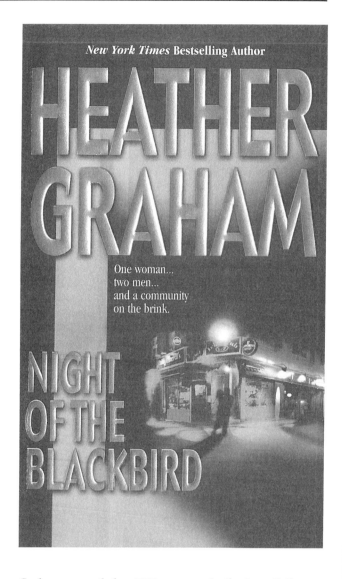

New York Times Bestselling Author

HEATHER GRAHAM

One woman... two men... and a community on the brink.

NIGHT OF THE BLACKBIRD

Graham grounds her 2001 romance in the twentieth century as Moira Kelly joins her family for a St. Patrick's Day celebration that propels her into a romantic quandary tinged with suspense.

Once again combining elements of mystery and romance, *For All of Her Life* could be described as Graham's 1960s novel. It concerns the attempt to reunite a once-popular rock band, *Blue Heron,* for a charity concert. The group had dissolved ten years earlier following the violent and mysterious death of its drummer. The plot also involves the reuniting of the group's leader, Jordon Treveryan, with his former wife, Kathryn, who was a member of the band. Anonymous and threatening phone calls warn Jordon not to reform the band and hold the concert. Yet as he proceeds, both Jordon and Kathryn begin to learn more about the past, the drummer's death, and the changes they have undergone since their days as hippies. A reviewer for *Publishers Weekly* remarked: "This finely crafted, extremely credible love story is for those who survived the 60s and for anyone else who wants to understand them."

Personal history also impacts in the 2002 *Hurricane Bay,* another mystery/suspense thriller. When Sheila Warren goes missing, old friend Kelsey Cunningham vows to find her. Aided by Sheila's ex-boyfriend and private investigator, Dane Whitelaw, Kelsey pulls out all the stops to track Sheila down. The problem is that Sheila is already dead, a fact known only to Dane, who has received a photo of her body from the killer. He has kept quiet about this because it is obvious the killer is trying to frame him for the murder, and such is almost the case when Kelsey begins to suspect him. A reviewer for *Publishers Weekly* commented that even though the "prose often goes purple and the dialogue sags in spots, Graham builds jagged suspense that will keep readers guessing up to the final pages."

In *An Angel's Touch* Graham abandons romance in favor of fantasy. An automobile accident on Christmas Eve turns New York yuppies David and Cathy Angel into actual angels who must return to Earth and perform six miracles to earn their wings. The Angels' deeds include helping a bag lady and a terminally ill nun, and bringing an estranged couple back together. "Cramming a plethora of miseries into her slender tale," stated a reviewer for *Publishers Weekly,* "[Graham] veers unevenly between the sad circumstances of characters at various nadirs and the forced comic mayhem of the yuppie couple trying to get an afterlife."

Better received critically was *A Season of Miracles,* which similarly deals with reincarnation and fantasy. In this case a pair of modern lovers had a past life together in the seventeenth-century, an affair that went badly wrong. Now Robert Marston is hired by wealthy Douglas Llewellyn to watch out for the latter's granddaughter, Jillian. But when these two meet, the present begins to resemble the past they once shared and Robert now sees how much danger Jillian is really in. "With witchcraft, ghosts, and suspects aplenty, Graham's spooky romance is hard to put down," wrote *Booklist* reviewer Maria Hatton. Kristin Ramsdell, writing in *Library Journal,* also praised this "compelling, darkly magical tale of enduring love and reincarnation."

Writing as Shannon, Graham has also branched out into occult and vampire novels. *When Darkness Falls* finds travel writer Jade McGregor on holiday in Scotland and the victim of a vampire attack in a wind-swept cemetery. Back in New Orleans, Jade

has a publishing success, but any elation she feels is soon lost when reminders of the Scottish incident hit home. She finds that others attacked in Scotland are turning up very dead and bloodless, while her dreams are being taken over by visions of the man who saved her in Scotland. When Jade's boyfriend is attacked and is at death's door, she is forced to put all these pieces together. "Fans of vampire tales may find this novel entertaining," wrote a reviewer for *Publishers Weekly,* "but many will be turned off by the stiff dialogue, clumsy plotting and graphic gore."

Deep Midnight is another vampire tale, set in Venice during Carnival. Well-known book reviewer Jordan Riley, visiting Venice, witnesses a scene of carnage at a masked ball thrown by Nari, Contessa della Trieste, in which vampires feed on dinner guests. Nari subsequently tells Jordan that this was merely part of the night's staged entertainment, but Jordan is convinced what she saw was for real. So is Ragnor Wulfson, a thousand-year-old vampire who has come to Venice to stop the naughty deeds of Nari, his former lover and fellow vampire. When Jordan and Ragnor ultimately meet, Ragnor comes to believe Jordan is in danger. Together the two try to destroy the evil stalking Jordan and also begin to form a romantic bond. A reviewer for *Publishers Weekly* felt that the author's descriptions of Venice "are lush, and her colorful cast of characters will engage."

If you enjoy the works of Heather Graham, you might want to check out the following books:

Kathleen E. Woodiwuss, *Ashes in the Wind,* 1979.
Alexandra Ripley, *Scarlet,* 1991.
Micki Brown, *Once a Rebel,* 1992.

Graham, who produces three to four titles per year in various genres, maintains that she has no set schedule for her writing. "Writing revolves around life," she told *AAYA.* "I started writing when my children were toddlers and infants, and so, I don't mind music, commotion, or anything else going on while I work. Usually, anything on paper happens . . . in the dining room—homework and my writing. My children have introduced me to many of the subjects and people I have used in books." While she admitted to no set writing schedule, Graham also commented, "I am very disciplined. I know when what is due, and what it takes for me to do it. I love working in different genres now—suspense, vampire/occult, and history—and so, to keep up my schedule, I do work hard. I also play hard, and luckily, it's possible to juggle both very well in this field."

■ Biographical and Critical Sources

BOOKS

Twentieth-Century Romance and Historical Writers, 3rd edition, St. James Press (Detroit, MI), 1994.

PERIODICALS

Booklist, August, 1994, Denise Perry Donavin, review of *Runaway,* p. 2022; November 1, 1996, Melanie Duncan, review of *A Magical Christmas,* p. 481; February 1, 1999, Melanie Duncan, review of *Glory,* p. 966; April 1, 1999, Melanie Duncan, review of *Come the Morning,* p. 1390; November 15, 2001, Maria Hatton, review of *A Season of Miracles,* p. 559.

Library Journal, August, 1994, Barbara E. Kemp, review of *Runaway,* p. 128; November 15, 1995, Kristin Ramsdell, review of *An Angel's Touch,* p. 62; May 15, 1996, Mary K. Chelton, review of *No Other Woman,* p. 51; November 15, 1996, Kristin Ramsdell, review of *A Magical Christmas,* p. 48; November 15, 2001, Kristin Ramsdell, review of *A Season of Miracles,* p. 56.

New York Times Book Review, December 8, 1996, p. 102.

Publishers Weekly, March 1, 1985, p. 78; December 25, 1987, p. 69; October 28, 1988, p. 74; March 24, 1989, p. 63; January 27, 1992, p. 94; February 24, 1992, review of *And One Wore Gray,* p. 49; October 5, 1992, review of *And One Rode West,* pp. 66-67; November 1, 1993, review of *Spirit of the Season,* p. 68; February 14, 1994, p. 84; August 1, 1994, review of *Runaway,* p. 72; August 29, 1994, review of *Slow Burn,* p. 70; January 9, 1995, review of *Branded Hearts,* p. 60; April 17, 1995, review of *For All of Her Life,* p. 53; August 28, 1995, review of *Eyes of Fire,* p. 110; September 25, 1995, review of *An Angel's Touch,* p. 43; October 9, 1995, review of *No Other Man,* p. 82; May 20, 1996, review of *No Other Woman,* p. 255; February 3, 1997, review of *Rebel,* p. 100; June 23, 1997, review of *If Looks Could Kill,* p. 87, and *No Other Love,* p. 88; January 5, 1998, review of *Surrender,* pp. 64-65; June 1, 1998, review of *Never Sleep with a Stranger,* p. 48; July 27, 1998, review of *Drop Dead Gorgeous,* p. 74; January 4, 1999, review of *Glory,* p. 87; January 25, 1999, review of *Come the Morning,* p. 74; September 11, 2000, review of *When Darkness falls,* p. 74; August 6, 2001, review of *Deep Midnight,* p. 67; February 4, 2002, review of *Knight Triumphant,* p. 59; March 25, 2002, review of *Hurricane Bay,* pp. 43-44; May 13, 2002, review of *With a Southern Touch,* p. 57.

Romantic Times, July, 1991, pp. 10-11.

School Library Journal, January, 1995, Claudia Moore, review of *Runaway,* p. 146.

OTHER

eHarlequin.com, http://www.eharlequin.com/ (September 3, 2002), "Heather Graham: A Biography."

Heather Graham Home Page, http://www.booktalk.com/hgraham/ (September 3, 2002).

Graham, Heather, interview with J. Sydney Jones for *Authors and Artists for Young Adults,* August 26, 2002.*

Jenny Holzer

■ Personal

Born July 29, 1950, in Gallipolis, OH; married Michael Glier; children: one daughter. *Nationality:* American. *Education:* Attended Duke University, 1969-70, and University of Chicago; Ohio University, Athens, B.F.A., 1972; Rhode Island School of Design, M.F.A., 1977.

■ Addresses

Agent—c/o Barbara Gladstone Gallery, 99 Greene Street, New York, NY 10012.

■ Career

Independent artist, New York, NY, since 1977. *Exhibitions:* Individual shows include Project Studio, New York, NY, 1978; Franklin Furnace Window, New York, NY, 1978; Fashion Moda Window, Bronx, NY, 1979; Printed Matter Window, New York, NY, 1979; Galerie Rüdiger Schöttle, Munich, West Germany, 1980; Onze Rue Clavel, Paris, France, 1980;

Le Nouveau Musée, Lyon, France, 1981, 1984; Museum für (Sub) Kultur, West Berlin, Germany, 1981; Barbara Gladstone Gallery, New York, NY, 1982, 1983, 1985, 1994; Galerie Chantel Crousel, Paris, 1982; American Graffiti Gallery, Amsterdam, Holland, 1982; Artists Space, New York, NY, 1982; A Space, Toronto, Ontario, Canada, 1982; Lisson Gallery, London, England, 1983; Institute of Contemporary Arts, London, 1983, 1988; Institute of Contemporary Arts, Philadelphia, PA, 1983; *Sign on a Truck,* Grand Army Plaza/Bowling Green Plaza, New York, NY, 1984; Dallas Museum of Art, Dallas, TX, 1984, 1994; University of Massachusetts, Amherst, 1984; Kunsthalle, Basle, Switzerland, 1984; Galerie 't Venster, Rotterdam, Holland, 1984; Cranbrook Museum, Bloomfield Hills, MI, 1984; State University of New York, Old Westbury, 1984; Seattle Art Museum, Seattle, WA, 1984; Galerie Monika Spruth, Cologne, West Germany, 1985; Galerie Crousel-Husseonot, Paris, 1985; (with Cindy Sherman) Contemporary Arts Center, Cincinnati, OH, 1985; (with Keith Haring) Am Hof, Vienna, Austria, 1985; (with Barbara Kruger) Israel Museum, Jerusalem, 1985; Des Moines Art Center, Des Moines, IA, 1986; toured United States, 1986-88; Rhona Hoffman Gallery, Chicago, IL, 1987; Interim Art Gallery, London, 1988; Brooklyn Museum, New York, NY, 1988; Winnipeg Art Gallery, Winnipeg, Canada, 1988; Hoffman-Borman Gallery, Santa Monica, CA, 1988; Cleveland Center for Contemporary Arts, Cleveland, OH, 1988; Guggenheim Museum, New York, NY, 1988; Dia Art Foundation, New York, NY, 1989; Ydessa Hendeles Art Foundation, Toronto, 1989, 1992; Biennale, Venice, Italy, 1990; Stadische Kunsthalle, Dusseldorf, Germany, 1990; Laura Carpenter

Fine Art, Santa Fe, NM, 1991; Louisiana Museum, Humlebaek, Denmark, 1991; Albright-Know Gallery, Buffalo, NY, 1991; Walker Art Gallery, Minneapolis, MN, 1991; Hammond Galleries, Lancaster, OH, 1992; Claremont Graduate School, Claremont, CA, 1992; North Dakota Museum of Art, Grand Forks, 1992; St. Peters Church, Cologne, Germany, 1993; Haus der Kunst, Munich, Germany, 1993; Barry Whistler Gallery, Dallas, 1993; Bergen Museum of Art, Bergen, Norway, 1994; Galerie für Zeitgenössische Kunst, Leipzig, Germany, 1996; Kunstmuseum des Kantons Thurgau, 1997; Musée d'Art, Bordeaux, France, 2001; and Printed Matter Gallery, New York, NY, 2002. Selected group exhibitions include *Issue*, Institute of Contemporary Arts, London, England, 1980; *Westkunst*, Messehallen, Cologne, West Germany, 1981; *Documenta 7*, Museum Fridericianum, Kassel, West Germany, 1982 (and *Documenta 8*, 1987); *Biennale of Sydney*, Art Gallery of New South Wales, New South Wales, Australia, 1984; *Kunst mit Eigen-Sinn*, Museum Moderner Kunst, Vienna, Austria, 1985; *In Other Words*, Corcoran Gallery of Art, Washington, DC, 1986; *Committed to Print*, Museum of Modern Art, New York, NY, 1988; *High and Low*, Museum of Modern Art, New York, NY, 1990; *Metropolis*, Walter Gropius Bau, 1991; and *Virtual Reality*, Guggenheim Museum, New York, NY, 1993. Works included in permanent collections at Museum of Modern Art, New York, NY; Whitney Museum, New York, NY; Centro Cultural Arte Contemporaneo, Polanco, Mexico City; Tate Gallery, London, England; Musée d'Art Moderne, Paris, France; Kunsthalle, Berne, Switzerland; Kunsthaus, Zurich, Switzerland; Museum of Contemporary Art, Chicago, IL; Stedelijk Van Abbemuseum, Eindhoven, Holland; and National Gallery of Canada, Ottawa, Canada.

■ **Awards, Honors**

Blair Award, 79th Americans Show, Art Institute of Chicago, 1982; Golden Lion award for Best National Pavilion, Venice Biennale, 1990.

■ **Writings**

A Little Knowledge, 1978.
Black Book, 1979.
(With Peter Nadin) *Hotel*, 1980.
(With Peter Nadin) *Living*, 1980.
(With Peter Nadin) *Eating through Living*, Tanam Press (New York, NY), 1981.

(With Peter Nadin) *Eating Friends*, Tanam Press (New York, NY), 1981.
Abuse of Power Comes as No Surprise: Truisms and Essays, [Halifax, Nova Scotia], 1983.
Jenny Holzer: Kunsthalle Basle (exhibition catalogue), Kunsthalle (Basle, Switzerland), 1984.
Jenny Holzer and Cindy Sherman: Personae, Contemporary Arts Center (Cleveland, OH), 1986.
Jenny Holzer: Signs, Des Moines Art Center (Des Moines, IA), 1986.
Jenny Holzer/ Diane Waldman, Guggenheim Museum (New York, NY), 1989.
Laments, Dia Art Foundation (New York, NY), 1990.
Jenny Holzer: The Venice Installation, Albright-Knox Art Gallery (Buffalo, NY), 1991.
(With Noemi Smolik) *Jenny Holzer: Im Gespräch mit Noemi Smolik*, Kiepenheuer & Witsch (Cologne, Germany), 1993.
(With Matt Mullican and Lawrence Weiner) *Rosebud*, Kunstbau Lenbachhaus München (Munich, Germany), 1994.
Jenny Holzer: Lustmord, Cantz (Ostfildern-Ruit), 1996.
Writing/Schriften, edited by Noemi Smolik, Distributed Art Publishers, 1996.
Jenny Holzer, KriegsZustand, Die Galerie (Leipzig, Germany), 1997.
Jenny Holzer/ David Joselit, Joan Simon, Renata Saleci, Phaidon Press (London, England), 1998
Jenny Holzer: Oh, Reunion des musées nationaux (Paris, France), 2001.

■ **Sidelights**

Jenny Holzer has been called visual artist, poet, propagandist, aphorist, and crank. None of the descriptions actually get to the heart of her language installations, words chosen as parables and sayings which she has been displaying in public spaces, galleries, and museums for over a quarter of a century, printed in block letters on leaflets, engraved in plaques, carved in stone, bleeping on LED displays, emblazoned on T-shirts and caps, and flashed in television ads. One of her most quoted "Truisms," as she calls them, "ABUSE OF POWER COMES AS NO SURPRISE," has now entered the lexicon of the land, a phrase that—like the plethora of information Holzer implicitly criticizes in her art—has become internalized, part of the modern landscape. Holzer creates, Arthur C. Danto noted in *Nation*, a very "state-of-the-art art and a symbolic condensation of our national culture—up-to-the-minute in technology, populist in format, moralistic in tone."

In 1989 Holzer became the first female artist chosen to represent the United States at Italy's Venice Biennale, winning a Golden Lion award for her installation. In addition to shows at major museums around the world, her aphoristic displays have also graced high-impact public spaces such as Candlestick Park in San Francisco, Times Square in New York City, Caesar's Palace in Las Vegas, Dupont Circle in Washington, D.C., and the space around the Centre Georges Pompidou in Paris. As P. Plagens noted in *Newsweek,* Holzer makes a clear distinction between such contexts: "It's art when it's in a formal installation like [the Venice Biennale]. It's just pronouncements when it's in public places." But whether creating art or pronouncements, Holzer has transformed the conception of what makes art in the modern context.

From Heartland to New York

Holzer was born July 29, 1950, in Gallipolis, Ohio, into a family of two generations of Ford auto dealers. She attended Duke University from 1969 to 1970, then studied painting and printmaking at the University of Chicago before completing her undergraduate degree at Ohio University in Athens. While enrolled at the Rhode Island School of Design, Holzer experimented with an abstract painting style influenced by the painters Mark Rothko and Morris Louis. "When I was in graduate school I had done some public things, but they were unsuccessful," Holzer told Patrick J. B. Flynn in the *Progressive.* "They didn't mean anything, they were abstract. I started writing on my paintings, but that didn't work either." In 1976 she moved to Manhattan, participating in the Whitney Museum's independent study program. "When I came to New York the painting fell away and the writing became dominant," she told Flynn. "I then figured out how to take this writing public—I thought posters would be appropriate. It made sense as a public project."

Holzer's conception of language as art indeed began to emerge in New York, influenced by the Whitney Museum program, which included an extensive reading list of Western and Eastern literature and philosophy. Holzer felt that such writings could, and in fact should, be simplified to phrases everyone could understand. She printed these "Truisms" anonymously in black italic script on white paper and subsequently pasted them to building facades, signs, and telephone booths in lower Manhattan. Holzer arranged these summaries and pronouncements in alphabetical order in short sentences such as, "An elite is inevitable," "Any surplus is immoral," and "Money creates taste." These sayings also inspired passersby to scribble messages on the posters in response. Such interactivity affirmed for Holzer the provocative nature of her new art. "The reason I wrote from every point of view—Far Left, Far Right, common-sense, lunatic—was that I thought it was a more accurate way of portraying people's beliefs, and maybe a better way than always having didactic or dogmatic stuff." Thus Holzer accumulated sayings she both agreed with and was violently opposed to, but the power was in the pronouncement, that somebody, somewhere believed the statement.

"I came to language because I wanted to be explicit about things, but I didn't want to be a social realist painter," Holzer told Flynn. As Mark Stevens noted in a *New Republic* article, her new works "obviously shared much with the Dada and pop strains in modern American art, but more importantly they also tied into an increasingly popular view of the power of the media." For Stevens, an artist like Holzer represents a modern transformation not only in how landscapes are portrayed, but also what constitutes a landscape: "nature and paint have given way to a new environment created by the media and their means." To Danto, Holzer's early slogans "looked like the dubious accumulated wisdom of a self-taught evangelist who had appropriated the no-budget advertising strategy of the Off-Off-Off Broadway production." Danto further noted that Holzer's work had "the astringent shock of an unmodulated voice interrupting the commercials with irrelevant one-line sermons." It was not so much the message in Holzer's works, but the medium itself that was the art, the momentary disruption of the otherwise continuous flow of information in today's over-commercialized and information-bombarded world.

Language as Art

Holzer's second series of statements and sayings was the "Inflammatory Essays," which laid out more of her concerns about contemporary society. These "Essays" were printed in alphabetical order, first on small posters and then as a manuscript titled *The Black Book.* Turning to different media, Holzer printed the "Living Series" on aluminum and bronze plaques to resemble those used by medical and government buildings. "Living" moved away from overt social critique to talk about the necessities of daily life: eating, breathing, sleeping, and human relationships. Her words were accompanied with paintings by U.S. artist Peter Nadin, whose portraits of men and women attached to metal posts were meant to further demonstrate the shallowness if not emptiness in a modern life so permeated with information.

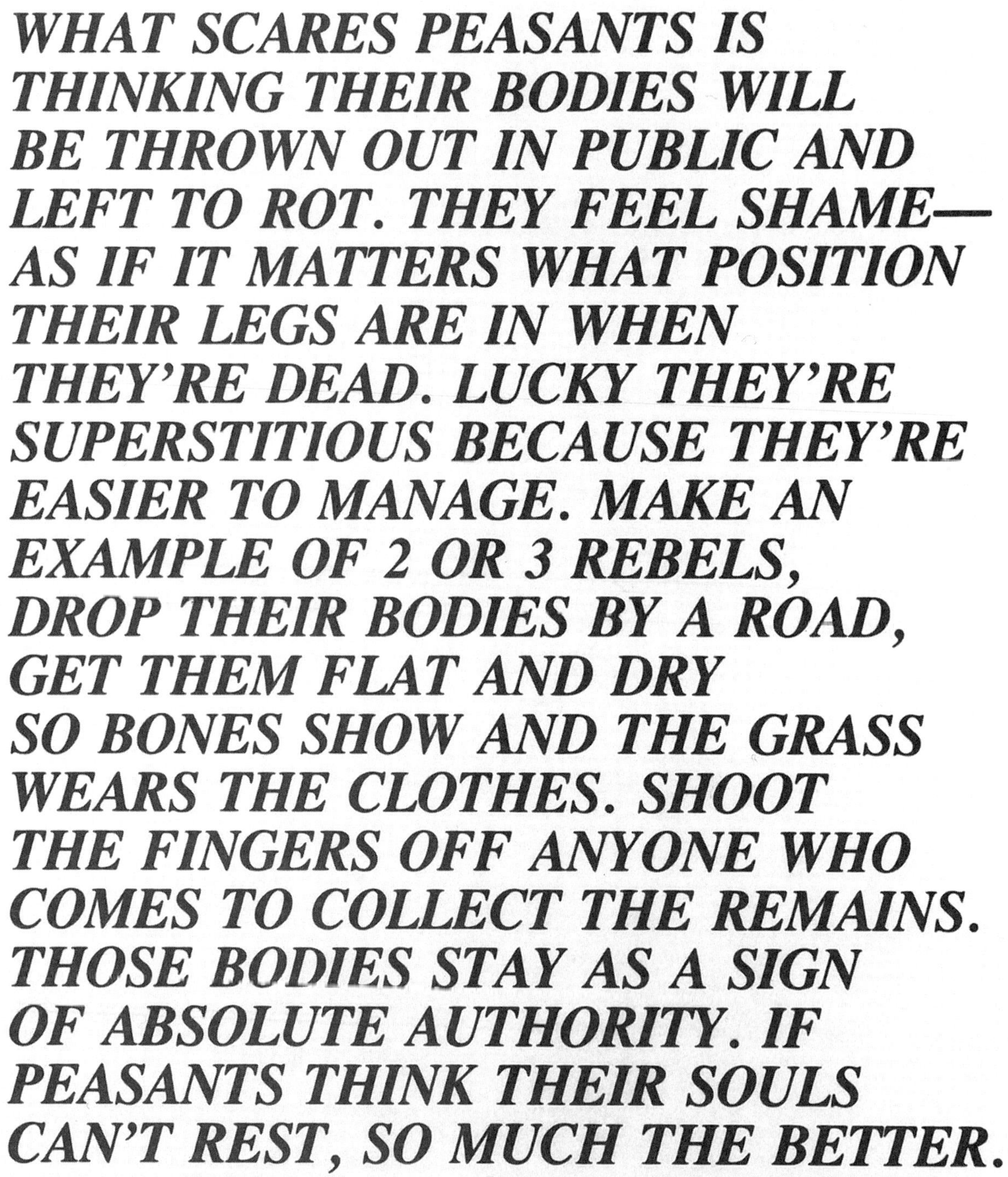

*WHAT SCARES PEASANTS IS
THINKING THEIR BODIES WILL
BE THROWN OUT IN PUBLIC AND
LEFT TO ROT. THEY FEEL SHAME—
AS IF IT MATTERS WHAT POSITION
THEIR LEGS ARE IN WHEN
THEY'RE DEAD. LUCKY THEY'RE
SUPERSTITIOUS BECAUSE THEY'RE
EASIER TO MANAGE. MAKE AN
EXAMPLE OF 2 OR 3 REBELS,
DROP THEIR BODIES BY A ROAD,
GET THEM FLAT AND DRY
SO BONES SHOW AND THE GRASS
WEARS THE CLOTHES. SHOOT
THE FINGERS OFF ANYONE WHO
COMES TO COLLECT THE REMAINS.
THOSE BODIES STAY AS A SIGN
OF ABSOLUTE AUTHORITY. IF
PEASANTS THINK THEIR SOULS
CAN'T REST, SO MUCH THE BETTER.*

Among artist Jenny Holzer's "Inflammatory Essays" is this lithograph, created in the early 1980s and currently in the collection of the Tate Gallery, London, England.

Holzer went techno in 1982 when many of her "Truisms" were computer-generated on a huge LED or light-emitting diode sign, the Spectacolor board, over New York's Times Square. This same electronic signboard was used to broadcast the statements in her next work, "Survival Series." Stated in a somewhat less authoritarian voice, these pronouncements dealt with more realities of everyday life.

More Monumental Approach

With her 1986 work, "Under a Rock," Holzer moved to a more monumental scale while maintaining similar content. In "Under a Rock" she blended the electronic signboard with a set of granite blocks and a marble bench engraved with gold lettering. Her messages contrasted an edgy fear with a mock objective journalistic voice: "CRACK THE PELVIS SO SHE LIES RIGHT, THIS IS A MISTAKE WHEN SHE DIES YOU CANNOT REPEAT THE ACT." The following year she projected her "Truisms" on the outside of the Centre Pompidou in Paris.

In 1989 Holzer had two major exhibitions in New York. Her installation at the Guggenheim Museum displayed her sayings as a continual tape loop on an electric band which wound its way up the helix-like display floors of the gallery. The show was the words. "They are like messages from an oracle, or a sibyl, or a fortuneteller or someone's slightly dotty aunt," wrote Danto, who concluded that Holzer's work is "consistently deeper than the words." "In Holzer's hands," commented Stevens of the Guggenheim show, a "good epigram inspires delight, an art-dart." But Stevens also noted that Holzer's art does not lie in the "wit" or "brilliance" of such sayings, for they cannot compete with those of the masters of language. "Instead," wrote Stevens, "she is a master of the almost-epigram, a clever magpie who collects the shiny thought-scraps that you think you've read somewhere but can't place." The content of such epigrams, according to Stevens, is "really not the point. The point is the glimpse, in the constant spooling out, in the unending stream of middling and junky insight."

Holzer's other 1989 installation, "Laments," was partly inspired by the birth of her daughter. In this series she dealt with themes from motherhood to torture and death in a variety of voices. These were longer poem-like creations, displayed vertically up the sides of columns on electronic strips. Other rooms displayed the same thirteen laments on sarcophagus-like granite blocks into which the words had been chiseled. Stevens felt that "this is not good poetry," no matter how genuine Holzer's intent or emotion. Danto, however, thought that "Laments" "expresses a singular symbolic imagination," and that it "provides an experience, in consequence of its symbolism and multidimensionality, well beyond anything that painting or sculpture alone are capable of." As Holzer explained to Flynn, the texts of "Laments" "were intended to be the final remarks of dead people. It was as if the people had a last chance to say what they wished had been different in their lives, or to describe what happened to them, or to talk about what hurt them. I wanted to give these people who had died unnecessarily a chance to say what they couldn't say."

The Biennale and Beyond

In 1990 Holzer became the first female artist to represent the United States in the Venice Biennale, and her installation there included pieces from many of her previous exhibitions, including "Truisms," "blazing across rows of LED . . . signs," according to Plagens, and "her Roman-letter "Laments," carved into marble floors and benches." Though *Time*'s Robert Hughes felt the installation was "lavish but mediocre," and that Holzer's works were "so faultlessly, limpidly pedestrian as to make no demands of any sort on the viewer, beyond the slight eyestrain induced by the LEDs," the panel of international judges disagreed, awarding Holzer the grand prize for the best national pavilion. Thereafter Holzer took a hiatus from the art world for a few years, devoting time to raising her young child. Also, criticism that her popularity had led her to become elitist as shown in the size and expense of her exhibition was beginning to sting. From a rebel on the fringes of the art camp, she had become part of the establishment, and now a younger generation of artists were beginning to challenge her because of her success.

After several years away, Holzer returned to the art world, exhibiting her series "Lustmord" in 1994. In this work she explored the idea of socially sanctioned violence against women, including rape. A multimedia exhibit, the central installation was a large sort of cave, outside of which a LED structure sent her words in random red snatches, while inside more words were hand-tooled on red leather. The messages included phrases such as "I am awake in the place where women die," and "The color of her inside out is enough to make me want to kill her." Another part of the exhibition included human bones banded with engraved silver which viewers were encouraged to handle. Jan Avgikos, reviewing the exhibition in *Artforum International*, found that the work "cleaves to both an antiquated past and a technological future," while Nancy Princenthal, writing in *Art in America*, noted that Holzer's "is not, of course, a formal art. It is driven by subject matter, and its focus remains squarely on the political realm." Princenthal concluded, "As Holzer moves ever further from her early Truisms, with their punchy ironies and simple invocations of political speech, she explores with increasing precision just what a word is worth, carved in stone or written on the air."

For her thirteenth text series, "Oh," held in 2001, Holzer "features the voice of a mother as she described the love and anxiety she feels for her daughter," according to Susan Harris in *Art in America*. These comments are scrolled next to comments about sexuality, rape, and incest, the words projected on four large LED signs in a vaulted space filled with blue light, on thirteen horizontal LEDs spanning the ceiling of the gallery, and also projected in beams that seemed to float in space. Harris felt that the text lacked the "impact and indispensability of Holzer's earlier texts," but that in fact her words were "secondary to the overall visual impression." Reviewing the same exhibition in the *New York Times*, Ken Johnson remarked that Holzer "lifts you up and then she brings you down," and that while the physical presentation in her signs was "hypnotically beautiful," the words, as poetry, "are leaden and portentous." Johnson found himself wishing that Holzer's poetry "were as inventive and light on its feet as her play with structure, light, space and motion."

If you enjoy the works of Jenny Holzer, you might want to check out the following:

Conceptual artists such as John Baldessari and Jan Dibbets.
Digital artists such as Ben Benjamin, John Klima, and Margot Lovejoy.
Video artists like Douglas Davis, Naim June Paik, and Bill Viola.

"If any single viewpoint emerges in Holzer's messages," wrote a contributor for *Scholastic Art*, "it is that truth is relative and that each viewer must decide what is valid and what is not. Her sayings compel the reader to question the messages we see around us every day." Concluding in *Art in America*, Harris noted that as Holzer "continues to develop her electronic media-and language-based art, she nonetheless defies categorization as an '80s artist by demonstrating a masterful facility at integrating sculptures, technology, color and architecture into optically stunning public presentations." Reviewing a 2002 retrospective of Holzer's art, Roberta Smith in the *New York Times* felt that the artist still had power in the new millennium. Smith commented, "Unfortunately, the world has caught up with her sense of apocalyptic foreboding and an imminent totalitarianism. Phrases like 'Abuse of Power Comes as No Surprise,' 'The Beginning of the War Will Be Secret,' and 'I Am Awake in the Place Where Women Die,' are all freshly pertinent, if cold comfort, in times like these."

This virtual reality representation of the "Lustmord" text, a series of texts in response to violence being perpetrated against women in Bosnia, appeared at the Guggenheim museum SoHo.

■ Biographical and Critical Sources

BOOKS

Auping, Michael, *Jenny Holzer,* St. Martin's Press (New York, NY), 1992.

Chilvers, Ian, *A Dictionary of Twentieth-Century Art,* Oxford University Press (Oxford, England), 1998.

Contemporary Artists, 4th edition, St. James Press (Detroit, MI), 1996.

Encyclopedia of World Biography, 2nd edition, Gale (Detroit, MI), 1998.

PERIODICALS

Art and Design, summer, 1994, Kevin Teixeira, "Jenny Holzer: Virtual Reality: An Emerging Medium," pp. 9-15; summer, 1994, Ben Snider, "Jenny Holzer: Multidisciplinary Dweeb," pp. 17-19.

Artforum, February, 1990, Donald Kuspit, "The Only Immortal."

Artforum International, September, 1989, p. 139; September, 1990, pp. 132-134; September, 1994, Jan Avgikos, "Jenny Holzer," p. 102.

Art in America, November, 1982, pp. 88-92; summer, 1983, pp. 7-11; December, 1986, Bruce Ferguson, "Wordsmith," pp. 108-116; September 1991, Lilly Wei, "Jenny Holzer," pp. 126-127; November, 1994, Nancy Princenthal, "Jenny Holzer at Barbara Gladstone," February, 2002, Susan Harris, "Jenny Holzer at Cheim and Read," p. 120.

ARTnews, summer, 1988, John Howell, "Jenny Holzer: The Message Is the Medium," pp. 122-127; January, 1997, Jonathan Turner, "Transporting Truisms," p. 29.

Arts, September, 1988, p. 91; April, 1990, p. 108; April, 1990, Marjorie Welish, "Who's Afraid of Verbs, Nouns, and Adjectives," pp. 79-84.

Esquire, December, 1989, Larkin Warren, "Jenny Holzer: Artist," p. 102.

Flash Art, March-April, 1990, Paul Taylor, "Jenny Holzer: I Wanted to Do a Portrait of Society," pp. 116-119.

Nation, February 12, 1990, Arthur C. Danto, "Jenny Holzer," pp. 213-215.

New Republic, March 26, 1990, Mark Stevens, "Jenny Take a Ride," pp. 30-33.

Newsweek, June 11, 1990, P. Plagens, "The Venetian Carnival," pp. 60-61.

New York, November 28, 1983, Kay Larson, "Jenny Holzer," pp. 98-99; April 8, 1985, Kay Larson, "Bad-News Bearers," pp. 72-73; September 4, 1988, Kay Larson, "Signs of the Times," pp. 48-53; January 8, 1990, Kay Larson, "Jenny Be Good," p. 69.

New York Times, May 17, 1985, p. C22; July 27, 1988, Michael Brenson, "Media Artist Is U.S. Choice for Biennale," p. N15; August 7, 1988, Michael Brenson, "Jenny Holzer: The Message Is the Message," p. H29; December 13, 1989, Roberta Smith, "Holzer Makes the Guggenheim a Museum of Many Messages," p. B1; October 21, 1990, p. H41; May 8, 1994, A. Schwartzman, "After Four Years, the Message Is Murder," p. 34; July 28, 2000, Carol Vogel, "Holzer Message," p. B26; November 9, 2001, Ken Johnson, "Jenny Holzer: 'Oh'," p. E35; September 6, 2002, Roberta Smith, "Jenny Holzer—'Protect Me from What I Want,'" p. E32.

New York Times Magazine, December 3, 1989, Grace Glueck, "And Now, a Few Words from Jenny Holzer," p. 42.

Parachute, summer, 1983, Elke Town, "Jenny Holzer."

Print Collector's Newsletter, November-December, 1982, Carter Ratcliff, "Jenny Holzer."

Progressive, April, 1993, Patrick J. B. Flynn, "Jenny Holzer," pp. 30-34.

Scholastic Art, April-May, 2002, "Digital Visions," pp. 4-6.

Splash, summer, 1988, Roy MacPherson, "Jenny Holzer."

Time, July 30, 1990, Robert Hughes, "A Sampler of Witless Truisms," p. 66.

Vogue, November 1988, Paul Taylor, "Jenny Holzer Sees Aphorism as Art," pp. 390-394.

OTHER

Ada Web, http://adaweb.walkerart.org/ (May 23, 1995), "Jenny Holzer."

Geocities, http://www.geocities.com/Paris/Rue/5047/ (September 12, 2002), "Jenny Holzer's Weapon Is Words."

Green Table, http://stuartcollection.ucsd.edu/ (September 12, 2002), "Jenny Holzer."

Guggenheim Museum, http://www.guggenheimcollection.org/ (September 12, 2002), "Jenny Holzer."

Wired, http://www.wired.com/ (February, 1994), "Jenny Holzer Interview."*

—Sketch by J. Sydney Jones

Joe R. Lansdale

vices, Nacogdoches, foreman, 1980-81; writer, 1981—. Proprietor and karate instructor at a martial arts studio, Nacogdoches; also worked variously as a bouncer, bodyguard, factory worker, carpenter, ditch digger, and plumber's helper.

■ Personal

Born October 28, 1951, in Gladewater, TX; son of Alcee Bee (a mechanic) and Reta (in sales; maiden name, Wood) Lansdale; married Cassie Ellis, June 25, 1970 (divorced, 1972); married Karen Ann Morton (a writer and editor), August 25, 1973; children: (second marriage) Keith Jordan, Kasey JoAnn. *Nationality:* American. *Education:* Attended Tyler Junior College, 1970-71, University of Texas at Austin, 1971-72, and Stephen F. Austin State University, 1973, 1975, 1976.

■ Addresses

Home and office-113 Timber Ridge, Nacogdoches, TX 75961. *Agent*—Barbara Puechner, 3121 Portage Rd., Bethlehem, PA 18017.

■ Career

Goodwill Industries, transportation manager, 1973-75; Stephen F. Austin State University, Nacogdoches, TX, custodian, 1976-80; LaBorde Custodial Ser-

■ Member

Horror Writers of America (vice president, 1987-88), Western Writers of America (treasurer, 1987).

■ Awards, Honors

Six Bram Stoker Awards, Horror Writers of America, including 1988 and 1989; American Horror award, 1989; British Fantasy Award, 1989, for novella; Notable Book designation, *New York Times,* 1994, for *Mucho Mojo;* Edgar Allan Poe Award for Best Novel, Mystery Writers of America, 2001, for *The Bottoms.*

■ Writings

MYSTERY/SUSPENSE NOVELS

Act of Love, Zebra (New York, NY), 1981.
The Nightrunners, illustrated by Gregory Manchess, introduction by Dean R. Koontz, Dark Harvest (Arlington Heights, IL), 1987.

Cold in July (also see below), Ziesing (Shingletown, CA), 1989.

Savage Season (also see below), Ziesing (Shingletown, CA), 1990.

Lansdale's Limited Edition: Cold in July [and] *Savage Season* (boxed set), Ziesing (Shingletown, CA), 1990.

Freezer Burn, Mysterious Press (New York, NY), 1999.

Waltz of Shadows, Subterranean Press (Burton, MI), 1999.

The Bottoms, Mysterious Press (New York, NY), 2000.

A Fine Dark Line, Mysterious Press (New York, NY), 2003.

"HAP COLLINS" MYSTERIES

Mucho Mojo, Mysterious Press (New York, NY), 1994.

The Two-Bear Mambo, Mysterious Press (New York, NY), 1995.

Bad Chili, Mysterious Press (New York, NY), 1997.

Rumble Tumble, Mysterious Press (New York, NY), 1998.

Captains Outrageous, Mysterious Press (New York, NY), 2001.

SCIENCE FICTION/FANTASY/HORROR NOVELS

The Drive-In: A "B"-Movie with Blood and Popcorn, Made in Texas, Doubleday (New York, NY), 1988.

The Drive-In 2: Not Just One of Them Sequels, Bantam (New York, NY), 1990.

Batman: Captured by the Engines, Warner (New York, NY), 1991.

On the Far Side of the Cadillac Desert with Dead Folks (chapbook), Roadkill Press (Denver, CO), 1991.

Terror on the High Skies (juvenile), illustrated by Edward Hannigan and Dick Giordano, Little, Brown (Boston, MA), 1992.

(With Andrew H. Vachss) *Drive-By,* Crossroads (Holyoke, MA), 1993.

The Drive-In: A Double Feature Omnibus (contains *The Drive-In: A "B"-Movie with Blood and Popcorn, Made in Texas* and *The Drive-In 2: Not Just One of Them Sequels*), Carroll & Graf (New York, NY), 1997.

WESTERNS

Dead in the West, Space & Time Books (New York, NY), 1986.

The Magic Wagon, Doubleday (Garden City, NY), 1986.

Jonah Hex: Two-Gun Mo (graphic novel), illustrated by Timothy Truman, Sam Blanzma, and others, DC Comics (New York, NY), 1994.

Jonah Hex: Riders of the Worm and Such (graphic novel), illustrated by Timothy Truman and Sam Glanzman, Vertigo/DC Comics (New York, NY), 1995.

Blood Dance, Subterranean Press (Burton, MI), 2000.

Zeppelin's West, Subterranean Press (Burton, MI), 2001.

HORROR; STORY COLLECTIONS

By Bizarre Hands, illustrated by Mark A. Nelson, introduction by Lewis Shiner, Ziesing (Shingletown, CA), 1989.

Stories by Mama Lansdale's Youngest Boy, Pulphouse (Eugene, OR), 1991, expanded as *Best Sellers Guaranteed,* Ace (New York, NY), 1993.

The Steel Valentine, Pulphouse (Eugene, OR), 1991.

Steppin' out, Summer '68, Roadkill (Denver, CO), 1992.

Tight Little Stitches on a Dead Man's Back, Pulphouse (Eugene, OR), 1992.

Writer of the Purple Rage, CD (Baltimore, MD), 1994.

Electric Gumbo, Quality Paperback Book Club (New York, NY), 1994.

A Fistful of Stories, CD (Baltimore, MD), 1997.

The Good the Bad, and the Indifferent, Subterranean Press (Burton, MI), 1997.

High Cotton, Golden Gryphon Press (Urbana, IL), 2000.

EDITOR

Best of the West, Doubleday (New York, NY), 1986.

The New Frontier: The Best of Today's Western Fiction, Doubleday (New York, NY), 1989.

(With Pat Lo Brutto) *Razored Saddles* (horror), illustrated by Rick Araluce, Dark Harvest (Arlington Heights, IL), 1989.

(With wife, Karen Lansdale) *Dark at Heart: All New Tales of Dark Suspense,* Dark Harvest (Arlington Heights, IL), 1992.

(With Thomas W. Knowles) *The West That Was,* Wings (New York, NY), 1994.

(With Thomas W. Knowles) *Wild West Show,* Wings (New York, NY), 1994.

(With Richard Klaw) *Weird Business* (horror), Mojo (Austin, TX), 1995.

OTHER

(Under pseudonym Ray Slater) *Texas Night Riders* (western), Leisure (Champaign, IL), 1983.

My Dead Dog Bobby (illustrated short story), Cobble-stone Books (Sacramento, CA), 1995.

Atomic Chili: The Illustrated Joe R. Lansdale (comic-strip adaptations), Mojo (Austin, TX), 1996.

(With Edgar Rice Burroughs) *Tarzan: The Lost Adventure,* Dark Horse (Milwaukee, OR), 1996.

Weird War Tales (short story), illustrated by Sam Glanzman, Vertigo/DC Comics (New York, NY), 1996.

Blood and Shadows (comic book), illustrated by Mark A. Nelson, Vertigo/DC Comics (New York, NY), 1996.

(With Neil Barrett) *Supergirl Annual #2* (comic book), illustrated by Robert Branishi and Stan Woch, DC Comics (New York, NY), 1996.

(With Rick Klaw) *Gangland #4* (crime comic), illustrated by Tony Salmons, Vertigo/DC Comics (New York, NY), 1998.

(With Lewis Shiner) *Private Eye Action as You Like It* (short stories), Cross Roads Press, 1998.

The Boar (young adult novel), Subterranean Press (Burton, MI), 1998.

Something Lumber This Way Comes (young adult novel), Subterranean Press (Burton, MI), 1999.

Contributor to anthologies, including *Fears,* 1984, and *Book of the Dead,* Bantam (New York, NY), 1989. Contributor of articles, stories, and reviews to magazines, including *Horror Show, Modern Stories, Espionage,* and *Mike Shayne.* Lansdale's manuscripts are held at Southwest Texas State University, San Marcos.

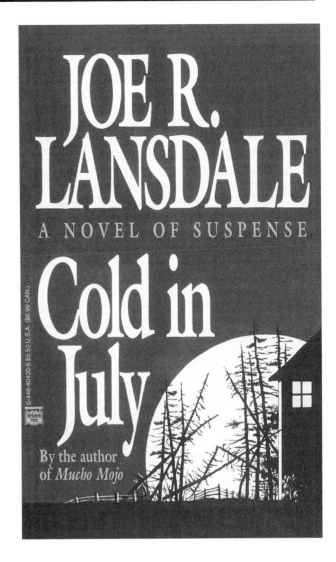

Award-winning author Joe R. Lansdale's 1989 novel focuses on a deadly game of cat-and-mouse that begins after Richard Dane shoots and kills a violent house-breaker he discovers in his living room.

■ Work in Progress

A novel, *Sunset and Sawdust,* for Knopf.

■ Sidelights

"The line dividing commerce and art, genre work and literary fiction is one that [Joe R.] Lansdale's many volumes of over-the-top horror, weird fantasy and pulp westerns have often tried to erase," noted James Hynes in a *Publishers Weekly* profile of the prolific author. Add science fiction, mystery, suspense, comics, graphic novels, young adult novels, and even television and movie scripts to that list and you would have the full complement of the Lansdale oeuvre. Lansdale's fiction encompasses all of the above, frequently combining several genres in the same story or novel while defining a distinctive voice of its own. "Lansdale is sui generis,"

wrote a contributor for *St. James Guide to Crime and Mystery Writers.* Though influences by many writers, "his voice remains distinctively original," the same contributor further noted, "and his novels and stories defy easy categorization." Lansdale's "preferred genre is the fantastic," the author once admitted, "but suspense runs a close second, followed by mystery, westerns, and the mainstream." "Actually," continued Lansdale, "much of my work and intended work is a combination of these things. . . . I like all kinds of horror and fantasy writing, especially the contemporary horror tale. I am not too fond, though, of the vague ending that seems so popular in many publications today. Much of what I write, although it is called horror, is really just oddball or weird fantasy, perhaps never becoming scary, but certainly striking a note of the unusual."

Speaking with Hynes, Lansdale railed against stereotyping by genres. "What is a genre? All of this is the American preoccupation with putting things in boxes. Am I a commercial writer? You bet. Is John Updike giving his books away? Did Hemingway cash his checks? I mean, come on, this is silly." Hynes commented, "No matter what his own books are, there's no mistaking the purely literary pleasure of reading Lansdale as he wrestles with the complicated world of East Texas," that patch of country the author calls his own and with which he has been dealing since his first short story.

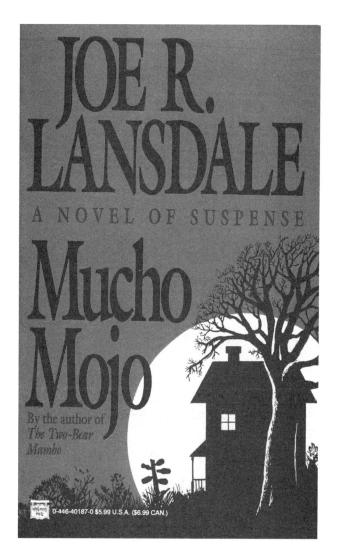

Lansdale captures the attention of thriller fans with his 1994 novel about an inherited house that divulges a few corpses among its many secrets.

Lansdale's work has been characterized by *New York Times Book Review* contributor Daniel Woodrell as "country noir" and the novelist likened to such authors as James M. Cain and Erskine Caldwell. Lansdale himself has listed Cain as a major influence. The "country" in this case is East Texas, where Lansdale was born, raised, and continues to reside. The "noir" refers to the dark vision of human nature and contemporary life that pervades nearly all of his work. Other writers Lansdale mentions as influential include Ray Bradbury, Robert Bloch, Flannery O'Connor, Dashiell Hammett, Raymond Chandler, and Richard Matheson. Lansdale departs from these literary icons on at least two counts, each of which reflects one of his stated non-literary influences: B-movies and comic books. No matter the genre in which he is writing, graphic violence and horror are usually present. No matter how dark the vision he is rendering, satirical and humorous elements often abound.

Texas Born and Raised

Lansdale was born in 1951 in Gladewater, Texas, about seventy miles from where he now makes his home. His father was a mechanic who never learned to read but who encouraged that activity in his precocious second son. "He is my hero," Lansdale told Hynes. "I've always felt like I've read the books he couldn't read." The world of books was also something his mother made available, reading to him regularly from Rudyard Kipling's *The Jungle Book*. Lansdale, at age nine, determined that he wanted to write similar books when he grew up. He read widely, from Shakespeare to the Bible and the works of Bloch and Edgar Rice Burroughs, the latter considered by Lansdale to be "the absolute best writer in the world" according to boys. He also began reading Southern writers such as O'Connor and Harper Lee, writers who allowed him to see the vernacular of the South and of East Texas as having worth in a literary sense.

Martial arts was also something Lansdale began at an early age, taught by his father, who had worked as a traveling boxer and wrestler during the Great Depression of the 1930s. From a skill that could help him to defend himself against school bullies, martial arts became a spiritual as well as physical exercise for the author. The movement centered him and filled him with self-confidence.

Lansdale went to various colleges in Texas in the early 1970s and also made a pilgrimage to Berkeley, California, to get in touch with the counterculture. It did not take him long, however, to find his way

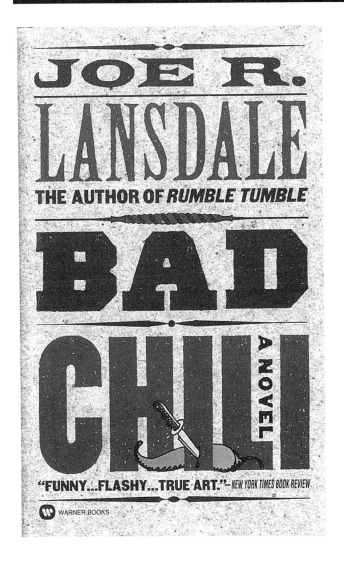

Lansdale rekindles the adventures of his sleuths Hap Collins and Leonard Pine in this 1997 page-turner that features dead bikers, inclement weather, and a renowned Texas chili king.

back to East Texas. There he sold his first article, co-written with his mother, to *Farm Journal.* He continued to publish in journals and magazines throughout the early 1970s, meanwhile earning a living in any manner he could, working variously as a roofer, bouncer, janitor, and farmer, all of them occupations that he would later give to his fictional protagonists. He also married and started a family, writing at night after a full day in the factory or the fields.

From Short Fiction to Horror and Westerns

The author of numerous stories, Lansdale first made his mark in the arena of short fiction by penning "quirky, violent, and blackly comic horror stories,"

according to Hynes. "I prefer the short story medium," the writer told Stanley Wiater in *Dark Dreamers: Conversations with the Masters of Horror.* "I think if I could make a living as a short story writer, I would do that primarily." Lansdale's stories began appearing widely in both commercial and alternative publications by the late 1970s. Some of this work was collected in *By Bizarre Hands* and *Stories by Mama Lansdale's Youngest Boy. Best Sellers Guaranteed* combines the stories from the second collection with "The Events concerning a Nude Fold-out Found in a Harlequin Romance," a previously anthologized novella. Writing in *Locus,* Ed Bryant described *Best Sellers Guaranteed* as "a first-rate retrospective, particularly of Lansdale's earlier career." Bryant went on to characterize "Lansdale's strong suit" as "whacked-out humorous melodrama with a distinctive voice (East Texas) and a keen sense of place (ditto)." Writing in the *Bloomsbury Review,* Bryant also credited Lansdale with having "a universal grasp of humankind's terrors."

Lansdale's novels began appearing in the early 1980s. Although marketed within specific genres, they transcend traditional genre definitions. Typical of a Lansdale western is *Dead in the West.* Set in pioneer days in Mud Water, Texas—a fictionalized version of Lansdale's own Gladewater—it relates a series of events involving animated corpses that would seem more at home in a contemporary horror tale than in a western. *The Magic Wagon,* set in East Texas in 1909, tells of a traveling medicine show that includes a wrestling chimpanzee and the corpse of Wild Bill Hickok. Critiquing *The Magic Wagon* for the *New York Times Book Review,* Anne Roston offered another example of how Lansdale's work defies simple categorization: "Behind this entertaining and seemingly innocent western . . . lies a subtle discussion of racism and the myths people create for themselves." Reviewing the novel, a critic for *Publishers Weekly* noted that the "true charm of the story . . . is in its telling, which melds laconic humor, colorful colloquialisms and outrageous figures of speech in a Twainesque tall tale." The same reviewer concluded that *The Magic Wagon* "endures as a western classic." Blending the western with fantasy and science fiction, Lansdale presents what another *Publishers Weekly* reviewer called an "irrepressible, irreverent and unpredictable" novel in *Zeppelin's West.* Buffalo Bill Cody leads his Wild West Show by zeppelin to Japan in this bizarre tale; problem is, Cody is only a head in a jar that sits atop a mechanical body after his wife caught him in bed with the singer Lily Langtry. Other figures from the Wild West make similar appearances: Wild Bill Hickok comes on stage in this book, too, romancing Annie Oakley and telling tall tales about Custer to his new friend, Sitting Bull. In Japan this "ribald tall tale gets wilder and wackier," according to the contributor for *Publishers Weekly*, as Cody meets up with Frankenstein. "This novel is one big joyride from start to finish," concluded the same reviewer. A more old-fashioned sort of pulp western from Lansdale is *Blood Dance*, a novel finally published in 2000, but one originally written in 1980 that languished for two decades as three successive publishers who were going to publish it went out of business. Set in 1875, the novel features Jim Melgrhue who ultimately has to avenge the death of his partner, Bob Bucklaw, after they are forced into joining a gang of train robbers. A reviewer called *Blood Dance* a "near-perfect model of the time-honored, much-cherished Zane Grey/Louis L'Amour classic western."

Prime examples of Lansdale's science fiction and fantasy/horror fiction can be found in *The Drive-In: A B-Movie with Blood and Popcorn, Made in Texas*, and *The Drive-In 2: Not Just One of Them Sequels*. In the first novel, the patrons of a Texas drive-in movie are whisked into another universe where the horror films they have been watching and the drive-in itself become the sum of their reality. Scenes of rape, cannibalism, and necrophilia are portrayed. In the sequel, the patrons leave the drive-in to enter the strange world surrounding it, where they encounter both dinosaurs and vampires. *Village Voice* contributor Richard Gehr called these two books "semiparodistic novels" that "turn the horror spectacle upon itself." With his 1994 collection *Writer of the Purple Rage*, featuring such grisly tales as "Steppin' Out, Summer '68," "Love Doll," "Godzilla's Twelve-Step Program," and "Drive-in Date," Lansdale "horrifies and amuses, sometimes within the same piece," wrote *Booklist* contributor Wes Lukowsky, who concluded that the Texas author's "newly acquired cult status stands only to be strengthened" with the collection.

With such books, Lansdale has become the "Stephen King of Texas," as Anne Dingus described him in *Texas Monthly*, winner of a half dozen Bram Stoker awards for novels and short stories which deal with "bizarre and horrific themes like rape, torture, bestiality, sexual mutilation, cannibalism, necrophilia, and (always) death." Lansdale won fans with tales such as "Tight Little Stitches in a Dead Man's Back," a story that "combines the themes of tattooing as sadism and roses as predators," Dingus wrote, and "On the Far Side of the Cadillac Desert with Dead Folks," a tale that "pays sick tribute to Amarillo's Cadillac Ranch."

Turns to Crime Novel

Despite his growing notoriety, a drawer full of awards, and cult following in fantasy and horror, beginning in the 1990s Lansdale increasingly turned

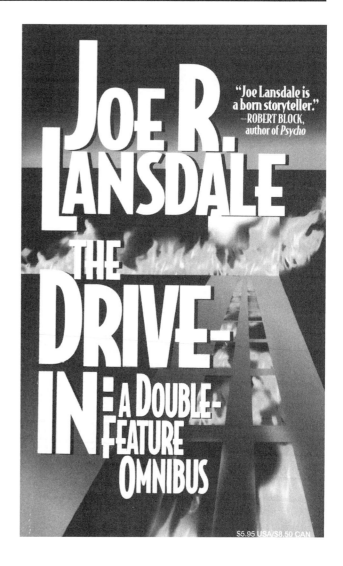

"Joe Lansdale is a born storyteller."
—ROBERT BLOCK, author of *Psycho*

$5.95 USA/$8.50 CAN

Containing both Lansdale's "Drive-In" novels, this omnibus edition follows a group of Texas moviegoers who become trapped in a local drive-in and are forced to battle horrific manifestations to forestall the end of the world.

to mystery and suspense fiction, still employing his fantastical plot twists and wild humor. Among his most popular mystery and suspense novels are his "Hap Collins" mysteries. *Savage Season*, set in the 1990s, relates the story of Hap Collins, a white, 1960s draft-dodger who is lured by his ex-wife, Trudy, into a scheme to locate stolen money at the bottom of the Sabine River in East Texas. Accompanied by his friend Leonard, a black, gay Vietnam veteran, Hap must eventually confront the nefarious gang with whom Trudy has become involved. Implicit in the relations between Hap and Leonard is an exploration of the dynamics of racism and of homophobia in America. As Liz Currie related in

With an image inspired by his popular "Drive-In" novels, Lansdale's author Web site welcomes readers to a wealth of information that should satiate even the most greedy fan.

Armchair Detective: "When 1960s idealism meets 1990s cynicism, the stage is set for a violent confrontation between good intentions and evil results."

Several years passed before Hap Collins and Leonard returned in *Mucho Mojo.* After Leonard inherits a house from his uncle, the skeleton of a murdered child is discovered under the floorboards. Suddenly Leonard's Uncle Chester becomes the posthumous prime suspect in the disappearance of several local children. As Hap and Leonard proceed to investigate, they discover that Chester and a friend of his were also the victims of homicide, busy with their own investigation of the real serial killer. "Hap and Leonard . . . wisecrack their way to a resolution," noted *Booklist* reviewer Lukowsky, who also felt that the relationship and dialogue between protagonists is "so real it's palpable," that the "plot is compelling, and the book overall "extraordinarily memorable."

Two-Bear Mambo is the next outing for Hap and Leonard, and it was with this book that Lansdale had his first commercial success, earning enough on sales and a movie option—that has since expired—to purchase a martial arts studio in his home town where he teaches at night after his five or six hours of daily writing. *Mambo* has Hap and Leonard— "two of the unlikeliest but most likable amateur detectives in crime fiction," according to Lukowsky— investigating the disappearance of Hap's one-time lover, Florida Grange. Grange, who was also Leonard's lawyer, has gone missing in Grovetown, a town with a strong Ku Klux Klan presence where she went to investigate a suicide in the local jail. Arriving in Grovetown, Hap and Leonard are confronted with a redneck haven and no leads to Florida's whereabouts. "Lansdale is an immense talent," Lukowsky further commented, praising the author's ability to "generate side-splitting laughter and gut-wrenching terror on the same page." A reviewer for *Publishers Weekly* felt that this tale was "just as funny and violent and gripping" as *Mucho Mojo,* and that though the plot followed what happened to Florida, the core of the story is the relationship between Hap and Leonard, which is "rendered by Lansdale in perfectly pitched, profanity-laced repartee and guided throughout by a strong moral compass."

Collins and Leonard appear again in *Bad Chili,* which follows the amateur sleuths as they track down the murderer of Leonard's gay lover. Bit by a rabid squirrel, the hapless Hap finds himself in the hospital being treated for rabies by an amorous nurse. Meanwhile, Leonard's lover, Raoul, leaves him for a biker until the new boyfriend turns up headless. Leonard is suspected of killing the biker out of jealousy, but when Raoul's body also turns up—very dead and obviously tortured—the local police begin to see there might be a small problem with the multiple homicides. Hap checks himself out of the hospital to help his gay buddy uncover who the real killer is. This "raucously funny mystery" was lauded by Lev Raphael in *Lambda Book Report* as "remarkable for its range of characters with no animus whatsoever towards gays. . . . Straight and gay characters [are] treated as equals." "The narrative, including a breathless finale, is droll, crude, touching and very nasty. . . . extravagant, lovable characters mix with outrageous, despicable actions to irresistible effect," commented a *Publishers Weekly* critic. Similarly, Lukowsky declared in *Booklist:* "Simultaneously funny and tragic . . . wildly profane yet invariably humane. In his unique way [Lansdale] reveals the human condition." With *Bad Chili,* proclaimed *People* contributor Pam Lambert, "Lansdale demonstrates just why he has become a cult figure in every genre from horror to humor."

In *Rumble Tumble* Collins and Leonard come to the aid of Collins's girlfriend's daughter who is involved in prostitution. Brett, the girlfriend in question, lost control of Tillie years ago, but now when she discovers that her daughter is essentially the property of one Big Jim in Hootie Hoot, Oklahoma, she determines to rescue her with the help of Hap and Leonard. "The language and the characters are as ripe as ever" in this adventure, noted a contributor for *Publishers Weekly,* who also felt that those readers unfamiliar with previous "Hap Collins" mysteries "should be amazed and dazzled by Lansdale's clod-kicking virtuosity." However, the same critic warned against "a hint of over-the-shoulder coyness that might eventually spoil the series." In contrast, Nikki Amdur's *Entertainment Weekly* review of *Rumble Tumble* maintained that each successive "Hap Collins" mystery "gets more heroic,"

while *Booklist* reviewer Lukowsky felt the book was "extraordinarily entertaining," and that the "friendship between Hap and Leonard belongs in the men's Hall of Fame."

Lansdale's fiction has often been praised and blamed for similar reasons. The extreme, graphic violence he depicts can be viewed as gratuitous, shock for its own sake, or as a pointed exaggeration of the violence in America. Depending on one's perspective and sensibilities, his humor on the darkest subjects can be perceived as poor taste or as satire on American popular culture. Critics do agree that there is far more to his work than run-of-the-mill genre fiction written for the sake of entertainment. In summing up *Mucho Mojo* for *Locus,* Edward Bryant felt that what "Lansdale proceeds to spin is not only a top-drawer thriller, but a social portrait of a society in painful evolution. His East Texas is a place of entrenched tradition in painful conflict with new ideas about race relations, gender politics, and more open choices in sexual preference." This compliment lends itself to Lansdale's own definition of "good fiction," as he defined for Kevin E. Proulx in *Fear to the World: Eleven Voices in a Chorus of Horror:* "Good fiction can actually tell you how people relate to one another. How they really feel about things. What life is all about. What makes it worth living, or, for some people, not worth living. I find a lot more truth in fiction than nonfiction, and that's why I prefer to write it."

Hap and Leonard—"Lansdale's popular Hardy boys on speed," according to *Library Journal*'s Bob Lunn—team up once again in the 2001 title *Captains Outrageous,* in which the pair are caught "in a bout of middle-aged angst," as Lunn described the novel. Brett, Hap's girlfriend, seems to have moved on to greener pastures, while Hap himself is going nowhere fast, working as a security guard at a chicken factory where his chief job is milking rooster sperm. But when he saves a young woman from a beating, things take a turn for the better, for the young woman turns out to be the daughter of the plant owner and Hap earns a nice bonus for his bravery. Money burning a hole in his pocket, Hap decides to get his buddy Leonard and set off on a Caribbean cruise. When the ship strands them behind at Playa del Carmen, however, they come up against muggers and fall ever more deeply into a miasma of violence and double-dealing, aided by a Mexican fisherman and his daughter. The ending to this book hints at Brett and Hap getting back together. This installment of Hap and Leonard met with uniformly positive response from critics and also helped earn a six-figure deal on a two-book contract with Knopf publishers. A contributor for *Publishers Weekly* felt that this "mystery marvel is sure to keep you laughing amid the carnage," and that this was one book you should "take along on your next cruise." Lukowsky, writing in *Booklist,* also had praise for the novel, noting that it was "funny, violent, peppered with profanity, oozing testosterone, and ultimately very satisfying."

Speaking with M. M. Hall in a *Publishers Weekly* interview, Lansdale was not sure whether *Captains Outrageous,* the sixth novel in the series, would be the last. "Never say never," Lansdale commented. "When I wrote *Savage Season,* it was three years later before I wrote the second Hap and Leonard novel. Whenever I wrote one, I never intended to write the next one." Lansdale also noted that, when writing, he identifies with both of the characters in the series. "Probably Hap would be the one I am most like," Lansdale continued, "his past and a lot of the events in his life are sort of similar to my own, and some of them are exactly my own. He might be the kind of guy I would've been had I not gotten married and gotten a little direction."

From Series to Stand-alone Mysteries, Thrillers

Lansdale has also written many non-series mysteries and thrillers, including the 1999 *Freezer Burn* and the Edgar Award-winning title *The Bottoms.* In the former, somewhat mentally-challenged Bill Roberts is making a meal of canned beets while sitting in the dark. The reason for such economies? He cannot afford to buy groceries or to pay the electric bill now that his mother is dead and the social security checks are uncashed. Bill cannot quite figure out how to forge her signature on the checks, but he did have enough smarts to keep her death a secret so that the checks keep arriving. Trouble is, her body—still hidden in the back bedroom—is beginning to stink. He figures it is time to come up with a better scheme, but everything that Bill puts his hand to turns to tragicomedy. Robbing a fireworks stand, things go decidedly south when the storeowner is shot, one of his buddies gets a Roman candle in the head, and another is killed by a water moccasin. Taking up with a traveling freak show, he soon gets in more hot water when the wife of the show's owner figures Bill should help her get rid of her husband. "The irrepressible Lansdale continues to amuse and astonish with his outrageous storytelling," wrote Lunn in a *Library Journal* review. Lukowsky also praised the novel in *Booklist,* concluding that Lansdale "may have a screw or two loose, but he is a master storyteller and an im-

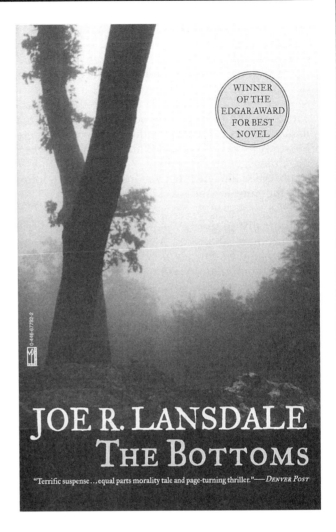

WINNER OF THE EDGAR AWARD FOR BEST NOVEL

0-446-67792-2

JOE R. LANSDALE
The Bottoms

"Terrific suspense...equal parts morality tale and page-turning thriller."—*Denver Post*

Taking place in Lansdale's beloved East Texas, this 2000 thriller finds two children determined to solve a mystery begun when the body of a murdered woman is discovered in a nearby flood plain.

mensely talented writer." And a contributor for *Publishers Weekly,* while noting that the humor "often misfires with overloaded similes and strained attempts to be outrageous," also found it a "page-turner suitable for bus or beach."

Lansdale's *The Bottoms* takes a more serious tack in a coming-of-age tale set in Depression-age Texas with overtones of *To Kill a Mocking Bird.* Told in a flashback from the point of view of octogenarian Harry Crane, the tale takes readers back to a day in 1933 when Harry, then thirteen, and his nine-year-old sister, Tom (short for Thomasina), find the mutilated corpse of a dead black woman, a prostitute as it turns out. Their father, Jacob Crane, a farmer, barber, and part-time constable, takes on the task of finding the woman's killer. Soon he learns that two other similarly mutilated bodies have been found in the past year-and-a-half, but because of the women's race and profession, no one cares. The population suddenly cares too much, however, when the next body to turn up is that of a white prostitute. Mob violence takes over, and despite the desperate efforts of both Jacob and his son, Harry, a black man named Moses is lynched as the supposed murderer. Moses has played an important part in the lives of the Cranes, being something of a stand-in father for Jacob. After the lynching, yet another body is found, and the hunt for the real killer goes on.

Universally praised, *The Bottoms* won the prestigious Edgar Allan Poe Award and brought Lansdale's name to entirely new groups of readers, including young adults. A critic for *Publishers Weekly* felt that the novel is "folksy and bittersweet, though rather rough-hewn and uneven," and also that it "treats themes still sadly pertinent today." Lunn, writing in *Library Journal*, compared Lansdale's writing to that of William Faulkner and Harper Lee, voicing the hope that this novel "just might at long last bring premier storyteller Lansdale to the attention of an even broader audience." *School Library Journal*'s Carol DeAngelo also lauded this "thought-provoking" and "wonderful" book, that "will capture and educate young adults about a shameful time in this country's history and the strength of an individual to make a difference."

In the *St. James Guide to Horror, Ghost, and Gothic Writers*, Darrell Schweitzer summarized Lansdale's work: "A sense of twisted realism is a leading characteristic of Lansdale's fiction, as is an intensely vulgar idiom and a tendency to pile outrageous and absurd situations on top of one another to such a degree that, in the hands of a lesser writer, the result would have to be either parody, or trash." "But," continued Schweitzer, "Lansdale's fiction is redeemed first, by an authentic regional voice, which captures the ways and mores (and seamy underside) of rural Texas life as no outsider ever could. Then there is a strong, uninhibited sense of macabre humour, which marks Lansdale as the funniest horror writer since Robert Bloch (whose influence Lansdale acknowledges). But he is also effectively satirical, enormously inventive, and genuinely grim when he chooses."

Lansdale once commented: "My writing is done to entertain and to please me. And to put bread on the table. I like to think my work has something going for it besides momentum. That there is some thematic depth that will ring in the reader's head afterwards like an echo. I'm attempting to blend the pacing and color of genre fiction with the character and style of the mainstream. And maybe doing a damn bad job of it. But I'm trying. . . . My work ranges from popular to literary. I believe the purpose of fiction is to entertain. Enlightening the reader is nice, but secondary. If you don't have a good tale to tell, no one is listening anyway."

If you enjoy the works of Joe R. Lansdale, you might want to check out the following books:

Stephen King, *Skeleton Crew*, 1985.
Peter Straub, *Koko*, 1988.
Nancy A. Collins, *Nameless Sins*, 1994.

■ Biographical and Critical Sources

BOOKS

Proulx, Kevin E., *Fear to the World: Eleven Voices in a Chorus of Horror* (interview), Starmont House (Mercer Island, WA), 1992, pp. 43-58.
St. James Guide to Crime and Mystery Writers, 4th edition, St. James Press (Detroit, MI), 1996.
St. James Guide to Horror, Ghost, and Gothic Writers, 1st edition, St. James Press (Detroit, MI), 1998.
Wiater, Stanley, *Dark Dreamers: Conversations with the Masters of Horror* (interview), Avon (New York, NY), 1990, pp. 111-118.

PERIODICALS

Antioch Review, winter, 1987, p. 117.
Armchair Detective, fall, 1989, p. 435; spring, 1991, Liz Currie, review of *Savage Season*, p. 227.
Bloomsbury Review, December, 1991, p. 27; June, 1992, p. 17.
Book, September, 2001, Randy Michael Signor, review of *Captains Outrageous*, p. 81.
Booklist, August, 1994, Wes Lukowsky, review of *Mucho Mojo*, p. 2028; January 15, 1995, Wes Lukowsky, review of *Writer of the Purple Rage*, p. 895; August, 1995, Wes Lukowsky, review of *The Two-Bear Mambo*, p. 1910; March 1, 1997, pp. 1113-1114; July, 1997, Wes Lukowsky, review of *Bad Chili*, p. 1775, and Wes Lukowsky, review of *Rumble Tumble*, pp. 1829-1830; July, 1999, Wes Lukowsky, review of *Freezer Burn*, p. 1928, and

Wes Lukowsky, review of *The Bottoms*, p. 1798; September 1, 2001, Wes Lukowsky, review of *Captains Outrageous*, p. 56.

Deathrealm, fall-winter, 1988, pp. 42-44.

Entertainment Weekly, November 6, 1998, Nikki Amdur, review of *Rumble Tumble*, p. 82.

Horror Show, January, 1987.

Lambda Book Report, March, 1998, Lev Raphael, review of *Bad Chili*, pp. 30-31.

Library Journal, July, 1997, Michael Rogers, review of *Tarzan: The Lost Adventure*, p. 132; October 15, 1998, Bob Lunn, review of *Rumble Tumble*, p. 99; July, 1999, Bob Lunn, review of *Freezer Burn*, p. 133; August, 2000, Bob Lunn, review of *The Bottoms*, p. 158; August, 2001, Bob Lunn, review of *Captains Outrageous*, p. 162.

Locus, April, 1993, p. 21; May, 1993, p. 23; July, 1993, p. 23; May, 1994, Edward Bryant, review of *Mucho Mojo*, p. 25.

Magazine of Fantasy and Science Fiction, April, 1999, Charles de Lint, review of *The Boar*, p. 32; January, 2001, Charles de Lint, review of *The Bottoms, Blood Dance,* and *High Cotton*, pp. 24-26.

Mystery Scene, August, 1987.

New York Times Book Review, December 14, 1986, Anne Roston, review of *The Magic Wagon*, p. 24; October 2, 1994, Daniel Woodrell, review of *Mucho Mojo*, p. 37; October 1, 1995, Marilyn Stasio, review of *The Two-Bear Mambo*, p. 28; September 21, 1997, Marilyn Stasio, review of *Bad Chili*, p. 36; September 23, 2000, Marilyn Stasio, review of *The Bottoms*, p. 29.

People, November 10, 1997, Pam Lambert, review of *Bad Chili*, p. 44.

Publishers Weekly, May 30, 1994, review of *Mucho Mojo*, p. 34; August 7, 1995, review of *The Two-Bear Mambo*, pp. 444-445; March 11, 1996, review of *Tarzan: The Lost Adventure*, p. 45; March 1, 1997, Wes Lukowsky, review of *A Fist Full of Stories*, pp. 1113-1114; July 7, 1997, review of *Bad Chili*, pp. 52-53; September 22, 1997, p. 70; September 29, 1997. James Hynes, "Joe R. Lansdale: Black Belt in Pulp Fiction," pp. 59-60; June 22, 1998, review of *Rumble Tumble*, p. 87; October 5, 1998, review of *The Boar*, p. 80; July 12, 1999, review of *Freezer Burn*, p. 72; August 30, 1999, review of *Waltz of Shadows*, p. 56; May 15, 2000, review of *Blood Dance*, p. 88; June 26, 2000, review of *The Bottoms*, p. 49; May 14, 2001, review of *The Magic Wagon*, p. 55; June 4, 2001, review of *Zeppelin's West*, p. 62; August 27, 2001, M. M. Hall, "PW Talks with Joe R. Lansdale," p. 58; August 27, 2001, review of *Captains Outrageous*, p. 57.

School Library Journal, January, 2001, Carol DeAngelo, review of *The Bottoms*, p. 160.

Small Press Review, April, 1990, p. 27.

Texas Monthly, March, 1997, Anne Dingus, review of *Atomic Chili*, pp. 100-102.

Village Voice, February 6, 1990, Richard Gehr, review of *The Drive-In: A B-Movie with Blood and Popcorn, Made in Texas,* and *The Drive-In 2: Not Just One of Them Sequels*, pp. 57-58.

OTHER

Joe R. Lansdale Home Page, http://www.joerlansdale.com (September 26, 2002).

Subterranean Press, http://www.subterraneanpress.com/ (September 26, 2002), "Interview: Joe R. Lansdale."

The Unofficial Joe R. Lansdale Homepage, http://www.geocities.com/Athens/Acropolis/3192/ (September 26, 2002).*

Juliet Marillier

■ Personal

Born July 27, 1948, in Dunedin, New Zealand; immigrated to Australia; daughter of William (a skilled tradesman) and Dorothy (a music teacher; maiden name, Johnston) Scott; married, 1969 (divorced); children: two daughters, two sons. *Nationality:* New Zealander; Australian. *Education:* Otago University, New Zealand, B.A. (languages; honor degree in music), 1970; studied music at Trinity College, London. *Politics:* Green Party. *Religion:* Pagan. *Hobbies and other interests:* Gardening, music, walking, animals.

■ Addresses

Home—Swann Valley, Western Australia. *Agent*—c/o Author Mail, Macmillan, Level 18, St. Martin's Tower, 31 Market St., Sydney, New South Wales, Australia 2000. *E-mail*—juliet@julietmarillier.com.

■ Career

Writer, 1998—. Has taught and lectured in music history, sung professionally, conducted choral groups, and assessed tax returns.

■ Awards, Honors

Aurealis Award shortlist for best fantasy novel, 1999, Australian Romantic Book of the Year shortlist and *Romantic Times* Readers' Choice Award for Best Fantasy Novel, both 2000, and Alex Award, American Library Association, all for *Daughter of the Forest*; Aurealis Award, 2000, for *Son of the Shadows*; Aurealis Award shortlist, 2001, for *Child of the Prophecy.*

■ Writings

"SEVENWATERS TRILOGY"

Daughter of the Forest, Macmillan (Sydney, New South Wales, Australia), 1999, Tor (New York, NY), 2000.
Son of the Shadows, Macmillan (Sydney, New South Wales, Australia), 2000, Tor (New York, NY), 2001.
Child of the Prophecy, Macmillan (Sydney, New South Wales, Australia), 2001, Tor (New York, NY), 2002.

Marillier's books have been translated into German, Dutch, and Portuguese.

OTHER

Wolfskin ("Saga of the Light Isles" series), Macmillan (Sydney, New South Wales, Australia), 2002, Tor (New York, NY), 2003.

Contributor to anthologies, including *The Road to Camelot,* Random House Australia, 2002; *Spinouts Sapphire,* Pearson Educational, 2002; and to magazines, including *Realms of Fantasy* and *Woman's Day.*

■ **Work in Progress**

Foxmask, the concluding volume of the "Saga of the Light Isles," Macmillan, 2003; *The Dark Mirror,* the first book in a new fantasy trilogy set in sixth-century Britain, due in 2004.

■ **Sidelights**

Called "Australia's high priestess of fantasy writing" by Carol George in the *Australian Women's Weekly,* Juliet Marillier is the author of folkloric fantasies that mine a Celtic vein. Despite this, Marillier might argue against the appellation "fantasy writer." As she told Michelle Cazzulino in Surry Hills, Australia's *Daily Telegraph,* her books are not typical fantasy adventures that take place an imaginary secondary world. Speaking of her 2002 title, *Wolfskin,* Marillier pointed out that it "is 90 per cent historical novel and about 10 per cent fantasy. It's really an historical novel, provided the reader can cope with a small amount of magic that's based on the beliefs of the people of the period." Marillier further commented, "I guess really my brooks bridge the gap between fantasy and history."

In an interview with *Authors and Artists for Young Adults (AAYA),* Marillier further described her work as "an unusual blend of history, romance and adventure, with a strong element of folkloric magic. Set in the Celtic twilight of Dark Ages Ireland ('The Sevenwaters Trilogy') and the early days of Viking Orkney (*Wolfskin*), the books are notable for their strong characterization, evocative historical settings, and flowing, easy style. The 'Sevenwaters' series features three generations of young women in one Irish family, while *Wolfskin* tells how a childhood promise between blood brothers leads to conflict, murder, and impossible choices."

Under whatever heading they are stored in the shelves of bookshops and libraries, Marillier's books have become popular with readers. From an amateur fantasy author struggling for her first publication at the age of fifty, Marillier has become a mainstay of fantasy readers, winning awards both in Australia in the United States. More than that, her "Sevenwaters Trilogy," as well as the first installment of the more action-oriented "Saga of the Light Isles," have attracted fans ranging from romance readers to devotees of historical fiction. "I believe there's a great power in traditional story telling and in our shared body of myth, legend, fable, folklore and fairy tale," Marillier told Iain Sharp in the Otago, New Zealand *Sunday Star Times.* "The codes, the symbolism, the distillation of fears, longings, aspirations and follies encapsulated in those traditional sources is the very lifeblood of fantasy, and cannot fail to touch something deep inside all but the most jaded listener." Marillier's first books feature strong female characters, but are in no way simply "women's" books; instead they deal with such harsh subject matter as rape, murder, and treachery.

Coming of Age down Under

Marillier was born in the town of Dunedin, New Zealand, an area with strong "Scottish roots" and home to the remnants of Celtic immigrants who originally settled the area. Far from the British Isles, Marillier grew up "surrounded by the music and stories of Scotland and Ireland," as she noted on her Web site; this influenced her strongly, creating the affinity for Celtic history and folklore she has maintained throughout her life. Another strong early influence was her love of reading and writing. Marillier noted in the *AAYA* interview, "As a small child I was cautious and a little insecure—once it was discovered I was severely short sighted and glasses were fitted, I did much better. My best friend's mother was a children's librarian and through her I was introduced to books from a very early age. My parents loved reading and music and surrounded me with both, especially traditional Scottish and Irish material." "I can't remember a time when I didn't want to be a writer," Marillier told an interviewer for *Slow Glass Books.* "I started writing stories when I was about five, and I still have my first extended piece, which was about scientists discovering a plesiosaur in Fiordland, New Zealand."

Marillier was educated in Dunedin, first at Arthur Street School, and then at Otago Girls School and Otago University, where she studied music and languages. "If there had been nerds in those days I would have been one," she admitted to *AAYA.* "I was an intellectual snob who only listened to classical music and spent most of the time with her nose in a book. I was academically inclined and highly competitive. I left school early and went straight to university because I was bored and couldn't handle being treated as a child. Socially I was rather inept,

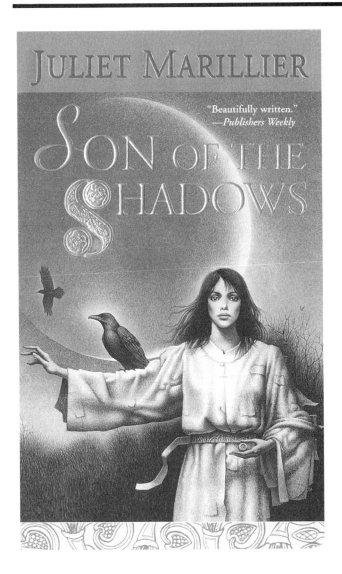

JULIET MARILLIER

"Beautifully written."
—*Publishers Weekly*

SON OF THE SHADOWS

The second installment in Julie Marillier's "Sevenwaters" trilogy, this 2000 novel follows the efforts of Liadan to fulfill her mother's quest to end the family curse and lift the spell that has turned her uncles into swans.

I think—that may have come from having no brothers and going to an all-girls school." As for early ambitions, Marillier added science and music to writing as one of her life goals during high school. "My first boyfriend and I both wanted to be veterinarians. I ended up as a music teacher and he ended up as a botanist. I probably would have been a writer much earlier if I hadn't made a last-minute decision to study music at university."

Marillier enjoyed college, noting that "It was great to meet like minds and have the freedom to pursue what, up till then, had been considered slightly weird interests. I shocked my parents by moving out of home into a share house with both male and female flat-mates (in the late '60s that was still considered pretty outrageous where I lived). I put myself through university partly on a scholarship and partly by working as a library assistant. My first job after university was classroom music teaching in a high school, followed by tutoring in the music department at the University of Otago."

Thereafter Marillier worked in a variety of other jobs, including in a children's library and in various dramatic capacities with a local theater. Married, she had four children and spent much of the 1970s and 1980s rearing her family. In 1976 the family moved from New Zealand to Australia, settling first in Melbourne. Marillier did not begin writing until after her children had grown up and her marriage had ended in divorce. "There were some very hard times during those years," the author recalled to Charmian Smith in the *Otago Daily Times,* "the sort of times when no-one would have had the creative energy to write, so I didn't. It was only after my marriage broke up and I got over that and started to establish myself as a person at last, that I started to do what I had always wanted to do, which was write." But once started, she vowed to become a published writer by age fifty or give it up.

Under the Wire with *Daughter of the Forest*

As it happened, Marillier narrowly made her goal, receiving a call from Macmillan on her fiftieth birthday telling her they wanted to publish her first novel, *Daughter of the Forest,* the beginning of trilogy. "The traditional story on which *Daughter of the Forest* is based, 'The Six Swans,' was a childhood favourite of mine, and writing the book was a healing activity," Marillier noted in her *AAYA* interview. "I sent my first book, and the first few chapters of the sequel, to Pan Macmillan as an unsolicited manuscript and it was picked up off the slush pile. I was pretty astonished to be offered a two-book contract. As first publishing experiences go, mine was great. There wasn't even very much editing, and they did their best to make it as painless as possible for me. I was very lucky."

"The underlying theme of the 'Sevenwaters Trilogy' is the preservation of what is most integral to survival: the forest, the islands, the spiritual values of which they are the physical manifestations," Marillier further noted on her Web site. She focused on one of the prime times in the Celtic world for this first novel: the ninth century when Christianity is overtaking and subsuming the last vestiges of Celtic paganism in Ireland. At the heart of the novel and its two companion pieces is the druidical sense of man's relationship with the environment—the ocean, sun, and moon. In writing this first novel, Marillier was not only inspired by, but also structured her novel around the fairy tale of "The Six Swans," the Celtic and indeed Europe-wide tale of the girl who saves her bewitched brothers by fashioning shirts which she throws over their heads as they fly by on swans' wings. The girl is thus able to counteract the spell and restore her siblings to their true human form. However, Marillier decided not to set her fantasy tale in the fantasy Otherworld, but in Ulster during the Dark Ages, using realistic, historically accurate details to fill out her family saga.

"In writing the series I blended a saga of tribal conflict, loyalty and treachery, romance and intrigue with a web of folklore and magic reflecting my own ancestral culture, that of the Celtic people of Europe," Marillier wrote for *Romantic Times Book Club.* The trials with which she confronted the family at Sevenwaters "are those of the human world of their age," she further explained, "and the magical elements in the books are based on what men and women of that time would have believed possible." Also, in contrast to many books of historical fantasy which reflect only the strong patriarchal times, Marillier decided to let her female characters grow and indeed take center stage in the trilogy: Sorcha as the female narrator in *Daughter of the Forest,* her daughter, Liadan, at the center of *Son of the Shadows,* and Fainne, her niece, at the heart of *Child of the Prophecy.*

Daughter of the Forest sets up the fictional world of Sevenwaters, ruled by Lord Colum, who has seven children: Liam who is a natural leader, Diarmid the adventurer, twins Cormack and Conor, rebellious Finbar with the gift of second sight, and compassionate Padriac. The seventh child is the daughter, Sorcha, whose mother died giving her birth. Their home, Sevenwaters, is a forest stronghold in Dark Age Ireland, at war with the Britons. Thus the Lord is away fighting, and the seven children grow up without parents, but their lives are idyllic nonetheless, and Sorcha becomes a competent herbalist and healer. This idyll ends, however, with the arrival of a stepmother, Lady Oonagh, who casts a spell on the six brothers, turning them into swans. The only salvation for her brothers, the Lady of the Fair Folk tells Sorcha, is for her to weave cloth from the starwort—a plant that blisters even worse than nettles—and from this sew each brother a shirt, and all this without the sorceress suspecting what Sorcha is up to. In order to succeed, she takes a vow of silence until the shirts are completed. At the outset of her ordeal, Sorcha, alone in the forest, is raped and then rescued by the British nobleman Hugh of Harrowfield, brother of Simon, a man whom Sorcha in fact earlier aided. But still under her oath of silence, she cannot tell Hugh of this. When they wed, she returns to England with him, where she continues her quest to transform her brothers. However, at Harrowfield, she is also caught in a deadly power struggle between Hugh and his mother and uncle, narrowly escaping being burned at the stake for witchcraft because of her magical powers, before returning to her native Ireland to end the family curse.

Marillier's debut novel received praise from many quarters. In a starred review, *Booklist*'s Patricia Monaghan lauded Marillier's "sterling characterizations, perfect pacing, appropriately marvelous fairy subplots, and vivid descriptive passages [that] make for a flawless launching of a fantasy trilogy." A reviewer for *Publishers Weekly* had similar praise, noting that Marillier "is a fine folklorist and gifted narrator who has created a wholly appealing and powerful character in this daughter of the forest." Focusing on the character of Sorcha, Kim Bates noted in *Green Man Review* that the protagonist "faces many dangers and finds unusual allies on the way, but she spends most of the time alone, disfigured, and bereft." Bates further commented, "But make no mistake, it is in and through this pain that growth comes, that life-changing realizations are made, where paths twist and turn and people make choices that affect the larger fabric of the world." Faren Miller, writing in *Locus,* likewise felt that Marillier "doesn't pull any punches in describing what her heroine must undergo. . . . But this Daughter of the Forest is more than a mere victim. As the book's central figure, she has or develops links to its many realms: Ireland, Britain, woodland, and the elusive otherworld of the gods." *Library Journal*'s Jackie Cassada praised Marillier's "keen understanding" of both the pagan Celt scene and of early Irish Christianity, elements which add "texture to a rich and vibrant novel."

"A remarkable new author makes a debut that is nothing short of brilliant," declared Melinda Helfer in the *Romantic Times Book Club.* Helfer went on to characterize Marillier as a "beautiful storyteller" who "brings a classic Celtic fairy tale to vibrant, glowing life with riveting prose and lyrical magic." Harriet Klausner, writing in *BookBrowser,* remarked that the "fast-paced" story line is "filled with action, and loaded with romance yet brimming with magical elements that seem real." And Laurie Thayer, reviewing the novel in *Rambles,* concluded that *Daughter of the Forest* "will keep you turning pages until there are no more, and leave you anxiously awaiting the next installment in the 'Sevenwaters Trilogy.'"

The Trilogy Continues

Readers did not have long to wait; the second volume in the series, *Son of the Shadows,* came out the following year. Liadan is the child of Sorcha and her British husband, and she has the power to heal others as well as to hear and see what other people cannot. When a tattooed outlaw threatens to destroy the fragile peace of Sevenwaters, it falls to Liadan to save her family and birthplace, even as she struggles to go out into the world and find her own identity. Kidnapped by these outlaws, who wear animal masks, she falls in love with their leader, Bran, and she must ultimately choose between her personal happiness and her duty to family.

Once again, Marillier's fiction was met with critical praise. *Booklist* reviewer Monaghan lauded *Son of the Shadows* for its "virtuosic pacing and vivid, filmic style," and also felt that it would "enthrall teen fans of the first book." *Library Journal* contributor Cassada dubbed it an "epic fantasy," and a reviewer for *Publishers Weekly* felt it was "beautifully written," and a "compelling story" that has fairies and earth magic aplenty, but that is not simply "a tale of the fey," but of one real human who has contact with the magical otherworld. "Adults who never lost the child within them will enjoy this marvelous epic," wrote Klausner in *BookBrowser,* further calling the novel a "powerful brew." Kelly Rae Cooper, writing in *Romantic Times Book Club,* commented on the "exquisite poetry of the story [which] is carefully balanced with strong characterizations and more than a nod to Irish mythology." And Erin Bush concluded in *Rambles* that the *Son of the Shadows* "is more than a continuation of the story begun in *Daughter of the Forest;* it is a fine work in its own right, brought to life by a gifted storyteller."

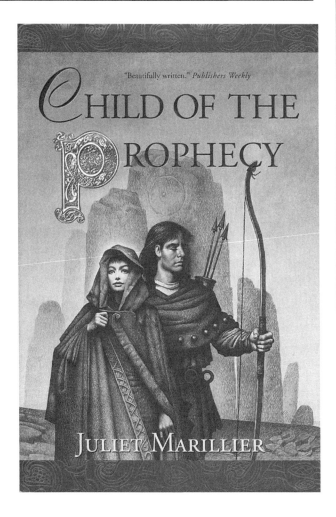

In the tradition of Celtic myth, Marillier spins a tale of sorcery and fate that finds a young woman searching for a way to break a spell of binding evil.

The trilogy is rounded off with *Child of the Prophecy,* featuring Fainne, daughter of Liadan's sister, Niamh, who has come to Sevenwaters from her isolated cove in Kerry to claim her rightful heritage. But in doing so she sparks the animosity of her evil fairy grandmother, especially as her love grows for her long lost kin. When she disobeys an order, this grandmother claims to torture Fainne's father in reprisal. On top of this there is Fainne's love for a young man that seems doomed from the start, as well as the cessation of the centuries old feud with the Britons. Another chorus of commendation was heard from reviewers for this final volume in the trilogy. Rachelle Bilz called this novel a "captivating finale to [Marillier's] richly imagined fantasy saga," in a *Voice of Youth Advocates* review, further labeling the entire trilogy an "incomparable fantasy tale." *Booklist* reviewer Monaghan felt the concluding novel in the series was a "rousing page-turner, a

heady blend of romance, magic, and battle," and that readers of the entire saga would sigh with both pleasure and regret "at bidding Marillier's perfectly realized world adieu." "Fans of powerfully intelligent fantasy novels with strong characterizations that deserves awards will want to read this book and its two previous tales," wrote Klausner in *Books & Bytes,* "because it is some of the genre's best in recent years," while Cooper concluded in *Romantic Times Book Club,* "Ms. Marillier creates a wondrous world with compelling characters and passages."

"I believe certain types of story have a great deal of power for change," Marillier explained in her *AAYA* interview. "The archetypal stories seen in myths, legends, folk tales and fairy tales, the stories that were once told around the camp fire, were a tool for making sense of life's dilemmas and challenges. They broke difficult and frightening things down into manageable codes. We still need those coded messages today, but we don't have much of a mechanism for sharing them any more in Western culture. Fantasy uses many of those archetypal themes and motifs, and often includes a personal journey for the protagonist in which she grows up and/or learns about herself and the world. That's the kind of story I love to write, and my readers often tell me the stories help them with their own life choices, as well as providing entertainment! My own spiritual beliefs, which are tied up with the desire to see mankind living in better harmony with the environment, are integral to my writing. I also find human behaviour fascinating, so I tend to focus strongly on character in my novels. I like to place real people in extraordinary situations and see how well they cope, and how their experiences change them."

"Saga of the Light Isles"

Upon finishing her Irish trilogy, Marillier immediately set to work on a pair of books set in Norway and on Scotland's Orkney Islands. The first volume, *Wolfskin,* deals with young Eyvind, who has childhood dreams of growing up to be an elite warrior known as a Wolfskin. It is his fondest wish is to serve Thor, the god of war. But a vow made to a childhood friend, Somerled, leads to astounding complications later in his life. Growing up, Eyvind's wishes are fulfilled, and he has become one of the most respected Wolfskins, but now he must accompany Somerled with a group of settlers to the magical islands across the sea where they will establish a new Viking community. There, in what later is called Orkney, Eyvind's boyhood oath is challenged by events, and by Nessa, kinswoman of the last great king of the Folk, the magical people who once lived so peacefully in this island kingdom.

"I guess it is quite a leap from the Celtic twilight and fairytale fantasy of my 'Sevenwaters' series to his saga-like Viking adventure," Marillier explained in an interview published on the Macmillan Web site. "The idea for the book was sparked off when I read about berserk warriors, who appear in the Norse sagas. . . . The central character of *Wolfskin,* Eyvind, is one of these elite soldiers. I had to get inside his head and show what forces drive him, and how a young man could live such an apparently crazy life and still be quite ordinary in other ways." Research for the book took Marillier to Orkney itself and through dozens of books on the Vikings and their military technology. "I guess what I wanted to show was how a young man of that time and culture could be placed under immense pressure because of his religious beliefs and because of

the codes of behaviour his society bound him to," Marillier further explained. George, writing in *Australian Women's Weekly,* called the novel "a potent mix of fine story-telling, rich imagination and meticulous research," and also noted that the book had started a bidding war for the foreign rights in both England and the United States. The second volume of the saga, *Foxmask,* features young Thorvald and his search for the father he has never known, aided by Creidhe.

"I get inspiration from my reading and study, particularly from old sources such as folklore, sagas, myths and legends," Marillier told *AAYA.* "And history—I love history, which is full of fascinating 'grey areas' to explore, those mysterious times that have very little in the way of contemporary records. I also do a lot of research. It includes reading reference books, using the Internet, including chat groups on specific topics, and also visiting some of the areas where my books are set (absolutely necessary as I currently live in Australia and generally write about my own ancestral cultures, which are in Europe)."

Marillier has been praised not only for her research, attention to detail, and lyrical writing, but also for the depth of her characterizations. Some have called her a feminist writer because of her strong heroines. As the author noted on her Web site, it remains important for her "to celebrate human strengths as well as exploring human follies and weaknesses in all of my work. Because I'm a woman and have made my share of the traditional mistakes, my work tends to focus particularly on women's journeys through the maze of life, and the way they deal with whatever surprises fate has in store for them." Marillier went on to note, "I don't so much write about men and women as about individual people."

Marillier works with aspiring writers in workshops, via e-mail, and through on-line chat groups. "The main piece of advice I give people is to write from the heart," she commented in her *AAYA* interview. "To write what you feel passionately about, because that is what writing is all about, expressing something that just has to come out. Don't sit down to write because you think it might make you rich and famous one day. Don't try to work out what is likely to sell. Write what you have inside you clamouring to get out. It might be a few words about something you think or feel, or something you saw on the way to school. It might be a daily journal or diary (these are really good discipline) or it might be a huge fantasy novel. It's the passion behind it that really counts. The reverse side of that piece of advice is that you should also be learning your craft, and one great way of doing that is to read a lot, and to read as many different kinds of writing as you can, fiction, both literary and popular, non-fiction, poetry, newspapers and magazines and so on. Study English, too, it helps to be able to spell and have a good grasp of grammar and structure. And good luck—the world needs more writers!"

If you enjoy the works of Juliet Marillier, you might want to check out the following books:

Donna Jo Napoli, *Zel,* 1996.
Mary Gentle, The Books of Ash series, 1998-2000.
Cynthia Voigt, *Elske,* 1999.

Interviewed on the Macmillan Web site about the Celtic influence in her work, she commented, "I was born in New Zealand, I live in Australia, and I have Scottish and Irish ancestry. It's no surprise, then, that I feel a need to explore the theme of colonisation and the destruction it can cause. Ancestral culture can disappear with frightening speed. That idea comes out in all the books. However, my main aim is just to tell a good story. If the reader can live in another world for a while, be it Celtic Ireland or Pictish Orkney, I feel that I've done my job."

■ Biographical and Critical Sources

PERIODICALS

Australian Women's Weekly, September, 2002, Carol George, "Fantastic Journey."
Booklist, April 15, 2000, Patricia Monaghan, review of *Daughter of the Forest,* p. 1534; April 1, 2001, Stephanie Zvirin, review of *Daughter of the Forest,* p. 1461; May 15, 2001, Patricia Monaghan, review of *Son of the Shadows,* p. 1738; February 15, 2002, Patricia Monaghan, review of *Child of the Prophecy,* p. 999; April 15, 2002, Ray Olson, review of *Child of the Prophecy,* p. 1387.
Daily Telegraph (Surry Hills, Australia), September 7, 2002, Michelle Cazzulino, "A Hit and Myth Affair," p. 3.

Library Journal, May 15, 2000, Jackie Cassada, review of *Daughter of the Forest,* p. 129; May 15, 2001, Jackie Cassada, review of *Son of the Shadows,* p. 167; March 15, 2002, Jackie Cassada, review of *Child of the Prophecy,* p. 111.
Locus, April, 2000, Faren Miller, review of *Daughter of the Forest.*
Otago Daily Times (Dunedin, New Zealand), October 20, 2001, Charmian Smith, "Tales That Tell of How the World Works."
Publishers Weekly, April 17, 2000, review of *Daughter of the Forest,* p. 57; April 16, 2001, review of *Son of the Shadows,* p. 49.
Sunday Star Times (Otago, New Zealand), December, 2001, Iain Sharp, "Fantasy Islands."
Voice of Youth Advocates, August, 2002, Rachelle Bilz, review of *Child of the Prophecy,* p. 204.

OTHER

BookBrowser, http://www.bookbrowser.com/ (April 27, 2000), Harriet Klausner, review of *Daughter of the Forest;* (March 25, 2001) Harriet Klausner, review of *Son of the Shadows.*
Books & Bytes, http://www.booksnbites.com/ (October 1, 2002), Harriet Klausner, review of *Child of the Prophecy.*
Green Man Review, http://www.greenmanreview. com/ (October 1, 2002), Kim Bates, review of *Daughter of the Forest.*
Juliet Marillier Web Page, http://www.julietmarillier. com/ (September 30, 2002).
Lunacat.net, http://www.lunacat.net/ (October 1, 2002), "Juliet Marillier."
Macmillan Web Site, http://www.panmacmillan. com.au/ (July, 2002), "Interview with Juliet Marillier."
Marillier, Juliet, interview with J. Sydney Jones for *Authors and Artists for Young Adults,* October 9, 2002.
Rambles, http://www.rambles.net (October 1, 2002), Laurie Thayer, review of *Daughter of the Forest;* (July 6, 2002) Erin Bush, review of *Son of the Shadows.*
Romantic Times Book Club, http://www. romantictimes.com/ (October 1, 2002), Melinda Helfer, review of *Daughter of the Forest;* (October 1, 2002), Juliet Marillier, "Expert Advice"; (October 1, 2002), Kelly Rae Cooper, review of *Son of the Shadows;* (October 1, 2002), Kelly Rae Cooper, review of *Child of the Prophecy.*
Slow Glass Books, http://wwwslowglass.com/ (September 30, 2002), "Interview with Juliet Marillier."*

—*Sketch by J. Sydney Jones*

Yukio Mishima

■ Personal

Born Kimitake Hiraoka, January 14, 1925, in Tokyo, Japan; died by his own hand, November 25, 1970, in Tokyo, Japan; son of Azusa (a public official) and Shizue (Hashi) Hiraoka; married Yoko Sugiyama, June 1, 1958; children: Noriko (daughter), Iichiro (son). *Nationality:* Japanese. *Education:* Tokyo University, degree in jurisprudence, 1947. *Religion:* Zen.

■ Career

Novelist, playwright, essayist, and author of short stories. Civil servant with Japanese Finance Ministry, 1948; writer, 1948-70. Lecturer, swordsman, singer, actor, director of plays, and director of motion pictures, including *Yukoku,* 1965, and *Enjo.*

■ Member

P.E.N. Club (Japan), Tate No Kai (Shield Society; founder).

■ Awards, Honors

Shincho Prize, Shinchsha Publishing, 1954, for *The Sound of Waves;* Kishida Prize for Drama, Shinchsha Publishing, 1955; Yomiuri Prize, Yomiuri Newspaper Co., for best novel, 1957, for *The Temple of the Golden Pavilion,* and for best drama, 1961, for *Toka no Kiku.*

■ Writings

Kamen no kpkuhaku, [Japan], 1949, English translation by Meredith Weatherby published as *Confessions of a Mask,* New Directions (New York, NY), 1958.

Ai no Kawaki, [Japan], 1950, translation by Alfred H. Marks published as *Thirst for Love,* introduction by Donald Keene, Knopf (New York, NY), 1969.

Kantan (also see below), [Japan], 1950, translation published in *Five Modern No Plays,* 1957.

Aya no tsuzumi (also see below), [Japan], 1951, translation published as *The Damask Drum* in *Five Modern No Plays,* 1957.

Sotoba komachi (also see below), [Japan], 1952, translation published in *Five Modern No Plays,* 1957.

Manatsu no shi (also see below), [Japan], 1952, translation by Edward Seidensticker published as *Death in Midsummer* in *Death in Midsummer and Other Stories,* 1966.

Yoru no himawari (four-act play), [Japan], 1953, translation by Shigeho Shinozaki and Virgil A. Warren published as *Twilight Sunflower,* Hokuseido Press (Tokyo, Japan), 1958.

Aoi no ue (also see below), [Japan], 1954, translation published as *The Lady Aoi*, in *Five Modern No Plays*, 1957.

Shigadera shonin no koi (also see below), [Japan], 1954, translation by Ivan Morris published as *The Priest of Shiga Temple and His Love* in *Modern Japanese Stories*, Tuttle (Rutland, VT), 1962, and in *Death in Midsummer and Other Stories*, 1966.

Kinjiki (fiction), two volumes, [Japan], 1954, translation by Alfred H. Marks published as *Forbidden Colors*, Secker & Warburg (London, England), 1968, Berkley Publishing (New York, NY), 1974.

Shiosai, [Japan], 1954, translation by Meredith Weatherby published as *The Sound of Waves*, Knopf (New York, NY), 1956.

Hanjo (also see below), [Japan], 1955, translation published in *Five Modern No Plays*, 1957.

Kindai nogaku shu, [Japan], 1956, translation by Donald Keene published as *Five Modern No Plays* (contains *The Damask Drum, Hanjo, Kantan, The Lady Aoi*, and *Sotoba komachi*), Knopf (New York, NY), 1957.

Kinkakuji, [Japan], 1956, translation by Ivan Morris published as *The Temple of the Golden Pavilion*, Knopf (New York, NY), 1959.

Nettaiju (play), [Japan], 1959, translation by Kenneth Strong published as *Tropical Tree* in *Japan Quarterly*, Volume XI, 1964.

Utage no ato, [Japan], 1960, translation by Donald Keene published as *After the Banquet*, Knopf (New York, NY), 1963.

Hyakuman-en sembei (also see below), [Japan], 1960, translation by Edward Seidensticker published as *Three Million Yen*, in *Death in Midsummer and Other Stories*, 1966.

Yukoku (also see below), [Japan], 1960, translation by Geoffrey Sargent published as *Patriotism* in *Death in Midsummer and Other Stories*, 1966.

Mahobin (also see below), [Japan], 1961, translation by Edward Seidensticker published as *Thermos Bottles* in *Death in Midsummer and Other Stories*, 1966.

Gogo no eiko (fiction), [Japan], 1963, translation by John Nathan published as *The Sailor Who Fell from Grace with the Sea*, Knopf (New York, NY), 1965.

Kinu to meisatsu (novel), [Japan], 1964, translation by Hiroaki Sato published as *Silk and Insight*, M. E. Sharpe (Armonk, NY), 1998.

Sado koshaku fujin (play), [Japan], 1965, translation by Donald Keene published as *Madame de Sade*, P. Owen (London, England), 1968.

Death in Midsummer, and Other Stories (contains *Death in Midsummer, Three Million Yen, Thermos Bottles, The Priest of Shiga Temple and His Love, The Seven Bridges, Patriotism, Dojoji, Onnagata, The Pearl*, and

Swaddling Clothes), translation by Edward Seidensticker, Donald Keene, Ivan Morris, and Geoffrey Sargent, New Directions (New York, NY), 1966.

Hagakure nyumon, [Japan], c. 1967, translation by Kathryn N. Sparling published as *The Way of Samurai: Yukio Mishima on Hagakure in Modern Life*, Basic Books (New York, NY), 1977.

Taido, [Japan], 1967, translation and introduction by Meredith Weatherby and Paul T. Konya published as *Young Samurai*, Grove (New York, NY), 1967.

Taiyo to tetsu, [Japan], 1968, translation by John Bester published as *Sun and Steel*, Grove (New York, NY), 1970.

Hojo no umi, [Japan], 1969-71, Volume I: *Haru no yuki*, Volume II: *Homba*, Volume III: *Akatsuki no tera*, Volume IV: *Tennin gosui*, translation of tetralogy published as *The Sea of Fertility: A Cycle of Four Novels*, Knopf (New York, NY), Volume I: *Spring Snow*, translated by Michael Gallagher, 1972, Volume II: *Runaway Horses*, translated by Michael Gallagher, 1973, Volume III: *The Temple of Dawn*, translated by E. Dale Saunders and Cecilia S. Seigle, 1973, Volume IV: *The Decay of the Angel*, translated by Edward Seidensticker, 1974.

Yukio Mishima on "Hagakure": The Samurai Ethic and Modern Japan, Souvenir Press (London, England), 1978.

IN JAPANESE; FICTION

Kofuku go shuppan, Sinchsha (Tokyo, Japan), 1956.

Bitoku no yoromeki (title means "A Misstepping of Virtue"), Kodansha (Tokyo, Japan), 1957.

Kyoko no ie (title means "Kyoko's House"), Shinchsha (Tokyo, Japan), 1959.

Natsuko no boken, 1960.

Ojosan, Kodansha (Tokyo, Japan), 1960.

Nagasugita haru, 1961.

Shisumoru taki, 1963.

Ai no shisso, 1963.

Nikutai no gakko, Shueisha (Tokyo, Japan), 1964.

Ongaku, Chu Kronsha (Tokyo, Japan), 1965.

Yakaifuku, Shueisha (Tokyo, Japan), 1967.

Mishima Yukio chohen zenshu, Shinchsha (Tokyo, Japan), 1967.

Inochi urimasu, Shueisha (Tokyo, Japan), 1968.

Kemono no tawamure, 1971.

Ao no jidai, 1971.

Mishima Yukio shu, Shinchsha (Tokyo, Japan), 1968.

SHORT STORIES

Hanazakari no mori (short stories and plays; title means "The Forest in Full Bloom"), 1944, reprinted, 1968.

Misaki nite no monogatari, 1947.

Toadai (short stories and plays), 1950.

Kaibutsu, 1950.

Seijo, 1951.

Kamen no kokuhaku sona ta, 1951.

Mishima Yukio tampen shu (short stories and plays), 1951.

Tonorikai, 1951.

Mishima Yukio shu, 1952, Kodansha (Tokyo, Japan), 1964.

Collections: Mishima Yukio sakuhinshu, six volumes, Shinchsha (Tokyo, Japan), 1953-71.

Mishima Yukio tampen senshu, six volumes, 1964-1971.

Koya yori (includes essays), 1967.

Shishi, 1971.

Mishima Yukio judai sakuhin shu, 1971.

Mishima Yukio, 1972.

Mishima Yukio shu (part of "Gendai Nihon no bungaku" series), 1976.

ESSAYS

Kari to emono, 1951.

Fudutoku kyoiku kosa, 1969.

Wakaki samurai no tame ni, 1969.

Mishima Yukio bungaku ronshu, 1970.

Ranryo O, 1971.

PLAYS

Wakodo yo yomigaere (title means "Young Man Back to Life"), 1954.

Rokumeikan, 1956.

Yoroboshi, 1960.

Toka no kiku, 1961.

Mishima Yukio gikyoku zenshu, 1962.

Kindai nogaku shu, 1968.

Gikyoku kurotokage, 1969.

CONTRIBUTOR

Fusao Hayashi, *Taiwa, Nihonjin ron,* 1966.

Katsuhiko Ito, *Taiwa, shiso no hassei,* 1967.

Kyutei no niwa, 1968.

Momo Iida, *Shichijunen e no kido,* 1969.

Koyo gunkan, Gorinsho, Hagakure shu, 1969.

Nihonjin no saiken, 1971.

Hayashi, *Rekishi e no shogen,* 1971.

Shimpen kyutei no niwa, 1971.

EDITOR

Rokusei nakamura utaemon, 1959.

Bungei tokuhon, Kawabata Yasunari (short stories), 1962.

Yoshitoshi Taiso, Chi no bansan, 1971.

(With Geoffrey Bownas) *New Writing in Japan,* Penguin (New York, NY), 1972.

OTHER

Magun no tsuka, 1949.

Aporo no sakazuki, 1952.

Koi no miyako, 1954.

Shosetsuka no kyuka, 1955.

Megami, 1955.

Seishun o do ikiru ka, 1955.

Shiroari no su, 1956.

Mishima Yukio senshu, nineteen volumes, 1957-1959.

Gendai shosetsu wa koten tari-uru ka, 1957.

Rara to kaizoku, 1958.

Hashizukushi, 1958.

Fudotoku kyoikukoza, 1959.

Bunsho tokuhon, 1959, new edition, 1969.

Hanteijo daigaku, 1966.

Mishima Yukio hyoron zenshu, 1966.

(With Mitsuo Nakamura) *Taidan, ningen to bungaku,* 1968.

Waga tomo Hittora, 1968.

Mishima Yukio reta kyoshitsu, 1968.

Toron Mishima Yukio vs. Todai Zenkyoto, 1969.

Raio no Terasu (drama), 1969.

Sado koshaku fujin (drama), 1969.

Chinsetsu yumiharizuki, 1969.

Bunka boei ron, 1969.

Mishima Yukio kenkyu, 1970.

Sakkaron, 1970.

Gensen no kanjo, 1970.

Mishima Yukio ten (exhibition catalog), 1970.

Kodogaku nyumon, 1970.

Shobu no kororo, 1970.

Mishima Yukio (volume of "Nihon bungaku kenkyu shiryo sosho" series), 1971.

Santao Yuchifu tuan p'ien chieh tso hsuan, 1971.

Mishima Yukio no ningenzo, 1971.

Mishima Yukio no ski o do miru ka, 1971.

Shosetsu to wa nani ka, 1972.

Nihon bungaku shoshi, 1972.

Mishima Yukio shonen shi, edited by Kazasuke Ogawa, 1973.

Waga shishunki, 1973.

Mishima Yukio, edited by Ken'ichi Adachi, 1973.

Daiichi no sei, 1973.

Mishima Yukio zenshu, thirty-six volumes, edited by Shoichi Saeki and Jun Ishikawa, 1973-1976.

Mishima Yukio goroku (title means "Invitation to Mishimalogy"), edited by Ken Akitsu, 1975.

(With Teiji Ito and Takeji Iwamiya) *Sento Gosho,* 1977.

Also author of screenplays, including *Yokoku,* 1965.

■ Adaptations

The Sailor Who Fell from Grace with the Sea was filmed in 1976 and starred Sarah Miles and Kris Kristofferson; *The School of Flesh,* starring Isabelle Huppert, 1999, was based on Mishima's *Nikutai no Gakko.*

■ Sidelights

Life magazine once called Yukio Mishima "the Japanese Hemingway," while Japan's first Nobel laureate, Yasunari Kawabata, "declared that a 'writer of his caliber appears only once every 200 or 300 years,'" as reported in the *Economist.* Mishima was a writer, poet, playwright, librettist, actor, bodybuilder, and right-wing political activist renowned for his flamboyant personality, eccentric political beliefs, and spectacular ritual suicide in 1970. At the time of his death at age forty-five, Mishima "was perhaps the most famous private citizen in Japan," according to James Fallows writing in the *Atlantic.* Fallows went on to note that Mishima's suicide "is often described as the most disturbing event of the postwar years [in Japan], since it was the most direct challenge to the modern religion of GNP."

Despite this public persona, Mishima is nevertheless best remembered for his contributions to Japanese literature, including novels such as *Confessions of a Mask* and *The Sea of Fertility,* as well as dozens of plays, many of which are still performed today. A prolific writer, Mishima's mastery of novels, essays, and plays earned him a reputation as the literary genius of Japan's postwar generation as well as a place among the world's finest authors, and for many years before his death it was rumored that he would be next in line for a Nobel Prize.

Samurai Ancestry

Mishima was born on January 14, 1925, to Azusa Hiraoka, a deputy director in the Japanese Agricultural Ministry, and Shizue Hara. Though of samurai background, Mishima's grandfather had run through most of the family wealth. While his mother was from a scholarly family, it was his maternal grandmother, Natsuko, who had the most influence on the young boy. She, in fact, forced a separation of Mishima, when still an infant, from his mother, having him live with her in her room. A semi-invalid, she stifled the young boy and even convinced him that he too was frail and sickly. She also encouraged his growing interest in Kabuki theater, and filled his head with dreams of the family's glorious past when they were among the elite.

Mishima also demonstrated an early interest in haiku and in writing. From an early age, one of his essays appeared in every issue of his school paper. He read widely as a child, beginning at age six with children's tales by Mimei Ogawa and Miekichi Suzuki, among others. When he was eight, his family and siblings moved to another home, but Mishima stayed with his grandmother, nursing her as her condition worsened. This strange arrangement lasted until he was twelve and he finally rejoined his family. His grandmother died the following year.

In middle school Mishima joined the literary club and began regularly attending both Kabuki and Noh plays. At age twelve he published his first essay, "Spring Grass: Recollections of Primary School Days," in the *Gakusyuin Hojinkai* journal and thereafter continued to publish plays, poems, short stories, novellas, and parts of novels in the same magazine throughout high school. Even as his country geared for war, Mishima continued with his study of literature, influenced heavily by the Japanese Romantic movement. His first novella, *A Forest in Full Flower,* was published in 1941 in the literary magazine *Bungeie Bunka,* but with the world at war, little notice was taken of it. Noteworthy, though, is the fact that with publication of this novella, he first used the pen name Yukio Mishima, loosely derived from that of the famous poet Sachio Ito. Ito is also the name of a resort with a view of Mt. Fuji; the neighboring resort of Mishima, however, has an even more lovely view, and thus the author stuck on this name as one adequate for a young writer who was set on challenging the greats of Japanese literature.

In 1942 Mishima went from the middle school to high school, graduating as class valedictorian in 1944. With all able-bodied men being called up for military duty, Mishima took a draft physical and failed, misdiagnosed as having tuberculosis. That year his novella *A Forest in Full Flower* was published as a bound book, and he entered the University of Tokyo to study law.

Mishima's university studies were delayed, however, until after the war, when the university re-

By the 1960s Mishima had become a militant activist who, as the charismatic leader of a Japanese youth group, worked to return his country to its traditional way of life.

opened. Meanwhile, the young writer continued to contribute numerous poems, stories, and essays to literary journals. Susan J. Napier, writing in *Dictionary of Literary Biography,* noted that the poems, stories, and even novels of the early postwar period "revel in a typically Romantic mixture of elements, among the most important being physically attractive young lovers; beautiful, youthful death; and the sea. These early elements remain constant throughout Mishima's oeuvre, although in his later stages they were often reworked with various degrees of irony."

Early Novels

Mishima's first novel appeared in 1948, but was largely ignored. Despite the lack of critical or popular interest in his debut work, the young man de-

cided to quit the bureaucratic position he held at the Japanese Finance Ministry in order to devote his full time to writing. Mishima's reputation was established the following year with *Confessions of a Mask.* Although not considered an autobiography, the book is an obvious chronicle of Mishima's life from early childhood through his wartime experiences. The novel focuses on the narrator's growing awareness that he would have to mask his sexual preferences from those around him. As Napier noted, the work shocked many at the time, for homosexuality was not something discussed in polite society. Additionally inflammatory, according to Napier, were the "highly explicit accounts of the young man's sadomasochistic and autoerotic fantasies, the most famous being his fascination with pictures of the arrow-pierced body of Saint Sebastian." So tightly and confidently does the narrator wear the public mask that he even courts a young woman. Rejected, he throws himself back into his world of sadomasochistic eroticism. A *Time* reviewer called *Confessions of a Mask* a "fierce portrait of homosexuality—a subject with which Mishima had a lifelong fascination and, some say, involvement." Writing in 1999, the critic Marjorie Rhine noted in *Studies in the Novel* that the book "not only catapulted [Mishima] into prominence as one of the top writers of postwar Japan when it was published in 1949, but also remains one of the most popular and most often taught and discussed of his novels."

In his next book, *Thirst for Love,* Mishima discards the self-confessional style in telling the story of a young widow who moves in with her father-in-law and becomes his mistress. She then develops an obsessive but unreciprocated passion for the household servant boy. Critics commented that Mishima's descriptions of a bourgeois Japanese household were well done. Napier described *Thirst for Love* as a novel that "privileges intensity over dreary quotidian responsibility," a Romantic notion that became part of Mishima's belief system. Michael Rogers, writing in *Library Journal,* noted the book's theme of "idealism destroyed by beauty," and concluded that several decades after Mishima's suicide, he continues to be a "compelling novelist." This novel, with its themes of sexual repression and violence, proved another literary success in its day, further solidifying Mishima's reputation as one of the finest novelists of his generation.

Forbidden Colors, written in 1954, is another "groundbreaking work," according to Napier. The novel explores the homosexual underground in postwar Tokyo, and also introduces an important theme Mishima continued to develop in later work, the "passive aging intellectual in implicit competition with a handsome young protagonist," as Napier described the dynamic.

Considered one of Mishima's best early books, *The Temple of the Golden Pavilion* won the Yomiuri prize in 1957. The novel is based on the true story of a young Buddhist acolyte whose ugliness and stutter make him grow to hate anything beautiful. He becomes obsessed with the idea that the golden temple where he studies is the ideal of beauty, and in envy he burns the temple to the ground. Mishima based his story on information he gathered from the actual court trial, with the protagonist acting as narrator. "But although Mishima has made use of the reported details of the real-life culprit's arrogant and desperate history, culminating in the final willful act of arson," wrote Nancy Wilson Ross in the book's introduction, "he has employed the factual record merely as a scaffolding on which to erect a

disturbing and powerful story of a sick young man's obsession with a beauty he cannot attain, and the way in which his private pathology leads him, slowly and fatefully, to self-destruction and a desperate deed of pyromania." Napier noted that *The Temple of the Golden Pavilion* is considered by many to be Mishima's "masterpiece," a "complex meditation on outsiderhood and alterity wrapped within a framework whose background is defeated postwar Japan." Napier further commented that the book "resounds with the sense of loss, of lost traditions, lost beauty, at the same time as it implicitly questions the viability of beauty in the real world." As such it is one of Mishima's strongest statements of the preference for the ideal over the real.

Novels of note from Mishima that remain untranslated into English include 1957's *Bitoku no yoromeki,* about an adulterous married woman and her younger lover, and *Kyoko no ie,* which deals with four heroes—a businessman, an artist, an actor, and a boxer—all different aspects of Mishima's own personality. The latter novel is considered prophetic for its themes of suicide, right-wing politics, and bodybuilding, all important in Mishima's own life. *Bitoku,* on the other hand, while one of Mishima's most popular novels, is also one of his least literary, a gossipy potboiler not usually ranked among his literary fiction.

Gogo no eiko, translated as *The Sailor Who Fell from Grace with the Sea,* deals with themes of violence and apocalypse in a tale of a group of preadolescents who kill a sailor so that they can return him to a more heroic position. Notable in this novel also are criticisms of Japan's materialistic postwar culture. Made into a successful movie in the 1970s, this book was hailed as Mishima's "greatest novel, and one of the greatest of the [twentieth] . . . century" by Rhoda Koenig in the *Independent.* Mishima's *After the Banquet* steers away from political messages as for the first time the author manages to create a sympathetic female character. With *Silk and Insight,* a 1998 English translation of a 1964 novel, Mishima departs from his usual aesthetic message in recounting one the most important labor strikes in postwar Japan at a silk textile mill. "Mishima's novelization demonstrates how paternalism was a wolf in sheep's clothing," remarked *Booklist* contributor Allen Weakland. Marleigh Grayer Ryan, reviewing the novel in *World Literature Today,* explained that the book "is awash in the grays and blacks of 1950s Japan, seething with malnutrition, disease, and ignorance, and has a bleakness and pessimism consistent with the ideological vacuum of the period."

Works in Drama and the Short Story

Nearly as popular as his novels have been Mishima's modernized versions of traditional Japanese Noh plays. Developed in the fourteenth century, Noh plays generally feature four or five actors who tell their story with a recitation and dance accompanied by flute and drums. The plays' stylized gestures and deliberate dialogues have become so much a ritual that audiences are able to detect the slightest variation in a performance.

Mishima was the first contemporary author to work successfully in this medium. In adapting some of the plays he painstakingly recreated the details of the story; in others, he followed only the general theme. The plot of *The Damask Drum,* for example, resembles that of the original play. Donald Keene, writing in *Landscapes and Portraits,* compared the two versions: In the original story an old gardener in a palace falls in love with a princess and is told he will win her favor if he can beat a drum loud enough for her to hear. But the drum is made of damask and can make no sound, so the old man commits suicide. Mishima's version concerns a janitor in a Tokyo law office who falls in love with "the client of a fashionable couturiere in the building across the way," stated Keene. The janitor, too, is told to beat the drum in order to win the girl's affection, but it makes no sound and he commits suicide. In the original play "the No ghost returns to torment the cruel princess with the ceaseless beating of the drum, but in the modern play the lady's inability to love makes her deaf to the beating of the drum, and the janitor's ghost is driven a second time to despair."

The Noh plays are considered among Mishima's most interesting works and his reworkings of Noh continue to be popular. Reviewing the 2002 performance of *Sotoba komachi* and *Yoroboshi* at London's Barbican Theater, Charles Spencer noted in the *Daily Telegraph* that *Sotoba komachi* "is mesmerisingly staged, brimming with sex, mystery and a powerful sense of transcendence. But, as in *Yoroboshi,* there is little doubt that Mishima was more than half in love with easeful death."

Ten of Mishima's best short stories and plays have been translated into English as *Death in Midsummer and Other Stories.* The longest entry is the title story about a woman whose two small children and sister-in-law drown at a beach. Mishima studies the jealousy, resentment, and guilt of the woman and her husband over their inability to mourn. Another notable inclusion in this volume is the short novella *Yukoku.* It describes the ritual suicides of a young army officer and his wife after a coup in which he is involved fails to overthrow reigning politicians. The couple, both "perfect specimens, of physique, of sexual beauty, of loyalty," make passionate love before their suicides.

The Sea of Fertility Tetralogy

Mishima's final work, considered by many his magnum opus, was *The Sea of Fertility* tetralogy, the final portions of which he completed and submitted to his publishers on the day of his suicide. In a letter written to an American friend just before his death, Mishima explained: "I wrote everything in it, and I believe I expressed in it everything I felt and thought about through my life. I just finished the novel on the very day of my action in order to realize my Bunbu-Ryodo." (Bunbu-Ryodo is a synthesis of the culture arts and the warrior arts.)

"After thinking and thinking through four years, I came to wish to sacrifice myself for the old, beautiful tradition of Japan, which is disappearing very quickly day by day."

—*Yukio Mishima*

The tetralogy begins with *Spring Snow,* a tragic love story of Kiyoaki and Satoko, both children of Japanese aristocrats. When Satoko is chosen to marry the emperor's grandson, each of Kiyoaki's liaisons with her becomes more dangerous yet all the more passionate. Continuing on from Kiyoaki's story in 1912, the rest of the series spans the history of Japan through the 1970s. Mishima connects the stories with the reincarnation of Kiyoaki as a different person in each new volume: as a political fanatic, a Thai princess, and then an evil young orphan. The final three volumes are told from the viewpoint of a school friend of Kiyoaki's, "a wonderfully subtle spiritual voyeur named Honda, a rationalist Japanese judge and lawyer" who follows the progress of Kiyoaki's spirit into three new bodies, each bearing a certain pattern of three moles and each dying at the age of twenty.

Although the simple love story of *Spring Snow* made it the most popular book of the tetralogy, the other volumes are also highly regarded. Many readers have been drawn to *Runaway Hero* because the suicide of its protagonist, Isao, foreshadowed in almost exact detail the author's own suicide.

Because Mishima knew this tetralogy was to be his last work, it is often considered a suicide note to the world. Critics disagree, however, on Mishima's intended message. Some reviewers have maintained that the tetralogy's theme is reincarnation and that Mishima evidently planned to return to this world, while others are convinced that the author did not actually believe in rebirth at all.

Critics have asserted that the two major themes of *The Sea of Fertility* tetralogy are the dissolution of the individual and of the old aristocratic values, both of which Mishima vigorously crusaded against during his lifetime. The tetralogy is therefore often considered a written expression of the beliefs for which its author lived and died. Reviewing the four-book sequence in *Atlantic,* Fallows noted that Mishima "clearly did believe in other themes of the series, and they are what make the books so fascinating now. Mishima writes as powerfully about the psychology of obsession as anyone since Dostoyevsky. Almost every figure in the book is undone by impulses he or she cannot control." Concluding his lengthy review, Fallows noted that neither Mishima's books nor his life could "be taken as literal guides to modern Japanese beliefs, any more than the raft scenes in Huckleberry Finn tell us explicitly about American race relations in the 1990s. But as Twain's books reveal general truths about our culture, so does *The Sea of Fertility,* for better or worse, about Japan."

Shield Society, Seppuku Shape Legacy

Mishima's fascination with death and suicide can be traced to his childhood. Born to a family of samurai nobility, he attempted even as a young man to follow the samurai tradition which emphasized expertise in the martial arts, control over mind and body, and a following of the bushido code of self-sacrifice, indifference to pain, and complete loyalty to Japan's emperor. Young Mishima had been convinced that he would die for the emperor during World War II, as did the kamikaze pilots, but because he failed the army physical his death wish remained unfulfilled. After his rejection, he began to build up his frail physique and thereafter maintained his body in the perfect physical condition of the samurai by lifting weights, practicing karate, and engaging in the ancient sword-fighting game of kendo.

When Japan was defeated by the Allies in World War II, the country was forced to adopt a new constitution that stripped the emperor of his power.

Under foreign influence Japanese culture began to change in ways that both pleased and horrified Mishima. His home, once described as "almost determinedly un-Japanese," was full of English antiques. Even his writing contained more references to classic French literature than to Japanese. But Mishima grew to hate the Westernization that he felt was causing the dissolution of traditional Japanese ideals. In 1968 he formed a private army of eighty-three university men who were also interested in the martial arts and who believed in the way of the samurai. The goal of the Tate No Kai, or Shield Society, was to return Japan to the samurai tradition.

One of the ancient samurai rituals that Mishima and his followers believed in was *seppuku,* a form of suicide reserved for the samurai warrior. In this painful ritual the subject kneels and slices open his abdomen, releasing the intestines. "Standing behind the subject is a samurai with a sword," a *New Yorker* writer explained, "whose function is to behead the subject at the first sign of pain, or even the slightest alteration of the traditional posture."

Apparently Mishima began to plan his suicide several years in advance. Perhaps to prove his perfect physical condition, he posed in 1969 for a photographic study of various postures of death, including death by drowning, by duel, and by *hara-kiri.* In addition, a few weeks before his suicide he displayed at a Tokyo department store a series of photographs of himself in the nude. The author was also prepared mentally for the final act. In a letter to Ivan Morris just before his death, Mishima wrote: "After thinking and thinking through four years, I came to wish to sacrifice myself for the old, beautiful tradition of Japan, which is disappearing very quickly day by day."

On November 25, 1970, Mishima and four of his followers from the Shield Society entered the headquarters of Japan's Eastern Ground Self-Defense Forces, took its commander, Lt. General Kanetoshi Mashida, hostage, and demanded that soldiers be assembled on a parade ground below. As 1,200 men quickly gathered, Mishima went out on a balcony, his kamikaze-style headband fluttering in the breeze, and shouted: "Listen to me! I have waited in vain for four years for you to take arms in an uprising. Are you warriors? If so, why do you strive to guard the constitution that is designed to deny the very reason for the existence of your organization? Why can't you realize that so long as this constitution exists, you cannot be saved? Isn't there anyone among you willing to hurl his body against the constitution that has turned Japan spineless? Let us stand up and fight together and die together for something that is far more important than our life. That is not freedom or democracy, but the most important thing for us all, Japan."

When his words were greeted with angry heckling by the soldiers, Mishima shouted "Tenno Heika Banzai!" ("Long live the Emperor!"), stepped back from the balcony, and proceeded to perform in exact detail the traditional seppuku ceremony. A *Time* reporter related the dramatic event: "Mishima stripped to the waist and knelt on the floor. . . . Probing the left side of his abdomen, he put the ceremonial dagger in place, then thrust it deep into his flesh. Standing behind him, Masakatsu Morita, 25, one of his most devoted followers, raised his sword and with one stroke sent Mishima's severed head rolling to the floor. To complete the ceremony, Morita plunged a dagger into his own stomach, and yet another student lopped off Morita's head. Shedding tears, the three surviving students saluted the two dead men and surrendered to the general's aides." The *New Yorker* writer pointed out later that Mishima's seventeen-centimeter incision displayed "a degree of mastery over physical reflex, and over pain itself, unparalleled in modern records of this ritual."

Ironically, this man so obsessed with death had been greatly admired for his charisma and vitality. Throughout his life he had followed a hectic schedule of writing, acting, singing, directing, exercising, running his private army, and pursuing an active social life. John Nathan, in his biography *Mishima*, described the energetic author: "Mishima has a rare capacity for enjoying himself, and he loves nothing better than a party. He has only to walk into a room full of people and it belongs to him. He is not a large man, but his presence is so palpable it can be stifling. . . . Mishima weighs into a party with gusto, delighting over the food, mixing experimental drinks, neighing hoarsely at all the jokes, including his own. . . . Mishima is clever, amusing, astute, catty."

Although many critics pointed out the paradox of Mishima's captivation with both life and death, East and West, Masao Miyoshi, writing in *Accomplices of Silence,* averred that the author "was an amazingly consistent person, who never forgot his wartime catechism—the myth of Japan as a ritually ordered state, the samurai way of life characterized by manly courage and feminine grace, and the vision of imminent death as the catalyst of life."

Since his death, Mishima's reputation has grown abroad with re-issuing of *The Sea of Fertility* as well as some of his earlier works. Similarly, his plays continue to be produced both in Japan and abroad,

If you enjoy the works of Yukio Mishima, you might want to check out the following books:

Junichiro Tanizaki, *The Makioka Sisters,* 1957.
Yasunari Kawabata, *The Master of Go,* 1972.
Kenzaburo Oe, *The Silent Cry,* 1974.

and Mishima has been called one of the literary giants of the twentieth century. Mishima's political legacy has also been almost as strong. While other right-wing politicians distanced themselves from Mishima after his dramatic double suicide, the very goals he purportedly died to propagandize have come to pass. As a contributor for the *Economist* pointed out, Mishima criticized the emperor for renouncing his divinity, and since 1970 "conservative governments have underwritten the resumption of ceremonies implying the emperor's godliness." Mishima's desire for Japanese rearmament likewise took root, and "Japan now has (on some accounts) the world's third biggest defence budget." Mishima also called for restoration of the country's pre-war symbols, and "bit by bit, the national flag and anthems . . . have resumed a central place in school events and public ceremonies." The *Economist* journalist concluded, "Mishima's gloom seems to many Japanese prophetic. Bizarre as he was, Mishima expressed a common sentiment that Japan was losing touch with its soul."

■ Biographical and Critical Sources

BOOKS

Appignanesi, Richard, *Yukio Mishima's Report to the Emperor* (novel), Sinclair-Stevenson (London, England), 2002.
Contemporary Literary Criticism, Gale (Detroit, MI), Volume 2, 1974, Volume 4, 1975, Volume 6, 1976, Volume 9, 1978.
Dictionary of Literary Biography, Volume 182: *Japanese Fiction Writers since World War II,* Gale (Detroit, MI), 1997, pp. 121-134.
Drama Criticism, Volume 1, Gale (Detroit, MI), 1991.
Encyclopedia of World Biography, 2nd edition, Gale (Detroit, MI), 1998.
Gay and Lesbian Biography, St. James Press (Detroit, MI), 1997.

Keene, Donald, *Landscapes and Portraits,* Kodansha International (Tokyo, Japan), 1971.

Keene, Donald, *Dawn to the West,* Holt, Rinehart (New York, NY), 1985.

Mishima, Yukio, *Temple of the Golden Pavilion,* translated by Ivan Morris, introduction by Nancy Wilson Ross, Knopf (New York, NY), 1959.

Miyoshi, Masao, *Accomplices of Silence: The Modern Japanese Novel,* University of California Press (Berkeley, CA), 1974.

Nathan, John, *Mishima: A Biography,* Little, Brown (Boston, MA), 1974.

Scott-Stokes, Henry, *Life and Death of Yukio Mishima,* Farrar, Straus (New York, NY), 1974, revised edition, Noonday Press (New York, NY), 1995.

Short Story Criticism, Volume 4, Gale (Detroit, MI), 1990.

Starrs, Roy, *Deadly Dialectics: Sex, Violence, and Nihilism in the World of Yukio Mishima,* University of Hawaii Press (Honolulu, HI), 1994.

Yourcenar, Marguerite, *Mishima: A Vision of the Void,* translated by Albert Manguel, Ellis (Henley on Thames, England), 1985.

PERIODICALS

AB Bookman's Weekly, January 4, 1971.

Atlantic, April, 1968; September, 1977; September, 1990, James Fallows, review of *The Sea of Fertility,* pp. 117-121.

Best Sellers, April 15, 1968; September 1, 1969.

Booklist, August, 1998, Allen Weakland, review of *Silk and Insight,* p. 1967.

Books Abroad, winter, 1968; spring, 1969; spring, 1971.

Books and Bookmen, August, 1970; February, 1971; December 1974.

Commonweal, March 19, 1971.

Contemporary Literature, winter, 1975.

Critique, Volume X, number 2, 1968; Volume XII, number 1, 1970.

Daily Telegraph, June 29, 2001, Charles Spencer, "Mishima at His Most Mesmerising."

Detroit News, August 20, 1972.

Economist, November 11, 1995, "The Man Japan Wants to Forget," pp. 85-86.

Encounter, May, 1975.

Esquire, May, 1972.

Harper's, September, 1972.

Independent (London, England), May 16, 2001, Rhoda Koenig, "The Family Who Fell from Grace with One Another," p. 10; June 29, 2001, Paul Taylor, "A Night of Fatal Love and Despair," p. 9; July 2, 2001, p. 12.

Library Journal, September 1, 1998, Michael Rogers, review of *Silk and Insight,* p. 224; May 1, 1999, Michael Rogers, review of *Thirst for Love,* p. 118.

Life, September 2, 1966; December 11, 1970.

Listener, May 5, 1967; April 25, 1968.

Nation, June 12, 1972.

New Republic, June 24, 1972; June 21, 1993, pp. 29-31.

New Statesman, April 7, 1967; November 30, 1973; July 19, 1974.

Newsweek, December 7, 1970; February 8, 1971.

New Yorker, June 15, 1968; December 12, 1970.

New York Review of Books, September 25, 1969; June 17, 1971.

New York Times, March 1, 1967; January 7, 1970; November 25, 1970; November 26, 1970; November 27, 1970; December 10, 1970; March 24, 1971; July 6, 1972; November 1, 1972.

New York Times Book Review, May 1, 1966; June 28, 1968; January 3, 1971; November 12, 1972; June 24, 1973; October 14, 1973; December 2, 1973; May 12, 1974.

Observer (London, England), June 8, 1967; May 31, 1970; July 28, 1974; July 1, 2001, Susannah Clapp, "When Noh Means Yes," p. 11.

Observer Review, September 1, 1968; May 31, 1970; March 14, 1971.

Paris Review, spring, 1995, pp. 140-160.

Saturday Review, May 7, 1966; December 12, 1970; June 10, 1972; December 2, 1972.

Saturday Review/World, June 1, 1974.

Spectator, August 30, 1968.

Studies in the Novel, summer, 1999, Marjorie Rhine, "Glossing Scripts and Scripting Pleasure in Mishima's *Confessions of a Mask,*" p. 222.

Time, May 24, 1968; December 7, 1970; October 15, 1973; June 10, 1974.

Times Literary Supplement, April 20, 1967; September 19, 1968; July 2, 1970; March 12, 1971; August 20, 1971; November 10, 1972; November 30, 1973; July 26, 1974.

Variety, July 15, 1970; December 9, 1970; December 30, 1970; April 7, 1971.

Virginia Quarterly Review, autumn, 1968; winter, 1970; autumn, 1973.

Washington Post Book World, June 2, 1968; September 21, 1969; July 2, 1972; July 22, 1973; May 19, 1974.

World Literature Today, spring, 1999, Marleigh Grayer Ryan, review of *Silk and Insight,* p. 389.

Yale Review, summer, 1975.

OTHER

Mishima Yukio Cyber Museum, http://www.vill.yamanakako.yamanashi.jp/bungaku/mishima/ (October 1, 2002).

Schrader, Paul, *Mishima: A Life in Four Chapters* (biographical film), 1985.

Yukio Mishima, http://www.kirjasto.sci.fi/ (October 1, 2002).*

Farley Mowat

Personal

Surname rhymes with "poet"; born May 12, 1921, in Belleville, Ontario, Canada; son of Angus McGill (a librarian) and Helen Elizabeth (Thomson) Mowat; married Frances Thornhill, 1947 (marriage ended, 1959); married Claire A. Wheeler (a writer), March, 1964; children: (first marriage) Robert Alexander, David Peter. *Nationality:* Canadian. *Education:* University of Toronto, B.A., 1949.

Addresses

Home—Port Hope, Ontario, Canada, and Cape Breton, Nova Scotia. *Agent*—c/o Key Porter Books Ltd., 70 The Esplanade, Toronto, Ontario M5E 1R2, Canada.

Career

Author. *Military service:* Canadian Army, Infantry and Intelligence Corps, 1940-46; became captain.

Awards, Honors

President's Medal for best Canadian short story, University of Western Ontario, 1952, for "Eskimo Spring"; Anisfield-Wolfe Award, 1954, for *People of the Deer*; Governor General's Medal (Canada) for juvenile literature, 1957, and Book of the Year for Children award, Canadian Association of Children's Librarians, and International Board on Books for Young People Honour List (Canada), both 1958, all for *Lost in the Barrens*; Canadian Women's Clubs award, 1958, for *The Dog Who Wouldn't Be*; Boys' Club Junior Book Award, Boys' Club of America, 1963, for *Owls in the Family*; National Association of Independent Schools Award, 1963, for juvenile books; Hans Christian Andersen Honour List, 1965, for juvenile books; Canadian Centennial Medal, 1967; Stephen Leacock Medal, Stephen Leacock Foundation, 1970, and L'etoile de la Mer Honours List, 1972, both for *The Boat Who Wouldn't Float*; honorary D.Lit., Laurentian University, 1970; Vicky Metcalf Award, Canadian Authors' Association, 1971, for body of work; Doctor of Law from Lethbridge University and University of Toronto, both 1973, and University of Prince Edward Island, 1979; Book of the Year, Canadian Association of Children's Librarians, 1976; Curran Award, 1977, for "contributions to understanding wolves"; Queen Elizabeth II Jubilee Medal, 1978; Knight of Mark Twain, 1980; New York Public Library's Books for the Teen Age, 1980, for *The Great Betrayal: Arctic Canada Now,* and 1981, for *And No Birds Sang*; Officer, Order of Canada, 1981; Doctor of Literature, University of Victoria, 1982, and Lakehead University, 1986; Author's Award, Foundation for the Advancement of

Canadian Letters, 1985, for *Sea of Slaughter;* Book of the Year designation, Foundation for the Advancement of Canadian Letters, and named Author of the Year, Canadian Booksellers Association, both 1988, both for *Virunga;* Gemini Award for best documentary script, 1989, for *The New North;* Torgi Talking Book of the Year, Canadian National Institute of the Blind, 1989, for *Virunga;* Canadian Achievers Award, Toshiba, 1990; Award of Excellence, Atlantic Film Festival, for outstanding achievement in narration, Conservation Film of the Year, Wildscreen Film Festival, and finalist, American Cable Entertainment Awards, all 1990, all for *Sea of Slaughter;* Take Back the Nation Award, Council of Canadians, 1991; L.H. D., McMaster University, 1994; L.L.D., Queen's University, 1995; D.Litt., University College of Cape Breton, 1996; Fourth National Prize for Foreign Literature Books, Beiyue Literature and Art Publishing House, 1999, for *Never Cry Wolf, Sea of Slaughter, A Whale for the Killing,* and *People of the Deer.*

■ **Writings**

FOR YOUNG ADULTS

Lost in the Barrens (novel), illustrated by Charles Geer, Atlantic/Little, Brown (Boston, MA), 1956, published as *Two against the North,* illustrated by Alan Daniel, Scholastic-TAB (New York, NY), 1977.

The Dog Who Wouldn't Be (nonfiction), illustrated by Paul Galdone, Atlantic/Little, Brown (Boston, MA), 1957.

Owls in the Family (nonfiction), illustrated by Robert Frankenberg, Atlantic/Little, Brown (Boston, MA), 1961, revised edition, McClelland & Stewart (Toronto, Ontario, Canada), 1973.

The Black Joke (novel), illustrated by D. Johnson, McClelland & Stewart (Toronto, Ontario, Canada), 1962, revised edition, 1973, American edition, illustrated by Victor Mays, Atlantic/Little, Brown (Boston, MA), 1963.

The Curse of the Viking Grave (novel), illustrated by Charles Geer, Atlantic/Little, Brown (Boston, MA), 1966.

NONFICTION FOR ADULTS

People of the Deer, Atlantic/Little, Brown (Boston, MA), 1952, revised edition, McClelland & Stewart (Toronto, Ontario, Canada), 1975.

The Regiment, McClelland & Stewart (Toronto, Ontario, Canada), 1954, revised edition, 1973.

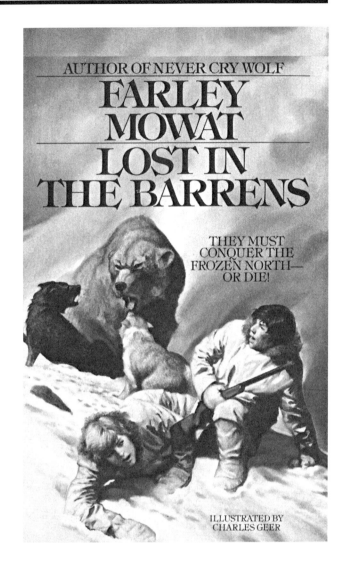

Released in the United States under the title *Two against the North,* Farley Mowat's first novel for young adults finds two teens using their survival skills in a fight to weather a winter on Canada's Arctic tundra.

(Editor) Samuel Hearne, *Coppermine Journey: An Account of a Great Adventure,* Atlantic/Little, Brown (Boston, MA), 1958.

The Grey Seas Under: The Perilous Rescue Missions of a North Atlantic Salvage Tug, Atlantic/Little, Brown (Boston, MA), 1958, reprinted, Lyons Press (New York, NY), 2001.

The Desperate People, Atlantic/Little, Brown (Boston, MA), 1959, revised edition, McClelland & Stewart (Toronto, Ontario, Canada), 1975.

(Editor) *Ordeal by Ice: The Search for the Northwest Passage* (also see below), McClelland & Stewart (Toronto, Ontario, Canada), 1960, Atlantic/Little, Brown (Boston, MA), 1961, revised edition, 1973.

The Serpent's Coil: An Incredible Story of Hurricane-battered Ships and the Heroic Men Who Fought to Save Them, McClelland & Stewart (Toronto, Ontario, Canada), 1961, Atlantic/Little, Brown (Boston, MA), 1962, reprinted, Lyons Press (New York, NY), 2001.

Never Cry Wolf, Atlantic/Little, Brown (Boston, MA), 1963, revised edition, McClelland & Stewart (Toronto, Ontario, Canada), 1973, reprinted, Holt (New York, NY), 2000.

Westviking: The Ancient Norse in Greenland and North America, illustrated by wife, Claire Wheeler, Atlantic/Little, Brown (Boston, MA), 1965.

(Editor) *The Polar Passion: The Quest for the North Pole* (also see below), McClelland & Stewart (Toronto, Ontario, Canada), 1967, revised edition, 1973, Atlantic/Little, Brown (Boston, MA), 1968.

Canada North, Atlantic/Little, Brown (Boston, MA), 1968.

This Rock within the Sea: A Heritage Lost, illustrated with photographs by John de Visser, McClelland & Stewart (Toronto, Ontario, Canada), 1968, Atlantic/Little, Brown (Boston, MA), 1969, new edition, McClelland & Stewart (Toronto, Ontario, Canada), 1976.

The Boat Who Wouldn't Float, McClelland & Stewart (Toronto, Ontario, Canada), 1969, Atlantic/Little, Brown (Boston, MA), 1970.

The Siberians, Atlantic/Little, Brown (Boston, MA), 1970, published in Canada as *Sibir: My Discovery of Siberia,* McClelland & Stewart (Toronto, Ontario, Canada), 1970, revised edition, 1973.

A Whale for the Killing, Atlantic/Little, Brown (Boston, MA), 1972.

Wake of the Great Sealers, illustrated by David Blackwood, Atlantic/Little, Brown (Boston, MA), 1973.

(Editor) *Tundra: Selections from the Great Accounts of Arctic Land Voyages* (also see below), McClelland & Stewart (Toronto, Ontario, Canada), 1973.

The Great Betrayal: Arctic Canada Now (sequel to *Canada North*), 1976, published in Canada as *Canada North Now: The Great Betrayal,* illustrated with photographs by Shin Sugini, McClelland & Stewart (Toronto, Ontario, Canada), 1976.

Top of the World Trilogy (includes *Ordeal by Ice, Polar Passion,* and *Tundra*), McClelland & Stewart (Toronto, Ontario, Canada), 1976.

And No Birds Sang (autobiography), Atlantic/Little, Brown (Boston, MA), 1979.

The World of Farley Mowat: A Selection from His Works, edited by Peter Davison, Atlantic/Little, Brown (Boston, MA), 1980.

Sea of Slaughter, McClelland & Stewart (Toronto, Ontario, Canada), 1984, Atlantic/Little, Brown (Boston, MA), 1985, reprinted, with a new afterword by the author, Chapters (Shelburne, VT), 1996.

My Discovery of America, McClelland & Stewart (Toronto, Ontario, Canada), 1985, Atlantic/Little, Brown (Boston, MA), 1986.

Woman in the Mists: The Story of Dian Fossey and the Mountain Gorillas of Africa, Warner (New York, NY), 1987, published in Canada as *Virunga: The Passion of Dian Fossey,* McClelland & Stewart (Toronto, Ontario, Canada), 1987.

The New Founde Land, McClelland & Stewart (Toronto, Ontario, Canada), 1989.

Rescue the Earth: Conversations with the Green Crusaders, McClelland & Stewart (Toronto, Ontario, Canada), 1990.

My Father's Son: Memories of War and Peace, Houghton Mifflin (Boston, MA), 1992.

Born Naked, Key Porter Books (Toronto, Ontario, Canada), 1993, Houghton Mifflin (Boston, MA), 1994.

Aftermath: Travels in a Post-War World, Key Porter Books (Toronto, Ontario, Canada), 1995, Roberts Rinehart (Boulder, CO), 1996.

A Farley Mowat Reader, Roberts Rinehart (Boulder, CO), 1997.

The Farfarers: Before the Norse, Key Porter Books (Toronto, Ontario, Canada), 1998, Steerforth Press (South Royalton, VT), 2000, published as *The Alban Quest: The Search for a Lost Tribe,* Weidenfeld & Nicolson (London, England), 1999.

Walking on the Land, Key Porter Books (Toronto, Ontario, Canada), 2000, Steerforth Press (South Royalton, VT), 2001.

OTHER

The Snow Walker (short story collection), Atlantic/Little, Brown (Boston, MA), 1975.

Author of television screenplays *Sea Fare,* 1963, and *Diary of a Boy on Vacation,* 1964. Contributor to *Cricket's Choice,* Open Court, 1974, and to magazines, including *Saturday Evening Post, Argosy, Maclean's,* and *Cricket.* Mowat's books have been translated into more than twenty languages and anthologized in more than 400 works. His manuscripts are held at McMaster University, Hamilton, Ontario, Canada.

■ **Adaptations**

Films include *A Whale for the Killing* (TV movie), American Broadcasting Co. (ABC-TV), 1980; *Never Cry Wolf* (feature film), Disney, 1983; *The New North* (documentary), Norwolf/Noralpha/CTV, 1989; *Sea of Slaughter* (documentary), Canadian Broadcasting Corp. (CBC-TV), 1990; *Lost in the Barrens* (TV

A pair of adopted owls named Weeps and Wol turn a small household upside down in Mowat's comic 1961 novel *Owls in the Family*, illustrated by Robert Frankenberg.

movie), Atlantis Films, 1992; and *Curse of the Viking Grave* (TV movie), Atlantis Films, 1992. Audio cassette recordings include *And No Birds Sang,* Books on Tape (Newport Beach, CA), 1991; *Grey Seas Under,* Books on Tape (Newport Beach, CA), 1994; *Lost in the Barrens,* Books on Tape (Newport Beach, CA), 1994; *Never Cry Wolf,* Books on Tape (Newport Beach, CA), 1994, *People of the Deer,* Books on Tape (Newport Beach, CA), 1994; *The Snow Walker,* Books on Tape (Newport Beach, CA), 1994; *A Whale for the Killing,* Books on Tape (Newport Beach, CA), 1994; and *Born Naked,* Books on Tape (Newport Beach, CA), 1995.

■ Sidelights

Farley Mowat is considered by many to be "Canada's most famous author of nature lore," according to John Bemrose writing in *Maclean's.* With nearly forty published books and fourteen million copies of his works printed in thirty-five languages, Mowat's influence stretches far beyond the borders of his native country. Dubbed an "environmentalist and literary 'agent provocateur,'" by Ben Macintyre in the London *Times,* Mowat writes for both adults and children and is known for his vivid powers of observation and the flair of his nonfiction storytelling technique, employing what he himself calls "subjective nonfiction" effects. Winner of dozens of awards and honors, Mowat infuses his work with an affection for the Canadian wilderness and its inhabitants, both human and other animals. His books offer tragic glimpses of the extinction of species at the hand of so-called "civilized" humans as well as strong warnings about the future of a human race that devours natural resources unchecked. "Mowat has a remarkably humble view of his place—of man's place in general—in the scheme of things," noted Valerie Wyatt in *Profiles.* "He believes that man is no more and no less important than any of the other animals that inhabit the planet, and he has lived by this philosophy, elaborating on it in his books."

Many of Mowat's works—like *Never Cry Wolf, People of the Deer,* and *A Whale for the Killing*—are written for adult audiences but can also be understood and appreciated by young adult readers. On the other hand, Mowat's children's books—like *The Dog Who Wouldn't Be, Owls in the Family,* and *Lost in the Barrens*—offer stories adults can enjoy. "Mowat is a natural writer for children," claimed Sheila Egoff in *The Republic of Childhood: A Critical Guide to Canadian Children's Literature in English.* "He writes from his own experience, both childhood and adult. With his direct, simple, and lively style he can reveal aspects of life that are necessary in good children's literature if it is to have any enduring value. Qualities such as cruelty, irony, satire—gentled of course—give life and depth to children's literature and they are present in all Mowat's animal stories. They are implied in the style and confronted squarely in the realistic details."

Early Love of Nature

Mowat was born in Belleville, Ontario, the son of Angus, a librarian and frustrated novelist, and Helen, and the great-grandson of Sir Oliver Mowat, premier of Ontario from 1872 to 1896. The author once described himself in an interview as "pretty much an outcast" who spent much of his time reading, wandering in the woods, and writing about nature. While Mowat was still young his family moved frequently. Eventually they found themselves in Saskatoon, Saskatchewan, where his father became head librarian. "It seemed we were always picking up and leaving," Mowat told the interviewer. Still, he made the best of the situation. "I spent monstrous amounts of time in the libraries my father directed," he said. "To his everlasting credit, he never directed my reading. . . . In some of his libraries they kept the 'bad books' under the counter. These I would spirit home by the armful and devour in solitary splendor. My father, of course, knew full well and gave me nothing but encouragement for my writing as well as for my reading."

His father, an avid outdoorsman, introduced his son to sailing and hunting expeditions, instilling in young Farley "a taste for the wild," as Bemrose noted in *Maclean's.* The father was something of a free spirit—Mowat once described him as the original hippie—and was not faithful to his wife, who increasingly found refuge in invalidism. Wayne Grady, writing in the *Globe and Mail,* called Mowat's mother "long-suffering," and a woman "who believed she had married beneath her station." A bit of a loner and unable to find many friends as a youth because of his frequent moves and his small size, Mowat found his own solace in observing birds and animals, collecting pets such as his dog, Mutt, and in writing—a calling he pursued from his earliest years. While living in Windsor, Ontario, the seven year old was happily composing verse; when they moved to Saskatoon, the thirteen year old had his own column in the local paper detailing his observations of birds.

Another inspirational figure was Mowat's uncle Frank Farley, who was an avid naturalist and tireless traveler. Under his uncle's tutelage, Mowat learned to collect specimens the old-fashioned way: he shot wildlife and stuffed the skins with cotton and took birds' eggs from nests to be sent to museums. "As a lad I felt quite the scientist tromping through the woods murdering things and contemplating corpses in the hallowed halls of museums," Mowat recalled. Time altered his perspective, however, and by fifteen he was banding birds rather than shooting them. In fact, he was the youngest Canadian ever to be issued a permit to band birds.

"It was my uncle Frank Farley who first took me to the far north where I saw the great herds of caribou migrating across the tundra," Mowat remembered. "It would prove momentous in my life." Mowat became more and more entranced by a region of the Canadian Arctic known as "the barrens." His chance to explore was cut short by history, however. Just as he was graduating from high school, World War II broke out, and he joined his father's old regiment, the Hastings and Prince Edward, which saw brutal

fighting during the invasion of Italy. "The war changed my thinking radically," Mowat noted. "I had had no real sense of fear, cruelty, madness, and horror before seeing combat in Italy. . . . I saved myself during the last part of my infantry experience by writing what would eventually become *The Dog Who Wouldn't Be.* Amid the bombs, grenades, strafing, death, and dying, I tried to steep myself in the funny, idyllic world of my childhood." Mowat was discharged in 1946, having advanced to the rank of captain. Back in Canada, Mowat went to college at the University of Toronto, graduating in 1949.

Seeks Solitude of Nature

"After the war, I deliberately sought out solitude," Mowat said. "I wanted to get away from my own species. I didn't like myself for being one of them." Mowat headed for the Canadian wilderness and spent some time in the company of various Eskimo and Native American tribes, especially the Ihalmiut ("People of the Deer"). During 1947 and 1948, while still a student, he worked in the Northwest Territories as a student biologist, and it was chiefly this experience which led to the author's first book, *People of the Deer,* which chronicles the Ihalmiuts' near extinction as a tribe due to the interference of white traders and the Canadian government. The work was extremely controversial—Mowat condemned his government for its insensitivity to Native American problems. *New York Times Book Review* critic Walter O'Hearn called Mowat "Canada's angriest young man" and added: "If we are at last fumbling toward a grasp of the Eskimo problem, the goading of Farley Mowat is one of the reasons. He has convictions and he can express them in prose that sears the conscience."

Seven years after the publication of his first book, *People of the Deer,* Mowat returned to its tragic story of the Ihalmiut in *The Desperate People,* and then again in the year 2000 he dealt with the same topic in *Walking on the Land.* In "this passionate account," as Margaret W. Norton called it in *Library Journal,* he recounts the effects of disease, starvation, and violence on the gentle Inuit band a decade after his first visit. Explaining why he chose to revisit the plight of the Ihalmiut, Mowat wrote in the prologue: "My principal reason for doing so is the same as that of writers who continue to tell the story of the Holocaust: to help ensure that man's inhuman acts are not expunged from memory, thereby easing the way for repetitions of such horrors." Reviewing *Walking on the Land* in *Booklist,* Gilbert Taylor noted that Mowat's "skillful writing, familiar to many fans, should also engage new readers as well as

NEVER CRY WOLF | FARLEY MOWAT

The Amazing True Story of Life Among Arctic Wolves

"AN ENGAGING BOOK... WRITTEN WITH GRACE AND SKILL... FASCINATING." —*NEW YORK TIMES*

Naturalist Mowat's multi-award-winning account of a summer during which he studied the wolf packs making their home on the Arctic tundra was first published in 1963.

anyone concerned about indigenous people." Susan Salter Reynolds, reviewing the same book in the *Los Angeles Times,* found Mowat's story of government abuse and Ihalmiut debilitation "shocking."

Mowat also spent the early postwar years studying wolf behavior in the barrens. He set out to determine what role the wolves were playing in the dwindling numbers of caribou. After months of detailed observation, Mowat discovered that the wolves ate more mice than caribou. In order to convince himself that an animal the size of a wolf could subsist on mice, he began to eat a diet of mice too. When he survived the experiment in good health, he made a report to the government—and was fired.

Mowat's experience among the wolves is chronicled in *Never Cry Wolf,* perhaps his best-known adult

work. "Much of what I discovered about wolves flies in the face of our received notions about this species," he told an interviewer. "I learned that wolves mate for life, live in devoted family groups which absorb widowed relations as members of the nuclear family unit, are extremely affectionate and playful, and are far less violent than man. I never saw a wolf commit a wanton act of destruction, cruelty, or maliciousness." *Never Cry Wolf* was published in the Soviet Union as *Wolves, Please Don't Cry!* There it had a significant impact on the treatment of wolves—the government legislated an end to wholesale slaughter of the animals. Mowat himself admitted that he took poetic license with the writing of the book, blending fact and fiction somewhat for effect and to make his message stronger. A reviewer for *Maclean's* later called the book a "spoof and a potboiler," but also a "passionate defence of the wolf." Publication of the book made Mowat, according to the same contributor, "a true celebrity" in both Canada and the United States, elevating his name to the status of Rachel Carson as "one of the truly great crusaders defending the integrity of the planet against government and corporate interests. . . . A latter-day prophet who railed against the rapid destruction of humanity's bonds to animals, plants, and the earth itself."

A Voice in the Wilderness

Other Mowat titles about man's mistreatment of wildlife followed. *A Whale for the Killing,* published in 1972, recounts the slow torture of a marooned whale in a cove in Newfoundland. This book was inspired by an actual event that took place in the small Newfoundland town of Burgeo, where he and his wife, Claire, had taken refuge from the negative effects of civilization in 1962. Five years later a seventy-foot female fin whale was trapped in a cove near the town, which during the same time had begun to feel the creeping effects of modernity. When word of the whale leaked out, men from a local factory started using the animal for target practice. Soon thirty shooters were out, enjoying their perverse sport of shooting the mammal. By the time Mowat found out about the creature and its plight, it was too late to save her. The Mowats left their "idyllic" village soon thereafter, but it took Mowat five more years before he could digest the barbarity of the act in order to write about it in *A Whale for the Killing.* Writing in *Dictionary of Literary Biography,* Eric Thompson noted that "the book did arouse international attention to the plight of the whale as an endangered species, and that, more than anything else, is the true measure of its value."

Sea of Slaughter, another of Mowat's most popular titles, offers a wider view of extinction along the Eastern Seaboard of North America, and *Woman in the Mists: The Story of Dian Fossey and the Mountain Gorillas of Africa* chronicles one field biologist's attempts to save the species she studied. Mowat told *Authors and Artists for Young Adults* that his purpose in these books "was not simply to depress everyone, including myself, but [to warn] that we must change our attitudes toward the species with which we inhabit this earth. We must, in every sense, *share* the planet with them, or we will become its ultimate destroyers. . . . The earth was once *very different and much richer* than it presently is. . . . We have a responsibility to look back in anger and to use that anger to try to salvage the present and ensure the future."

Mowat has gone on to write books on many subjects, ranging from books about the far North, such as *Ordeal By Ice, The Polar Passion, Tundra,* and *Sibir: My Discovery of Siberia,* to the history of salvage operations in *The Grey Seas* and *The Serpent's Coil,* called Mowat's "paean to tugboats of the North Atlantic" by Michael Rogers in a *Library Journal* review.

Mowat has also written memoirs, including *Born Naked,* and books of personal history and travel regarding the Second World War, such as *The Regiment, And No Birds Sang, My Father's Son: Memories of War and Peace,* and *Aftermath: Travels in a Post-War World.* Reviewing *Born Naked,* a *Publishers Weekly* contributor found the book to be "delightful," while *Booklist*'s John Mort called it a "mostly sweet memoir." In an *Atlantic* review of *My Father's Son,* Phoebe-Lou Adams found this war memoir in parts "hilarious," while a *Publishers Weekly* contributor found the same gathering of correspondence "a fine portrait of a young man's coming-of-age." However, reviewing Mowat's *Aftermath,* a travelogue of his European war haunts, Bemrose noted in *Maclean's* that "too often [Mowat's] descriptions are conventional, while his dialogue sounds lifted from an industrial training film." Bemrose went on to note, though, that sometimes "the sheer originality of the material . . . asserts itself."

In 1996 a minor scandal broke out surrounding Mowat's use of facts in his work. A writer for the Ca-

Charles Martin Smith stars in the film adaptation of Mowat's classic nonfiction work *Never Cry Wolf,* which was directed by Carroll Ballard and released in 1983.

On the set of the film adaptation of *Never Cry Wolf;* from left to right, actor Charles Martin Smith, author Farley Mowat, and producer Lewis Allen.

nadian magazine *Saturday Night* accused Mowat of playing fast and loose with factual material in his books. John Goddard maintained that Mowat "has broken a trust with his public." The prolific author, in his mid-seventies at the time, brushed off the criticism by saying that he had always admitted to certain factual errors in his books, changing names and locations in his nonfiction books, and reworking some of the tales he had heard to achieve the proper effect. The debate did not last long, and Mowat was soon on to another book, *The Farfarers: Before the Norse,* in which he spins a new tale of the discovery of America: not by the ancient Norse Vikings, but by ancient Scots, or Albans. According to Mowat's recounting, based on stone structures in the Arctic as well as the tales of ancient sailors which he has long been collecting, these inhabitants of ancient Britain were first forced from their homes by the Vikings and then went to Iceland in skin-covered boats. When the Vikings came to Iceland,

the Albans moved on to Greenland; then when the Vikings came to Greenland, the Albans moved on to the west, reaching Newfoundland in the tenth century.

"Is this a crank theory?" asked Christopher Moore in a review of *The Farfarers* in *Maclean's.* "The difference between Mowat and crank theorist, perhaps, is that Mowat is not a crank." Based in part on research he had done for his 1965 title, *Westviking: The Ancient Norse in Greenland and North America,* Mowat's *The Farfarers* had other critics posing questions, as well. For Moore, however, on balance the book is a work of the "historical imagination," but nonetheless one "worth the voyage." Peter Schledermann, writing in *Canadian Geographic,* remarked that Mowat "spins a great yarn and does it well—a true saga writer." But ultimately Schledermann found the theory behind the work to be "an enormous stretch of the best imaginations." Other reviewers followed this tack. A contributor for *Pub-*

lishers Weekly commented that the book "is best enjoyed as a richly detailed and imaginative reconstruction," while *Booklist*'s Julia Glynn concluded, "Mowat has written a fascinating account of his contentious and latest concept."

Writer for Many Audiences

Mowat's message of responsibility is echoed in his books for children, but in a more lighthearted vein. In his novel *Lost in the Barrens,* for instance, a pair of teenaged boys faces a winter alone on the tundra. Their survival depends on a knowledge of the wilderness (on the part of the Indian boy) and an innovative spirit (in the city-bred boy). *Lost in the Barrens* won the prestigious Governor General's Award in Canada and helped to establish Mowat's literary reputation. The book remains, according to Thomp-

son, "an exciting yarn of two boys' discovery of the Arctic wilderness."

Two other books Mowat wrote for juveniles, *The Dog Who Wouldn't Be* and *Owls in the Family,* are memoirs of rather eccentric family pets. Mutt, the dog, has a penchant for climbing fences and trees, while his owl companions, Wol and Weeps, bring dead skunks to the dinner table and feud with cats and crows. Alec Lucas, writing in his *Farley Mowat,* called *The Dog Who Wouldn't Be* an "ingenious mixture of beast fable, tall tale, and satire." Thompson called three of Mowat's autobiographical tales—*The Dog Who Wouldn't Be, Never Cry Wolf,* and *The Boat Who Wouldn't Float*—books with a "strangely elegiac quality, not dissimilar to the motif of the loss of innocence which is a natural element in the war books." In an essay for the *British Columbia Library Quarterly,* Joseph E. Carver contended that Mowat "knows children and what they like and can open

A photograph of Mowat's parents, Angus and Helen Mowat, from the naturalist's autobiography *Born Naked,* published in 1993.

doors to adventures both credible and entertaining to his young readers. His stories are credible because Mowat wanted to write them to give permanence to the places, loyalties and experiences of his youth; entertaining because the author enjoys the telling of them. . . . Because almost all of his writing is autobiographical, . . . he relives his experiences so vividly and exuberantly that the action rings with an authenticity the reader cannot help but enjoy."

According to Theo Hersh in *Children's Books and Their Creators*, "Mowat's great gift to children's literature is twofold: He brings his own love of nature to his stories, and he spices it up with his wry sense of humor." Mowat is certainly one of the best-known Canadian writers for children outside the bounds of his own country. His works have been translated and sold in the millions all over the world. In the *Canadian Library Journal*, Mowat stated that "it is an absolute duty" for authors to devote a significant part of their time to writing for youngsters. "It is of absolutely vital importance if basic changes for the good are ever to be initiated in any human culture," he noted. For his own part, he concluded, "the writing of young people's books has been fun—and some of the best and most enduring fun I have ever known."

If you enjoy the works of Farley Mowat, you might want to check out the following books:

Gary Paulsen, *Hatchet*, 1987.
Mette Newth, *The Abduction*, 1989.
Lynn Hall, *Halsey's Pride*, 1990.

Speaking of Mowat's work in general, Thompson called the writer "essentially romantic in outlook," and a man who "despises the cramping influence of the modern metropolis, preferring the simpler, older rhythms of life in small towns and traditional societies. Sometimes his nostalgia leads him into bathetic pronouncements, but more often it allows him to express something of the truth and beauty of existence as it has been known by ordinary men and women through the ages."

■ **Biographical and Critical Sources**

BOOKS

Beacham's Guide to Literature for Young Adults, Volume 2, Beacham Publishing (Osprey, FL), 1990.

Benson, Eugene, and William Toye, editors, *Oxford Companion to Canadian Literature*, 2nd edition, Oxford University Press (Toronto, Ontario, Canada), 1997.

Children's Literature Review, Volume 20, Gale (Detroit, MI), 1990.

Contemporary Heroes and Heroines, Gale (Detroit, MI), 1998.

Contemporary Literary Criticism, Volume 26, Gale (Detroit, MI), 1983.

Dictionary of Literary Biography, Volume 68: *Canadian Writers, 1920-1959*, Gale (Detroit, MI), 1988, pp. 253-258.

Egoff, Sheila, *The Republic of Childhood: A Critical Guide to Canadian Children's Literature in English*, 2nd edition, Oxford University Press (Don Mills, Ontario, Canada), 1975.

King, James, *Farley: The Life of Farley Mowat*, HarperFlamingo (Toronto, Ontario, Canada), 2002.

Lucas, Alex, *Farley Mowat*, McClelland & Stewart (Toronto, Ontario, Canada), 1976.

Mowat, Farley, *Walking on the Land*, Key Porter Books (Toronto, Ontario, Canada), 2000.

St. James Guide to Young Adult Writers, 2nd edition, St. James Press (Detroit, MI), 1999.

Silvey, Anita, editor, *Children's Books and Their Creators*, Houghton (Boston, MA), 1995.

Wyatt, Valerie, *Profiles*, Canadian Library Association (Ottawa, Ontario, Canada), 1975.

PERIODICALS

Atlantic, February, 1993, Phoebe-Lou Adams, review of *My Father's Son*, pp. 117-118.

Beaver: Exploring Canada's History, December-January, 1998, Christopher Moore, "Farley's Far-out *Farfarers*," pp. 54-55.

Booklist, January 1, 1994, John Mort, review of *Born Naked*, p. 787; September 1, 1996, Alice Joyce, review of *Aftermath*, p. 59; November 15, 1997, Gilbert Taylor, review of *A Farley Mowat Reader*, p. 537; February 1, 2000, Julia Glynn, review of *The Farfarers: Before the Norse*, p. 1006; March 15, 2001, Gilbert Taylor, review of *Walking on the Land*, p. 1330.

British Columbia Library Quarterly, April, 1969, Joseph E. Carver, "Farley Mowat: An Author for All Ages," pp. 10-16.

Canadian Geographic, November-December, 1998, Peter Schledermann, "Is *The Farfarers* Simply Far-Fetched?," p. 18; November, 2000, Stephen Smith, "Horror on the Barrens," p. 107.

Canadian Library Journal, September-October, 1973, Farley Mowat, "A Message from the Patron," p. 391.

Chicago Tribune, May 6, 1985.

Globe and Mail (Toronto, Ontario, Canada), Wayne Grady, review of *Farley: The Life of Farley Mowat.*

Library Journal, January, 2000, Harry Frumerman, review of *The Farfarers,* p. 132; May 1, 2001, Margaret W. Norton, review of *Walking on the Land,* p. 99, June 1, 2001, Michael Rogers, review of *The Grey Seas Under* and *The Serpent's Coil,* p. 226.

Los Angeles Times, December 13, 1985; February 27, 2000, Susan Salter Reynolds, review of *The Farfarers;* June 24, 2001, Susan Salter Reynolds, review of *Walking on the Land,* p. 1.

Maclean's, October 11, 1993, John Bemrose, review of *Born Naked,* p. 76; December 11, 1995, John Bemrose, review of *Aftermath,* p. 68; May 20, 1996, "Sticks and Stones," p. 16; November 23, 1998, Christopher Moore, review of *The Farfarers,* p. 139; August 12, 2002, "Latter-Day Prophet," p. 48.

New York Times, November 8, 1999, "Ha! Taking the Wind out of Leif Ericsson's Sails," p. A4.

New York Times Book Review, November 1, 1959, Walter O'Hearn, review of *People of the Deer;* February 27, 2000, Richard Ellis, review of *The Farfarers,* p. 37.

People, March 31, 1980.

Publishers Weekly, November 23, 1992, review of *My Father's Son: Memories of War and Peace,* p. 47; February 7, 1994, review of *Born Naked,* p. 78; January 3, 2000, review of *The Farfarers,* p. 63.

San Francisco Chronicle, David Crary, "Canadian Author Accused of Pumping Up His Arctic Adventures," p. A8.

Saturday Night, May, 1996, John Goddard, "A Real Whopper," pp. 46-53.

Sunday Times (London, England), York Membery, "Wolf Man of the Arctic Accused of Faking Eskimo Adventures," p. 20.

Time, February 18, 1980; May 6, 1985; October 26, 1987.

Times (London, England), November 8, 1999, Ben Macintyre, "Scots 'Beat Vikings to North America,'" p. 17.

Washington Post, October 9, 1983; April 25, 1985; October 25, 1985; November 6, 1998, "Rethinking the Story of North America's First Inhabitants," p. D8.

OTHER

CBC 4 Kids, http://www.cbc4kids.ca/ (January, 1999), author profile and bibliography.

Farley Mowat Web site (unofficial author home page), http://www.farleymowat.com/(December 2, 2001).

Independent, http://www.eastnorthumberland.com/news/ (December 8, 1998), Lorraine Dmitrovic, "Under Full Sail: At Thirty-six Books and Counting, Northumberland's Most Famous Author May Have a Few Books in Him Yet."

In Search of Farley Mowat (film), National Film Board of Canada, 1981.

Salon.com, http://www.salon.com/ (May 11, 1999), Steve Burgess, "Northern Exposure."*

Octavio Paz

bridge University, 1970-71; Charles Eliot Norton Professor of Poetry, Harvard University, 1971-72; Professor of comparative literature, Harvard University, 1973-80. Regent's fellow at University of California—San Diego.

■ Member

American Academy and Institute of Arts and Letters (honorary).

■ Awards, Honors

Guggenheim fellowship, 1944; Grand Prix International de Poesie (Belgium), 1963; Jerusalem Prize, Critics Prize (Spain), and National Prize for Letters (Mexico), all 1977; Grand Aigle d'Or (Nice, France), 1979; Premio Ollin Yoliztli (Mexico), 1980; Miguel de Cervantes Prize (Spain), 1982; Neustadt International Prize for Literature, 1982; Wilhelm Heinse Medal (West Germany), 1984; German Book Trade Peace prize, 1984; T. S. Eliot Award for Creative Writing, Ingersoll Foundation, 1987; Tocqueville Prize, 1989; Nobel Prize for Literature, 1990.

■ Writings

POETRY

Luna silvestre (title means "Sylvan Moon"), Fabula (Mexico City, Mexico), 1933.
No pasaran!, Simbad (Mexico City, Mexico), 1936.

■ Personal

Born March 31, 1914, in Mexico City, Mexico; died of cancer, April 19, 1998, in Mexico City, Mexico; son of Octavio Paz (a lawyer) and Josephina Lozano; married Elena Garro (a writer), mid-1930s (marriage ended, mid-1950s); married Maria-Jose Tramini, 1964; children: one daughter. *Nationality:* Mexican. *Education:* Attended National Autonomous University of Mexico, 1932-37. *Politics:* "Disillusioned leftist." *Religion:* Atheist.

■ Career

Writer. Government of Mexico, Mexican Foreign Service, posted to San Francisco, CA, and New York, NY, secretary at Mexican Embassy in Paris, beginning 1945, charge d'affaires at Mexican Embassy in Japan, beginning 1951, posted to Mexican Secretariat for External Affairs, 1953-58, extraordinary and plenipotentiary minister to Mexican Embassy, 1959-62, ambassador to India, 1962-68. Visiting professor of Spanish-American literature, University of Texas at Austin and University of Pittsburgh, 1968-70; Simon Bolivar Professor of Latin American Studies, 1970, and fellow of Churchill College, Cam-

Raiz del hombre (title means "Root of Man"; also see below), Simbad (Mexico City, Mexico), 1937.

Bajo tu clara sombra y otros poemas sobre España (title means "Under Your Clear Shadow and Other Poems about Spain"; also see below), Españolas (Valencia, Spain), 1937, revised edition, Tierra Nueva (Valencia, Spain), 1941.

Entre la piedra y la flor (title means "Between the Stone and the Flower"), Nueva Voz (Mexico City, Mexico), 1938, 2nd edition, Asociacion Civica Yucatan (Mexico City, Mexico), 1956.

A la orilla del mundo y primer dia; Bajo tu clara sombra; Raiz del hombre; Noche de resurrecciones, Ars (Mexico City, Mexico), 1942.

Libertad bajo palabra (title means "Freedom on Parole"), Tezontle (Mexico City, Mexico), 1949.

Aguila o sol? (prose poems), Tezontle (Mexico City, Mexico), 1951, 2nd edition, 1973, translation by Eliot Weinberger published as *Aguila o sol?/Eagle or Sun?* (bilingual edition), October House (New York, NY), 1970, revised, New Directions (New York, NY), 1976.

Semillas para un himno, Tezontle (Mexico City, Mexico), 1954.

Piedra de sol, Tezontle (Mexico City, Mexico), 1957, translation by Muriel Rukeyser published as *Sun Stone/Piedra de sol* (bilingual edition; also see below), New Directions (New York, NY), 1963, translation by Peter Miller published as *Sun-Stone,* Contact (Toronto, Ontario, Canada), 1963, translation by Donald Gardner published as *Sun Stone,* Cosmos (New York, NY), 1969, translation by Eliot Weinberger published as *Sunstone—Piedra de sol,* New Directions (New York, NY), 1991.

La estacion violenta, Fondo de Cultura Economica (Mexico City, Mexico), 1958, reprinted, 1978.

Agua y viento, Ediciones Mito (Bogota, Colombia), 1959.

Libertad bajo palabra: Obra poetica, 1935-1958, Fondo de Cultura Economica (Mexico City, Mexico), 1960, revised edition, 1968.

Salamandra (1958-1961) (also see below), J. Mortiz (Mexico City, Mexico), 1962, 3rd edition, 1975.

Selected Poems of Octavio Paz (bilingual edition), translation by Muriel Rukeyser, Indiana University Press (Bloomington, IN), 1963.

Viento entero, Caxton (Delhi, India), 1965.

Blanco (also see below), J. Mortiz (Mexico City, Mexico), 1967, 2nd edition, 1972, translation by Eliot Weinberger published under same title, The Press (New York, NY), 1974.

Disco visuales (four spatial poems), Era (Mexico City, Mexico), 1968.

Ladera este (1962-1968) (title means "Eastern Slope [1962-1968])"; also see below), J. Mortiz (Mexico City, Mexico), 1969, 3rd edition, 1975.

La centena (Poemas: 1935-1968), Seix Barral (Barcelona, Spain), 1969, 2nd edition, 1972.

Topoemas (six spatial poems), Era (Mexico City, Mexico), 1971.

Vuelta (long poem), El Mendrugo (Mexico City, Mexico), 1971.

Configurations (contains *Piedra de sol/Sun Stone, Blanco,* and selections from *Salamandra* and *Ladera este*), translations by G. Aroul and others, New Directions (New York, NY), 1971.

(With Jacques Roubaud, Edoardo Sanguinetti, and Charles Tomlinson; also author of prologue) *Renga* (collective poem written in French, Italian, English, and Spanish), J. Mortiz (Mexico City, Mexico), 1972, translation by Charles Tomlinson published as *Renga: A Chain of Poems,* Braziller (New York, NY), 1972.

Early Poems: 1935-1955, translations by Muriel Rukeyser and others, New Directions (New York, NY), 1973.

3 Notations/3 Rotations (contains fragments of poems by Paz), Carpenter Center for the Visual Arts, Harvard University (Cambridge, MA), 1974.

Pasado en claro (long poem), Fondo de Cultura Economica (Mexico City, Mexico), 1975, revised edition, 1978, translation included in *A Draft of Shadows and Other Poems* (also see below), New Directions (New York, NY), 1979.

Vuelta, Seix Barral (Barcelona, Spain), 1976.

(With Charles Tomlinson) *Air Born/Hijos del aire* (sonnets written in Spanish and English), Pescador (Mexico City, Mexico), 1979.

Poemas (1935-1975), Seix Barral (Mexico City, Mexico), 1979.

A Draft of Shadows and Other Poems, edited and translated by Eliot Weinberger, with additional translations by Elizabeth Bishop and Mark Strand, New Directions (New York, NY), 1979.

Selected Poems (bilingual edition), translations by Charles Tomlinson and others, Penguin (New York, NY), 1979.

Octavio Paz: Poemas recientes, Institucion Cultural de Cantabria de la Diputacion Provincial de Santander, 1981.

Selected Poems, edited by Eliot Weinberger, translations by G. Aroul and others, New Directions (New York, NY), 1984.

Cuatro chopos/The Four Poplars (bilingual edition), translation by Eliot Weinberger, Center for Edition Works (New York, NY), 1985.

The Collected Poems, 1957-1987: Bilingual Edition, New Editions, 1987.

One Word to the Other, Latitudes Press (Fort Worth, TX), 1991.

La casa de la presencia, Fondo de Cultura Economica (Mexico City, Mexico), 1994.

A Tale of Two Gardens: Poems from India, 1952-1995, edited and translated by Eliot Weinberger, Harcourt (New York, NY), 1997.

Delta de cinco brazos, Galaxia Gutenberg (Barcelona, Spain), 1998.

(With Maria-Jose Paz) *Figures and Figurations*, translated by Eliot Weinberger, New Directions (New York, NY), 2002.

PROSE

El laberinto de la soledad (also see below), Cuadernos Americanos (Mexico City, Mexico), 1950, revised edition, Fondo de Cultura Economica (Mexico City, Mexico), 1959, reprinted, 1980, translation by Lysander Kemp published as *The Labyrinth of Solitude: Life and Thought in Mexico*, Grove (New York, NY), 1961.

El arco y la lira: El poema; La revelacion poetica; Poesia e historia, Fondo de Cultura Economica (Mexico City, Mexico), 1956, 2nd edition includes text of *Los signos en rotacion* (also see below), 1967, 3rd edition, 1972, translation by Ruth L. C. Simms published as *The Bow and the Lyre: The Poem, the Poetic Revelation, Poetry and History*, University of Texas Press (Austin, TX), 1973, 2nd edition, McGraw-Hill (New York, NY), 1975.

Las peras del olmo, Universidad Nacional Autonoma de Mexico (Mexico City, Mexico), 1957, third edition, Seix Barral (Barcelona, Spain), 1978.

Tamayo en la pintura mexicana, Universidad Nacional Autonoma de Mexico (Mexico City, Mexico), 1959.

Cuadrivio: Dario, Lopez Velarde, Pessoa, Cernuda, J. Mortiz (Mexico City, Mexico), 1965.

Los signos en rotacion, Sur (Buenos Aires, Argentina), 1965, expanded as *Los signos en rotacion y otros ensayos*, edited and with a prologue by Carlos Fuentes, Alianza (Madrid, Spain), 1971.

Puertas al campo (also see below), Universidad Nacional Autonoma de Mexico (Mexico City, Mexico), 1966.

Claude Levi-Strauss; o, El nuevo festin de Esopo, J. Mortiz (Mexico City, Mexico), 1967, translation by J. S. Bernstein and Maxine Bernstein published as *Claude Levi-Strauss: An Introduction*, Cornell University Press (Ithaca, NY), 1970, published as *On Levi-Strauss*, J. Cape (London, England), 1970.

Corriente alterna, Siglo Veintiuno (Mexico City, Mexico), 1967, translation by Helen R. Lane published as *Alternating Current*, Viking (New York, NY), 1973.

Marcel Duchamp; o, El castillo de la pureza, Era (Mexico City, Mexico), 1968, translation by Donald Gardner published as *Marcel Duchamp; or, The Castle of Purity*, Grossman (New York, NY), 1970.

Conjunciones y disyunciones, J. Mortiz (Mexico City, Mexico), 1969, 2nd edition, 1978, translation by Helen R. Lane published as *Conjunctions and Disjunctions*, Viking (New York, NY), 1974.

Mexico: La ultima decada, Institute of Latin American Studies, University of Texas (Austin, TX), 1969.

Posdata (also see below), Siglo Veintiuno (Mexico City, Mexico), 1970, translation by Lysander Kemp published as *The Other Mexico: Critique of the Pyramid*, Grove (New York, NY), 1972.

(With Juan Marichal) *Las cosas en su sitio: Sobre la literatura española del siglo XX*, Finisterre (Mexico City, Mexico), 1971.

Traduccion: Literatura y literalidad, Tusquets (Barcelona, Spain), 1971.

Aparencia desnuda: La obra de Marcel Duchamp, Era (Mexico City, Mexico), 1973, enlarged edition, 1979, translation by Rachel Phillips and Donald Gardner published as *Marcel Duchamp: Appearance Stripped Bare*, Viking (New York, NY), 1978.

El signo y el garabato (contains *Puertas al campo*), J. Mortiz (Mexico City, Mexico), 1973.

(With Julian Rios) *Solo a dos voces*, Lumen (Barcelona, Spain), 1973.

Teatro de signos/Transparencias, selection and montage by Julian Rios, Fundamentos (Madrid, Spain), 1974.

La busqueda del comienzo: Escritos sobre el surrealismo, Fundamentos (Madrid, Spain), 1974, 2nd edition, 1980.

El mono gramatico, Seix Barral (Barcelona, Spain), 1974, translation by Helen R. Lane published as *The Monkey Grammarian*, Seaver (New York, NY), 1981.

Los hijos del limo: Del romanticismo a la vanguardia, Seix Barral (Barcelona, Spain), 1974, translation by Rachel Phillips published as *Children of the Mire: Modern Poetry from Romanticism to the Avant-Garde*, Harvard University Press (Cambridge, MA), 1974.

The Siren and the Seashell, and Other Essays on Poets and Poetry, translations by Lysander Kemp and Margaret Sayers Peden, University of Texas Press (Austin, TX), 1976.

Xavier Villaurrutia en persona y en obra, Fondo de Cultura Economica (Mexico City, Mexico), 1978.

El ogro filantropico: Historia y politica, 1971-1978 (also see below), J. Mortiz (Mexico City, Mexico), 1979.

In/mediaciones, Seix Barral (Barcelona, Spain), 1979.

Mexico en la obra de Octavio Paz, edited by Luis Mario Schneider, Promexa (Mexico City, Mexico), 1979.

El laberinto de la soledad; Posdata; Vuelta a el laberinto de la soledad, Fondo de Cultura Economica (Mexico City, Mexico), 1981.

Sor Juana Ines de la Cruz; o, Las trampas de la fe, Seix Barral (Barcelona, Spain), 1982, translation by Margaret Sayers Peden published as *Sor Juana; or,*

The Traps of Faith, Harvard University Press (Cambridge, MA), 1988.

(With Jacques Lassaigne) *Rufino Tamayo,* Ediciones Poligrafia (Barcelona, Spain), 1982, translation by Kenneth Lyons published under same title, Rizzoli (New York, NY), 1982.

(With John Golding) *Gunther Gerzo* (Spanish, English, and French texts), Editions du Griffon (Switzerland), 1983.

Sombras de obras: Arte y literatura, Seix Barral (Barcelona, Spain), 1983.

Hombres en su siglo y otros ensayos, Seix Barral (Barcelona, Spain), 1984, translation by Michael Schmidt published as *On Poets and Others,* Seaver Books (New York, NY), 1987.

Tiempo nublado, Seix Barral (Barcelona, Spain), 1984, translation by Helen R. Lane published with three additional essays as *On Earth, Four or Five Worlds: Reflections on Contemporary History,* Harcourt (New York, NY), 1985.

The Labyrinth of Solitude, The Other Mexico, Return to the Labyrinth of Solitude, Mexico and the United States, [and] *The Philanthropic Ogre,* translated by Lysander Kemp, Yara Milos, and Rachel Phillips Belash, Grove Press (New York, NY), 1985.

Arbol adentro, Seix Barral (Barcelona, Spain), 1987, translation published as *A Tree Within,* New Directions (New York, NY), 1988.

Convergences: Essays on Art and Literature, translation by Helen R. Lane, Harcourt (New York, NY), 1987.

The Other Voice: Essays on Modern Poetry, Harcourt (New York, NY), 1991.

La llama doble: Amor y erotisma, Seix Barral (Barcelona, Spain), 1993, translation by Helen R. Lane published as *The Double Flame: Love and Eroticism,* Harcourt (New York, NY), 1995.

Essays on Mexican Art, Harcourt (New York, NY), 1994.

Fundacion y disidencia: Dominio hispanico, Fondo de Cultura Economica (Mexico City, Mexico), 1994.

Generaciones y semblanzas: Dominio mexicano, Fondo de Cultura Economica (Mexico City, Mexico), 1994.

Los privilegios de la vista, Fondo de Cultura Economica (Mexico City, Mexico), 1994.

Obras completas, Fondo de Cultura Economica (Mexico City, Mexico), 1994-1999.

Vislumbres de la India, Seix Barral (Barcelona, Spain), 1995, translated by Eliot Weinberger as *In Light of India,* Harcourt Brace (New York, NY), 1997.

An Erotic Beyond: Sade, Harcourt Brace (New York, NY), 1998.

Itinerary: An Intellectual Journey, translated by Jason Wilson, Harcourt (New York, NY), 1999.

Rufino Tamayo: Tres ensayos, Colegio Nacional (Mexico City, Mexico), 1999.

Sueño en libertad: Escritos politicos, selection and prologue by Yvon Grenier, Planeta (Mexico City, Mexico), 2001.

El camino de la passion, Lopez Velarde, Seix Barral (Mexico City, Mexico), 2001.

EDITOR

Voces de España, Letras de Mexico (Mexico City, Mexico), 1938.

(With others) *Laurel: Antologia de la poesia moderna en lengua española,* Seneca (Mexico), 1941.

Antologie de la poesie mexicaine, Nagel (Geneva, Switzerland), 1952, translation by Samuel Beckett published as *Anthology of Mexican Poetry,* Indiana University Press (Bloomington, IN), 1958.

Antologia poetica, Revista Panoramas (Mexico City, Mexico), 1956.

(And translator, with Eikichi Hayashiya) Matsuo Basho, *Sendas de Oku,* Universidad Nacional Autonoma de Mexico (Mexico City, Mexico), 1957, 2nd edition, Seix Barral (Barcelona, Spain), 1970.

Tamayo en la pintura mexicana, Imprenta Universitaria (Mexico City, Mexico), 1958.

Magia de la risa, Universidad Veracruzana (Veracruz, Mexico), 1962.

Fernando Pessoa, *Antologia,* Universidad Nacional Autonoma de Mexico (Mexico City, Mexico), 1962.

(With Pedro Zekeli) *Cuatro poetas contemporaneos de Suecia: Martinson, Lundkvist, Ekeloef, y Lindegren,* Universidad Nacional Autonoma de Mexico (Mexico City, Mexico), 1963.

(With others, and author of prologue) *Poesia en movimiento: Mexico, 1915-1966,* Siglo Veintiuno (Mexico City, Mexico), 1966, translation edited by Mark Strand and published as *New Poetry of Mexico,* Dutton (New York, NY), 1970.

(With Roger Caillois) *Remedios Varo,* Era (Mexico City, Mexico), 1966.

(And author of prologue) Xavier Villaurrutia, *Antologia,* Fondo de Cultura Economica (Mexico City, Mexico), 1980.

Mexico: Splendors of Thirty Centuries, Metropolitan Museum of Art (New York, NY), 1990, translated as *Mexico: Esplendores de treinta siglos,* Friends of the Arts of Mexico, 1991.

TRANSLATOR

(And author of introduction) William Carlos Williams, *Veinte poemas,* Era (Mexico City, Mexico), 1973.

Versiones y diversiones (translations of poems from English, French, Portuguese, Swedish, Chinese, and Japanese), J. Mortiz (Mexico City, Mexico), 1974.

Apollinaire, *15 Poemas,* Latitudes (Mexico City, Mexico), 1979.

OTHER

La hija de Rappaccini (one-act play; based on a short story by Nathaniel Hawthorne, first produced in Mexico, 1956), translation by Harry Haskell published as *Rappaccini's Daughter* in *Octavio Paz: Homage to the Poet,* Kosmos (San Francisco, CA), 1980.

(Author of introduction) Carlos Fuentes, *Cuerpos y ofrendas,* Alianza (Madrid, Spain), 1972.

(Author of introduction) *Antonio Pelaez: Pintor,* Secretaria de Educacion Publica (Mexico), 1975.

(Author of foreword) *A Sor Juana Anthology,* translation by Alan S. Trueblood, Harvard University Press (Cambridge, MA) 1988.

(Author of introduction) James Laughlin, *Random Stories,* Moyer Bell (Wickford, RI), 1990.

(Author of introduction) Elena Poniatowska, *Massacre in Mexico,* translation by Helen R. Lane, University of Missouri Press (Columbia, MO), 1991.

In Search of the Present, Harcourt (New York, NY), 1991.

Al Paso, Seix Barral (Barcelona, Spain), 1992.

(Author of essay) *Nostalgia for Death/ Hieroglyphs of Desire: A Critical Study of Villaurrutia,* edited by Eliot Weinberger, Copper Canyon Press (Port Townsend, WA), 1993.

Excursiones/Incursiones: Dominio extranjero, Fondo de Cultura Economica (Mexico City, Mexico), 1994.

My Life with the Wave (children's book), Lothrop (New York, NY), 1994.

Contributor to *In Praise of Hands: Contemporary Crafts of the World,* New York Graphic Society, 1974; *Avances,* Fundamentos, 1978; *Democracy and Dictatorship in Latin America: A Special Publication Devoted Entirely to the Voices and Opinions of Writers from Latin America,* Foundation for the Independent Study of Social Ideas, 1982; *Instante y revelacion,* Fondo Nacional para Actividades Sociales, 1982; *Frustraciones de un destino: La democracia en America Latina,* Libro Libre, 1985; and *Nineteen Ways of Looking at Wang Wei: How a Chinese Poem Is Translated,* edited by Eliot Weinberger, Moyer Bell, 1987.

Contributor to numerous anthologies. Founder of literary review *Barandal,* 1931; member of editorial board and columnist, *El Popular,* late 1930s; co-founder of *Taller,* 1938; co-founder and editor, *El Hijo Prodigo,* 1943-46; editor of *Plural,* 1971-75; founder and editor, *Vuelta,* 1976-98.

■ Sidelights

Nobel laureate Octavio Paz was a Mexican author who enjoyed a worldwide reputation as a master poet and essayist. Although Mexico figures prominently in Paz's work—one of his best-known books, *The Labyrinth of Solitude,* for example, is a comprehensive portrait of Mexican society—*Los Angeles Times* contributor Jascha Kessler called Paz "truly international." *World Literature Today*'s Manuel Duran felt that Paz's "exploration of Mexican existential values permit[ted] him to open a door to an understanding of other countries and other cultures" and thus appeal to readers of diverse backgrounds. "What began as a slow, almost microscopic examination of self and of a single cultural tradition widens unexpectedly," Duran continued, "becoming universal without sacrificing its unique characteristic." That transformation from micro to macro included the growth of his poetry from his first book of poems, *Luna silvestre,* to the visionary mapping of the past, present, and future of Mexico in the sequence of prose poems *Aguila o sol?* and the long poem *Piedra del sol,* the latter of which uses the structure of the Aztec calendar. Those collections plus *The Labyrinth of Solitude* placed Paz in the forefront of Mexican literature by the close of the 1950s, yet he failed to gain an international reputation until his work was translated into English in the 1960s and 1970s. For another four decades Paz continued to deepen his thought and expression in poetry and essays which continued to examine philosophical, moral, religious, historical, political, and artistic themes.

Paz, who died in 1998 at the age of eighty-four, wore many hats during his lifetime. Not only was he a leading writer, but also a translator, editor, playwright, and major intellectual voice on the Mexican and world stage. A tireless defender of democracy and the freedom of expression, Paz viewed language as a central concern and characterized the role of the writer as a guardian of language. Additionally, for almost two decades he was in the Mexican diplomatic corps, beginning in France in the 1940s as cultural attaché. In 1962 Paz was made Mexico's ambassador to India, a post which he resigned in 1968 following a government massacre of student protestors in Mexico City. During his lifetime he was honored by the Cervantes Award in 1981, the Neustadt Prize in 1982, and the Nobel Prize for Literature in 1990. Paz's passing was mourned as the end of an era for Mexico. According to his obituary in *Americas,* "Paz's literary career helped to define modern poetry and the Mexican personality."

Throughout his life, despite his international repute, Paz continued to think of himself as a Mexican poet first. In a 1993 *New Yorker* profile, he noted that when he began to write poetry, "the first thing I did was learn my craft from the Spanish classics. I then read the great Latin Americans who came before me. Then suddenly I discovered the Indian past

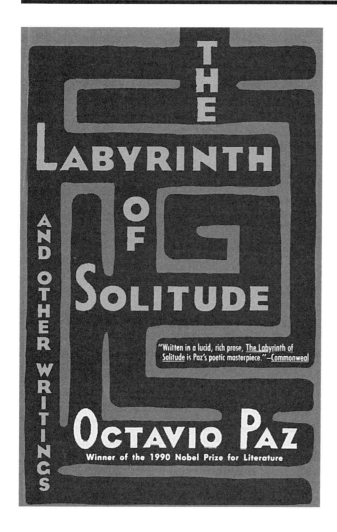

THE Labyrinth OF Solitude AND OTHER WRITINGS

"Written in a lucid, rich prose, The Labyrinth of Solitude is Paz's poetic masterpiece."—Commonweal

Octavio Paz

Winner of the 1990 Nobel Prize for Literature

Hailed as the first modern collection of prose poetry when it appeared in the original Spanish in 1951, this set of poems was later revised and appeared in this bilingual edition in 1976.

through modernity." Still Paz was not through with his studies. He discovered that his education was not complete without the lessons that world literature could teach him, and he imbibed the poetry of Walt Whitman, T. S. Eliot, Ezra Pound, and William Carlos Williams. "But despite all this, I am not a foreign writer, I am a Mexican poet."

The Making of a Mexican Poet

Paz was born in 1914 near Mexico City, into a prominent family with ties to Mexico's political, cultural, and military elite. His father—of Mexican and Native descent—was a journalist and lawyer who served as assistant to Emiliano Zapata, the

leader of a popular revolution in 1911, while his mother's family had come from Andalusia, Spain. Many Zapatistas were forced into exile when their leader was slain a few years later, and the Paz family relocated to Los Angeles, California, for a time. Upon their return to Mexico City, the family's economic situation declined, and soon they could no longer afford the large city house, moving instead to Mixcoac, outside the capital. The father, because of his political affairs, spent little time at home, and the young Paz was raised mostly by his religious mother, Josephina Lozano, and by his paternal grandfather, a novelist and former soldier. The house at Mixcoac had a well-stocked library, and between this and the Marist brothers who were his formal teachers, Paz benefitted from a solid early education. This childhood did much to inspire in Paz a love for the Mexican past. As he told Marilyn Snell in *New Perspectives Quarterly,* "One day, while on a picnic with my friends, we found a small pyramid . . . this was the Mexico of my childhood—a Mexico right in pre-Columbian art, in the art of the colonists, and the flowering of modern Mexican art."

Early on, Paz began writing poetry, and as a teen, he found increasing success for his poems and short stories in local publications, including his own literary review, *Barandal,* in which he published his first poem at age seventeen. In 1932 he attended the National Autonomous University of Mexico, and his first volume of poetry, *Luna silvestre,* appeared in 1933. While attending law school, however, Paz found himself drawn to leftist politics. When he sent some of his work to famed Chilean poet Pablo Neruda, the senior writer gave it a favorable review and encouraged Paz to attend a congress of leftist-thinking writers in Spain.

In Spain, Paz was drawn into that country's raging civil war and joined a brigade fighting the armies of fascist dictator Francisco Franco. He returned to Mexico with a mission to popularize the Spanish Republican cause, and spent time in both Berkeley, California, and New York City over the next few years as a graduate student, journalist, and translator. In 1946 he was offered a post as Mexico's cultural attaché to France, and served in his country's diplomatic corps for the next two decades. The work left him enough time to write prodigiously, and during the course of his career he published dozens of volumes of poetry and prose.

Poet and Essayist

In France, Paz met and was influenced by surrealist poet André Breton. Slowly Paz began to find his own poetic voice, and an early example of this came with the collection *Aguila o sol?*, published in 1951. In this collection Paz employs the surrealist technique of connecting seemingly unrelated images to break down the barriers between dream and reality. The visionary prose poems in this early collection explore the past, present, and future of Mexico—a major theme for Paz.

Critics have pointed to several repeated contrasting images which dramatically capture the essence of Paz's work. Ronald Christ, for example, commented in a *Nation* review of *Aguila o sol?/Eagle or Sun?* (the title refers to the images on a Mexican coin and is the equivalent of the English expression "heads or tails?"): "The dual image of the Mexican coin which gives *Eagle or Sun?* its title epitomizes Paz's technique and credo, for we see that there is no question of eagle *or* sun, rather of eagle *and* sun which together in their oppositeness are the same coin." Another of the poet's images which reviewers have

Seventeenth-century Mexican poet and intellectual Sor Juana Ines de la Cruz is the subject of Paz's acclaimed biography *Sor Juana; or, The Traps of Faith*, both a critical study and a meditation on the role of the poet within society.

frequently mentioned is "burnt water," an ancient Mexican concept that appears in Paz's work in both Spanish and in the Aztec original, "atl tlachinolli." Grace Schulman maintained in the *Hudson Review* that "burnt water" is "the dominant image of [Paz's] poetry" and found that the image fulfills a role similar to that of the two sides of the coin in *Eagle or Sun?* She noted: "Paz sees the world burning, and knows with visionary clarity that opposites are resolved in a place beyond contraries, in a moment of pure vision: in that place, there are no frontiers between men and women, life and death." Frances Chiles, writing in *World Literature Today,* called the Aztec combination of fire and water "particularly apt in its multiple connotations as a symbol of the union of all warring contraries."

One of Paz's best-known prose works was *El laberinto de la soledad,* which appeared first in 1950 and in English translation as *The Labyrinth of Solitude: Life and Thought in Mexico* eleven years later. This work has been interpreted by critics and reviewers as a melange of autobiography, a study of Mexican history, a psychological study, and a work of existential philosophy. "In it Paz argues that Mexicans see themselves as children of the conquering Spanish father who abandoned his offspring and the treacherous Indian mother who turned against her own people," explained a contributor in an *Americas* essay. "Because of the wounds that Mexicans suffer as a result of their dual cultural heritage, they have developed a defensive stance, hiding behind masks and taking refuge in a 'labyrinth of solitude.'" Pete Hamill, writing in *Esquire,* declared that *The Labyrinth of Solitude* "explained the Mexican character and identity both to the world and to other Mexicans." The volume became standard reading for students of Latin-American history and literature, and has also been viewed as a seminal work in understanding Mexican-U.S. relations.

After an eleven-year sojourn out of his native country, Paz returned to Mexico and wrote two more influential works in the late 1950s. The prose *The Bow and the Lyre* is an attempt to resolve the use of language—the very thing that has kept man separated from the world—as a sort of bridge to take him back into the world. Another major work of poetry from Paz is *Sun Stone,* composed as a single circular sentence of 584 eleven-syllable lines. This long poem is a lyrical exploration of time and memory, erotic love, myth, and the art of writing. The number 584 was chosen because it is based on the Aztec calendar. *Sun Stone* is generally considered Paz's finest verse achievement.

Passage to India

In 1962 Paz was posted to India as Mexico's ambassador, and the six years he spent there were highly influential to his developing spiritual thought. He became an avid student of Eastern philosophy. His *Eastern Slope (1962-1968)* is an experimental compilation based on such new beliefs, dealing with love and poetry. Paz also integrated such new thinking into the rest of his work. Through juxtaposition of contrasting thoughts or objects Paz created a more harmonious world, one based on the complementary association of opposites found in the Eastern concept of yin and yang. Schulman explained Paz's proclivity for Eastern philosophy in *Hudson Review:* "Although he had embraced contraries from the beginning of his writing career . . . [Paz] found in Tantric thought and in Hindu religious life dualities that enforced his conviction that history turns on reciprocal rhythms. In *Alternating Current,* he writes that the Hindu gods, creators or destroyers according to their names and region, manifest contradiction. 'Duality,' he says, 'a basic feature of Tantrism. . . . In Eastern thought, these opposites can co-exist; in Western philosophy, they disappear for the worst reasons: far from being resolved into a higher synthesis, they cancel each other out.'"

One aspect of Paz's work often mentioned by critics is his tendency to maintain elements of prose —most commonly philosophical thought—in his poetry, and poetic elements in his prose. Perhaps the best example to support this claim can be found in Paz's exploration of India, titled *The Monkey Grammarian,* a work *New York Times Book Review* contributor Keith Botsford called "exceedingly curious" and described as "an extended meditation on the nature of language." In separate *World Literature Today* essays, critics Jaime Alazraki and Jose Miguel Oviedo discussed the difficulty encountered in assigning the book to a literary genre. "It is apparent," Alazraki noted, "that *The Monkey Grammarian* is not an essay. It is also apparent that it is not a poem, at least not in the conventional sense. It is both an essay and a poem, or perhaps neither." Oviedo similarly stated that the book "does not belong to any specific genre—although it has a bit of all of them—because it is deliberately written at the edge of genres."

According to Oviedo, *The Monkey Grammarian* is the product of Paz's long-stated quest "to produce a text which would be an intersection of poetry, narrative and essay." The fusion of opposites found in this work is an important element in nearly all Paz's literary production. In many instances both the work's structure and its content represent a blending of contradictory forces: *Renga,* for example, is written in four languages, while *Air Born/Hijos del*

1990 Nobel Laureate

poems by OCTAVIO PAZ

EAGLE OR SUN?

Containing Paz's most famous work, "The Labyrinth of Solitude," this 1985 essay collection showcases the poet's extensive understanding of history and his penetrating intellect.

aire, is written in two. According to *World Literature Today* contributor Chiles, Paz strove to create in his writing "a sense of community or communion" which he found lacking in contemporary society. In his Neustadt Prize acceptance speech reprinted in *World Literature Today,* Paz attempted to explain his emphasis on contrasting thoughts: "Plurality is Universality, and Universality is the acknowledging of the admirable diversity of man and his works. . . . To acknowledge the variety of visions and sensibilities is to preserve the richness of life and thus to ensure its continuity."

Later Work

Paz met his wife, Maria-Jose Tramini, when he was posted to India. His diplomatic career came to an end in 1968 when government forces killed three hundred student protestors at the university in Mexico City. Paz resigned his post in protest, and from that time he and his wife lived in many places around the world while he served as a visiting professor, and also returned to Paz's native Mexico, where he continued to work in verse and prose, writing on a wide range of topics, including politics, religion, anthropology, archaeology, and poetry. Among others, Paz wrote respected works on Marcel Duchamp and Claude Levi-Strauss, and also founded *Vuelta,* a literary magazine that helped to introduce European writing to Latin American intellectuals.

In *Sor Juana; or, The Traps of Faith* Paz examines the literary achievement of Sor Juana Ines de la Cruz, a seventeenth-century New Spain nun and poetess who produced masterful verse from a convent in Mexico City. *New York Times Book Review* contributor Frederick Luciani wrote, "Her extant works . . . are of such abundance and variety, in such a range of styles, voices and manners, as to be simultaneously seductive and bewildering. With characteristic lucidity, Mr. Paz sorts through this textual morass and arrives at an admiring and sympathetic portrait, but an honest and demythologizing one, too." To understand his subject, Paz addressed the complex and turbulent civilization of colonial Mexico. "It is, after all," according to Jonathan Keates in the London *Observer,* "not only the nun's tale but that of Mexico itself, the kingdom of New Spain, its imposed framework of ideal constructs eroded by mutual resentment between governors and governed and by a chronic fear of change." According to Electa Arenal in *Criticism,* "*Sor Juana; or, The Traps of Faith* is a tour de force—biography, cultural history and ideological criticism all in one. It describes the intellectual, political and religious climate of sixteenth-and seventeenth-century Mexico; comments on the poet as rebel against orthodoxy, then and now; and studies the life, times, and art of a woman with whom Paz identifies and to whom he implicitly compares himself."

With *La llama doble: Amor y erotisma,* translated as *The Double Flame,* Paz provides a social and literary history of love and eroticism, comparing modern manifestations to those of earlier ages, while noting the special relationship between eroticism and poetry. "This book is a product of immense wisdom and patient observation, an approach to passion from the vantage of maturity," wrote Ilan Stavans in *Washington Post Book World.* "His ultimate thesis is that our society is plagued by erotic permissiveness, placing the stability and continuity of love in jeopardy, and that the difficult encounter between two humans attracted to each other, has lost importance, a development that he believes threatens our psy-

chological and cultural foundations." According to Paz, "Both love and eroticism—the double flame—are fed by the original fire: sexuality." A reviewer for *Publishers Weekly* called this a "gem of a book" which "calls for a dialogue between science and philosophy" in order to reestablish "the centrality of love and the soul." Amanda Hopkinson, writing in the *New Statesman,* felt that Paz "makes this love story the culmination of an intellectual and sentimental journey through the greater part of our century and world," and further noted that Paz does so in a language at once "visionary as well as passionate." Paz explores much the same theme in *An Erotic Beyond: Sade,* an examination of the life and work of the Marquis de Sade that "offers an original insight into Sade's sexually charged works," according to *Library Journal* contributor Robert Kelly.

In *The Other Voice: Essays on Modern Poetry* Paz offers a critique of contemporary poetry, including an analysis of the Romantics and Symbolists and a forceful objection to postmodernism and consumerism. Though noting Paz's conservative New Critic perspective, Raymond Leslie Williams wrote in *American Book Review,* "The breadth of Paz's literary repertoire in this volume, as in all his writing, is impressive. His understanding of Pound, Eliot, Apollinaire, and many other modern poets is vast." Paz emphasizes the unifying power of poetry and asserts the importance of a public audience. "The volume's prevailing theme," wrote Ilan Stavans in a *Nation* review, is "poetry as a nonconformist, rebellious force of the modern age." Stavans observed, "Paz argues that while poets are elitists by nature, despite the tiny circulation of their craft it has a profound impact on society." For Paz, as John Butt wrote in the *Times Literary Supplement,* "the poem aspires to be all-encompassing, an image of what a unified theory of life might be, 'a miniature, animated cosmos' which 'unites the ten thousand things' that swirl around us."

Critics have agreed that Paz's great theme of a blended reality situated his work in the forefront of modern literature. As Christ noted: "By contraries then, by polarities and divergences converging in a rhetoric of opposites, Paz established himself as a brilliant stylist balancing the tension of East and West, art and criticism, the many and the one in the figures of his writing. Paz is thus not only a great writer: he is also an indispensable corrective to our cultural tradition and a critic in the highest sense in which he himself uses the word." Enrique Fernandez similarly viewed Paz as a writer of enormous influence. "Not only has he left his mark on world poetry, with a multilingual cortege of acolytes," Fernandez wrote in a *Village Voice* essay, "he is a force to be reckoned with by anyone who chooses that modernist *imitaio Christi,* the Life of the Mind."

A HARVEST/HBJ BOOK

1990 NOBEL LAUREATE IN LITERATURE

OCTAVIO PAZ

CONVERGENCES
ESSAYS ON ART AND LITERATURE

"An excellent collection . . . elegantly translated."
—*New York Times*

Paz exhibits his wide-ranging interests in this work, which focuses on such diverse topics as the relationship between linguistics and culture and the works of Spanish artists Pablo Picasso and Joan Miró.

tiny treasures—delicate, suggestive, and profound." A reviewer for *Publishers Weekly* called this collection of essays "masterful," while a contributor to the *Economist* found Paz to be both "knowledgeable and passionate" about his subject.

Paz was an active critic of politics for nearly all of his career. Unlike some other leftist Latin American writers—Gabriel García Marquéz, for example—Paz was not a supporter of Communist Cuban leader Fidel Castro. He also criticized Nicaragua's Sandinista guerrilla movement; Mexican demonstrations of solidarity with the Sandinista movement sometimes included the burning of an effigy of Paz. Nor was he a champion of the Zapatista uprising which fomented in a mountainous Mexican state in 1994. The writer, in both his writings and public utterances, defended his views ardently. "Revolution begins as a promise," Paz wrote, according to the *New Republic,* "is squandered in violent agitation, and freezes into bloody dictatorships that are the negation of the fiery impulse that brought it into being. In all revolutionary movements, the sacred time of myth is transformed inexorably into the profane time of history."

Paz died in April of 1998, after suffering from cancer of the spine. His death was announced by no less than the president of Mexico, Ernesto Zedillo. "This is an irreplaceable loss for contemporary thought and culture—not just for Latin America but for the entire world," Notimex, the government news agency, quoted Zedillo as saying. Gabriel Zaid, who co-founded the literary journal *Vuelta* with Paz, recalled the writer's final public appearance in December of 1997 in a piece for *Time International.* "The day was overcast and gray," Zaid wrote. "Octavio spoke of the sun, of gratitude and of grace. And the sun, as if engaged in conversation, peered down on him through the clouds."

Though Paz left the Asian subcontinent in 1968, his time there continued to hold sway over him creatively. In 1997 his collection *A Tale of Two Gardens: Poems from India, 1952-1995* appeared. A review from Barbara Mujica in *Americas* described the poet as "obsessed with India. Although many American and European writers have been fascinated with the subcontinent, none has studied its culture with the intensity and thoroughness of Paz." Some of the poems in the collection were written in a short Sanskrit form called *kayva;* the form was also used for some verse that appeared in Paz's prose memoir, *In Light of India,* also published in 1997. As Mujica noted, "In the kayva, Paz evokes exquisite and fleeting erotic images—a young bather emerging from the river, silks slipping off bodies and fluttering in the breeze. . . . These verses are

If you enjoy the works of Octavio Paz, you might want to check out the following books:

Frederico Garcia Lorca, *Gypsy Ballads,* 1951.
Pablo Neruda, *Twenty Love Poems and a Song of Despair,* 1969.
Antonio Machado, *Selected Poems,* 1982.

In a *New York Times* summary of Paz's poetry, Edward Hirsch praised the Mexican writer as a man who "practiced poetry like a secret religion." Hirsch further noted, "Writing was for him a primordial act, and he stared down at the blank page like an abyss until it sent him reeling over the brink of language. And the poems he brought back are fill with ancient wonder and strangeness, hermetic wisdom, a dizzying sense of the sacred." Paz was, Hirsch concluded, the "poet of separation and fusion, this mind of the Americas." Also writing in the *New York Times,* Jonathan Kandell called Paz "Mexico's premier poet and essayist and one of the towering men of letters in the second half of [the twentieth] century."

■ Biographical and Critical Sources

BOOKS

Bloom, Harold, editor, *Octavio Paz,* Chelsea House (New York, NY), 2002.
Contemporary Literature Criticism, Gale (Detroit, MI), Volume 3, 1975, Volume 4, 1975, Volume 6, 1976, Volume 10, 1979, Volume 19, 1981, Volume 51, 1989, Volume 65, 1990; Volume 119, 1999.
Dictionary of Hispanic Biography, Gale (Detroit, MI), 1996.
Encyclopedia of World Biography, 2nd edition, Gale (Detroit, MI), 1998.
Hispanic Literature Criticism, Gale (Detroit, MI), 1989.
Ivask, Ivar, *The Perpetual Present: The Poetry and Prose of Octavio Paz,* University of Oklahoma Press (Norman, OK), 1973.
Poetry Criticism, Gale (Detroit, MI), Volume 1, 1989.
Roman, Joseph, *Octavio Paz,* Chelsea House (New York, NY), 1994.
Wilson, Jason, *Octavio Paz,* Twayne (Boston, MA), 1986.

PERIODICALS

American Book Review, August-September, 1992, Raymond Leslie Williams, review of *The Other Voice: Essays on Modern Poetry,* p. 3.
Americas, August, 1998, Barbara Mujica, review of "A Tale of Two Gardens," p. 60.
Booklist, November 15, 1991, p. 595; March 15, 1997, Donna Seaman, review of *In Light of India* and *A Tale of Two Gardens,* p. 1223; April, 1998, Donna Seaman, review of *An Erotic Beyond: Sade,* p. 1297.
Commonweal, January 27, 1989, p. 50.
Comparative Literature, fall, 1989, p. 397.
Criticism, Volume 31, number 4, Electa Arenal, review of *Sor Juana; or, The Traps of Faith,* p. 463.

Economist, June 21, 1997, review of *In Light of India,* pp. R3-R4.
Esquire, March, 1991, Pete Hamill, "The World According to Octavio Paz," pp. 46-47.
Hudson Review, autumn, 1974; summer, 1989, pp. 314-320.
Interview, October, 1989.
Journal of Youth Services in Libraries, summer, 1990, p. 311.
Kirkus Reviews, January 1, 1995, p. 62.
Library Journal, January, 1995, p. 79; February 15, 1997, James F. DeRoche, review of *In Light of India,* p. 146; April 1, 1998, Robert Kelly, review of *An Erotic Beyond: Sade,* p. 89; December, 2000, Silvia Heredia, review of *Itinerary: An Intellectual Journey,* p. 134.
London Review of Books, May 18, 1989, p. 20.
Los Angeles Times, November 28, 1971.
Los Angeles Times Book Review, September 18, 1988, p. 3; April 30, 1995, p. 6.
Nation, August 2, 1975, Ronald Christ, review of *Aguila o sol/Eagle or Sun;* February 17, 1992, Ilan Stavans, review of *The Other Voice: Essays on Modern Poetry,* pp. 205-207.
New Criterion, February, 2001, Stephen Schwartz, "Octavio Paz," p. 68.
New Perspectives Quarterly, fall, 1988, pp. 46-51; summer, 1990, Marilyn Snell, "The House of Glances," pp. 50-55; winter, 1991, pp. 36-41; spring, 1992, pp. 5-9.
New Republic, March 14, 1988, pp. 36-39; October 9, 1995, p. 40.
New Statesman, Amanda Hopkinson, review of *The Double Flame,* p. 48.
New Yorker, April 4, 1988, pp. 97-101; December 27, 1993, Octavio Paz, "The World after NAFTA," pp. 57-58; May 15, 1995, p. 93.
New York Times, June 7, 1998, Edward Hirsch, "Octavio Paz: In Defense of Poetry."
New York Times Book Review, December 27, 1981, Keith Botsford, review of *The Monkey Grammarian;* December 25, 1988, Frederick Luciani, review of *Sor Juana; or, The Traps of Faith,* p. 12; April 19, 1998, Laura Jamison, review of *An Erotic Beyond;* June 7, 1998, Edward Hirsch, "Octavio Paz: In Defense of Poetry."
Observer (London, England), January 15, 1989, Jonathan Keates, review of *Sor Juana; or, The Traps of Faith,* p. 49.
Paris Review, summer, 1991, pp. 82-123.
Publishers Weekly, January 16, 1995, review of *The Double Flame,* p. 444; January 13, 1997, review of *In Light of India,* p. 59; June 9, 1997, review of *My Life with the Wave,* pp. 44-45.
Small Press, winter, 1994, p. 89.
Times (London, England), June 8, 1989.

Times Literary Supplement, December 30, 1988-January 5, 1989, p. 1435; July 24, 1992, John Butt, review of *The Other Voice: Essays on Modern Poetry,* p. 6; August 2, 1996, p. 7.

Tribune Books (Chicago, IL), September 11, 1988, p. 24.

Village Voice, March 19, 1985.

Washington Post Book World, July 23, 1995, Ilan Stavans, review of *The Double Flame,* p. 11.

World Literature Today, autumn, 1982; winter, 1991, Manuel Duran, "Octavio Paz: Nobel Laureate in Literature, 1990," pp. 4-7; autumn, 1994, Naomi Lindstrom, review of *The Double Flame,* p. 795; winter, 1995, H. Mojica, review of *Nostalgia for Death/ Hieroglyphs of Desire: A Critical Study of Villaurrutia,* p. 111.

■ Obituaries

PERIODICALS

Americas, August, 1998, p. 62.

Chicago Tribune, April 21, 1998, p. 1.

Los Angeles Times, April 20, 1998, p. A18; April 21, 1998, p. A1.

New Republic, May 11, 1998, "A Poet Passes," p. 10.

New York Times, April 21, 1998, Jonathan Kandell, "Octavio Paz, Mexico's Literary Giant, Dead at 84," p. A1.

Time, May 4, 1998, p. 27.

Time International, May 4, 1998, "Global Conversationalist Octavio Paz: 1914-1998," p. 52.

Washington Post, April 21, 1998, p. B6.*

Chaim Potok

■ Personal

Born Herman Harold Potok, Hebrew given name, Chaim (pronounced "Hah-yim") Tzvi, February 17, 1929, New York, NY; died of cancer, July 23, 2002, in Merion, PA; son of Benjamin Max (a businessman) and Mollie (Friedman) Potok; married Adena Sara Mosevitzky (a psychiatric social worker), June 8, 1958; children: Rena, Naama, Akiva. *Nationality:* American. *Education:* Yeshiva University, B.A., (summa cum laude), 1950; Jewish Theological Seminary, ordination, M.H.L., 1954; University of Pennsylvania, Ph.D., 1965. *Religion:* Conservative Judaism. *Hobbies and other interests:* Painting, photography.

■ Career

Writer. Leaders Training Fellowship, Jewish Theological Seminary, national director, 1954-55; Camp Ramah, Los Angeles, CA, director, 1957-59; Har Zion Temple, Philadelphia, PA, scholar-in-residence, 1959-63; Jewish Theological Seminary, member of faculty of Teachers' Institute, 1963-64; *Conservative Judaism,* New York, NY, managing editor, 1964-65; Jewish Publication Society, Philadelphia, associate editor, 1965-66, editor-in-chief, 1966-74, special projects editor, 1974—. Instructor, University of Judaism, Los Angeles, 1957-59; visiting professor of philosophy, Bryn Mawr College, 1985, University of Pennsylvania, 1983, 1991-2002, and Johns Hopkins University, 1995-2002. Occasional commentator for National Public Radio. *Military service:* U.S. Army, chaplain in Korea, 1956-57; became first lieutenant.

■ Member

Rabbinical Assembly, PEN, Authors Guild, Artists Equity.

■ Awards, Honors

National Book Award nomination for *The Chosen,* and Edward Lewis Wallant Prize, both 1967; Athenaeum Award, 1969, for *The Promise;* Professional and Scholarly Publishing Division special citation, AAP, 1984, for collaborating in new translation of the Hebrew Bible; National Jewish Book Award, 1990, for *The Gift of Asher Lev;* National Foundation for Jewish Culture Achievement Award, 1997; O. Henry Short Story Prize, 1998; Books in the Middle: Outstanding Titles of 1998 designation, *Voice of Youth Advocates,* and Best Books for Young Adults, American Library Association, both 1999, both for *Zebra and Other Stories.*

■ Writings

FICTION

The Chosen, Simon & Schuster (New York, NY), 1967, reprinted, Knopf (New York, NY), 1992.

The Promise (sequel to *The Chosen*), Knopf (New York, NY), 1969.

My Name Is Asher Lev, Knopf (New York, NY), 1972.

In the Beginning, Knopf (New York, NY), 1975.

The Book of Lights, Knopf (New York, NY), 1981.

Davita's Harp, Knopf (New York, NY), 1985.

The Gift of Asher Lev (sequel to *My Name Is Asher Lev*), Knopf (New York, NY), 1990.

I Am the Clay, Knopf (New York, NY), 1992.

Hanukkah Lights: Stories from the Festival of Lights, Dove, 1997.

Zebra and Other Stories (for young adults), Knopf (New York, NY), 1998.

Old Men at Midnight, Knopf (New York, NY), 2001.

NONFICTION

The Jew Confronts Himself in American Literature, Sacred Heart School of Theology (Hales Comers, WI), 1975.

Wanderings: Chaim Potok's History of the Jews, Knopf (New York, NY), 1978.

Ethical Living for a Modern World, Jewish Theological Seminary of America (New York, NY), 1985.

Tobiasse: Artist in Exile, Rizzoli (New York, NY), 1986.

The Gates of November: Chronicles of the Slepak Family, Knopf (New York, NY), 1996.

(With Isaac Stern) *My First Seventy-nine Years,* Knopf (New York, NY), 1999.

PLAYS

The Chosen (musical), first produced on Broadway, 1988, produced as a drama in Philadelphia, PA, 1999.

Also author of *Sins of the Fathers* (two one-act plays), and *The Play of Lights,* both produced in Philadelphia.

OTHER

The Tree of Here (picture book), illustrated by Tony Auth, Knopf (New York, NY), 1993.

The Sky of Now (picture book), illustrated by Tony Auth, Knopf (New York, NY), 1995.

(Editor, with Nahum M. Sarna) *JPS Torah Commentary,* Jewish Publication Society (Philadelphia, PA), 1996.

Contributor to *Jewish Ethics* (pamphlet series), Leaders Training Fellowship, 1964-69. Also contributor to *May My Words Feed Others,* edited by Chayym Zeldis, Barnes, 1974; *Literature and the Urban Experience,* edited by Michael C. Jaye and Ann C. Watts, Rutgers University Press, 1981; *From the Corners of the Earth,* by Bill Aron, Jewish Publication Society, 1985; *The Jews in America,* edited by David C. Cohen, Collins, 1989; *Tales of the Hasidim,* by Martin Buber, Pantheon, 1991; *A Worthy Use of Summer,* edited by Jenna Weissman Joselitt with Karen S. Mittelman, National Museum of American Jewish History, 1993; *Graven Images,* by Arnold Schwartzman, Abrams, 1993; and *I Never Saw Another Butterfly,* edited by Hana Volavkova, Pantheon, 1993. Contributor to periodicals, including *Ladies' Home Journal, Commentary, American Judaism, Saturday Review, Kenyon Review, New York Times Book Review,* and *New York Times Sunday Magazine.*

■ Adaptations

The Chosen, a film based on Potok's novel and starring Maximilian Schell, Robby Benson, Rod Steiger, and Barry Miller, was produced by Twentieth Century-Fox, 1982. *Hanukkah Lights* was produced on audiocassette by Dove Audio, 1996.

■ Sidelights

Chaim Potok "wrote of what he knew best, Jewish-Americans in the 20th century struggling with two contradictory yet valid points of view," according to Shirley Saad writing for the *United Press International.* In such popular and award-winning books as *The Chosen, The Promise, My Name Is Asher Lev,* and *Davita's Harp,* Potok reached an audience of millions of readers all ages throughout the United States and around the world. An ordained rabbi, Potok never saw himself in a traditional religious role. He worked as a writer, rabbi, and professor, often concerning himself with Orthodox and Hasidic Jews and how they merge their beliefs with twentieth-century life. Robert J. Milch wrote in the *Saturday Review:* "Judaism was at the center of all [Potok's] works. . . . [It motivated] his characters and provided the basis for their way of looking at themselves, each other, and the world." For Liz

Stevens, writing in the *Knight Ridder/Tribune News Service,* "confrontation" gave form to Potok's world. He found such confrontation in his discovery of secular fiction as a teenager, a discovery that challenged his Orthodox religious beliefs. His time served as a U.S. Army chaplain after the Korean War further "rattled everything he thought he knew," according to Stevens. "Clash of cultures fills the . . . author's numerous novels, including *The Choice, The Promise,* and *My Name Is Asher Lev,*" Stevens remarked. Potok used such seminal experiences as well as his rabbinical training to invent a believable world often populated by highly educated Jewish leaders and students. Above all, the writer's "primary concern is the spiritual and intellectual growth of his characters—how and what they come to believe," observed Hugh Nissenson in the *New York Times Book Review.*

Some critics have compared Potok to Sholom Aleichem, a turn-of-the-twentieth-century Russian-Yiddish author of short stories and novels, in that the conflicts contained in Potok's books are cultural, religious, and scholarly. "That his novels have been best-sellers requires some explanation given the rather esoteric nature of his subject matter," commented Edward Abramson in *Chaim Potok.* "Many non-Jews think that the Jewish community is a homogeneous one with each member having substantially the same beliefs as the other." The critic further explained that "there is a wide divergence in the interpretation of law and ritual among Liberal, Reform, Conservative, Orthodox and Hasidic Jews." Alex Rubin noted in *Newsweek* that though Potok's "fictional characters remained bound within the insular world of Hasidic Judaism, . . . his powerfully human prose transcended religious denomination."

An Orthodox Upbringing

Potok's father, Benjamin Max Potok, was born a Hasidic Jew in Poland at a time when tensions were rising between Jewish and gentile residents. (Hasidism, a sect originating in Poland in the eighteenth century, arose in reaction to growing Jewish formalism. The Hasids formed tight communities that did not merge with the rest of society.) The elder Potok served in World War I, fighting in a Polish unit of the Austrian Army despite the fact that most of the other soldiers were gentiles. When his service was over, Benjamin came home to find a *pogrom*—an organized massacre of Jewish residents—decimating his community. Fortunately, Potok was able to leave Poland for the United States, eventually marrying and settling in New York City.

Chaim Potok grew up in a close-knit Jewish community in the Bronx. Life in the city was frequently hard and sometimes violent, notably toward the re-

gion's growing population of immigrant Jews. In addition, the Potok family had to deal with the economic difficulties brought on by the Great Depression. Young Potok found happiness, however, in a variety of things. "There were books and classes and teachers; there were friends with whom I invented street games limited only by the boundaries of the imagination," Potok once wrote.

Art appealed to Potok from childhood. One summer, his parochial school hired an artist to teach a painting class. Potok's father and teachers dissuaded the boy from the idea of pursuing of art as a career, in large part because Hasids see art as a frivolous pursuit, or a rebellion against God. Potok commented: "Scholarship—especially Talmudic scholarship—is the measure of an individual. Fiction, even serious fiction—as far as the religious Jewish tradition is concerned—is at best a frivolity, at worst a menace." While Potok's parents generally disregarded their son's writing impulses, they nevertheless allowed him to write short pieces.

"A novel is really a way of presenting a particular world universally. It's about particulars, but the writer's hope is that it can be crafted in a way that will enable all people to lock with it if they are willing to invest some time and energy getting into that world."

—*Chaim Potok*

Potok attended an Orthodox Jewish day school, or yeshiva, where the studies included traditional Jewish writings. As Potok biographer Abramson explained, "This learning was largely restricted to discussion and study of the Talmud, a collection of sixty-three books usually set out in eighteen folio volumes" that consist of civil, religious, and ethical laws based upon Jewish teaching and biblical interpretation, originally passed down orally over the ages from Israel's earliest history. In addition, Potok's high-school teachers assigned such traditional reading matter as *Ivanhoe* and *Treasure Island.* In 1945, however, Potok read with great enthusiasm *Brideshead Revisited,* Evelyn Waugh's popular story of early twentieth-century British upper-class life. After completing *Brideshead Revisited,* Potok decided to become a writer. "I remember finishing the book and marveling at the power of this kind of creativity," the author once wrote. As Potok told Abramson: "Somehow Evelyn Waugh reached across the chasm that separated my tight New York Jewish world from that of the upper-class British Catholics in his book. . . . From that time on, I not only read works of literature for enjoyment but also studied them with Talmudic intensity in order to teach myself how to create worlds out of words on paper. . . . In time I discovered that I had entered a tradition—modern literature." Another important influence on Potok was James Joyce's *Portrait of the Artist as a Young Man.* The novel truly effected the young man's opinion of his place in the world. "Basic to [the novel] was . . . the iconoclast, the individual who grows up inside inherited systems of value and [will not tolerate] . . . the games, masks, arid hypocrisies he sees all around," Potok remarked. In an interview with Laura Chavkin for *MELUS,* Potok recalled that he decided to become a writer when he was sixteen. "My father wasn't very happy over it," Potok noted in his interview. "He wanted me to teach Talmud at an academy of higher Jewish learning. My mother thought it might be a difficult way to make a living, and friends thought it was sort of odd, except for one friend who was very encouraging."

As he grew older, Potok realized that his close religious community clashed with modern society in many areas. He later reflected in *Literature and the Urban Experience* that he was "deep inside [the Jewish world], with a child's slowly increasing awareness of his own culture's richness and shortcomings. . . . [However] there was an echoing world that I longed to embrace. . . . It seemed to hold out at the same time the promise of worldly wisdom . . . and . . . the creations of the great minds of man."

Potok combined his interests in the religious and secular worlds by pursuing both conservative Jewish and gentile studies, receiving his bachelor's degree in English literature from Orthodox Yeshiva University. Soon after, the author abandoned fundamentalist Judaism in favor of Conservatism, a decision made with great difficulty. Nevertheless, Potok needed to find new fields of knowledge that could intertwine with his religious beliefs, and such knowledge turned up in the commentaries and methods of gentile critics. "It was just this . . . that made it possible for him to achieve a reconciliation with Judaism," Abramson noted. As Potok remarked in *Chaim Potok:* "The problems that troubled me [were] resolved by . . . the scientific approach to the sacred texts of Judaism. . . .They give the sources a form, a vitality which is impossible within a fundamentalist stance."

Potok eventually attended the Jewish Theological Seminary in New York City, and was ordained as a conservative rabbi in 1954. As a young rabbi, he traveled to the Far East immediately after the Korean War. Once there, he served in the U.S. Army with a medical then a combat engineer battalion. Potok's experiences in the Orient upset all his former convictions concerning civilization and religion. "In the shattered villages of Korea . . . in the teeming Chinese hovels of Hong Kong, in the vile back streets of Macao, all the neat antique coherence of my past came undone," he once explained. "It was not the anguish of my own people that sundered me . . . but the loveliness and the suffering I saw in the lives of pagans." Asked by Chavkin how seminal an influence Korea had been on him, Potok replied that it was "crucial, fundamental, pivotal." Further elaborating, he commented, "It was a transforming experience. I was not the same person coming out of the army and Korea as I was going in. It was an experience that took me to the brink of death. I lost a dear friend in Korea and came very close to my own death on a number of occasions." Soon after, the author drew on his Korean experiences for his first novel.

A Novelist Comes of Age

In 1958 Potok married Adena Mosevitzky; he also finished and submitted his Korean novel, but publishers rejected it, claiming the work lacked commercial value. Potok began a second novel despite the failure of the first. Soon after his daughter Rena was born, the author and his family moved to Israel where Potok wrote his doctoral dissertation; he also worked on the first draft of his second novel. Upon returning to the United States the family settled in Brooklyn and Potok went back to the Jewish Theological Seminary, now as a member of the Teachers' Institute. At about the same time, he took a position at the journal *Conservative Judaism* that ultimately led to his position as managing editor. In 1965 Potok's daughter Naama was born, and the author received his doctorate in philosophy from the University of Pennsylvania; he also wrote a series of pamphlets under the umbrella title *Jewish Ethics* for the Leaders Training Fellowship and became editor at the Jewish Publication Society. Much of Potok's long-term work with the Society would involve the translation of the Hebrew Bible into English.

It wasn't until 1965 that Potok completed his best-selling novel, *The Chosen.* The book explores the conflict between the world of the Hasidim and that of Orthodox Jews. In the *Dictionary of Literary Biography,* essayist S. Lillian Kremer explained that "The Crown Heights-Williamsburg section of Brooklyn, an area heavily populated by Jews, is the setting for a drama of religious commitment. . . . Potok's descriptive and dramatic portrayal of scholarly endeavor brings new depth and breadth to American-Jewish fiction." Kremer also commented that the novel "captures the joy and intensity of Talmudic learning."

The two main characters in *The Chosen* are Reuven Malter, son of a progressive Talmudic scholar, and Danny Saunders, heir-apparent to the position of *Zaddik,* or spiritual leader, of the Hasidic community. A *Commentary* reviewer explained further: "Hasidism is hardly intelligible without . . . the Zaddik, the spiritual superman whose holy living not only provides . . . inspiration for [his followers] lives' but who raises them aloft with him through [his] spiritual powers. . . . The Zaddik's prayer on behalf of his followers can achieve results far beyond the scope of their own puny efforts at prayer." Two forces run at odds in Danny's life: the encouragement of his Conservative tutor—Reuven's father, who guides the boy's intellectual growth—and Reb Saunders's tightly proscribed rules for his heir. Saunders has brought Danny up in a world of silence, where the only conversations occur during discussions of Scripture.

One of Potok's strong points in fashioning *The Chosen* is his explanation of Talmudic scholarship. "The elder Malter, patterned after the novelist's beloved father-in-law . . . is the idealized Jewish teacher," wrote Kremer. "Just as he fuses the best in Judaic scholarship with the best in secular culture, Reuven combines intellectual excellence in sacred and secular studies." No one was more amazed at the positive reaction to that book than Potok. "I was very surprised by the tremendous success of *The Chosen,*" the author told Chavkin. He had attempted to describe in the book what he terms as "core-to-core culture confrontation." Danny Saunders faces such a confrontation head on when his Hasidism meets the psychoanalytic theories of Sigmund Freud. Such cultural confrontations attracted non-Jewish readers to his work, just as earlier he had been attracted to the upper class English Catholic world of Waugh or the middle class Dublin world which Joyce presented. "A novel is really a way of presenting a particular world universally," Potok told Chavkin. "It's about particulars, but the writer's hope is that it can be crafted in a way that will enable all people to lock with it if they are willing to invest some time and energy getting into that world." For Potok, the novel became an "instrument that bridged cultures."

In 1969 Potok completed *The Promise,* a sequel to *The Chosen.* Reuven prepares to become a rabbi, but clashes with apostate scholar Abraham Gordon. Simultaneously Danny, now a student of clinical psychology, treats young Michael Gordon, the scholar's disturbed son. The family achieves unity, however, through Danny Saunders's betrothal and marriage to Rachel Gordon, his young patient's sister. The book's theme, said Kremer, focuses on how "each character defines himself, understands himself, and celebrates himself as a twentieth-century Jew." In the *New York Times Book Review,* Nissenson wrote that "despite an occasional technical lapse, Potok has demonstrated his ability to deal with a more complex conception and to suffuse it with pertinence and vitality."

My Name Is Asher Lev is the third of Potok's early popular novels. Once again it is set in the world of Hasidim, this time dealing with an artist. As in his earlier books, Potok relates Asher's experiences in the first person and sets his character in the midst of a "core-to-core culture confrontation, as the protagonist encounters Western art. Asher's story is "the mature artist's retrospective portrait of his childhood [and] a reexamination of his attitudes," explained Kremer. Asher's parents dislike his interest in art, often scolding him for his apathy towards Biblical scholarship. Asher often dreams of his deceased grandfather, a noted scholar. In the dreams, his grandfather condemns Asher for his devotion to art. Some members of the Hasidic community even consider Asher's gifts demonic, but the Rebbe—who leads the community and also employs Asher's father—unexpectedly champions the boy.

Asher's goal is "to develop his aesthetic sense through painting," observed Abramson in *Chaim Potok.* Like Danny Saunders, Asher is born into the role of heir-apparent. In the latter case, Asher's future position entails working as an international emissary for the Rebbe. The tumult over Asher's studies increases when he begins to paint nudes and crucifixions. Although Asher sees the cross as a non-religious symbol, his father sees it as a figure for antisemitism. The crisis comes to a head over Asher's painting the "Brooklyn Crucifixion." Eventually, Asher must choose between his community and his painting. With publication of this third book, Potok had assured himself of a large and loyal reading public.

In Two Worlds

In 1973 Potok and his family left the United States to live in Jerusalem for three years before settling permanently in Marion, Pennsylvania, just outside Philadelphia. In 1975 he published his next work, *In the Beginning.* As with many of his other novels, *In the Beginning* deals with antisemitism. "Rarely has the rage of the Jew been so honestly portrayed," remarked Nissenson, who added that "by the power of his own intellect [Potok comes] to grips with the theme implicit in all of his previous work: the problem of sustaining religious faith in a meaningless world. . . . It successfully recreates a time and a place and the journey of a soul." The author goes beyond America's treatment of Jews and looks at its historical precedence.

In the Beginning focuses on the relationship between David Lurie, a Jewish boy, and Eddie Kulanski, a gentile. Other main themes in the work revolve around Biblical scholarship and the State of Israel. "The narrator here is a brilliantly gifted Orthodox Jewish boy who eventually accommodates himself to modern life," explained Nissenson. Through David, Potok uses stream-of-consciousness writing to depict the tragedies endured by the Jews in Europe. When David hears of the losses sustained by Jews during World War II, he enters a dreamland where an imaginary hero fights Nazi oppressors. David deeply loves the Torah, and sees it as a symbol of hope for all Jews. He alienates his family, however, when he adopts the shocking belief that using gentile scholarship will bridge the gulf separating Jew and gentile.

A *Time* reviewer wrote that *In the Beginning* makes the reader "wholly aware of what it must have been like to belong to such a family and such a religion at such a time. Conveying vividly the exact feel of unfamiliar territory is a job almost exclusively performed by journalists. . . . That novels can accomplish that task superlatively is one of the reasons why they are still written—and read." Michael Irwin, writing in the *Times Literary Supplement,* noted that Potok "catches beautifully the atmosphere of a family party or a school quarrel. Rarer than this is the skill with which he shows how what a child learns and what it experiences are fused and transformed by the imagination." Daphne Merkin stated in *Commentary* that while Potok tends to stick to "fertile Jewish territory," he has hit "a formula for success . . . in which the only limits to artistic achievement are the limits of his own imagination." She also noted, however, that "Potok's rendition of Orthodox life is entertaining and informative, but his work does not expand to the dimensions it reaches for."

In 1978 the author saw publication of the nonfiction work *Wanderings: Chaim Potok's History of the Jews.* In *The Christian Science Monitor,* Michael J. Bandler described the book: "Using hundreds of eminent sources and texts in several languages . . . [Potok] has fashioned an intelligent, thorough and credible one-volume chronicle that breathes with a passion

that is more common to fiction than history. . . . It should be savored, scene by provocative scene, mulled over and retained." A *Maclean's* contributor noted a different consideration: "Behind Potok's account of the Jewish struggle to stay alive . . . is [his] own moral search: to understand how a people managed to survive both the seduction of comfort . . . [and] diabolical tortures . . . to remain Jews."

Three years later, Potok finished *The Book of Lights.* Steeped in the Jewish mysticism of the Kabbalah and full of moral decisions fraught with anguish, the work marked a new departure for the author. Johanna Kaplan, writing in the *New York Times Book Review,* called the novel "The story of [a] dark and baffling inner journey." *The Book of Lights* tackles the subject of moral responsibility and the atom bomb, a dilemma epitomized by the characters Gershon Loran and Arthur Leiden. In the novel, Potok's characters work to incorporate their faith with a secular society. The book culminates in Jerusalem, where Gershon works to resolve his spiritual dilemmas. Potok noted to Chavkin that the problems he dealt with in his later books, such as *The Book of Lights,* "are far more complex than those in the earlier books, and lead to resolutions that are mired in ambiguity."

Over the years, Potok developed a rigid work schedule. He would rise at 6:30 in the morning and work from 8:00 until 1:00, break for lunch, and then work again until five in the afternoon. After that he would go out for a long walk and then have dinner, and in the evening read or perhaps go out for a movie with his wife. He would follow this same schedule five-and-a-half days a week, working on one fiction project at a time, interrupting his work only to write a review if requested. For Potok, as he commented to Chavkin, writing was "painful and exhausting, that's true. But it's also exhilarating. And very frustrating."

Much of the impetus for Potok's sixth work of fiction, *Davita's Harp,* was an experience of sexism his wife suffered while in her teens. The novel takes place in Depression-era New York. Both of Davita's parents—her Protestant newspaperman father and Jewish mother—have abandoned religious beliefs for Communism. Seeking security, the girl explores Judaism and attends a yeshiva. Once there, Davita discovers a prejudice against female scholars; when she makes top marks, the young girl is denied a highly coveted school award because she is female. "Davita's commitment to patriarchal Judaism is deeply shaken at her graduation," explained Patty Campbell in *Wilson Library Bulletin.* The school gives the Akiva award "to a boy to save the school the public shame of a girl as best student," Campbell noted. Critics praised the book's use of common-place items to establish the setting. "The idealistic underworld of American communism in the thirties leaps out in evocative details," remarked Campbell.

Toward the end of the 1980s Potok adapted *The Chosen* as a musical. He felt the time-consuming project was worthwhile, even though it took over a year. As he told Mervyn Rothstein of the *New York Times,* "there was potentiality for seriousness here." Simultaneously, Potok felt that "it didn't have to be heavy-handed, because the novel itself is not heavy-handed." In his theater adaptation Potok centers on "a sense of the way a particular core culture confronts the world outside, and the dimensions of that confrontation," Rothstein reported. Many theater critics, however, found the production disappointing. *New York Times* contributor Mel Gussow noted that "the relationship between Reuven and Danny moves perilously close to a love that dare not speak its name . . . one that would clearly contradict the author's intent."

As a sequel to *My Name Is Asher Lev,* Potok wrote *The Gift of Asher Lev.* The author picks up the narrative many years after the first book. Lev has left New York and the Hasidic world to live with his family on the Cote d'Azur. A funeral brings the Lev family back to Asher's old home. Matters become complicated when Lev's wife and son prefer the tight-knit Hasidic community to life on the Mediterranean. In the end, Lev's father resolves the conflict. As the elderly Rebbe's successor, Lev's father turns his attention to Asher's son, Avrumel. The older man decides that Avrumel shall take his father's place and continue the dynasty. The sad conclusion is that "the price of Lev's restoration to his people is his physical and personal exclusion," noted Brian Morton in the *Times Literary Supplement.* "Much as Christ was a sacrificed 'missing generation' between God and mankind, Lev's self-sacrificing art is a personal crucifixion. . . . [it also guarantees] that the tradition will pass on."

Reaching Children and Adults

In 1992 Potok published his only novel without a Jewish setting, *I Am the Clay,* "a bleak portrayal of uneducated Korean war refugees," according to Eric Homberger writing in the *Guardian.* The following year he created another first for himself with *The Tree of Here,* his first picture book for young children. Potok also completed a second picture book for young readers, *The Sky of Now,* in 1995. These books received mixed reviews. A contributor for *Publishers Weekly* felt that in *The Tree of Here* and *The Sky of*

Now neither Potok's nor political cartoonist Tony Auth's "talents translate clearly to children's books." However, *Booklist* contributor Julie Corsaro called *The Sky of Now* "well-crafted," containing an "eloquently expressed story line."

More successful was *Zebra and Other Stories,* Potok's 1998 collection of six short tales for young adults. Each story features a teenage protagonist in transition, like B. B., whose father leaves the family the same day the teen's mother goes into labor; and Isabel, whose widowed mother marries a widowed man with a daughter the same age as she. "All the stories are thought-provoking and gripping," wrote Susan Scheps in *School Library Journal.* "The characters and their personal dilemmas" added the reviewer, "will linger with readers." More praise for the collection came from *Booklist* contributor Stephanie Zvirin who felt that this anthology "is a wonderful introduction" to Potok's work. Zvirin described the tales as "quiet, spare, intimate, about children and teens who experience something that pushes them one step closer to the adult world." *Horn Book* reviewer Nancy Vasilakis also had kind words for the award-winning collection, noting that Potok does not condescend in his writing for young adults. "Though simple on the surface," wrote Vasilakis, "the stories carry layers of meaning, and teens will discover that one reading won't be enough."

Turning his hand to nonfiction again, Potok explores the plight of Jews in the former Soviet Union with *The Gates of November: Chronicles of the Slepak Family.* He records the difficulties of this Jewish family, representative of millions more. The father, Solomon, manages to navigate the treacherous waters of the Russian Revolution of the early twentieth century, surviving the purges of dictator Josef Stalin and rising high in the Communist bureaucracy. When his son Volodya decides to immigrate to Israel, the family is torn apart. It takes Volodya eighteen years to get such permission, and during this time he loses his job, is divorced from his wife, and is sent into internal exile. *Booklist* contributor Nancy Pearl felt that there is a "great deal of interesting history" contained in the book, but criticized Potok's "plodding writing style" which lacks "emotional punch." A contributor for *Publishers Weekly,* however, found the same book a "compelling account," and Rena Fowler, writing in *Library Journal,* remarked that *The Gates of November* is a "well-written, thought-provoking book."

In the late 1990s Potok again turned his hand to nonfiction, working with virtuoso violinist Isaac Stern to tell the story of that musician's life in *My First Seventy-nine Years.* Ray Olson, writing in *Booklist,* thought that Potok makes the narrative line of the book "flow beautifully, in a voice that is vital and exciting as well as excited," while Carol J. Binkowski, writing in *Library Journal,* found the book to be a "sensitive and engrossing history of a man and an era."

Potok's final book, *Old Men at Midnight,* appeared in 2001, a collection of three novellas which share a common character, Ilana Davita Dinn. Dubbed an "inquisitive Jewish woman" by *Book* reviewer Chris Barsanti, Ilana is a teenager in "The Ark Builder," tutoring concentration camp survivors in New York City. One of her students, a teenage boy who is the only survivor of his Polish village, begins to open up to Ilana and tells her of his friendship with the man who was the caretaker of his local synagogue. Ilana is a graduate student in "The War Doctor"; as such she persuades a visiting lecturer from Russia to write about his experiences living under Stalin. It turns out that this lecturer, Leon Shertov, was saved by a Jewish doctor in World War I, later became a KGB interrogator, and met the same doctor as a prisoner. In "The Trope Teacher" Ilana has become famous in her own right, as an author, and works with a well-known academic to help him write his memoirs. *Old Men at Midnight* was, on the whole, warmly received by critics. Though a contributor for *Publishers Weekly* had problems with Potok's narration of Ilana as a teenager, there were no such reservations for "The War Doctor," "the grimmest and most nuanced of the stories, [which] alone is worth the price of admission." Barsanti found the same story "the most engrossing," and further noted that all the tales are "masterfully written" and "delicately realized." Kristine Huntley added to the praise in *Booklist,* calling *Old Men at Midnight* a "moving and powerful book." And Deborah King, writing for *Knight Ridder/Tribune News Service,* found the collection to be, "in the best sense, a return to familiar ground for Chaim Potok. . . . perhaps the foremost chronicler of the Jewish-American experience." Potok died of brain cancer at age seventy-three.

If you enjoy the works of Chaim Potok, you might want to check out the following books:

Kathryn Lasky, *Beyond the Divide,* 1983.
Aidan Chambers, *NIK: Now I Know,* 1988.
Brock Cole, *Celine,* 1989.

In her *Dictionary of Literary Biography* essay, Kremer summarized the general response to Potok's body of work by noting that the criticism "ranged from denunciation to acclaim." Some critics have called the author's approach, plots, and characters narrow and dry, pointing to a sometimes labored style and pompous narrative tone; these reviewers also maintained that Potok's brilliant theology students often seem too good to be true. Other assessors, however, have noted the author's thoughtful, careful deliberation of important issues. Potok likewise received praise for his piercing visions into Orthodox Jewish life and culture; by comparison, many contemporary Jewish authors appear topical in their treatment of the variety of Jewish experience. Overall, the author saw as his mission to bring meaning to a nonsensical world. He once commented that doing this "specifically . . . is the task of the artist." In his interview with Rothstein, Potok clarified, "You deal with a small and particular world. . . . You dig into that world with as much honesty as you can, and if you do it honestly and skillfully enough, somehow you're going to bridge the gap." With his death in 2002, Potok was remembered by critics and friends alike, but Saad perhaps summed up his contribution best: "His work will ensure that he is not forgotten."

■ Biographical and Critical Sources

BOOKS

Abramson, Edward A., *Chaim Potok,* Twayne (Boston, MA), 1986.
Authors in the News, Gale (Detroit MI), Volume 1, 1976, Volume 2, 1976.
Contemporary Literary Criticism, Gale (Detroit MI), Volume 2, 1974, Volume 7, 1977, Volume 14, 1980, Volume 26, 1983, Volume 112, 1999.
Dictionary of Literary Biography, Volume 28: *Twentieth-Century American-Jewish Fiction Writers,* Gale (Detroit, MI), 1984, pp. 232-243.
Dictionary of Literary Biography Yearbook: 1984, Gale (Detroit MI), 1985.
Jaye, M. C and A. C. Watts, editors, *Literature and Urban Experience: Essays on the City and Literature,* Rutgers University Press (New Brunswick, NJ), 1981.

PERIODICALS

Book, November-December, 2001, Chris Barsanti, review of *Old Men at Midnight,* pp. 65-66.
Booklist, February 1, 1990, p. 1050; April 1, 1992, p. 1413; January 1, 1996, Julie Corsaro, review of *The Sky of Now,* p. 848; November 1, 1996, Nancy

Pearl, review of *The Gates of November,* p. 480; July, 1998, Stephanie Zvirin, review of *Zebra and Other Stories,* p. 1878; September 15, 1999, Ray Olson, review of *My First Seventy-nine Years,* p. 196; September 15, 2001, Kristine Huntley, review of *Old Men at Midnight,* p. 195.

Christian Science Monitor, December 16, 1969, Michael J. Bandler, "Faith's Long Journey," p. 13.

Commentary, September, 1967, review of *The Chosen,* p. 107; February, 1976, Daphne Merkin, "Why Potok Is Popular," pp. 73-75.

Horn Book, November-December, 1998, Nancy Vasilakis, review of *Zebra and Other Stories,* p. 739.

Kirkus Reviews, April 1, 1992, p. 423; September 15, 1996, p. 1383.

Knight Ridder/Tribune News Service, October 7, 1998, Liz Stevens, "Writer Chaim Potok Struggles to Reconcile Religion, Modern World," p. 1007K5428; November 21, 2001, Deborah King, review of *Old Men at Midnight,* p. K0003.

Library Journal, November 1, 1996, Rena Fowler, review of *The Gates of November,* p. 90; November 1, 1999, Carol J. Binkowski, review of *My First Seventy-nine Years,* p. 86.

Maclean's, January 1, 1979, review of *Wanderings: Chaim Potok's History of the Jews,* p. 47.

MELUS, summer, 1999, Laura Chavkin, "A MELUS Interview: Chaim Potok," p. 147.

New York Times, January 3, 1988, Mervyn Rothstein, "Crafting a Musical from *The Chosen*"; January 7, 1988, Mel Gussow, "Theater: *The Chosen* as a Musical"; December 1, 1996, p. 33.

New York Times Book Review, May 7, 1967, Hugh Nissenson, "The Spark and the Shell," pp. 4-5, 34; September 14, 1969, Hugh Nissenson, review of *The Promise*; October 19, 1975, Hugh Nissenson, "My Name Is David Lurie"; October 11, 1981, Johanna Kaplan, "Two Ways of Life," pp. 14-15, 28.

Publishers Weekly, March 30, 1992, p. 89; November 27, 1995, review if *The Sky of Now,* p. 69; October 28, 1996, review of *The Gates of November,* p. 7;

July 20, 1998, review of *Zebra and Other Stories,* p. 222; November 5, 2001, review of *Old Men at Midnight,* p. 43.

Saturday Review, April 15, 1972, Robert J. Milch, review of *My Name Is Asher Lev,* pp. 65-66.

School Library Journal, October, 1993, p. 108; September, 1998, Susan Scheps, review of *Zebra and Other Stories,* p. 208.

Time, November 3, 1975, review of *In the Beginning,* p. 94.

Times Literary Supplement, April 9, 1976, Michael Irwin, "A Full-Time Condition," p. 413; November 2, 1990, Brian Morton, "Banished and Banished Again."

Wilson Library Bulletin, June, 1985, Patty Campbell, review of *Davita's Harp,* pp. 688-689.

OTHER

Books and Writers, http://www.kirjasto.sci-fi/potok/ (October 26, 2002), "Chaim Potok."

Chaim Potok Home Page, http://www.lasierra.edu/ ˜ballen/potok (October 26, 2002).

McDougal, Littell Author Profile, http://www. mcdougallittell.com/ (October 26, 2002), "Chaim Potok."

■ Obituaries

PERIODICALS

Guardian (London, England), July 31, 2002.

Newsweek, August 5, 2002, p. 6.

People, August 5, 2002, p. 77.

Time International, August 5, 2002, p. 13.

United Press International, July 24, 2002, Shirley Saad, "Chaim Potok Is Dead."

U.S. News and World Report, August 5, 2002, "Chaim's Choice," p. 6.*

Rembrandt

Personal

Full name Rembrandt Harmensz van Rijn; born July 15, 1606, in Leiden, Netherlands; died, October 4, 1669, in Amsterdam, Netherlands; son of Harmen (a miller) and Cornelia Neeltgen Willemsdochter (van Zuidbroeck) van Rijn; married Saskia van Uylenburgh, 1634 (died 1642); lived with Hendrickje Stoffels, from late 1640s (died 1663); children: (first marriage) Titus; (with Stoffels) Cornelia. *Nationality:* Dutch. *Education:* Studied at University of Leiden; studied art with Jacob van Swanenburgh, 1621-24, and Pieter Lastman, 1624-25.

Career

Painter and etcher. *Exhibitions:* Work included in permanent collections at major museums worldwide, including Metropolitan Museum of Art and Frick Collection, New York, NY; Louvre, Paris, France; Rijksmuseum, Amsterdam, Netherlands; National Gallery, London, England; Prado, Madrid, Spain; Hermitage, St. Petersburg, Russia; Gemaldegalerie, Berlin, Germany; and Kunsthistorisches Museum, Vienna, Austria.

Writings

Seven Letters, edited by Horst Gerson, translated by Yda D. Ovink, Boucher (The Hague, Netherlands), 1961.

Sidelights

Both creation and creator of Holland's Golden Age of art, Rembrandt van Rijn is considered one of the most famous Western painters of all time as well as the finest portrait painter in the world. Even those unfamiliar with the classics of world painting will likely know the name if not the somewhat murky and mysterious surfaces of his famous series of self-portraits—of which the artist painted nearly a hundred. In oil, drawing, and etching, Rembrandt left a legacy of upwards of 2,000 items, a rich storehouse of images which include portraits, landscapes, biblical and mythical scenes, and historical representations.

Known for the manipulation of light and shadow that gives his works emotional impact, Rembrandt produced works of art that transcend their subject matter. Never content with mere surface, Rembrandt, more than any of his contemporaries, exposes the viewer to the inner, private person. And his ability to manipulate paint creates the illusion of texture in depictions of hair, clothing, and jewelry, lending his paintings a solid, sculpted effect. "Apart from his immense gifts as a pure painter and illustrator," wrote art critic Kenneth Clark in *An Introduction to Rembrant,* the painter "digs down to the roots of life; and he seems to open his heart to us. We have the feeling he is keeping nothing back." Clark further noted in *Civilization* that the "psychological truth in Rembrandt's paintings goes beyond that of any other artist who ever lived." In addition to his prowess in painting, his etchings are equally famous and are often compared by critics to the work of German artist Albrecht Dürer. Many contend that even if Rembrandt had never painted a picture, his prints alone would have been enough to secure his fame.

Among Rembrant's most famous paintings are "The Anatomy Lessons of Dr. Tulp," "Portrait of Maerten Soolmans," "The Blinding of Samson," "Titus at His Desk," "Militia Company of Captain Frans Banning Cocq and Lieutenant Willem van Ruytenbuch" (known popularly as "The Night Watch"), "Hendrickje Bathing," "Aristotle Contemplating a Bust of Homer," "Syndics of the Cloth Guild," "The Return of the Prodigal Son," "The Jewish Bride," and numerous self-portraits. Famous during his own lifetime, Rembrandt earned a healthy living with his portrait commissions, although his penchant for speculating and for collecting artwork led to his bankruptcy in middle age. His final years, though productive, were also characterized by reduced economic circumstances and loneliness, for he had outlived one wife, and another life companion, as well as his son.

The Early Years

Rembrandt Harmensz van Rijn was born on July 15, 1606, in Leiden, the ninth of ten children of Harmen van Rijn, a miller, and Cornelia Neeltgen Willemsdochter van Zuidbroeck, daughter of a prosperous baker. Rembrandt was fortunate in his birth not only for family but also for the era he was born into. Years of war had finally resulted in a peaceful time for the Netherlands, and the van Rijn family benefitted from such tranquility. His father was half owner of the mill De Rijn, and the family was thus solidly middle class. Rembrandt, like his older brothers, attended the city's Latin school, where he learned Greek, Latin, literature, and history. The most promising of all his siblings intellectually, Rembrandt spent seven years in this school environment, where pupils conversed in Latin. In 1620, just shy of fourteen years of age, he was sent on to Leiden University, where his parents hoped he would prepare for the life of a scholar. This would be a first in the family, for the other brothers had all

studied for a trade. However, after only a few months at the university, Rembrandt's real love took priority. He had already been painting and sketching for several years by this time, and his parents finally agreed that he could quit the university and take an apprenticeship with local artist Jacob van Swanenburgh.

For three years the young Rembrandt worked in Swanenburgh's studio, where he learned basic painting techniques as well as the fundamentals of etching. Swanenburgh, the son of a well-known painter and former mayor of Leiden, had studied in Italy, though his painting—architectural and religious scenes—does not seem to have hugely benefitted from such an education. No attributed works from Rembrandt remain from these apprenticeship years, though it is known that he practiced his skills at portraiture by using his parents and various residents of Leiden during this time.

Of more lasting influence was painter Pieter Lastman, with whom Rembrandt worked for a half year immediately following his apprenticeship with Swanenburgh. Typically, young artists might round out their education by traveling to Italy to absorb its influences; instead, Rembrandt opted to study with Lastman, a celebrated painter in Amsterdam who had himself studied in Italy. Known for historical scenes which blended elements of the Bible and mythology, Lastman deeply affected Rembrandt's compositional style, kindling the young artist's own interest in biblical and historical paintings. Like Lastman, Rembrandt infuses such paintings with a strong narrative and dramatic approach. Additionally, Lastman, while studying in Rome, had come under the influence of the painter Caravaggios, who created revolutionary effects with the use of shadow and light, and the influence of Caravaggio thus can be seen clearly in the mature work of Rembrandt as well. Early paintings from Rembrandt that directly reflect the Lastman style include "Stoning of St. Stephen," "Paul and Barnabas at Lystra," "Balaam and the Ass," and "Baptism of the Eunuch," all from 1625 and 1626. Like a sponge, Rembrandt absorbed these early influences, and soon began creating a body of work of his own. As B. P. J. Broos noted in a *Grove Art* entry on Rembrandt, "even at the outset of his career, Rembrandt displayed a tremendous zest for work and a profusion of new ideas."

Rembrandt returned to Leiden in 1626, there to set up a studio that he shared with fellow artist Jan Lievens. The two did not collaborate on paintings; rather they shared models and often painted the same scenes. By 1628 Rembrandt was already tak-

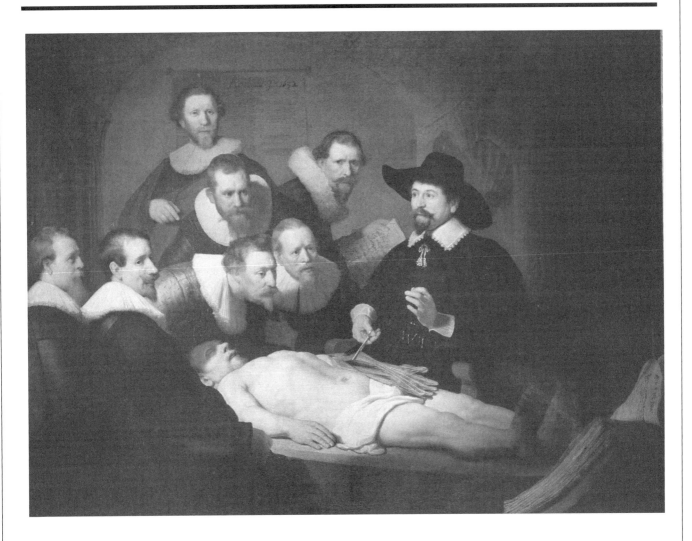

Considered one of Rembrandt's most famous paintings, "The Anatomy Lesson of Dr. Tulp" was completed in 1632 for Amsterdam's surgeon's guild.

ing pupils, a practice he continued all his life and which also helped support him. Rembrandt's paintings were small in size in these Leiden years, and he also sketched and utilized the etcher's needle to create works which depicted human emotions as shown in the facial expressions of his subjects. Together, Rembrandt and Lievens developed a new sort of portrait painting, the *tronie*, in which the subject was dressed in "exotic garments, with a turban or an ornamental cap and a golden necklace or the like," according to Broos. Among such tronies was Rembrandt's first self-portrait of 1629. According to Broos, the "high point" in Rembrandt's Leiden years was the 1631 painting "Presentation in the Temple." In Broos' opinion, "This multi-figured history piece in the style of Lastman combines the latter's attention to detail and thorough composition with Rembrandt's own powerful means of ex-

pression, the concentrated fall of light that dramatically illuminates the main figures." By the time Rembrandt decided to leave Leiden in 1631, his dramatic chiaroscuro technique had already been developed.

Earns Fame in Amsterdam

Toward the end of 1631 Rembrandt left the more provincial confines of Leiden for the bustling commercial center of Amsterdam. He had already begun painting portraits of the rich and powerful in Leiden, and his reputation had spread to Amsterdam, earning him portrait commissions from there as well. Amsterdam, at the time, was the perfect place for a portraitist such as Rembrandt, for it had a solid middle class with enough disposable income to not only encourage the arts but also indulge the vanity of the nouveau riche with portraits. Coming to the metropolis, Rembrandt resumed a commercial relationship with the art dealer van Uylenburgh, whom he had met on his earlier stay in Amsterdam. The artist invested money in van Uylenburgh's business, living with the dealer and virtually worked for him while the art dealer obtained portrait commissions for the young artist. His first major group portrait commission came in 1632, a painting for the Amsterdam surgeons' guild, "Anatomy Lesson of Dr. Tulp." This initial corporate portrait features a group of students gathered around a cadaver while a doctor instructs them in anatomy. Writing about this painting in *Grove Art*, Broos noted that Rembrandt "knew how to tell a story," and more importantly, he "broke with all existing traditions" in this composition. Rembrandt's dramatic use of light and shadow comes to the fore in "Anatomy Lesson." "Bright light falls on the demonstrating hands of Dr. Tulp, who commands the complete attention of his audience," according to Broos. Other individual portraits followed, including those of businessmen such as "Martin Looten" and "Maerten Soolmans." During his years with van Uylenburgh, Rembrandt painted about fifty portraits, or almost one per month, leaving little time for drawing or etching.

One double portrait of note is "Rembrandt and Saskia," one of many oils featuring his new wife, Saskia van Uylenburgh, the niece of the art dealer. Saskia was an orphan from the age of twelve who alternately lived with relations in Friesland and in Amsterdam, where Rembrandt met her. Another well-known painting featuring his wife, "Saskia as Flora," depicts her as the goddess of love and gave Rembrandt the opportunity to indulge in his gift for painting rich damask and embroidery in the clothing of the goddess. His use of pigments and overpainting—in a technique still imperfectly understood—allowed him to add rich textures to fabric as well as sparkle to glass and jewelry and sheen to satin and silk.

Saskia brought a dowry to their wedding in June of 1634 that helped make Rembrandt an independent painter. However, it appears that Rembrandt also left behind his own family at this time. His mother, for example, did not attend her son's wedding nor was she in attendance at the baptism of any of his children. The couple set up in their own house in 1635 and had three daughters in five years, each of who died in infancy.

During these years Rembrandt also indulged his passion for collecting the work of other artists, both contemporary and classical. His private collection of paintings, etchings, drawings, and objects of art grew into the hundreds of items over the years, and increasingly ate into the artist's income. However, he was also able to use such pieces as inspiration for his own work. This collection, along with the large house he purchased in 1639, pushed him into debt. For the rest of his life he remained bothered by the financial problems encountered at this time.

In 1639 Rembrandt reached the high point in his career, with five scenes from the passion of Christ recently finished for a wealthy client and a bevy of other commissions contracted. The well-known "Self-Portrait Leaning on a Stone Sill," both an etching and an oil painting, clearly shows how he identified himself with the wealthy and elegant class of his clients. He branched out into landscape painting at this time, also, as with "Landscape with the Good Samaritan," and also continued to paint historical and biblical subjects. With the latter, he was famous for depicting the subjects of such narratives in contemporary dress, in an effort to make their stories more relevant not only to himself, but also to other viewers of his day. Most critics agree that "The Blinding of Samson" is the pinnacle of this early dramatic style, a painting heavily influenced by Rubens.

Then came the commission for what has become one of his most famous paintings, the "Militia Company of Captain Frans Banning Cocq," also known, erroneously, as "Night Watch." This scene of a military company or platoon of musketeers decked out in swords, guns, drums, and banners, was meant to decorate the hall of the civic guards. Because of Rembrandt's dramatic use of lighting, the scene is often misinterpreted as taking place at night, though the militia never paraded at night. During a restoration of the painting in 1975, it was discovered that the scene really takes place during daylight. This group portrait was hung in the Kloveniersdoelen in Amsterdam until 1715, after which it was moved to the Stadhuis and the canvas was reduced in size. When Amsterdam's Rijksmuseum opened in 1885, "Night Watch" became the centerpiece of the entire collection. Rembrandt adopted a novel approach to this group portrait, catching the individual characters in action rather than in static poses. His use of light is also unique; illumination seems to come from within the painting itself, spotlighting some of the characters and casting others into shadow and partial obscurity. Other elements add to the interest: a young girl with a chicken dangling from her belt, a man with a drum, a pointing man, and a barking dog. The viewer is left to wonder what it all means, to try and understand the dramatic scene captured in this canvas. The small details Rembrandt adds to this group portrait of eighteen militiamen take it far beyond the bounds of typical group portraits.

Rembrandt's 1652 etching "Faust in His Study" depicts the legendary German doctor who sold his soul to the Devil in exchange for never-ending youth and infinite knowledge.

Though the painting has no discernable theme, it still seems to convey a message. The drama here is not staged, but real and created by the use of light, and of strong vertical, horizontal, and diagonal lines that lead the viewer's eye from subject to subject.

Legend has it that Captain Cocq and his company were highly dissatisfied with Rembrant's portrait and that the poor reception of the painting marked a reversal in the artist's fortunes. In fact, as numerous critics have pointed out, the painting was highly praised in his own lifetime. Broos, for example, noted that critics "admired the treatment of form and the animated composition, which gives the effect of a narrative or subject picture as opposed to a static portrait." Broos also went on to remark that Rembrandt not only provided "a number of excellent portraits," but also "cleverly used the group to demonstrate the operation of a militia company."

Years of Adversity

After the death of several children, Rembrandt and his wife finally had a healthy child, Titus, in 1641. A year later, along with the completion of "Night Watch," Saskia died of tuberculosis and Rembrandt was left alone with a small son to raise. Saskia's fortune was divided equally between Rembrandt and Titus, though it appears that the painter also went through his son's inheritance quickly with his penchant for a high lifestyle. Another feature of Saskia's will was that Rembrandt could not remarry after her death without losing his inheritance. Therefore, to help care for his child, Rembrandt employed Geertge Dircx, widow of a ship's bugler and popular local musician. The widow clearly grew attached to the young boy and to his father. By 1648, Geertge had drawn up a will of her own in which she left her possessions to Titus, which possessions included Saskia's jewels, given to her by Rembrandt. When in 1649 Rembrandt's attentions strayed to a younger woman named Hendrickje Stoffels, the artist made a separation agreement with Geertge. The terms of the agreement, however, were not to the spurned woman's liking and she sued Rembrandt. The artist, admitting he had been intimate with Geertge but had never promised to marry her, was ordered to support her with an annual allowance of 200 guilders, an amount that was increasingly difficult for him to afford. Angered, Rembrandt conspired with Geertge's brother to have her committed to a reformatory in Gouda where she remained until 1655, dying the following year. Meanwhile, Rembrandt had a daughter with Hendrickje, whom he never married, but who remained his domestic partner until her death in 1663.

Attributed to Rembrandt, "The Apostle Bartholomew" is one of many paintings the Dutch artist completed based on religious subjects, and shows his ability to use light and dark to dramatic effect.

In addition to domestic problems, Rembrandt also suffered from financial difficulties and by 1654 was unable to meet the mortgage payments on his house. Despite such affairs, Rembrandt continued to create some of his most powerful work in oil, drawings, and etchings throughout the later 1640s and the 1650s. With his 1648 etching "Self-Portrait Drawing at a Window," a sea change in his self-depiction occurs, however. No longer is he the dandy of the earlier self-portraits, looking over one shoulder and attired in the finest clothes. Instead, he presents himself frontally, with the painter's beret replaced by solid brimmed hat. He is now dressed in simple clothing with his hair cut short and his flowing beard gone. At forty-two, Rembrandt was suddenly transformed into a simple artist at work. Donald Bruce, writing in *Contemporary Review,* noted that "Rembrandt's personal disaster increased his introspection, ever present in his early canvases and etchings."

Notable paintings from the 1650s include "Aristotle with the Bust of Homer," a contemplative painting that continues to confound scholars looking for the correct interpretation or meaning, and "Titus at his Desk," a rendering of his son as a fourteen-year-old. Rembrant also used his new partner in several paintings, including "Hendrickje Bathing." Another imposing painting of the time is "Anatomy Lesson of Dr. Deyman," later largely destroyed by fire. Religious subjects comprised a large part of Rembrandt's total output and continued to figure prominently in his creative life. The "Blessing of Jacob," which Broos referred to as "an artistic zenith," came from 1656, and "Risen Christ," "Jacob Wrestling with the Angel," and "Moses with the Tablets" are among other biblical scenes from the late 1650s.

Rembrandt's financial problems worsened with unwise speculation, and in 1656 he was forced to declare insolvency. His property was put up for auction in order to pay his creditors, both his house in the Jodenbreestraat where he had lived for almost two decades, as well as his considerable art collection, which included ancient sculpture, Italian, German, Dutch, and Flemish prints and drawings, Far Eastern artwork, weapons and armor, as well as his own work. In all, his collection contained 360 pieces, enough for a small museum. He had once paid hundreds of guilders for just one of the prints; now the entire collection was auctioned for less than 500 guilders. An economic recession at the time was in part responsible for such an undervaluing, and there are also historians who claim that the auction was fixed by a rival painter. With the sale of the collection and later of the house, Rembrandt's creditors were mostly paid off, and the artist, together with Titus, Hendrickje, and the couple's daughter, Cornelia, moved to a more modest house in another district of Amsterdam. Here, in 1660, Hendrickje and son Titus formed an art business and Rembrandt became their "employee" in an attempt to shield him from future creditors.

The Final Years and Legacy

Saved from creditors, Rembrandt was free to create again and resumed taking on pupils. He painted daily until his death nine years later, but in this late period made few drawings or etchings. In 1662 he received another important commission for a group portrait, this time from the Amsterdam Drapers' Guild. Titled "Syndics of the Cloth Guild," the painting is recognized as his last great group portrait. Each of the six men represented in the painting have real presence and depth. As Richard G. Tansey and Fred S. Kleiner noted in *Gardner's Art through the Ages,* "Rembrandt applied all that he knew of the dynamics and the psychology of light,

the visual suggestion of time, and the art of pose and facial expression" in this work. Five syndics or members of the board of directors of a business are shown, going over the books of a corporation. These five notables in hats are attended to by a bareheaded assistant, and all look up as if a visitor has just arrived in their boardroom. "Rembrandt gives us the lively reality of a business conference as it is interrupted," according to Tansey and Kleiner. The arrangement of the figures was no accident. As X-ray analysis has shown, the position of these six was changed several times during the course of the painting. The same authors concluded that the result is a "superb harmony of light, color, movement, time, and pose [which] has few rivals in the history of painting."

Other late paintings of note include "Jewish Bride," a picture of two unknown subjects that has become "world-famous thanks to the magical fall of light,

The drypoint etching "The Rising of Lazarus" may have served as a study for Rembrandt's subsequent painting of the same subject.

the wonderful impasto and the tender gestures of the man and his bride," according to Broos. Also from the final years is "Return of the Prodigal Son," showing a son crouching in front of his father, who in turn embraces him. This painting is, as Tansey and Kleiner remarked, "one of the most moving pictures in all religious art." Fittingly, Rembrandt ended his painting life with three more self-portraits in 1669, these last revealing a "faded, pouched and collapsed Rembrandt, oppressed almost to tears, perhaps by the loss of his loyal Titus and Hendrickje," according to Bruce writing in *Contemporary Review*. All his life he created such personal portraits, forever experimenting with human expression in the model that was closest to hand. Other theories abound about his continual use of the self-portrait, some critics contending that it was a blatant form of self-promotion, while others argued that it was a form of self-analysis. "Whatever his reasons for producing them," wrote Susan Fegley Osmond in *World and I*, "the nearly ninety self-portrayals of Rembrandt that remain today are eloquent testimony to the human spirit, in all its nobility, imperfection, and grandeur." And Hilton Kramer, writing in the *New York Observer*, commented that "no master of the Western pictorial tradition has ever equaled Rembrandt either in the sheer quantity of masterworks he produced in this genre of self-portrayal or in the exalted union of existential candor and esthetic grandeur he brought to its realization."

Popular tradition has Rembrandt dying alone and in poverty, completely forgotten by the art world of his day. The truth is less dramatic. He continued working right up to the end, not as hugely popular as earlier, but still earning a decent living. His companion, Hendrickje, died in 1663, and he continued living with his son until Titus died of the plague in 1668, recently married and leaving behind him a pregnant wife. His granddaughter was born in March of 1669; Rembrandt himself died on October 4 of that same year and was buried next to Hendrickje.

At the time of his death, though he was receiving important commissions such as "Syndics of the Cloth Guild," Rembrandt's paintings were not as well-received as they once had been. Many of his contemporaries found them too unique and personal. Since that time, however, the reputation of Rembrandt has grown to make him one of the foremost names in Western art. The biggest shift in critical appreciation occurred in the nineteenth century, when his style—once thought rather clumsy and ugly—found acceptance and respect among a generation of painters who were themselves breaking new territory in painting. For a time Rembrandt was also looked upon as the classic misunderstood

artist, a Romantic conceit. More recent scholarship, though, has placed him firmly in his time and has acknowledged predecessors and contemporaries who influenced him.

At the same time, through the auspices of the Rembrandt Research Project centered in Amsterdam since 1968, there has been a major re-examination of paintings attributed to the master. As a columnist for the *Economist* wrote, that group's findings "have sent waves of shock through the genteel world of museums and connoisseurs," for they have discovered scores of falsely attributed paintings in noted collections. Famous among such "casualties" have been "The Polish Rider," "The Man in the Golden Helmet," and "The Girl at the Door." These paintings and many others have been attributed to some of Rembrandt's pupils, such as Willem Drost, Gerrit Dou, and Samuel van Hoogstraten. It was a usual practice in Rembrandt's studio that the master would sign his pupils' paintings to show that they had in fact studied with him and that such paintings had been produced under his auspices. The Research Project has projected the actual Rembrandt output of paintings, once numbered close to 700, at closer to half that number. Writing in *Time* magazine, Otto Friedrich noted that the re-evaluation of "The Man in the Golden Helmet" "promptly lowered its theoretical value from . . . $8 million . . . to about one-twentieth of that amount."

If you enjoy the works of Rembrandt, you might want to check out the following:

The masterpieces of Italian painter Titian, whose work influenced Rembrandt.
The works of the great Italian Renaissance artists like Michelangelo and Leonardo da Vinci.
The paintings of the Impressionists, such as Claude Monet and Pierre-Auguste Renoir, who revived and extended the ideas found in Rembrandt's work.

None of the changes wrought by contemporary scholarship takes away from the real legacy of Rembrandt in his exploration of emotional states of his subject, the subtle use of light and shadow for emotional effect, and the innovative techniques by which he portrayed all sorts of materials, from fabrics to metal. His self-portraits alone make him a painter par excellence, and his attention to detail give modern viewers a priceless insight into the world of the seventeenth century.

■ **Biographical and Critical Sources**

BOOKS

Alpers, Svetlana, *Rembrandt's Enterprise: The Studio and the Market,* University of Chicago Press (Chicago, IL), 1988.

Benesch, Otto, *Rembrandt,* edited by Eva Benesch, Phaidon (London, England), 1970.

Benesch, Otto, *The Drawings of Rembrandt,* Phaidon (London, England), 1973.

Bonafoux, Pascal, *Rembrandt, Master of the Portrait,* Abrams (New York, NY), 1992.

Brion, Marcel, *Rembrandt,* A. Michel (Paris, France), 1946.

Chapman, H. Perry, *Rembrandt's Self-Portraits: A Study in Seventeenth-Century Identity,* Princeton University Press (Princeton, NJ), 1990.

Clark, Kenneth, *Rembrandt and the Italian Renaissance,* New York University Press (New York, NY), 1966.

Clark, Kenneth, *Civilization,* Harper and Row (New York, NY), 1970.

Clark, Kenneth, *An Introduction to Rembrandt,* J. Murray (London, England), 1978.

Descargues, Pierre, *Rembrandt van Rijn,* Archipel (Paris, France), 1999.

Fowkes, Charles, *The Life of Rembrandt,* Hamlyn (London, England), 1978.

Gerson, Horst, *Rembrandt Paintings,* Harrison House (New York, NY), 1976.

Haak, Bob, *Rembrandt: His Life, His Work, His Time,* translated by Elizabeth Willems-Treeman, Abrams (New York, NY), 1969.

Haak, Bob, *Rembrandt Drawings,* translated by Elizabeth Willems-Treeman, Thames & Hudson (London, England), 1976.

International Dictionary of Art and Artists, St. James Press (Detroit, MI), 1990.

Koot, Ton, *Rembrandt's "Night Watch," Its History and Adventures,* Cassel (London, England), 1953.

Mee, Charles L., Jr., *Rembrandt's Portrait: A Biography,* Simon & Schuster (New York, NY), 1988.

Nash, J. M., *The Age of Rembrandt and Vermeer,* Holt, Rinehart (New York, NY), 1972.

Pescio, Claudio, *Rembrandt and Seventeenth-Century Holland,* Peter Bedrick Books (New York, NY), 2000.

Roberts, Keith, *Rembrandt Master Drawings,* Dutton (New York, NY), 1976.

Rosenberg, Jakob, *Rembrandt: Life and Work,* Phaidon (London, England), 1964.

Schama, Simon, *Rembrandt's Eyes,* Knopf (New York, NY) 1999.

Schwartz, Gary, *Rembrandt: His Life, His Paintings,* Viking Press (New York, NY), 1985.

Silver, Larry, *Rembrandt,* Rizzoli (New York, NY), 1992.

Stearns, Monroe, *Rembrandt and His World,* F. Watts (New York, NY), 1967.

Tansey, Richard G., and Fred S. Kleiner, *Gardner's Art through the Ages,* 10th edition, Harcourt Brace (San Diego, CA), 1996, pp. 857-862.

Velasquez, Louis Richard, *Rembrandt: The Man in the Golden Helmet,* Vela Press (San Diego, CA), 1994.

Weigert, Hans, *Rembrandt,* translated by John Garrett, Crown (New York, NY), 1966.

Westerman, Mariet, *Rembrandt,* Phaidon (London, England), 2000.

White, Christopher, *The Drawings of Rembrandt,* British Museum (London, England), 1966.

White, Christopher, *Rembrandt and His World,* Viking Press (New York, NY), 1974.

White Christopher, *Rembrandt,* Thames & Hudson (London, England), 1984.

White, Christopher, *Rembrandt as an Etcher: A Study of the Artist at Work,* 2nd edition, Yale University Press (New Haven, CT), 1999.

White, Christopher, and Quentin Buvelot, *Rembrandt by Himself,* Yale University Press (New Haven, CT), 1999.

Wright, Christopher, *Rembrandt and His Art,* Hamlyn (New York, NY), 1975.

PERIODICALS

Art Bulletin, June, 2000, Stephanie S. Dickey, review of *Rembrandt by Himself,* pp. 366-368.

Contemporary Review, August, 1999, Donald Bruce, "Winter Sunlight: Rembrandt's Self-Portraits at the National Gallery," pp. 94-99; February, 2002, Donald Bruce, "Rembrandt's Women and Painted Ladies," pp. 98-103.

Economist, October 22, 1988, "Rembrandt Revised," pp. 100-101; December 7, 1991, "What Not Rembrandt?." p. 109.

Library Journal, October 15, 1999, Sandra Rothenberg, review of *Rembrandt by Himself,* p. 68.

New Criterion, November, 2000, Karen Wilkin, "Rembrandt and Venice," p. 48.

New York Observer, July 19, 1999, Hilton Kramer, "Rembrandt Is Still a Genius, despite Professor's Rantings"; July 26, 1999, Hilton Kramer, "Rembrandt Painted Himself with Total Lack of Vanity."

Spectator, September 29, 2001, Martin Gayford, "Rembrandt's Women," p. 43.

Time, December 16, 1985, Otto Friedrich, "The Man with the Golden Helmet," p. 100.

Variety, October 18, 1999, Lisa Nesselson, review of *Rembrandt,* p. 37.

World and I, January, 2000, Susan Fegley Osmond, "Shadow and Substance: Rembrandt Self-Portraits," pp. 110-115.

OTHER

Artcyclopedia, http://www.artcyclopedia.com/ (August 28, 2002), "Rembrandt van Rijn."

Grove Art Online, http://www.groveart.com/ (August 28, 2002), B. P. J. Broos, "Rembrandt (Harmensz) van Rijn [Rhyn]."

Webmuseum, http://www.ibiblio.org/ (August 28, 2002), "Rembrandt."*

—*Sketch by J. Sydney Jones*

Harriette Gillem Robinet

■ Personal

Surname is pronounced "ro-bi-*nay*"; born July 14, 1931, in Washington, DC; daughter of Richard Avitus (a teacher) and Martha (a teacher; maiden name, Gray) Gillem; married McLouis Joseph Robinet (a health physicist), August 9, 1960; children: Stephen, Philip, Rita, Jonathan, Marsha, Linda. *Education:* College of New Rochelle, B.S., 1953; Catholic University of America, M.S., 1957, Ph.D., 1963. *Politics:* Democrat. *Religion:* Roman Catholic. *Hobbies and other interests:* Pets, bird watching, growing orchids and other plants, knitting, crocheting, sketching; loves dogs and cats and enjoys camping with her family.

■ Addresses

Home and office—214 South Elmwood, Oak Park, IL 60302.

■ Career

Children's Hospital, Washington, DC, bacteriologist, 1953-54; Walter Reed Army Medical Center, Washington, DC, medical bacteriologist, 1954-57, research bacteriologist, 1958-60; Xavier University, New Orleans, LA, instructor in biology, 1957-58; U.S. Army, Quartermaster Corps, civilian food bacteriologist, 1960-62. Freelance writer, 1962—.

■ Member

Society of Children's Book Writers and Illustrators, Mystery Writers of America, National Writers Union, Sisters in Crime, Society of Midland Authors.

■ Awards, Honors

Award from Friends of American Writers, 1991, for *Children of the Fire;* Carl Sandburg Award, 1997, for *Washington City Is Burning;* Midland Authors Award, 1998, for *The Twins, the Pirates, and the Battle of New Orleans;* Scott O'Dell Award for historical fiction for children, 1999, for *Forty Acres and Maybe a Mule;* Edgar Allan Poe Award nomination, Mystery Writers of America, 2001, for *Walking to the Bus-Rider Blues; Mississippi Chariot* named a Book for the Teen Age, New York Public Library; *Mississippi Chariot* and *Children of the Fire* were named Notable Children's Trade Books in Social Studies.

■ Writings

Jay and the Marigold, illustrated by Trudy Scott, Children's Press (Danbury, CT), 1976.

Ride the Red Cycle, illustrated by David Brown, Houghton Mifflin (Boston, MA), 1980.

Children of the Fire, Maxwell Macmillan International (New York, NY), 1991.

Mississippi Chariot, Atheneum (New York, NY), 1994.

If You Please, President Lincoln, Atheneum (New York, NY), 1995.

Washington City Is Burning, Atheneum (New York, NY), 1996.

The Twins, the Pirates, and the Battle of New Orleans, Atheneum (New York, NY), 1997.

Forty Acres and Maybe a Mule, Atheneum (New York, NY), 1998.

Walking to the Bus-Rider Blues, Atheneum (New York, NY), 2000.

Missing from Haymarket Square, Atheneum (New York, NY), 2001.

Twelve Travelers, Twenty Horses, Atheneum (New York, NY), 2003.

Contributor to magazines.

■ Sidelights

Harriette Gillem Robinet grew up in Washington, D.C. and lived her childhood summers in Arlington, Virginia, near the home of Confederate general Robert E. Lee, where her ancestors had been slaves. In 1960 she and her husband moved to suburban Chicago, Illinois, where she began writing. The birth of a disabled son proved to be an influential experience for Robinet; the main character of *Jay and the Marigold* suffers from cerebral palsy, as was the case with Robinet's own child. Much of her other writing has been influenced, she once explained, by meeting other handicapped children and adults, who "have shared some of their anger, dreams, and victories." The focus of Robinet's more recent work, however, has shifted to American historical events, such as the Chicago fire, the Battle of 1812, the emancipation of the slaves during and after the U.S. Civil War, and the Montgomery, Alabama, bus boycott of 1956, events she depicts through the lives of her fictional and predominantly African-American characters.

As in *Jay and the Marigold,* the protagonist of *Ride the Red Cycle* is disabled, in this case due to a viral infection received when he was two years old. Eleven-year-old Jerome faces a number of obstacles, of which race is a relatively minor one. Confined to a wheelchair, he cannot speak without slurring his words, but he is determined to participate in a Labor Day parade. "Among the countless recent books about handicapped children," wrote Karen M. Klockner in *Horn Book, Ride the Red Cycle* "stands out for its psychological acuity and compassion without sentimentality."

Writes First Historical Novel

The great Chicago fire of 1871 forms the backdrop for *Children of the Fire,* whose main character is named Hallelujah because she was born on an Easter morning. The child of runaway slaves, Hallelujah is an orphan who grows through her experience in the vast conflagration that sweeps the city: "Selfish and callous at first," Zena Sutherland noted in the *Bulletin of the Center for Children's Books,* "Halle-

Harriet Gillem Robinet's 1995 novel finds a young, newly freed house slave named Moses humbled after relocating to Haiti when he realizes that he knows less about survival than many of the field workers he had once looked down on.

lujah gains sympathetic insight during the course of the fire and the start of the rebuilding." According to a reviewer in *Publishers Weekly,* "Hallelujah emerges as a likeable, spunky heroine who discovers her self-worth during the course of events."

Robinet's *Mississippi Chariot,* as its name suggests, takes place farther south. Set in rural Mississippi during the Great Depression, its title is taken from a code phrase—itself a reference to the spiritual "Swing Low, Sweet Chariot"—used by slaves to warn each other of impending danger. Twelve-year-old Abraham Lincoln "Short'ning Bread" Jackson is trying to bring his father, Rufus, home from a chain gang, where the man has been serving time for a crime he did not commit. Short'ning Bread goes to great lengths to help his father, but ultimately the family has to face the fact that in the South in the 1930s the deck is stacked against them. Despite the help of a white postmaster who helps to free Rufus, the Jacksons are forced to head north to Chicago. A commentator in *Kirkus Reviews* concluded that "Robinet's . . . character, Short'ning, is ingenious and endearing."

Like several of her other books, Robinet's *If You Please, President Lincoln* offers not merely a story, but an education in U.S. history. The book involves an actual but little-known scheme to deport freed slaves—whom white workers feared would present dangerous competition for jobs—to Haiti in the Caribbean. The title refers to President Abraham Lincoln's Emancipation Proclamation of 1863, which freed the slaves—but only those in the Confederate states—thus doing little to help Robinet's protagonist, Moses, a slave in the pro-Union state of Maryland. Because he is a house servant, Moses is more sophisticated than many of the former "field hands" with whom he finds himself, and he has to overcome feelings of superiority. Like them, he is fooled by the promise of free land in Haiti, and when the former slaves find themselves deported to a virtual desert island, he has to rethink some of his attitudes toward the people around him. Moses becomes a leader among the group, and helps them return to America, where he sets about to gain a college education. Carolyn Phelan in *Booklist* called *If You Please, President Lincoln* "a historical novel with an exciting plot, convincing characters, and a most original setting." A reviewer in *Publishers Weekly* wrote, "Robinet combines desert-island drama with an insightful story of a mind gradually freeing itself." "Moses is a complex protagonist," Elizabeth Bush observed in the *Bulletin of the Center for Children's Books,* adding that his "struggle to control his own arrogance toward his less gifted and educated comrades lends insight into a legacy of slavery that threatened solidarity within new free black communities."

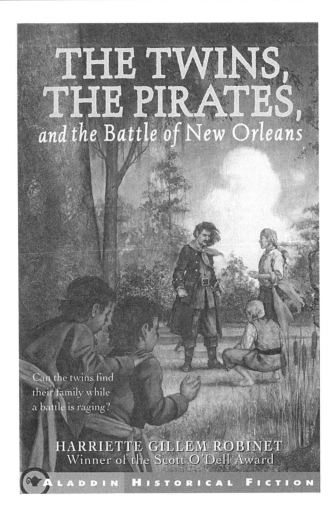

Robinet makes American history come alive for young readers with her story of two boys who work to save their mother and sister from being sold into slavery as war with England rages around them.

A Slave at the White House

Virginia, the heroine of *Washington City Is Burning,* is also a house servant with conflicting loyalties. She works for the family of James and Dolley Madison, and when Madison is elected president, she is proud of the fact that she will be a slave in the White House. She is, though, a slave nonetheless, and she cannot ignore the terrible conditions that confront many of her people. Like Hallelujah in *Children of the Fire,* Virginia is present at the scene of a great conflagration, the burning of Washington, D.C. by the British during the War of 1812. Again, critics noted the deft manner in which Robinet handled complex emotions and loyalties: a critic in *Kirkus Reviews,* who pronounced the book, "A fine, multilayered novel," cited the manner in which she portrayed "Dolley, who was brought up to believe

This 1998 novel draws readers into the Reconstruction-era South as a black family is determined to gain their own land on Georgia's Sea Islands.

slavery was wrong, yet keeps slaves out of political expediency." *Washington City Is Burning* is, in the words of Marie T. Wright in *School Library Journal,* "an above-average choice for historical-fiction shelves."

The War of 1812 also provides the setting for *The Twins, the Pirates, and the Battle of New Orleans.* Twins Pierre and Andrew have not spent much time together because their master has attempted to play one against the other—an example of one of the many ways in which slavery divided the African-American community. When their father leaves them in the middle of Gulf Coast swampland after an escape attempt, the two are forced to work together to find him, as well as the rest of their family. Challenges abound as the boys must overcome not only war conditions, but pirates as well. A commen-

tator in *Kirkus Reviews* called the book "an exciting and unusual story about runaway slaves," and noted that "young readers will relish the marvelous details of their diet (in which live snails play a large part), their adventurous expeditions across the swamps . . . and many other fascinating features of their unconventional life." Kay Weisman in *Booklist* wrote: "Filled with believable characters spun from thorough research," Robinet's *The Twins, the Pirates, and the Battle of New Orleans* is "a welcome addition to the historical fiction shelves."

Forty Acres and Maybe a Mule also combines a history lesson with a compelling narrative. This time, the story is set in the spring of 1865 and General William T. Sherman has promised both blacks and whites the land that was abandoned after the U.S. Civil War. Along with some friends and his brother Gideon, a runaway slave who joined the Union army, twelve-year-old Pascal sets out for Georgia to find a Freedman's Bureau and claim a farm. The ragtag family begins to grow cotton, but encounters night riders and eventual eviction from the farm due to the reversal of the act that declared blacks could own free land. Not to be deterred, Pascal and company set out to buy land on the Georgia Sea Islands. A reviewer in *Publishers Weekly* noted that "Robinet's resilient characters lend immediacy to the early events of Reconstruction." Of *Forty Acres and Maybe a Mule, School Library Journal* reviewer Kathleen Issacs said, "Once again, Robinet has humanized a little-known piece of American history." Hazel Rochman in *Booklist* called *Forty Acres and Maybe a Mule* a "landmark novel."

Tells of Early Civil Rights Boycott

Walking to the Bus-Rider Blues is set in Montgomery, Alabama in 1956, during a period when the local black community, inspired by Rosa Parks, is boycotting the bus system until blacks are treated as equal passengers. Young Alfa Merryfield has a different problem, however; someone has been stealing money from his hard-pressed family, spiriting the rent money out of a secret hiding place in their tar paper house. When the family in turn is accused of stealing from a rich woman whose house they clean, Alfa must solve the mystery of the missing money on his own to save the reputation of his great-grandmother and sister. Following the non-violent teachings of Martin Luther King, Jr., the civil rights leader leading the Montgomery bus boycott, Alfa eventually thwarts some thieving bullies and gets to the bottom of the mystery. Michael Cart in *Booklist* especially praised "Robinet's quietly dramatic, often poignant re-creation of the early days of the civil rights movement." Similarly, the critic for *Publishers Weekly* found that "the novel is at its strongest when filling in historical details of the time, such as the volunteer taxi service for bus boycotters, and may well inspire readers to discover more about this important chapter in civil rights history." Jean Westmoore, reviewing the book for the *Buffalo News,* explained that "Robinet presents a little-explored side of the bus boycott—its impact on poor working folk of Montgomery—in this interesting and suspenseful novel." *Walking to the Bus-Rider Blues* was nominated for the Edgar Allan Poe Award of the Mystery Writers of America.

Robinet turns to the city of Chicago in 1886 in her novel *Missing from Haymarket Square.* Dinah Bell's father, a union organizer in the windy city, goes missing and the girl and two immigrant friends must find out what has happened to him. "That

The nonviolence promoted by civil rights leader Martin Luther King is not lost upon young Alfa Merryfield during the 1950s as he turns his back on neighborhood bullies and brings a local crook to justice by peaceful means.

If you enjoy the works of Harriet Gillem Robinet, you might want to check out the following books:

Ann Rinaldi, *Wolf by the Ears,* 1991.
Walter Dean Myers, *The Glory Field,* 1994.
Sandra Forrester, *Sound the Jubilee,* 1995.

simple plot," Denise Wilms explained in *Booklist,* "is a vehicle . . . to portray the terrible poverty and social injustice that plagued the city's newly arrived immigrants." Dinah and her friends work twelve-hour shifts in a factory, but cannot earn enough money to pay the rent or buy food. They resort to pickpocketing to supplement their income. Eventually the friends find and release Dinah's father, who is being held prisoner by detectives bent on stopping the city's union organizers. A critic for *Publishers Weekly* concluded that "young readers willing to accept some unlikely twists will appreciate the relationship of the three sympathetic and resourceful friends and learn about a lesser-known aspect of U.S. history."

■ Biographical and Critical Sources

PERIODICALS

Booklist, October 15, 1991, p. 441; November 15, 1994, p. 591; August, 1995, Carolyn Phelan, review of *If You Please, President Lincoln,* p. 1947; November 1, 1996, p. 501; November 15, 1997, Kay Weisman, review of *The Twins, the Pirates, and the Battle of New Orleans,* p. 561; January 1, 1999, Susan Dove Lempke, review of *Forty Acres and Maybe a Mule,* p. 879; February 15, 1999, Hazel Rochman, review of *Forty Acres and Maybe a Mule,* p. 1068; May 1, 2000, Michael Cart, review of *Walking to the Bus-Rider Blues,* p. 1670; October 1, 2001, Denise Wilms, review of *Missing from Haymarket Square,* p. 319.

Buffalo News (Buffalo, NY), February 27, 2001, Jean Westmoore, review of *Walking to the Bus-Rider Blues,* p. N12.

Bulletin of the Center for Children's Books, November, 1980, p. 63; September, 1991, Zena Sutherland, review of *Children of the Fire,* p. 20; September, 1995, Elizabeth Bush, review of *If You Please, President Lincoln,* p. 27.

Children's Book Review Service, November, 1996, p. 35.

Horn Book, June, 1980, Karen M. Klockner, review of *Ride the Red Cycle,* p. 303.

Kirkus Reviews, November 15, 1994, review of *Mississippi Chariot,* p. 1541; July 15, 1996, review of *Washington City Is Burning,* p. 1055; October 1, 1997, review of *The Twins, the Pirates, and the Battle of New Orleans,* p. 1536; November 1, 1998, p. 1603.

Publishers Weekly, October 18, 1991, review of *Children of the Fire,* pp. 62-63; June 26, 1995, review of *If You Please, President Lincoln,* p. 107; November 2, 1998, review of *Forty Acres and Maybe a Mule,* p. 83; June 5, 2000, review of *Walking to the Bus-Rider Blues,* p. 94; June 18, 2001, review of *Missing from Haymarket Square,* p. 81.

School Library Journal, December, 1994, pp. 112-113; June, 1995, p. 132; November, 1996, Marie T. Wright, review of *Washington City Is Burning,* p. 110; December, 1997, p. 130; November, 1998, Kathleen Issacs, review of *Forty Acres and Maybe a Mule,* p. 128.

Voice of Youth Advocates, October, 1995, p. 223; Delia A. Culberson, review of *Twelve Travelers, Twenty Horses,* February, 2003, pp. 481-482.

OTHER

Harriette Gillem Robinet Web site, http://www.hgrobinet.com (August 26, 2002).*

Jerry Siegel and Joe Shuster

■ Personal

Jerry Siegel: Born Jerome Siegel, October 17, 1914, in Cleveland, OH; died of heart failure, January 28, 1996, in Los Angeles, CA; married Joanne Carter, 1948; children: Laura. *Nationality:* American. *Education:* Graduated from Glenville High School (Cleveland, OH).

Joe Shuster: Born July 10, 1914, in Toronto, Ontario, Canada; died July 30, 1992 in Los Angeles, CA; son of Julius (a tailor) and Ida Shuster. *Nationality:* American. *Education:* Studied art at John Huntington Polytechnical Institute and Cleveland School of Art.

■ Career

Jerry Siegel: Comic strip writer. *Cosmic Stories* (first science-fiction fanzine), founder, 1929; *Science Fiction,* co-creator (with Joe Shuster), 1932; co-creator (with Shuster) of comic book character "Superman," c. 1934; worked as a comic artist for *Cleveland Shopping News,* 1936; sold "Superman" character to DC Comics, 1938; comic-book director for Ziff-Davis Publications, c. early 1950s; worked at various jobs in Los Angeles, CA, including mail clerk. *Military service:* U.S. Army, 1943-46; served as a reporter for *Stars and Stripes.*

Joe Shuster: Cartoonist. Co-creator (with Jerome Siegel) of comic stories and books for DC-National, including "Henri Duval," Spy," "Radio Squad,"

"Slam Bradley," "Federal Men," "Dr. Occult," 1934-38, and "Superman" and "Superboy," 1938-47; co-creator (with Siegel) of "Funnyman" for Magazine Enterprises, 1948.

■ Awards, Honors

Jerry Siegel: Inkpot Award.

■ Writings

JERRY SIEGEL AND JOE SHUSTER: COMIC BOOKS

Creators of comic stories and books for DC-National, including "Henri Duval," "Spy," "Radio Squad," "Slam Bradley," "Federal Men," and "Dr. Occult," 1934-38. Creators and authors of numerous "Superman" and "Superboy" comic book stories, DC Comics, 1938-43, 1946-48, including Superman's origin and debut in *Action Comics,* no. 1, June, 1938, and stories appearing in *Superman Comics, New York World's Fair Comics, Adventure Comics,* and *Superboy.* Creators and authors of "Funnyman" comic book stories, including Funnyman's debut in *Funnyman,* no. 1, January, 1948.

JERRY SIEGEL: COMIC BOOKS

Creator (with artist Bernard Bailey) and author of "The Spectre" comic book stories, including thse Spectre's debut in *More Fun Comics,* no. 52, February, 1940. Creator (with artists Bill Smith and Stan Aschmeier) and author of "Red, White, and Blue" comic book stories, including Red, White, and Blue's debut in *All-American Comics,* no. 1, April, 1939. Creator (with artist Hal Sherman) and author of "The Star-Spangled Kid and Stripesy" comic books stories, including their debut in *Action Comics,* no. 40, September, 1941. Author of numerous "Superman" and "Superboy" comic book stories, DC Comics, 1959-66. Creator (with artist Leo Nowak) and author of "Robotman" comic book stories, including Robotman's debut in *Star-Spangled Comics,* no. 7, April, 1942. Author of comic book stories for Ziff-Davis, c. early 1950s including "Amazing Adventures," "Lars of Mars," "G.I. Joe," and "Kid Cowboy"; author of comic book stories for Toby, Farrell, and Prize; creator of comic book characters Nature Boy, Zara the Mystic, and Mr. Muscles for Charlton Publications; author of comic book stories for Archie Comics, 1964-66; author of comic book stories featuring the Phantom and Mandrake the Magician for King Comics, Woody Woodpecker for Western/Gold Key, and X-Men for Marvel Comics, c. late 1960s-early 1970s; author of comic book stories for Fleetway and Mondadori. Contributor of satirical stories to *Cracked* and *Lunatickle.*

JERRY SIEGEL: OTHER

High Camp Super Heroes (collection), Belmont (New York, NY), 1966.

Contributor to *Superman from the 'Thirties to the 'Seventies,* Crown (New York, NY), 1971. Author of article in *Inside Comics,* c. 1976.

■ **Adaptations**

The character of Superman was adapted into a Mutual Radio Network radio series, beginning 1940; seventeen cartoons directed by Dave Fleischer, beginning 1941; the novel *The Adventures of Superman* by George Lowther, 1942; the film serials *Superman,* Columbia, 1948, and *Atom-Man vs. Superman,* Columbia, 1950; the feature film *Superman and the Mole Men,* 1952; the television series *The Adventures of Superman,* starring George Reeves, 1953-58; the musical *It's a Bird . . . It's a Plane . . . It's Superman!,* produced on Broadway, 1966; the cartoon series *The New Adventures of Superman,* CBS, 1966, *The Superman/Aquaman Hour,* CBS, 1967, and *The Superman/Batman Hour,* CBS, 1968; films starring Christopher Reeve, including *Superman,* 1978, *Super-*

man II, 1981, *Superman III,* 1983, and *Superman IV,* 1987; the television series *Superboy,* syndicated, 1988-92; the cartoon series *Superman,* CBS, 1988-89; the television series *Lois and Clark: The New Adventures of Superman,* ABC, 1993-97; the animated series *Superman,* Warner, 1996—; television series *Smallville;* and toys and merchandise, including the Superman Krypto-Raygun (which projects movies on a wall), c. 1940, and a Superman hood ornament for automobiles.

■ **Sidelights**

Jerry Siegel and Joe Shuster were co-creators of *Superman,* the cartoon character which, more than any other superhero, revolutionized comics, turning them from a sideshow in American media into a multi-million-dollar industry. "I conceived a character like Samson, Hercules and all the strong men I heard tell of rolled into one. Only more so," Siegel once said of his Superman creation. Such a fanciful if not fantastical creation seems almost prosaic today, but in 1934, when Siegel had his summertime brainstorm, superheroes were a thing of the future, and the Man of Steel was initially laughed at and rejected by dozens of publishers as too strange and too fanciful before finally being picked up by DC publishers for its new *Action Comics* line in 1938. Since then, Superman has taken on mythic cultural as well as mercantile implications, spawning not only comic books, comic strips, television and radio series, movies, cartoons, a Broadway musical, dolls, puzzles, costumes, T-shirts, rings, bed sheets, lunch buckets, and fan clubs, but also a cottage industry in doctoral dissertations, cultural debates, and critical analyses about every aspect of the character, from his impregnable skin to his virginal status and Christ-like history. Superman has, indeed, entered the realm of heroic myth to become one of the most recognizable fictional characters in the world.

Dubbed the "most important cartoonist in the history of comic books," by Ron Goulart in *The Encyclopedia of American Comics,* and known for his simple, rather stiff artwork, Shuster also almost single-handedly changed the format of the comic book, adapting it from the comic strip image of the newspapers to fit the new medium of the comic book, breaking panels up in novel and interesting ways to fit the new format.

Boyhood friends, Siegel and Shuster manufactured Superman partly out of thin air and partly from the pulp heroes of their youth, creating one of the most enduring characters of American pop culture. Superman means something different to every reader. For screenwriter David Newman, who worked on the Broadway musical and three *Superman* films, the Man of Steel "is our myth, the American myth," as he noted in *Time* magazine. Newman further remarked that when friends found out he was writing the screenplay for *Superman I,* they asked him why he was involved in the project. Newman told them, "If I were an English writer and I were writing about King Arthur, you wouldn't be asking me that." John Byrne, a more recent scripter and artist for *Superman* comics, also noted in *Time* that the superhero is the "ultimate American success story—a foreigner who comes to America, and is more successful here than he would ever be anywhere else." Depending on the source, there is the Superman of hidden psychological motivations, the Nietzche-like Super-man with Nazi overtones (a rather ironic conjecture given that he was created by a pair of Jewish kids), or the Superman of the mall, the twentieth century's ultimate consumer product. Superman, the ultimate good-guy hero, has battled the forces of evil for many decades, but at heart he is the alter ego of a kid from Cleveland with dreams of being a hero himself.

Jerry Siegel, with the typewriter that he used to type his first "Superman" stories.

The Early Years

Born in Cleveland, Ohio in 1914, Siegel was the son of parents who ran a men's clothing store. Not a great student, Siegel was shy and nearsighted, and found a refuge in reading science fiction and fantasy, especially in pulp magazines such as *Amazing Stories.* Soon he began submitting his own work to these pulps, but his stories were all rejected. Defiant, he decided to self-publish. As a fifteen-year-old student at Cleveland's Glenville High School, Siegel began publishing his own science-fiction fan magazine, *Cosmic Stories.* As a writer for *Comic Art & Graffix Gallery* noted, this "is recognized as the first sci-fi fanzine, and it was just a prelude to future accomplishments." A booklet-sized publication, *Cosmic Stories* was filled with Siegel's own stories. Increasingly Siegel thought he would become a writer of science-fiction novels and stories, but when he read an article on comics creators, he discovered that some of them made very good incomes. Thereafter he began experimenting with scripts for comic strips.

Shuster was born in 1914, in Toronto, Canada, to parents who had only recently immigrated to North America. His tailor father, Julius, was from Rotterdam, Netherlands, while his mother, Ida, was from Kiev, Russia. By the age of four, Shuster displayed a penchant for drawing, sketching on the walls of the family's Toronto apartment house. Money was tight for the family, but the mother sometimes managed to get white butcher paper for her son to sketch on. Most of the time, however, Shuster had to salvage whatever paper he could find discarded by businesses. "I would go from store to store in Toronto and pick up whatever they threw out," he once recalled in an interview with Henry Mietkiewicz of the *Toronto Star.* "One day I was lucky enough to find a bunch of wallpaper rolls that were unused and left over from some job." Shuster used the reverse, blank side of the wallpaper. "So it was a gold mine for me, and I went home with every roll I could carry." The wallpaper saw him through for years, even after the family moved from Canada to Cleveland, Ohio, in 1924.

While still in Toronto, Shuster discovered another passion: the movies. He and his cousin went to the silent pictures whenever they could, spending entire days in the theater where the cousin's father worked as a projectionist. Many of the comic book characters he later drew were influenced by the actors he saw as a young boy in Toronto. When he was nine years old, Shuster got a job selling the *Tor-*

onto Star on the streets of the city, looking up at the soaring buildings all around him. It was this urban scene of metropolis that he would later reproduce in his famous comic books.

In the pages of the newspaper Schuster was introduced to that world of comics. As a very young boy he recalled sitting on his father's knee while the latter read the daily comics to him. On weekends there was the special treat of the Sunday comics, the bright, vivid colors appealing to the child. Before he started reading, Shuster and his father shared the Sunday papers. "We had a ritual," Shuster told Mietkiewicz. "We would both open up the color comics and my father would read all the dialogue and balloons." Favorite strips included the "Kaatzenjammer Kids," "Boob McNutt," "Happy Hooligan," "Barney Google," and best of all "Little Nemo" by Winsor McCay. In fact the fanciful world of McCay "was among the things that turned me on to fantasy and science fiction," Shuster explained.

A Fateful Meeting

In 1931 Shuster and Siegel met. The two became good friends and collaborators, together putting out the fanzine *Science Fiction* which combined reprints of stories from the pulp magazines, as well as original work by both Siegel and Shuster. In the January, 1933, issue Siegel published a story he had written under the pen name Herbert S. Fine called "The Reign of the Superman," with illustrations by Shuster. In this early take on the Superman character, Siegel makes him a villain after he has been granted super-powers by a mad scientist. Later that same year, Siegel saw one of the first comic books published, *Detective Dan,* and suddenly he thought that his Superman might make a good comic book character. He and Shuster set to work on "The Superman," a prototype comic book featuring Superman now as a hero rather than villain, but after it was rejected by the publishers of *Detective Dan* Shuster became so dejected that he destroyed all the illustrations for that early effort except for the cover art. "Creating comics was easy," Siegel noted on *Su-*

Joe Shuster, described by a family member as "a stereotypical 90-pound weakling," drew the original Superman with the muscular physique of a circus strongman.

perman through the Ages. "Selling them wasn't. Joe's eyes troubled him. Despite this, he drew panel after panel after panel." Thereafter Shuster found part-time work away from illustration, selling ice-cream bars on the streets and working as a delivery boy for a grocery store.

Siegel remained undeterred, however. He still felt they had a great comic book potential with Superman. One hot summer night in 1934, when the young Cleveland high-school graduate couldn't sleep, he thought up the final version of the character. As he was lying awake thinking of girls he wished would date him and imagining that if he had some special power they would do so, the character took shape in his imagination. Superman was born partly out of the popular culture images of heroes such as Tarzan, Buck Rogers, and Flash Gordon, the last two of which inspired Superman's famous tights and cape. Another contributing factor to the Superman genesis was Hugo Danner, hero of the 1930 novel *Gladiator* by Philip Wylie, a character who was bulletproof, able to leap great distances, and bend steel, all as a result of an experiment done by his biologist father. Additionally the pulp magazine character of Doc Savage, known as "The Man of Bronze," added a wrinkle to the character who would become known as "The Man of Steel." Partly too, perhaps, the character of Superman was influenced by the literary use of the word "superman" by German philosopher Friedrich Nietzsche and Irish playwright George Bernard Shaw.

Whatever the ancestry of Superman, he became an original character in his own right, with traits and a history almost every American child since has been able to recite by heart: babyhood on the planet Krypton; transition to Earth by his scientist father when Krypton exploded; a boyhood with an old couple named Kent in Smallville; adulthood as mild-mannered newspaper reporter Clark Kent (whose name came from Clark "Doc" Savage and from The Shadow's alter ego, Kent Allard) in Metropolis; romantic possibilities with colleague Lois Lane (whose prototype came from several Lois's whom Siegel and Shuster had gone to school with; one woman, Joanne Carter, who posed for the prototype of Lois Lane, later became Siegel's wife); opposition by villain Lex Luthor; and vulnerability to Kryptonite. These traits accumulated gradually around Superman over the years, and indeed many of the secondary details, such as Superman's virginity or lack thereof, would be changed back and forth; the super hero was even killed in 1992, but resurrected shortly afterward.

"Supie, you know and I know that much of that premise came out of my own personal frustrations," Siegel wrote in *Superman through the Ages.* "I wore

spectacles and was a high school boy who wrote for the school newspaper. Introverted, my thoughts kept dwelling on science-fiction, thriller pulp magazines and the movies." But Siegel had a vivid picture of the character in mind in 1934 when he dashed over to his friend's house to ask Shuster to draw the hero. Siegel suggested the "S" in the triangle in Superman's chest, and together the two came up with the rest of the distinctive and bright red, yellow, and blue costume with its cape that very day.

The two young friends created twelve comic strips at that time. They hawked them to comic-book publishers—who universally rejected the idea for the new hero. But when attempting to sell the strip to DC comics in 1935, the duo did get work writing for other stories, including "Slam Bradley," about a rough-hewn detective; "Spy," and "Dr. Occult," about a ghostly detective, prototype of such mystical characters of Dr. Fate and Dr. Strange. The two also worked for New Fun comics, writing and illustrating the adventures for "Henri Duval." Other comics from Siegel and Shuster at this time included "Radio Squad" and "Federal Men."

It was during the mid-1930s that Shuster revolutionized the look of comic books, reducing the number of panels per page from six to four, then to three or two, and even down to one, depending on time constraints. In the event, editors finally stopped Shuster from such an unorthodox approach, claiming that readers were not getting their money's worth. However, young readers responded warmly to the new techniques, and later Shuster's full-page "splash" panel would become one of the standard tricks of the comic book trade.

In 1938 DC Comics finally bought the rights to Superman in order to help launch its new *Action Comics* line. To meet the first deadline, however, Shuster actually cannibalized the weekly comic-strip versions to fit the demands of the comic book format, filling thirteen pages of the first issue of *Action Comics* in June, 1938. This effort provided a one-page introduction to Superman, and then readers were thrown into the midst of the action. Superman is faced with several separate problems in this debut outing: preventing a woman from dying in the electric chair, teaching a wife-beater a painful lesson, rescuing Lois Lane from being kidnapped, and racing off to Washington, D.C. to help out in the U.S. Senate. Readers also meet Lois, who is liable to get in trouble, and is fickle where it comes to superheroes, as well as Clark Kent, the timid newspaper man whom nobody suspects is a superhero beneath his milquetoast facade.

When Superman appeared in print he was an instant success, quickly spawning imitators (the hero

A promotional poster for the 1948 film series adaptation of Siegel and Shuster's popular crime-fighting creation, Superman, released by Columbia Pictures.

Batman appeared in 1939.) Within four months sales of *Action Comics* had skyrocketed to 500,000 copies a month, and by 1941 that number had doubled. In 1939 the vastly popular *Superman* radio show was inaugurated; that same year the *Superman* magazine also was started, selling over a million copies a month; and also in 1939, Superman got his own syndicated comic strip, which was ultimately published in over two thousand newspapers and reached twenty million readers. The Superman industry had been launched with a vengeance, yet Siegel and Shuster would never take a rightful part of the resulting profits, for they signed away copyright to their creation for the initial payment of $130 in 1938—ten dollars per page of that first story.

Life with Superman

From the outset, the Superman craze was recognized as a social and cultural phenomenon. "It was only two years ago that Superman was first revealed to the youth of this country," wrote Slater Brown in a 1940 *New Republic* article. "But the response which greeted his appearance was so enthusiastic and so immediate that already Superman has surpassed such long established classics as Little Orphan Annie, Dick Tracy and Popeye." In explaining the comic book character's popularity, Brown further commented that Superman was "handsome as Apollo, strong as Hercules, chivalrous as Lancelot, swift as Hermes," and that, in fact, he "embodies all the traditional attributes of a Hero God." John Kobler, writing in the *Saturday Evening Post* in 1941, declared that the "young creators of the Man of Steel would have been hailed by [Sigmund] Freud as perfect clinical illustrations of psychological compensation," and further noted that "besides being the greatest soliloquizer since Hamlet, Superman is also a humorist full of whimsy and light banter." Martin Sheridan, in his *Comics and Their Creators: Life Stories of American Cartoonists,* noted that the appeal of Superman "is due to the fact that America is a land of hero worshippers. . . . Superman is for the right and against the wrong." Coulton Waugh saw the man in tights as a "national figure, perhaps the most adored of our time," in his book *The Comics.* Calling Superman a "modern cousin to Paul Bunyan," Waugh went on to praise Siegel and Shuster for turning "the big guy's enormous influence into a number of socially useful channels; he has taught young people to keep clean and healthy, and he has held up our national ideals in a very definite manner."

As the praise grew, so did sales. Even as employees of DC, Siegel and Shuster began to reap the rewards of the Superman craze. A *Saturday Evening Post* con-tributor reported that by 1941 the pair was splitting a $150,000 annual income, still only peanuts, however compared to what DC was raking in for all its Superman spin-offs, including motion pictures. To meet increased production needs, Siegel and Shuster also expanded their initial Cleveland studio, bringing in other artists to help Shuster, whose eyesight continued to fail.

Over the years, Superman's legend has become such that a copy of *Action Comics* number one, originally priced at ten cents, was auctioned at Sotheby's in June of 1995 for over 75,000 dollars. According to the *World Encyclopedia of Comics,* Superman is "unquestionably the most lucrative character ever to appear in comic books." In the view of an *Economist* contributor, Superman is "second perhaps only to Mickey Mouse in imaginative renown." A seventeen-episode animated series, made by the legendary Max and Dave Fleischer, was produced by Paramount in 1941 and revived on videotape in 1993; there have been several more recent movie, radio, and television series, and a Broadway musical in addition to the comic books, newspaper comic strips, and related merchandise.

While Siegel and Shuster were paid decently for their work on *Superman,* compared to rates usually paid to comic book writers and artists during the 1940s, they became disgruntled over DC Comics' handling of the character. Siegel was drafted in 1943, returning to civilian life in 1946. During that time, DC had moved the production of Superman products from Cleveland to New York, in breach of what Siegel felt the company and he had agreed upon when he left for the Army. Returning, Siegel discovered that the publishers had also initiated a new feature, Superboy, the adventures of Superman as a youth. While the Superman property—which included by 1947 comics, a comic strip, movies, cartoons, a radio show, and assorted merchandising—was reportedly earning over 15 million dollars a year, Siegel and Shuster were then splitting under $50,000. Represented by attorney Albert Zugsmith, who later went on to produce movies in Hollywood, the two sued DC to regain their creations and recoup what they saw as millions of dollars in lost income. The pair also challenged ownership of the character Superboy, whom they had created in 1944. Immediately fired by National Comics, parent company of DC, Siegel and Shuster saw their names removed from the comic. The court ruled against them, except in the case of Superboy. "With neither party happy over the rulings, Siegel and Shuster agreed to a settlement in which DC paid them $94,013.16. In return, they abandoned claims to Superboy and once again signed away their rights to

Christopher Reeve stars in the popular 1978 screen adaptation of the comic-book marvel in the Richard Donner-directed *Superman: The Movie.*

Superman," stated Michael Catron in the *Comics Journal.* However, as Catron noted, "a key point not specifically addressed . . . was the matter of who was entitled to renew the original Superman copyrights when they became eligible for renewal in 1966. That oversight set the stage for a later court battle."

In fact, Siegel and Shuster sued DC again in 1969, claiming they had the right to renew the copyright. The case dragged on until 1976, when Warner Communications (who now owned DC Comics and was planning to make a movie about Superman) agreed to grant the pair an annual stipend of $20,000 a year, and medical insurance, for life. According to Catron in the *Comics Journal,* "the amount of [Siegel and Shuster's] payments from Warner was raised quietly over the years. When Shuster died in 1992, he was reportedly receiving eighty-five thousand dollars. A Reuters report placed Siegel's annual stipend at his death at 'six figures.'"

Life after Superman

Following their dismissal from DC in 1948, Siegel went to work for other comic book companies, becoming comics director at publisher Ziff-Davis during the early 1950s. As a freelancer Siegel wrote prolifically for other comic book publishers. He had already worked on other characters and with other artists in the early 1940s. Some of his more popular creations were the Spectre, for More Fun Comics, the Star Spangled Kid, and Robotman. After he was separated from Superman, Siegel, along with Shuster and John Sikela, created Funnyman, a mock-superhero who failed to make it in either comic-book form or as a comic strip. Throughout the 1950s he wrote for many books, including "G.I. Joe," "Kid Cowboy," "Joe Yank," and "Nature Boy." Shuster, on the other hand, in his mid-30s by the 1950s, left the world of comics.

Times became tough for Siegel and his family. His wife reportedly went to the head of DC and asked him to take her husband back; otherwise they might see in the newspaper that the co-creator of Superman had died of starvation. In 1959 he quietly and anonymously went back to work for DC as a writer on the Superman family of titles. "His reunion with Superman was far from a joyous one," Catron commented in the *Comics Journal,* quoting a 1962 letter from Siegel to Shuster: "As you know, I am doing a lot of scripting for Superman again on a freelance basis . . . at a fraction of my former script rates (I get no royalties at all), but though I work hard, I get a lot of scorn, belittlement and hot-tempered abuse." Siegel complained about the poor treatment he received from the editor in charge of the "Superman" titles. "This is really making a buck the hard way, but it's the only way I can support my family," he concluded. At DC he wrote scripts not only for Superman, but also for "Adam Strange" and "Legion of Super-Heroes," but was never allowed to sign his name to his work. Siegel's last writing in comics came with Marvel in the 1970s, scripting "X-Men" and "Human Torch." By the mid-1970s Siegel was living in California, near his former collaborator, Shuster, and working as a clerk typist for the state of California.

Actor and writer Bill Mumy spoke out about Siegel in the *Comics Journal:* "More than anyone I've ever known, Jerry Siegel deserved to have lived a richer life. As the co-creator of one of the most universally recognized and loved images that this planet has cherished for more than fifty years, he received little of the fame and fortune he was due." Shuster, in contrast, remained completely out of the comic book industry for the last forty years of his life. He spent his time mostly enjoying classical music and died in 1992, almost totally blind.

Siegel died in 1996 of heart failure, and his death made headlines internationally. In the *Economist,* a contributor remarked that "seldom has so powerful and popular a legend had such an identifiable author or so dateable a birth." Three years after his death, it was determined that under copyright law that both the Siegel estate and DC comics were the co-owners of Superman and any and all characters attaching to him. After more than sixty years, then, it appeared that one of the creators of Superman was finally being acknowledged.

Meanwhile, the character Siegel and Shuster created morphed, changing persona as the public psyche changed. From do-gooder of the 1930s, Superman became a Nazi-buster in the 1940s. With the end of the war, the public demanded increasingly dramatic activities from the superhero, and Superman took on more daring adventures, defeating not just Earthly hoodlums, but flying into outer space to stop the very course of planets. In the 1950s when the critics of comic book heroes were warning against the psychological damage such entertainment might be doing to young readers, Superman was toned down to follow the Comic Book Code. Never an overtly violent superhero, Superman did not resort to death rays or magical cannon. Instead he used his brains, his speed, and brawn. By the 1960s, embattled by counter-culture heroes, Superman began to lose his popularity as well as his mythic proportions in the face of the Vietnam War and domestic discontent. As Ted White noted in an essay for *All in Color for a Dime,* at his outset in the 1930s "Superman was a myth-figure—he was our dreams personified, even as he must have been Siegel and Shuster's. Superman was, almost literally, the perfect Boy Scout. We still believed in Boy Scouts then."

If you enjoy the works of Jerry Siegel and Joe Shuster, you might want to check out the following:

The work of Jack Cole, creator of "Plastic Man."

Will Eisner's work on the detective adventure strip "The Spirit."

The work of Bob Kane, creator of the mythic hero "Batman."

The 1970s craze for nostalgia—"including nostalgia for things the nostalgia lovers were too young to know," as Otto Friedrich noted in *Time* magazine—kicked in, leading to a Superman revival and the first of the blockbuster "Superman" movies starring Christopher Reeves. Throughout the 1980s and 1990s and into the new millennium, the caped warrior has continued to right wrongs. According to Friedrich, the character created by Siegel that muggy summer night in 1934 remains a "figure who somehow manages to embody the best qualities in that nebulous thing known as the American character. He is honest, he tells the truth, he is idealistic and optimistic, he helps people in need. . . . And not only is he good, he is also innocent, in a kind and guileless way that Americans have sometimes been but more often have only imagined themselves to be."

■ Biographical and Critical Sources

BOOKS

All in Color for a Dime, edited by Dick Lupoff and Don Thompson, Arlington House (New Rochelle, NY), 1970, pp. 20-43.

Becker, Stephen, *Comic Art in America: A Social History of the Funnies, the Political Cartoons, Magazine Humor, Sporting Cartoons, and Animated Cartoons,* Simon & Schuster (New York, NY), 1959.

Contemporary Literary Criticism, Volume 21, Gale (Detroit, MI), 1982, pp. 352-364.

Daniels, Les, *Comix: A History of Comic Books in America,* Dutton (New York, NY), 1971.

The Encyclopedia of American Comics, edited by Ron Goulart, Facts on File (New York, NY), 1990, pp. 333-334, 351-353.

The Encyclopedia of Science Fiction, edited by John Clute and Peter Nicholls, St. Martin's Press (New York, NY), 1993, pp. 1104, 1183-1185.

Feiffer, Jules, *The Great Comic Book Heroes,* Dial Press (New York, NY), 1965.

Legends in Their Own Time, Prentice Hall (New York, NY), 1994.

Sheridan, Martin, *Comics and Their Creators: Life Stories of American Cartoonists,* R. Hale, 1944, pp. 233-236.

Steranko, James, *Steranko's History of Comics,* Volume 1, Supergraphics (Reading, PA), 1970.

Superman from the 'Thirties to the 'Seventies, Crown (New York, NY), 1971.

Twentieth-Century Literary Criticism, Volume 66, Gale (Detroit, MI), 1997.

Waugh, Coulton, *The Comics,* Macmillan (New York, NY), 1947, pp. 247-263.

Wertham, Fredric, *Seduction of the Innocent,* Holt (New York, NY), 1954.

The World Encyclopedia of Comics, edited by Maurice Horn, Chelsea House (New York, NY), 1976.

PERIODICALS

Atlantic Monthly, January, 1966, pp. 104-105.

Boston Magazine, February, 1997, pp. 168-171.

Comics Journal, February, 1996, pp. 25-39.

Entertainment Weekly, June 8, 2001, Jeff Jensen, "Heroic Effort," p. 80.

Human Behavior, January, 1979, pp. 63-65.

Library Journal, February 1, 1993, p. 123.

Nemo: The Classic Comics Library, August, 1983, pp. 6-19.

New Republic, September 2, 1940, Slater Brown, "The Coming of Superman," p. 301.

New York Times, December 28, 1980, p. N14; June 14, 1981, p. D1.

New York Times Book Review, September 5, 1976.

New York Times Magazine, December 29, 1996, pp. 14-15.

Partisan Review, winter, 1966, pp. 111-115.

Saturday Evening Post, June 21, 1941, John Kobler, "Up, Up and Awa-a-y! The Rise of Superman, Inc.," pp. 14-15, 70, 73-74, 76, 78.

Time, March 14, 1988, Otto Friedrich, "Up, Up, and Away!!!," pp. 66-74.

OTHER

Comic & Graffix Gallery, http://www.comic-art.com/ (September 19, 2002), "Jerry Siegel, Co-Creator of Superman" and "Joe Shuster, Co-Creator of Superman."

Joe Shuster Web site, http://www.superman.nu (September 22, 2002).

Lambiek.net, http://www.lambiek.net/ (September 22, 2002), "Jerry Siegel" and "Joe Shuster."

Nashville.com, http://www.nashville.com/ (September 22, 2002), "Siegel and Shuster's Superman."

Superman through the Ages, http://www.superman.nu/ (1983), Jerry Siegel, "Happy 45th Anniversary, Superman!"; (September 22, 2002) "Jerry Siegel."

Zap Cartoons, http://www.zapcartoons.com/ (September 19, 2002), "Jerry Siegel and Joe Shuster."

■ Obituaries

PERIODICALS

Economist, February 17, 1996 (Jerry Siegel), p. 83.

Entertainment Weekly, August 14, 1992 (Joe Shuster), Ty Burr, "Man and Superman," pp. 55; February 16, 1996 (Jerry Siegel), p. 14.

Los Angeles Times, August 3, 1992 (Joe Shuster), p. B1; January 31, 1996 (Jerry Siegel), p. A10.

New York Times, August 3, 1992 (Joe Shuster), p. B8; January 31, 1996 (Jerry Siegel).

Time, February 12, 1996 (Jerry Siegel), p. 25.

Times (London, England), February 1, 1996 (Jerry Siegel), p. 21.

Washington Post, August 3, 1992 (Joe Shuster), p. B6.*

John Singleton

◼ Personal

Born January 6, 1968, in Los Angeles, CA; son of Danny Singleton (a mortgage broker) and Sheila Ward (a sales executive); married Akosua Busia, October 12, 1996 (divorced, 1997); children: Hadar. *Nationality:* American. *Education:* University of Southern California, B.A., 1990.

◼ Addresses

Home—Baldwin Hills, CA. *Office*—New Deal Productions, 10202 West Washington Blvd., Metro Bldg., Room 203, Culver City, CA 90232-3119. *Agent*—Bradford W. Smith, Creative Artists Agency, 9830 Wilshire Blvd., Beverly Hills, CA 90212-1804.

◼ Career

Screenwriter and producer. Director of films, including *Rosewood,* Warner Brothers, 1997; and *The Fast and Furious 2,* Universal Pictures, 2003.

◼ Member

Academy of Motion Picture Arts and Sciences.

◼ Awards, Honors

Three awards from University of Southern California School of Cinema-Television, including Jack Nicholson Award (twice); New Generation Award, Los Angeles Film Critics Association, 1991, New Director Award, NYFCC, 1991, Academy Award nominations for best director and best original screenplay, Academy of Motion Picture Arts and Sciences, 1992, nomination for Best Screenplay, Writers Guild of America, 1992, and Screenwriter of the Year and Directorial Debut of the Year awards, ShoWest, 1992, all for *Boyz N the Hood;* Golden Berlin Bear award nomination, 1997, and Black Film Award, 1998, both for *Rosewood;* special mention for innovative concept and ensemble acting, Locarno Film Festival, 2001, for *Baby Boy;* Career Achievement Award, Acapulco Black Film Festival, 2001.

◼ Writings

SCREENPLAYS; AND DIRECTOR

Boyz N the Hood, Columbia, 1991.
(And co-producer) *Poetic Justice,* Columbia, 1993.

(And producer) *Higher Learning,* Columbia, 1995.

(With Shane Salerno) *Shaft,* Paramount Pictures, 2000.

Baby Boy, New Deal Productions, 2001.

OTHER

(With Veronica Chambers) *Poetic Justice: Film-Making South Central Style,* Delta (New York, NY), 1993.

(Author of introduction) Michael D'Orso, *Like Judgment Day: The Ruin and Redemption of a Town Called Rosewood,* Boulevard Books (New York, NY), 1996.

■ Sidelights

At age twenty-four, John Singleton became the youngest person ever to receive an Academy Award nomination for best director for the 1991 film *Boyz N the Hood,* which he also wrote. The movie chronicles the struggles of three black friends growing up in South Central, a neighborhood of Los Angeles. While Singleton addresses issues and themes of specific relevance to African Americans in *Boys N the Hood,* the motion picture proved commercially successful with diverse audiences. With this venture, Singleton became one of a number of young black filmmakers redefining mainstream cinema in the mid-1980s. Shunning the traditional Hollywood formula which resolves conflicts happily, artists such as Spike Lee, Matty Rich, and Singleton strive to tell authentic black urban stories in which problems defy simple solutions. Intrigued by this new cinematic trend, critics as well as audiences have responded favorably to Singleton's work. "No first film in the new wave of films by and about black Americans states the case for the movement's longevity more forcefully than *Boyz N the Hood,*" declared *Detroit News* film critic Susan Stark. Singleton has gone on from that initial success to write and direct several more movies—none of which have proved to be quite as successful with box-office crowds—including *Poetic Justice, Higher Learning, Rosewood, Shaft,* and *Baby Boy.*

"I grew up in South Central Los Angeles," Singleton told Cynthia Fuchs in *Pop Matters.* Born in 1968, he was raised in separate households by his father and mother. The author has noted that it was his father who took him to see movies—such as George Lucas's *Star Wars*—leaving him determined at the age of nine to become a filmmaker. " went to see *Star Wars,* like ten times, and I started breaking down how they made the shots, and studying how to make a film," Singleton told Fuchs. Soon the

young boy was doodling animated films on the sides of school notebooks "because the power of the moving image was very intriguing for me." As a teenager he played basketball as a youth, but soon saw that for him movie making was the proper right of passage, not athletics. In high school Singleton began spending more time in Hollywood and in movie theaters. Discovering that the film business revolved around screenplays, he began working on his writing skills. He enrolled in film school at the University of Southern California, and by the time he graduated he had made a few eight-millimeter films, received several writing awards, and signed a contract with influential talent company Creative Artists Agency. Soon after graduation, Singleton's screenplay for *Boyz N the Hood* won him a three-year contract with Columbia Pictures.

Singleton accepted the contract, but, fearing that another director would distort his point of view, insisted that he direct *Boyz N the Hood* himself. "It's my story, I lived it," he explained in *New York Times Magazine.* "What sense would it have made to have some white boy impose his interpretation on my experience?" In *Elle,* he added, "Having a black man directing raw street-life narratives gives them a certain credibility." It was important to Singleton that every aspect of the production be marked by authenticity. After securing the position of director, Singleton hired a nearly all-black crew and solicited three black Los Angeles gang members to help him fine-tune the dialogue and select the wardrobe. Singleton wanted to deliver his message in language that the average black audience member could understand, because, as he expressed in *Interview,* "I made my film for the regular brother off the street." *Time* contributor Richard Corliss noted the success of this venture, calling the film "a harrowing document true to the director's south-central Los Angeles milieu; he paints it black."

Boyz N the Hood

In *Boyz N the Hood,* the main characters—Tre Styles and his friends Ricky and Doughboy—attempt to live through adolescence despite the constant threat of violence and the temptation to profit from the illegal drug business. Opening with the statistic that one out of every twenty-two black males will be murdered—most by other black males—the film emphasizes the difficulty of survival in the "hood" (slang for neighborhood). Singleton believes that the proliferation of black-on-black crime is partially due to the absence of adult male role models in black communities. The author argues in *Boyz* that the chain of violence can only be halted by concerned fathers who set an example for their sons.

Rapper and actor Ice Cube stars in the 1991 film *Boyz N the Hood,* a dramatic profile of urban culture written and directed by John Singleton.

Singleton advocates this solution because his own life is evidence of its success. Although he lived with his mother, Singleton considers the weekends he spent with his father paramount to his development and success as a filmmaker. He believes that having a dream—and a father to encourage it—kept him out of trouble. "A young boy needs a man to show him how to be a man," Singleton stated in *Elle.* "Black men need to be responsible fathers for their sons."

Boyz N the Hood portrays "a tragic way of life," according to *New York* contributor David Denby. The hood is an inner-city world in which constant gunshots, sirens, and police helicopter searchlights serve as reminders that danger is never far away. Tre Styles adopts this environment as his new home when, as a troubled ten-year-old, he is sent by his divorced mother to live with his father, Furious. As Tre grows up, Furious teaches him responsibility and dignity, making him strong enough to resist the lure of the street and stay in school. Tre counts as

his friends athletic, college-bound Ricky and street-smart Doughboy, half-brothers who live with their mother. Transferring her feelings about their respective fathers on her sons, the mother favors Ricky but has little hope for Doughboy. Tre's friendships draw him into a violent confrontation from which he narrowly escapes. At film's end, Tre, guided by his father's example, manages to survive and go to college, while Ricky and Doughboy—who lack a male role model—are killed.

Though Singleton acted as both writer and director for *Boyz N the Hood,* he considers himself primarily a screenwriter. As he related in *New York Times Magazine,* "In this business, you get hired for your vision, and your vision begins with your script. I'm a writer first, and I direct in order to protect my vision." Although *Detroit Free Press* contributor Kathy Huffhines appreciated the fact that "he puts his anger into words, not just camera angles," Singleton considers the visual aspect of his screenplay more important than the spoken element. He

Laurence Fishburne and Omar Epps star in *Higher Learning,* a 1995 film directed and written by Singleton that profiles the diverse forces shaping black students on a college campus.

remarked in *New York Times Magazine,* "I strive toward saying things visually—that verbal stuff is for T.V."

Critics responded positively to Singleton's first writing and directing effort, which they found authentic and effective. *New York Times* contributor Janet Maslin commented, "Singleton's terrifically confident first feature places [him] on a footing with Spike Lee as a chronicler of the frustration faced by young black men growing up in urban settings." Responding to its style, subject matter, and direction, Stark, writing in the *Detroit News,* called *Boyz N the Hood* "a smart, smooth, astonishingly authoritative debut piece." Yet several reviewers, noting the many speeches which Furious Styles imparts to Tre, found the script verbose. Referring to "the ideological burden" of Singleton's script, Stark maintained that the

film "is over-stuffed with ideas." *People* contributor Ralph Novak, calling the film "pedantic," expressed, "Every issue is accompanied by a preachy piece of dialogue." Stark, however, believed Singleton was aware of this problem. She asserted that by adding a line in which Furious is compared to a preacher, Singleton "both anticipates and diffuses negative reaction" to Furious's speeches. Some critics also expressed concern about the attitudes toward women in Singleton's film. "In *Boyz N the Hood*," stated Corliss, "most of the women are shown as doped-up, career-obsessed or irrelevant to the man's work of raising a son in an American war zone." Huffhines observed that Singleton's "diamond-hard belief in the importance of fatherhood shortchanges motherhood," noting, "he's clearly down on Tre's mother for being coolly ambitious." She added, however, that Singleton's obvious respect for his main characters outweighs the problems with the minor characters, and named Singleton "the most impressive" of the year's young black filmmakers. The Academy Awards committee backed up this assertion with two nominations for Singleton's first feature film.

Life after the Hood

Singleton followed *Boyz N the Hood* with *Poetic Justice* in 1993. A love story, the movie features singer Janet Jackson and rap artist Tupac Shakur. Singleton had a hard act to follow as his debut had grossed $100 million and earned him two Oscar nominations. Thus he went in a somewhat new direction for this second feature. According to Veronica Chambers, writing in *Essence,* Singleton looked for a "little yin" to go with his "yang," making a "film about 'gyrlz N the hood.'"

"I wanted to do something street," Singleton told Chambers, "but something different." *Poetic Justice* thus became the tale of a "young sister and how all the tribulations of the brothers affect her," as Singleton described the picture. Jackson plays the young black woman, Justice, who has undergone more experiences of violence than a woman her age should ever have to. This South Central beautician hides from the world after her boyfriend is gunned down, and turns to poetry to try and express her feelings. Rapper Tupac Shakur plays a friendly mailman who tries to break through to young Justice. The movie was a disappointment at the box office and suffered the usual critical dissection of a second feature film from a writer/director who had scored a major debut success. Leonard Maltin, writing in his *Movie and Video Guide,* felt that Singleton "suffers the sophomore jinx in this ambitious but fatally pretentious saga." Stanley Kaufmann, reviewing the movie in *New Republic,* also found it disappointing, calling it a "steady boil of pointless bickering between run-of-the-mill young people." Grossing only $30 million, *Poetic Justice* was nowhere near as popular as Singleton's first movie.

In 1995 Singleton offered *Higher Learning,* a film set on a fictional college campus and dealing with issues of race, violence, and sex. The movie's characters include Malik Williams, a black track star who is convinced the university only wants him for his athletic abilities; Deja, Malik's confident and ambitious girlfriend; Kristen, a white freshman coping with date rape; Remy, a white student from Idaho who joins a Neo-Nazi group; and Professor Phipps, trying to educate his students and forestall violence. The film received mixed reactions from critics. Writing in *Commonweal,* Richard Aleva remarked that the film is "a work of good intentions, and these intentions seem to have leached every last ounce of originality out of Singleton and much of his intelligence [as] well." Similarly, commenting on the film's roles, *Time* reviewer Richard Schickel declared: "These aren't really characters; they are points on a rigidly conceived political spectrum." However, while conceding that the film is "seriously flawed," a *Rolling Stone* critic averred that "Compelling questions of identity are being addressed" in *Higher Learning.*

Racial Violence, Superheroes, and Mean Streets

The 1997 film *Rosewood,* directed by Singleton, is based on a factual incident of racial violence that occurred during the first week of 1923 in the black town of Rosewood, Florida, an incident that had largely been a secret until the 1982 discovery of the story by a Florida reporter. During that week of 1923, several white inhabitants of a neighboring town, Sumner, destroyed Rosewood with fire and murdered or tortured many of its black townspeople after a white woman falsely let on that a recent attack on her had been committed by a black stranger. For the production of *Rosewood,* Singleton and others involved in the film researched and built a replica of Rosewood, which was constructed in Lake County, Florida. Two of the film's main characters, one white and one black—played by actors Jon Voight and Ving Rhames—work together to attempt a rescue of the women and children forced out of Rosewood and into the surrounding woods and swamp lands by the white mob. In an article for the *Calgary Sun,* Louis B. Hobson said of the survivors' descendants, who, in 1994, were granted $2 million by the Florida state legislature, "Their ancestors' story has become a powerful, compelling film from 28-year-old John Singleton, the director of *Boyz N the Hood* and *Higher Learning.*" Hobson quoted

Singleton as saying, "I had vowed never to make a movie about the South or in the South but when I read the screenplay for Rosewood, I made an exception."

In his review for the *Los Angeles Times,* critic Kenneth Turan said of *Rosewood:* "The need to bear witness against atrocity, to testify that something wicked this way came, is the powerful drive that animates 'Rosewood,' the story of an American tragedy so horrific no one talked about it for more than half a century." Though mentioning the story's unforgettableness, Turan also pointed out his disappointments with the film's portrayal of it, commenting, for example, that "as written by Gregory Poirier and produced by Jon Peters, whose credits are mostly of the blockbuster variety, the film is broader and more simplistic than it needs to be, settling more than it should for obvious emotions and situations." *Variety*'s Todd McCarthy called *Rosewood* an "unblinking look at the wages of racism," and a movie that "absorbingly recounts a ghastly and little-known chapter of 20th-century American history." Not all critics had praise for the movie, however. A reviewer for *People* called Singleton's film a "portentous would-be epic." Michael Sauter, writing in *Entertainment Weekly,* felt the film was caught in an artistic no-man's land: "Too harsh to be a popcorn movie and too undermined by make-believe to be the Important Film it was intended to be, *Rosewood* is ultimately neither." But while *Time*'s Schickel takes Singleton and his screenwriter, Gregory Poirier, to task for blending the "relatively few known facts of this matter with a lot of very obvious, very movieish fictions," he also lauded the film for finding "in a shameful bygone moment, sources of pride for contemporary audiences." Owen Gleiberman, writing in *Entertainment Weekly,* had more unreserved praise for the film, noting that Singleton "has taken a great leap toward artistic maturity" in its creation, working with a "solid, emotionally heated craftsmanship that makes you think, Yes, it could have looked something like this." And Stanley Crouch noted in the *New York Times* that *Rosewood* was a "major American film."

Singleton next took on a sequel to the popular 1971 movie *Shaft,* about a savvy, black private eye who scores long on points with the ladies. In Singleton's adaptation, however, Shaft—played by Samuel L. Jackson—is no longer a private detective, but a New York City policeman. *Variety* reviewer Robert Koehler noted that Singleton "affectionately embraces the blaxploitation genre tradition" and applies "New Millennium speed and sleekness" to come up with a "smart, entertaining product." Koehler also felt that Singleton's "turn to pure popcorn fare after suffering a rough track record . . . results in his best filmmaking to date, technically as slick as they come but substantial and relevant at the core." In this update, the cop Shaft is investigating the beating murder of a young black man, and figures out that the wealthy son of a real estate developer is the perpetrator. But catching the man is harder than it would seem, and Shaft must get to a white waitress who witnessed the crime before the murderer kills her too. Things go from bad to worse, forcing Shaft at one point to turn in his badge and go it alone. A reviewer for the *Economist* called the popular summertime movie "a new cocktail to the popcorn crowd," while Schickel, writing in *Time,* felt this "is yet another urban action piece, well enough made but not essentially different from a hundred other movies just like it."

In 2001 Singleton returned to the mean streets he so creatively evoked and explored in his first feature film, this time with a movie about "a case of arrested development," as Phillip Williams described the film in *MovieMaker. Baby Boy* is Singleton's attempt to explain a phenomenon found in many black males. "My definition of a baby boy is that he's the most dangerous cat around, because he's hypersensitive," Singleton explained to Fuchs. Such a youth has been raised by a single mom and thus is always attempting to defend his masculinity, and is a ripe candidate for the usual "dysfunctional rite of passage" of crime, prison, and abandonment of his own children, just as he was abandoned by his father. Something of a companion piece to *Boyz N the Hood, Baby Boy* tells the story of Jody—played by R & B star Tyrese—as a twenty-year-old aimless youth who has no job, lives with his still young mother, and has fathered children by two separate girlfriends. When the mother's boyfriend—a reformed 'gangsta' played by Ving Rhames—moves in, sparks fly with two men in the house. Jody tries to get his life in order, but in a bungling way, hustling stolen women's clothing. Events spiral downward as Jody turns into "a human pinball, ricocheting among his two 'baby mamas,' the young women who have his children," according to Kirk Honey-

John Voight and Ving Rhames battle racism in 1920s Florida following a white woman's allegations of rape in the 1997 Singleton-penned and -directed film *Rosewood.*

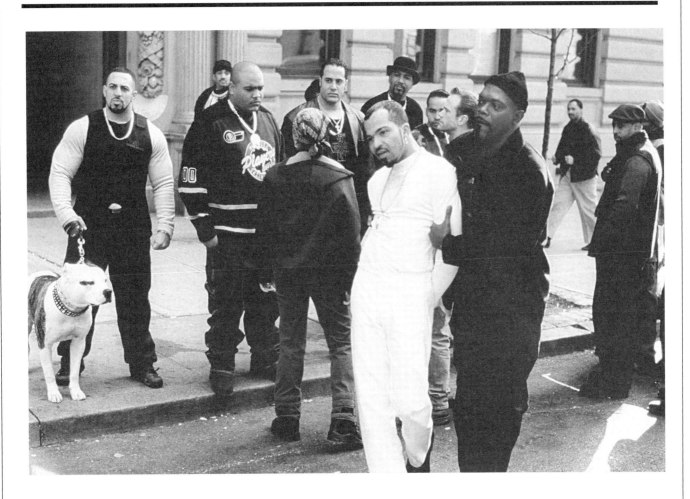

"Supercop" John Shaft, played by Samuel L. Jackson, puts the clamps on a suspect in Singleton's remake of the 1971 film *Shaft* that starred Richard Roundtree.

cutt in the *Hollywood Reporter.* At the end, however, Singleton does offer a bit of optimism, with Jody and his primary girlfriend once again pregnant and this time engaged.

Once more there were mixed reviews for Singleton's film, with most critics finding sincerity in a script which is also marred at times with an overly preachy tone. *Variety's* McCarthy called *Baby Boy* a "pungently argued civics lesson about the Peter Pan syndrome among contemporary young black men." McCarthy further felt that the movie "should play reasonably well with black audiences and presents a measure of crossover interest due to Singleton's name." Honeycutt noted that the movie "will certainly create a stir on the op-ed pages and in the black media that could translate into a minor success," but faulted Singleton's "awkwardly written scenes, ham-fisted direction and forced drama [which] crop up all the time." Daniel Eagan, writing in *Film Journal International,* thought *Baby Boy* "lacks

the drama and urgency" of *Boyz N the Hood,* and though "entertaining, [it] is too lightweight to win over broad audiences."

Other critics found more to like in the film. Owen Gleiberman, reviewing *Baby Boy* in *Entertainment Weekly,* called it "ambling yet impassioned." Michael Wilmington, writing in *Knight Ridder/Tribune News Service,* had more positive words, noting that while many "will recoil" from the sex, violence, and foul language, and other critics might "damn it as another exploitive collection of negative stereotypes," still other reviewers "may applaud Singleton's daring, returning to this rough-hewn territory." Irv Slifkin called the film an "uneven, often electrifying study of modern urban life," in a *Video Business* review, applauding the "strong performances" and "surprising plot twists." Crouch, reviewing *Baby Boy* in the *New York Times,* called it a "brave work," and one with a feeling of "depth" from a "sense of tragedy, of violence, of passing on the bloody heritage of abuse." For Couch, a film like *Baby Boy,* which was not a box office success, "stands tall in times like these."

If you enjoy the works of John Singleton, you might want to check out the following:

Do the Right Thing, a film by Spike Lee, 1989.
Fresh, a film starring Samuel L. Jackson, 1994.
Love Jones, a film starring Larenz Tate and Nia Long, 1997.

Singleton, hailed as a protean talent a la Orson Welles for making such a statement as a young filmmaker, has over the years developed his filmmaking talents, taking on new risk with each movie. Sometimes succeeding, sometimes failing, he has, as he told an interviewer for *Ebony,* continued "challenging Black people. I want people to have a sense of what we are as a people. I want to keep making people think." As Singleton told Fuchs, "I have a hard row to hoe, because not only do I have to make films that make money, I also feel inspired to make films that say something."

■ Biographical and Critical Sources

BOOKS

Contemporary Black Biography, Volume 30, Gale (Detroit, MI), 2001.

Maltin, Leonard, *Leonard Maltin's Movie and Video Guide,* Signet (New York, NY), 1995, p. 1024.

Newsmakers 1994, Gale (Detroit, MI), 1994.

PERIODICALS

Advocate, July 27, 1993, p. 77.

Calgary Sun, February 18, 1997, Louis B. Hobson, review of *Rosewood.*

Commonweal, February 24, 1995, Richard Aleva, review of *Higher Learning,* p. 55.

Detroit Free Press, July 12, 1991, Kathy Huffhines, review of *Boyz N the Hood,* pp. 1C, 4C.

Detroit News, July 12, 1991, pp. 1D, 3D; July 20, 1991, pp. 1C, 3-4C.

Detroit News and Free Press, July 14, 1991, pp. 1A, 8A.

Ebony, November, 1991; April, 1995, p. 122.

Economist, July 1, 2000, "Black Leather," p. 87.

Elle, June, 1991, pp. 52-61.

Emerge, March, 1996, p. 38.

Entertainment Weekly, July 23, 1993, pp. 28, 43; August 13, 1993, p. 12; January 13, 1995, p. 32; July 28, 1995, p. 68; March 7, 1997, Owen Gleiberman, review of *Rosewood,* p. 46; September 5, 1997, Michael Sauter, review of *Rosewood,* pp. 78-79; July 13, 2001, Owen Gleiberman, "Man Child," p. 56; July 27, 2001, Owen Gleiberman, review of *Baby Boy,* p. 48.

Esquire, August, 1993, pp. 59-65, 108.

Essence, September, 1991, p. 43; November, 1991, pp. 64, 112; August, 1993, Veronica Chambers, "John Singleton: After Directing 'Boyz N the Hood,' He Has Made a Movie for the Sisters," p. 48.

Film Journal International, August, 2001, Daniel Eagan, review of *Baby Boy,* p. 77.

Hollywood Reporter, June 27, 2001, Kirk Honeycutt, review of *Baby Boy,* p. 10.

Insight on the News, August 12, 1991, p. 44.

Interview, July, 1991, p. 20; July, 1993, p. 36.

Jet, July 15, 1991, p. 56; September 2, 1991, p. 11; June 1, 1992, p. 56; July 19, 1993, p. 54; January 23, 1995, p. 14; March 24, 1997, pp. 56-59; July 12, 1999, "John Singleton Pleads No Contest in Battery Case," p. 36.

Journal of Men's Studies, November, 1996, David Seelow, "Look Forward in Anger: Young, Black Males and the New Cinema," pp. 153-178.

Journal of Popular Film and Television, summer, 2002, Matthew Henry, "He's a Bad Mother *$%@!#\": Shaft and Contemporary Black Masculinity," pp. 114-119.

Knight Ridder/Tribune News Service, June 26, 2001, Michael Wilmington, review of *Baby Boy,* p. K2649.

Los Angeles Magazine, February, 1991, p. 18.

Los Angeles Times, February 21, 1997, Kenneth Turan, review of *Rosewood;* June 27, 2001, Kenneth Turan, review of *Baby Boy,* p. F1.

Los Angeles Times Book Review, August 8, 1993, p. 11.

Maclean's, July 29, 1991, p. 47.

National Review, September 23, 1991, pp. 54-56.

New Republic, September 2, 1991, pp. 26-27; August 23 and August 30, 1993, Stanley Kaufmann, review of *Poetic Justice,* pp. 30-31.

New Statesman, October 25, 1991, pp. 30-31.

Newsweek, July 29, 1991, pp. 48-49.

New York, July 22, 1991, pp. 40-41; July 29, 1991, p. 49.

New Yorker, August 2, 1993, pp. 76-78.

New York Times, July 12, 1991, Janet Maslin, review of review of *Boyz N the Hood,* pp. C1, C15; July 14, 1991, p. 10; June 27, 2001, A. O Scott, "Be a Man? But Where Are the Role Models?," p. B3; August 21, 2001, Stanley Crouch, "A Lost Generation and Its Exploiters," p. AR8.

New York Times Magazine, July 14, 1991, pp. 15-19, 38-40, 44.

People, July 22, 1991, Ralph Novak, review of *Boyz N the Hood,* pp. 14-15; January 23, 1995, p. 83; March 3, 1997, review of *Rosewood,* pp. 19-20; July 30, 2001, "Point of Departure," p. 83.

Premiere, November, 1991, p. 128; August, 1993, p. 70.

Rolling Stone, August 19, 1993, pp. 81-83; January 26, 1995, review of *Higher Learning,* p. 66.

Time, June 17, 1991, Richard Corliss, "Boyz of New Black City," pp. 64-68; December 7, 1992, p. 21; January 23, 1995, Richard Schickel, review of *Higher Learning,* p. 57; March 3, 1997, Richard Schickel, review of *Rosewood,* p. 83; June 26, 2000, Richard Schickel, "Has Shaft Been Shafted?," p. 70.

Variety, July 26, 1993, pp. 28-29; January 9, 1995, p. 71; February 17, 1997, Todd McCarthy, review of *Rosewood,* p. 68; June 12, 2000, Robert Koehler, review of *Shaft,* p. 13; July 9, 2001, Todd McCarthy, review of *Baby Boy,* p. 22.

Velvet Light Trap, fall, 1996, Glen Masato Mimura, "On Fathers and Sons, Sex and Death: John Singleton's *Boyz N the Hood,*" pp. 14-27.

Video Business, October 1, 2001, Irv Slifkin, review of *Baby Boy,* p. 17.

Washington Post, June 27, 2001, Stephen Hunter, review of *Baby Boy,* p. C1.

Wilson Library Bulletin, October, 1991, pp. 70-71.

OTHER

MovieMaker/Hands on Pages, http://www.moviemaker.com/ (October 2, 2002), Phillip Williams, "Life Lessons: An Interview with John Singleton."

MovieWeb, http://movieweb.com/movie/ (September 20, 1999).

Pop Matters, http://www.popmatters.com (October 2, 2002), Cynthia Fuchs, "Interview with John Singleton."*

Zadie Smith

■ Personal

Original first name Sadie; name changed in 1990; born 1976, in Hampstead, England; daughter of an advertising executive and a child psychologist. *Education:* Cambridge University, B.A., 1998; graduate study, Radcliffe College, 2002.

■ Addresses

Home—London, England. *Office*—c/o Author Mail, Random House, 299 Park Ave., New York, NY 10171-0002.

■ Career

Novelist. Writer-in-residence, Institute for Contemporary Arts, London, England, 2000.

■ Awards, Honors

Whitbread Award and *Guardian* Prize, both 2000, both for *White Teeth.*

■ Writings

White Teeth: A Novel, Random House (New York, NY), 2000.
The Autograph Man, Random House (New York, NY), 2002.

■ Adaptations

White Teeth was adapted for television by the British Broadcast Corporation in 2002; film rights were sold to Miramax.

■ Sidelights

British writer Zadie Smith has published only two novels: *White Teeth,* winner of two major literary awards and with over one million copies in print, and *The Autograph Man.* Smith burst into the international fiction scene with the publication of her debut novel, *White Teeth,* in 2000, and was immediately hailed as a new voice in British literature. The half-Jamaican Smith has since been lauded for her multicultural exploration in *White Teeth,* which was written during her years as an undergraduate at Cambridge University.

Smith grew up in Willesden Green, a multiethnic neighborhood northwest of London. Her English father and Jamaican mother divorced when she was fourteen years old. "I didn't always write stories when I was young," Smith admitted in an online interview with *Bold Type Magazine*. "I wrote some, but I've never been prolific. From the age of five to fifteen, I really wanted to be a musical movie actress. I tap danced for ten years before I began to understand people don't make musicals anymore. All I wanted to do was be at MGM working for Arthur Freed or Gene Kelly or Vincent Minelli. Historical and geographical constraints made this impossible. Slowly but surely the pen became mightier than the double pick-up timestep with shuffle."

Smith began writing *White Teeth* while attending Cambridge University. "The novel began as a short story which expanded," Smith told *Bold Type Magazine*. While in college, she regularly contributed short stories to the *May Anthologies,* an annual compilation of prose and poetry written by Cambridge and Oxford undergraduates. One of these stories later became the basis for *White Teeth*. That story caught the eye of a literary agent who wanted to discuss with its author the possibility of expanding the story into a full-length novel. Consequently, the agent secured for Smith a rumored 250,000-pound (approximately 400,000-dollar) advance, an extraordinary sum for a first-time author and an incomplete manuscript which contained only a plot synopsis and two chapters.

"I didn't always write stories when I was young. . . . From the age of five to fifteen, I really wanted to be a musical movie actress. I tap danced for ten years before I began to understand people don't make musicals anymore. . . . Slowly but surely the pen became mightier than the double pick-up timestep with shuffle."

—Zadie Smith

Publishes *White Teeth*

Addressing racial, cultural, and generational issues with wit and irony, *White Teeth* is the story of the "lifelong friendship between Archie, a white, working-class Londoner, and Samad, a Muslim from Bangladesh, with issues of race, religion, generational conflict and genetically modified mice thrown spicily into the pot," summarized Sarah Lyall in the *New York Times Book Review*. "Theirs is a relationship born of World War II, forged on a lie and nourished on the greasy eggs served at O'Connell's Pool House, which, by the way, is neither Irish nor a pool hall. In fact, nothing in their lives has turned out as it seemed it would," added Susan Horsburgh in *Time*. By its end, *White Teeth* exposes the dangers of labeling others and illustrates the universal striving to maintain self-identity in pluralistic contemporary society, despite cultural heritage or ethnic origin.

Critics were enthusiastic in their response to the book. "When Zadie Smith published her first book in Britain earlier this year, the press and literati agreed: the novel and the novelist were 'drop-dead cool,'" commented Jeff Giles in *Newsweek*. A *Publishers Weekly* critic called the book a "stunning, polymathic debut. . . . Smith's novel recalls the hyper-contemporary yet history-infused work of Rushdie, sharp-edged, fluorescent and many-faceted." A critic for the *Economist* found the work clever, continuing: "But lots of novels are clever, and what makes this one true and original is the way the comedy fizzes up through the characters. Dickens, not Salman Rushdie, comes to mind, with all his theatricality and exuberance."

Though Giles felt that the plot is "tortured" and the work as a whole has too many characters, he lauded Smith as an "astonishing intellect. She writes sharp dialogue for every age and race—and she's funny as hell." Anthony Quinn in the *New York Times Book Review,* wondering if Smith has taken on a task beyond her reach with *White Teeth,* found that "aside from a rather wobbly final quarter, Smith holds it all together with a raucous energy and confidence that couldn't be a fluke." "Imagine Charlie Parker with a typewriter, Coltrane with a laptop," wrote Greg Tate in *Village Voice*. "Incredibly enough, Smith just might be even smarter than her smackdown writing declares her to be."

With the success of *White Teeth* came international media attention, something Smith is uncomfortable with. She told Malcolm Jones in *Newsweek:* "I remember once being in the street in London and watching a bus go by with my face on it, when *White Teeth* had just come out, and the way that made me feel. It was a sort of mixture of pumped-up, false power, vanity and terror. And to multiply that, and to actively want it in your life, seems to me horrifying. It's about the emptiest thing on this planet, and I wanted to write about that."

Examines Limits of Fame

The public's obsessive interest in celebrities is one of the subjects in Smith's second novel, *The Autograph Man.* Alex-Li Tandem, half-Jewish and half-Chinese, is a dealer in the autographs of famous people. He is on a quest to find the autograph of his favorite screen star, Kitty Alexander, but she is retired now, reclusive, and was always reluctant to give out autographs. Once a week, Alex writes a letter to Kitty's fan club, hoping she will someday respond to his pleas. As time goes by without a response, Alex's obsession leads him to increasingly erratic behavior, including the sorting out of all behavior by whether it is "Jewish" or "Goyish." Among the novel's other characters are Alex's girlfriend Esther, his two closest childhood friends—now a rabbi and an insurance salesman—and Adam, a black friend who combines Jewish mysticism with marijuana. "Smith's lively, descriptive prose drives a comic plot of labyrinthine complexity," wrote Shannon Olson in the *Minneapolis Star-Tribune.* A *Kirkus* reviewer found the novel to be "an uneasy mix of [the film] *Sunset Boulevard,* J. P. Donleavy's *The Ginger Man,* and James McCourt's fey romantic comedies about dementedly self-absorbed beautiful people." But Brad Hooper in *Booklist* concluded that Smith's second novel is "as bracingly intelligent and humorous as her first."

In *The Autograph Man* Smith paints a portrait of a society in which racial, religious, and ethnic distinctions are confused. "Smith likes to trample over the usual delimiters of identity," Laura Miller wrote in *Salon.com,* "on her way to portraying a new kind of mongrel world citizen: little bit of this, little bit of that." A critic for *Publishers Weekly* noted: "Smith paints portraits of a very multiculti Judaism: Adam, for instance, is a black Jew, while Alex is a disbelieving Chinese one." "His unusual ethnicity aside, Alex is a safe choice for a character," explained Daniel Zalewski in the *New York Times Book Review.* "He is the prevailing stereotype of his generation, the pop-culture-addled trivialist." Don McLeese in *Book* pointed out that "Alex is Smith's English Everyman, his ethnicity more matter-of-fact than life-defining." Sean Rocha of *Library Journal* concluded that "the novel's real pleasure lies in the masterfully crafted characters and the small insights that capture something so true of the world that they make the reader sit up in startled recognition." McLeese summed up: "Smith remains a virtuosic master of voices, a stylist who can be both playful and profound."

Smith told Jones in *Newsweek* that, with the publication of *The Autograph Man,* she intended to take a break from novel writing. In the fall of 2002, she enrolled in graduate literature classes at Radcliffe: "I'm enormously ambitious about being a part of English writing. But I don't feel as though I've written a book that has even a long shot of doing that."

If you enjoy the works of Zadie Smith, you might want to check out the following books:

Salman Rushdie, *Midnight's Children,* 1981.
Michael Chabon, *The Amazing Adventures of Kavalier & Clay,* 2000.
Richard Russo, *Empire Falls,* 2001.

■ Biographical and Critical Sources

PERIODICALS

Black Issues Book Review, September, 2000, Askhari Hodari, "The Mystique of Zadie Smith," p. 26.
Book, November-December, 2002, Don McLeese, review of *The Autograph Man,* p. 78.
Booklist, April 1, 2000, Danise Hoover, review of *White Teeth,* p. 1436; October 1, 2002, Brad Hooper, review of *The Autograph Man,* p. 276.
Commonweal, August 11, 2000, Anita Mathias, review of *White Teeth,* p. 27.
Daily Telegraph (London, England), February 19, 2000, Philip Hensher, "Write First Time," p. 6.
Denver Post, May 28, 2000, Rob Stout, "Faces of Greatness Smile on British Novelist," p. F5.
Economist, February 19, 2000, review of *White Teeth,* p. 5.
Guardian, January 22, 2000, Maya Jaggi, "In a Strange Land," p. 9.
Harper's Bazaar, May, 2000, Laura Winters, "Great Expectations," p. 112.
Hudson Review, winter, 2001, Tom Wilhelmus, review of *White Teeth,* p. 694.
Kirkus Reviews, September 1, 2002, review of *The Autograph Man,* p. 1261.
Library Journal, April 1, 2000, Rebecca A. Stuhr, review of *White Teeth,* p. 132; October 15, 2002, Sean Rocha, review of *The Autograph Man,* p. 95.
London Review of Books, September 21, 2000, Daniel Soar, review of *White Teeth,* p. 30.
Los Angeles Times, June 26, 2000, Lynell George, "Author Purposeful with Prose, Fidgety with Fame," p. E1.

Los Angeles Times Book Review, May 7, 2000, Mark Rozzo, "Who's English Now?," p. 10.

Minneapolis Star-Tribune, October 13, 2002, Shannon Olson, review of *The Autograph Man.*

New Republic, July 24, 2000, James Wood, "Human, All Too Inhuman: The Smallness of the 'Big' Novel," p. 41.

New Statesman, January 29, 2001, Jason Cowley, "The Tiger Woods of Literature?," p. 57.

Newsweek, May 1, 2000, Jeff Giles, review of *White Teeth,* p. 73; September 30, 2002, Malcolm Jones, "Zadie Smith. Honest. Her Second Novel May Be Her Last—For Now."

New Yorker, October 18-25, 1999, Kevin Jackson, "Next Generation, Zadie Smith," p. 182.

New York Review of Books, February 8, 2001, John Lanchester, review of *White Teeth,* p. 28.

New York Times Book Review, April 30, 2000, Anthony Quinn, review of *White Teeth,* pp. 7-8; April 30, 2000, Sarah Lyall, "A Good Start" (interview), p. 8; October 6, 2002, Daniel Zalewski, "Star Turn: In Zadie Smith's Second Novel, the Chinese-Jewish-British Protagonist Worships an Aging Movie Actress," p. 13.

Observer (London, England), January 16, 2000, Stephanie Merritt, "Interview: Zadie Smith."

Publishers Weekly, March 13, 2000, review of *White Teeth,* p. 60; September 30, 2002, review of *The Autograph Man,* p. 47.

St. Louis Post-Dispatch, May 28, 2000, Susan C. Thomson, "Cultures and Generations Clash in Absorbing First Novel by Zadie Smith," p. F9.

Spectator, January 29, 2000, Zenga Longmore, "Fairy-Sweary-Land," p. 47.

Time, May 8, 2000, "Of Roots and Family Trees," p. 94.

Times Literary Supplement, January 21, 2000, Sukhdev Sandhu, "Excremental Children," p. 21.

Village Voice, May 16, 2000, Greg Tate, review of *White Teeth,* p. 75.

Washington Post Book World, May 21, 2000, Esther Iverem, "London Calling," p. 7.

Women's Review of Books, October, 2000, Kathleen O'Grady, "The Empire Strikes Back," p. 19.

World & I, September, 2000, Merritt Mosley, review of *White Teeth,* p. 220.

World Literature Today, winter, 2001, Bruce King, review of *White Teeth,* p. 116.

Yale Review, July, 2000, Meghan O'Rourke, review of *White Teeth,* p. 159.

OTHER

Bold Type Magazine, http://www.randomhouse.com/boldtype/ (November 10, 2002), interview with Zadie Smith.

Flak Magazine, http://www.flakmag.com/ (October 31, 2002), Cory O'Malley, review of *The Autograph Man.*

Salon.com, http://www.salon.com/ (September 5, 2002), Laura Miller, review of *The Autograph Man.**

Alfred Lord Tennyson

■ Personal

Born August 6, 1809, in Somersby, Lincolnshire, England; died, October 6, 1892, in Haslemere, England; son of George Clayton (a reverend) and Elizabeth (Fytche) Tennyson; married Emily Sellwood, June 13, 1850; children: Hallam, Lionel. *Nationality:* British; English. *Education:* Attended Trinity College, Cambridge, 1827-31.

■ Career

Poet and playwright.

■ Awards, Honors

Chancellor's Gold Medal, Cambridge University, for *Timbuctoo*; named poet laureate of Great Britain, 1850; made a peer of the realm, 1883. Honorary doctorate degrees from Oxford University and Edinburgh University.

■ Writings

POETRY

(With Frederick and Charles Tennyson) *Poems by Two Brothers*, Simpkin & Marshall/Louth (London, England), 1827.

Timbuctoo: A Poem (in Blank Verse) Which Obtained the Chancellor's Gold Medal at the Cambridge Commencement, Smith (Cambridge, England), 1829.

Poems, Chiefly Lyrical, Effingham Wilson (London, England), 1830.

Poems, Moxon (London, England), 1832.

Poems, two volumes, Ticknor (Boston, MA), 1842.

The Princess: A Medley, Moxon (London, England), 1847, Ticknor (Boston, MA), 1848.

In Memoriam, Ticknor, Reed & Fields (Boston, MA), 1850.

Ode on the Death of the Duke of Wellington, Moxon (London, England), 1852.

Maud, and Other Poems, Ticknor & Fields (Boston, MA), 1855.

Idylls of the King, Ticknor & Fields (Boston, MA), 1859.

Enoch Arden, etc., Moxon (London, England), 1864, Ticknor & Fields (Boston, MA), 1865.

The Holy Grail and Other Poems, Moxon (London, England), 1869, Fields, Osgood (Boston, MA), 1870.

Gareth and Lynette, etc., Osgood (Boston, MA), 1872.

Ballads and Other Poems, Osgood (Boston, MA), 1880.

Tiresias and Other Poems, Macmillan (London, England), 1885.

Locksley Hall Sixty Years After, etc., Macmillan (New York, NY), 1886.

Demeter and Other Poems, Macmillan (New York, NY), 1889.

The Death of Oenone, Akbar's Dream, and Other Poems, Macmillan (New York, NY), 1892.

COLLECTIONS

Numerous collections of Tennyson's poetry are available, including *The Poems of Tennyson,* edited by Christopher Ricks, Longmans, Green (London, England), 1969; *Alfred Lord Tennyson: Selected Poems,* Penguin (New York, NY), 1992; and *Tennyson's Poetry: Authoritative Texts, Contexts, Criticism,* edited by Robert W. Hill, Jr., Norton (New York, NY), 1998.

OTHER

Queen Mary: A Drama, Osgood (Boston, MA), 1875.

Harold: A Drama, King (London, England), 1876, Osgood (Boston, MA), 1877.

Becket, Macmillan (London, England), 1884, Dodd, Mead (New York, NY), 1894.

The Cup and the Falcon, Macmillan (New York, NY), 1884.

The Foresters, Robin Hood and Maid Marian, Macmillan (New York, NY), 1892.

The Letters of Alfred Lord Tennyson: 1821-1850, Volume 1, edited by Cecil Y. Lang and Edgar F. Shannon, Jr., Harvard University Press (Cambridge, MA), 1981.

Author's major collection of correspondence and manuscripts is housed at the Tennyson Research Centre, Lincoln, England; a family archive is housed at the Lincolnshire Archives Office, Lincoln; other important collections are housed at Trinity College, Cambridge; Houghton Library, Harvard University; Beinecke Library, Yale University, Perkins Library, Duke University; and the British Library.

■ Sidelights

Alfred Lord Tennyson has the dubious honor of being one of the most critically disputed great poets in the English language. The very term "Tennysonian" has taken on, in many quarters, the negative complaint of sentimentality, conservatism, too-easy rhyme, and shallow thinking. Praised during his lifetime, honored as a poet laureate whose every word became instant news, whose every new poem was eagerly awaited by the British populace, Tennyson suffered from his success after death. Poet W. H. Auden called him "the great English poet of the Nursery," while Irish playwright, George Bernard Shaw quipped that he had the "brains of a third-rate policeman." Poet T. S. Eliot, commenting on Tennyson's role as the poet of death, called him the "saddest of all English poets." After Tennyson's own death, critics from Matthew Arnold to F. R. Leavis condemned the poet as a "second-rater," according to Brian Southam in *British Writers.* Southam characterizes "Tennysonian" verse as "polished, melodious, and decorative; and in this artistry marooned, isolated from the central vitality of English poetry." In this light, the poetry of W. B. Yeats, Eliot, and Ezra Pound, at the beginning of the twentieth century, serves as an unromantic, unsentimental, subtle, and complex palliative to this Victorian master.

However, a plethora of other critics have also championed Tennyson for penning verse able to reach the man on the street with its direct messages and themes, its vibrant, rhythmic language, and its celebration of an earlier England, closer to nature. "Tennyson suffered particularly as the representative Victorian poet," Southam wrote. "His rejection was part of the historical process. . . . Although there is a good deal of Tennyson that is pompous, banal, grotesquely sentimental, and in many other ways laughably or unpleasantly Victorian, there is a sufficient body of his finest work to place him among the great poets of English literature."

Tennyson is perhaps best known for *In Memoriam,* a long poem in remembrance of a friend who died young. Most readers could also quote parts of his famous poem "Crossing the Bar." These two pieces, as well as other elegiac verses, however, managed to stereotype the poet as the voice of eulogy and death. But in other poem cycles, such as *Maud* and *Idylls of the King,* Tennyson taps psychological states or reawakens bygone times, passing on his love for the countryside and nature to future generations in a direct manner, with no need for postmodern analysis. Whatever critical analysis future generations put on Tennyson, he bestrode the Victorian age as no other writer in any other epoch; his name became synonymous with poetry. "More than any other Victorian writer, Tennyson has seemed the embodiment of his age," wrote a contributor for *Dictionary of Literary Biography.* "Even his most severe critics have always recognized his lyric gift for sound and cadence, a gift probably unequaled in the history of English poetry, but one so absolute that it has sometimes been mistaken for mere facility."

Bleak Beginnings

Tennyson was born on August 6, 1809, at Somersby, Lincolnshire, England, the fourth of twelve children born to Reverend George Clayton Tennyson and Elizabeth Fytche Tennyson. Tennyson's father was a bitter man, forced into a vocation in the church by a father intent on establishing the Tennyson clan as one of the splendid family dynasties of England. To that end, this grandfather of Alfred Tennyson passed over his older son, George, for the younger, more ambitious second son as the heir. The Reverend George Tennyson had already been mentally unstable before this slight; disinheritance pushed him further over the brink into the abuse of both alcohol and drugs. Thus, far from experiencing an idyllic Victorian childhood, Tennyson grew up in fear of his father's black moods, which grew ever worse in the late 1820s. Tennyson also witnessed the huge disparity in wealth between his father and his uncle, Charles, who lived in a castle and lorded it over his older brother. In ways, this comparison affected him his entire life, leading him to worry about money and financial arrangements. A third hereditary influence was a family strain of epilepsy and mental disease. Several members of his family had to be confined for periods of time: one of his brothers was in an asylum most of his life, another was addicted to drugs, one to alcohol, and still another died young but had been confined to asylums intermittently. In fact, all the children who reached maturity had at least one serious breakdown. Tennyson himself was under a doctor's care on and off throughout the 1840s.

Tennyson began composing poetry at an early age, as did many of his siblings. He used verse as a way to take his mind off his problems, making up phrases as he was doing other activities, then memorizing them for future use. From 1816 to 1820 he studied at the Louth grammar school, and was thereafter educated at home by his father, "In his first miserable year at home after Louth," wrote Robert Bernard Martin in *Tennyson: The Unquiet Heart,* "Alfred found himself at eleven acting as virtual head of the family. Both elder brothers were away, his mother was loving but ineffectual, and his father was constantly aggravating his epilepsy by drink until his mind seemed to be cracking." When well, Tennyson's father proved to be a demanding tutor, but his frequent illnesses insured that the boy had lots of time to write poetry. He began composing a six-thousand-line poem inspired by Sir Walter Scott, and by 1823 had written a three-act comedy in blank verse, *The Devil and the Lady,* a play "full of a clear kind of fun and an uncomplicated acceptance of sex that were sadly not to be repeated in Tennyson's later works," according to Martin. The play also shows influences from Shakespeare and

An illustration from the 1859 edition of Tennyson's *Idylls of the King,* depicting King Arthur's sister Vivien as she secretly watches the conjurer Merlin perform his magic.

Milton, and as Martin noted, "the confidence of the language, the freedom of versification, and the success of the comic sections are startling in so young a writer."

Increasingly, the health of Tennyson's father declined, "an agonizing series of temporary recoveries and deep relapses," according to Martin, that were made more severe by the addition of laudanum to his drinking affliction. In the midst of these difficulties, Tennyson's first volume of poetry, *Poems by Two Brothers,* was published. Actually the combined work of his brothers Frederick and Charles, as well as his own, the book appeared in 1827, earning the unknown young poets twenty pounds in cash and books. Most of Tennyson's contributions to this volume were inspired by his readings rather than from direct life experiences, for he was only eighteen at the time of publication, even younger when writing the verses. That same year, Tennyson entered Trinity College, Cambridge, along with his brother Charles. He finally had managed to escape from Somersby.

From Student to Poet

Tennyson's years at Trinity were happy ones, as for the first time he was able to be among young men his own age. He was happy to make new friends, and with his intelligence, humor, and good looks he soon was at the center of a group of close friends. He joined the discussion group, the Apostles, in 1829, whose members included Arthur Henry Hallam, James Spedding, Edward Lushington, and Richard Monckton Milnes, all of whom became well known in their time. With Hallam, Tennyson formed a particularly close bond. He was a gifted young man who became close to the entire Tennyson household, engaged to Tennyson's sister Emily. Meanwhile, Tennyson continued to compose poetry, winning the Chancellor's Medal for his blank-verse poem "Timbuctoo" and publishing a further collection of poetry, *Poems, Chiefly Lyrical*, in 1830. Such an accomplishment made him the hero of Cambridge undergraduates, and according to James D. Kissane in his *Alfred Tennyson*, the young poet "looked the part, with his loose, powerful physique; dark, gypsy-like face; and careless attire." Martin commented that the contents of this volume "are uneven in quality," but also noted that there are "a handful of poems that show for the first time that Tennyson was a great poet in the bud." Included in this list are the poems "The Kraken," "Ode to Memory," and "Mariana," the last of which is "one of the staples of English poetry," according to Martin. In this poem Tennyson deals with the theme of melancholy indirectly by a depiction of a landscape reminiscent of his native Lincolnshire. According to the contributor for *Dictionary of Literary Biography*, "Mariana" is the "first of Tennyson's works to demonstrate fully his brilliant use of objects and landscapes to convey a state of strong emotion." The collection earned respectful reviews in major newspapers and magazines of the day.

Later that same year Tennyson and Hallam were involved in a scheme to bring money and secret messages to Spanish revolutionaries in the Pyrenees. These men were plotting to overthrow the Spanish king, a cause sympathetic to the Apostles and Tennyson. However, in the end the meeting was a letdown for Tennyson, for he saw that the revolutionaries were not much better than the Royalists.

Still, this first trip abroad was important for Tennyson, especially his travels in the mountains. It was there he began the long poem "The Lotus-Eaters," and thereafter "the mountains remained as a model for the classical scenery that so often formed the backdrop of his poetry," according to the contributor for *Dictionary of Literary Biography*.

Tennyson's father died in 1831, and as a result, the allowance the family had enjoyed from the grandfather came to an end. There was thus no money to support Tennyson or his two brothers at Cambridge, so Tennyson left the university without a degree. An annual gift from an aunt allowed him to live modestly, but Tennyson steadfastly refused his grandfather's insistence that he become ordained in the church. He was, Tennyson told friends and relatives alike, a poet, not a man of the church.

In 1832 Tennyson published *Poems*, a collection containing the original versions of some of the poets most-loved works, including "The Lady of Shalott," his earliest Arthurian poem and one that expresses both the magic and necessity of art; "The Palace of Art," which is a discussion of an artist's responsibilities in the real world; "A Dream of Fair Women"; "The Hesperides"; and three poems begun on his trips to the Pyrenees: "Oenone," "The Lotus-Eaters," and "Mariana in the South." According to the contributor for *Dictionary of Literary Biography*, the volume "is notable for its consideration of the opposed attractions of isolated poetic creativity and social involvement." The reviews of this collection were, however, largely negative, the worst of the lot appearing in the *Quarterly Review* courtesy of John Wilson Croker, who questioned the masculinity of Tennyson and his work, dubbing him a Cockney poet and an imitator of Keats. Kissane noted that this single review "undoubtedly impeded Tennyson's rise to popularity and damaged his self-confidence." Tennyson did not publish another poem for a decade.

The Middle Period

Southam explained that Tennyson's poetry can be divided into three chronological periods: "the poetry written before the death of Arthur Hallam in September, 1833; the poetry written from the autumn of 1833 to the publication of *Maud* in 1855, including *The Princess* and *In Memoriam*; and the later writing, including his largest and most ambitious work, *Idylls of the King*." Most definitely, Tennyson's middle period was inaugurated by the death of his friend Hallam. Traveling in Vienna with his father, the young man suddenly died of apoplexy and his death shook Tennyson to his core. The previous year his brother Edward had suffered a mental collapse and his brother Charles became addicted to opium. Beset by fears for his own sanity, grieving his dead friend, injured by reviews to his latest publication, and desperate to escape poverty, Tennyson was in a deeply fragile condition. He determined to have no more of his poetry published, though he did continue to write. Hallam's death proved the inspiration for some of his best poetry, including "Ulysses," "Morte d'Arthur," "Tithonus," "Tiresias," "Break, Break, Break," and "Owe! That 'twere Possible," "all of which owe their inception to the passion of grief he felt but carefully hid from his intimates," according to the contributor for *Dictionary of Literary Biography*.

From 1833 to 1837 Tennyson lived at Somersby with his family, making attachments with several women, including Emily Sellwood, whom he would eventually marry over a dozen years later. In 1837 the Tennyson family was forced to move, first to Epping Forest, then to Tunbridge Wells, and finally to Boxley. Meanwhile, Tennyson had become engaged to Sellwood, but worried about his financial position and the possibility of passing on epilepsy to future generations, he broke off the relationship in 1840. Tennyson also managed to lose the small allowance he had with a bad investment in a woodworking scheme.

Finally, in 1842, he lifted his self-imposed ban on publishing, releasing a long-awaited two volumes of poetry, *Poems*, the "best-loved books Tennyson ever wrote," according to the critic for *Dictionary of Literary Biography*. Part of the offering was vastly revised and rewritten versions of some poems from his earlier volume of the same name. There were additionally poems inspired by Hallam's death, and also new and innovative verses in a variety of styles, such as the dramatic monologue "St. Simeon Stylites," a grouping of Arthurian poems, an autobiographical narrative and one of Tennyson's most famous, "Locksley Hall," and even an early attempt at dealing with sexuality in "The Vision of Sin." "The year 1842, marks . . . the beginning of Tennyson's success," wrote Kissane. Reviewers on both sides of the Atlantic praised this work. Suddenly, from complete neglect, Tennyson had been elevated to one of the most important poets of his day.

Ironically, in the midst of success Tennyson suffered deep depression, brought on in part because of the money he had lost in the woodworking scheme. In 1843 he went into a rest home for seven months in hopes of withdrawing from a deep melancholia. Such depression was alleviated by the reception of a government pension—awarded him at the instiga-

tion of Arthur Hallam's father—of 200 pounds a year for his poetic achievement. This pension was enough for him to live on, but for the rest of his life he would continue to complain of financial difficulties, even when he became a rich man and the toast of England.

The Princess, published in 1847, was Tennyson's first attempt at a long poem. Ostensibly about the establishment of female colleges, the poem veers sharply off course before its conclusion, making it, as Kissane remarked, a "poetic freak, unlikely in subject as in narrative conception." The following year, Tennyson made his final visit to the "hydropathic" hospital he had been entering on and off for several years, the doctor pronouncing him cured and convincing him that he had not been experiencing epileptic events, but rather the effects of gout. Relieved, Tennyson began reconsidering his decision not to marry.

THE

DEATH OF ŒNONE,

AKBAR'S DREAM,

AND OTHER POEMS

BY

ALFRED
LORD TENNYSON
POET LAUREATE

WITH FIVE STEEL PORTRAITS OF THE AUTHOR

London
MACMILLAN AND CO.
AND NEW YORK
1892

All rights reserved

Tennyson's 1892 collection was published in the year of the poet's death.

In Memoriam

In June of 1850 Tennyson anonymously published the elegies he had been writing about his friend Hallam for the past seventeen years. One of the major long works of his career, *In Memoriam* is a series of over 130 lyrics—plus prologue and epilogue—of different length, all of which have the same stanzaic form. Southam described the work as "Tennyson's most ambitious structure and most embracing countervision." He wrote the first of the elegies in 1833 and at that time had no thought of publishing them in some larger design. But over time he continued to write elegies in stanzas of four tetrameter lines with a rhyme scheme of "a b b a." In the 1840s he began arranging the poems sequentially and also introduced interposing narrative-chronological sections. Taken individually, the verses read like a journal, but overall the full poem begins with the death of Hallam, who was engaged to one of Tennyson's sisters, and ends with the marriage of another sister. Tennyson himself described the sequence as a sort of *Divine Comedy* "ending with happiness." The time period covered in the poem is about three years, announced by three Christmas celebrations, and the forward emotional movement goes from utter grief through resignation and acceptance, and ends with joy. In all, the poem has over seven hundred stanzas, all with the same rhythm and rhyme scheme. As Kissane noted, "The resulting monotony . . . is less damaging than it might be; for stanzaic regularity gives an element of cohesion to what is otherwise an extremely diffuse work." Kissane also praised the shifting emotions of the poem, "contained within the unvaried frame by Tennyson's fine ear and by his ability to modulate rhythms to catch the mood of the occasion." An example of such modulation can be seen in the following stanza: "Calm on the seas, and silver sleep, / And waves that sway themselves in rest, / And dead calm in that noble breast / Which heaves but with the heaving deep."

One of the major themes of the poem is the need not only to honor one's grief, but also to go beyond it. The contributor for *Dictionary of Literary Biography* felt that this three-thousand-line poem has a size "appropriate to what it undertakes," which is, "coming to terms with loss." In dealing with this theme, Tennyson also "touches on most of the intellectual issues at the center of the Victorian consciousness: religion, immortality, geology, evolution, the relation of the intellect to the unconscious, the place of art in a workaday world, the individual versus society, the relation of man to nature, and as many others." To readers of its day, *In Memoriam* was not only a work of beauty, but a work of reference, to be consulted for a myriad of topics and as a source of inspiration. It was an instant success, with edition following edition. The poem became "the most widely read and most profoundly admired . . . of its time in the English language," according to Charles W. French, writing in the introduction to a 1917 edition of *Idylls of the King.*

Tennyson was at the peak of his powers as a poet, and now felt that he could marry. Only weeks after the publication of *In Memoriam,* he and Sellwood were wed. When the couple returned from their honeymoon, Tennyson found that he had become famous overnight with his long poem, and with the death of Poet Laureate William Wordsworth he became his successor to that position.

Two years later, Emily Tennyson gave birth to a baby boy who was named Hallam in honor of Tennyson's valued friend. In 1853 the family moved into Farringford, a large house on the secluded Isle of Wight suitable to a man of Tennyson's position. In 1854, interested in the events of the Crimean War, Tennyson wrote his famous poem, "The Charge of the Light Brigade," which became inspirational to the British troops fighting in Sebastopol. With his 1855 poem, *Maud,* Tennyson completed the work of his middle period with a narrative verse piece about a hero who makes up for a life badly lived by volunteering to serve in the Crimea. Such a decision is in part influenced by the return of Maud, the proud daughter of a neighboring family who breaks through the self-absorbed facade of the hero. When the hero is forced to kill Maud's brother in a duel, the young woman dies of grief, and the hero decides to sacrifice himself in war as a form of noble self-redemption. Tennyson thought of his creation as a "monodrama," something between a monologue and a verse play. It is also remarkable for its dramatization of a neurotic state of mind. "*Maud* was an act of catharsis," noted Southam, and for the public is was something of an "aberration." The very experimental qualities which made it problematic to critics of Tennyson's day, however, have endeared the poem to modern critics, who generally hold it in high regard.

The Later Period

Tennyson's later work comprises chiefly the cycle of poems he wrote about King Arthur and the Round Table, most of them composed between 1856 and 1876. Tennyson considered the Arthurian tales the pinnacle of subjects for a poet and had long been a fan of Thomas Malory's *Morte d'Arthur.* For decades he planned such a huge undertaking, his own "Morte d'Arthur" appearing as early as 1842. Starting in 1859, he published four separate volumes which were finally collected and placed in their proper order in the definitive collection of twelve idylls, *Idylls of the King,* in 1885. These blank verse narratives deal with Arthur, Merlin, Lancelot, Guinevere, and other characters from the court of King Arthur. These narratives are in turn framed by a dedication to the Prince consort and an epilogue addressed to Queen Victoria, and are linked by the primary theme of the negative effects of lust and sexual passion on society. As Tennyson shows, the Round Table was destroyed by the affair between Lancelot and Guinevere. In its twelve episodes, the long poem follows the seasons of the year. In the "Coming of Arthur," it is early springtime, and the young king takes his queen in marriage. In "Gareth and Lynette," we move to June, with the busy energies of early summer and Arthur is establishing the order of law. With "Geraint Idylls" summer has advanced to early harvest time, and in "Merlin and Vivian" and "Balin and Balan" it is high, hot summer, time of destructive thunder storms. "Lancelot and Elaine" takes place in late summer with the feel of fall and winter in the offing, while the "Holy Grail" happens in a fall that is not heavy with the bounty of harvest, but desolate because of a fruitless year. "Pelleas and Etarre" and the "Last Tournament" take us deeper into dark autumn, while "Guinevere" introduces bleak winter, "disappointment and death," as French noted. And with the "Passing of Arthur," "doom has fallen," French commented. "Thus the story of human life is told from the springtime of youth to the snows of age."

While the long cycle of poems in *Idylls of the King* appealed to the general public, critical assessment was mixed. Most critics have agreed that it is Tennyson's most ambitious work, though not all agree that the poem succeeds. The visual imagery of the poem has long been praised, though critics fault the characterization as well as stilted dialogue. However, others have praised Tennyson's use of the Arthurian myth to express his own fears for an industrialized, nineteenth-century England seduced by materialism. The consensus of opinion is, however, that Tennyson did not quite bring off the epic poem he had envisioned. French, among others, commented on this: "The *Idylls* contain many of the elements of a great epic poem, but are lacking in that essential unity which, with the final triumph of the hero and the principles for which he contends, are the necessary elements of all great epic poems."

Throughout the decades of the 1850s through the 1880s, Tennyson's fame grew. He became a familiar of Queen Victoria, invited for informal visits to her own Isle of Wight estate, Osborne. He numbered other great Victorians among his friends, including Thomas Carlyle, Robert Browning, and Charles Dickens, for whose son he stood as a godfather. Politicians such as William Gladstone were also in his circle. In the midst of his social rounds and in the composition of his *Idylls,* he also found time to pen the 1864 volume *Enoch Arden,* which contains the long narrative poem "Aylmer's Field." The poems in this collection are "full of the kinds of magnificent language and imagery that no other Victorian poet could have hoped to produce," according to the critic for *Dictionary of Literary Biography.* From this volume alone, Tennyson earned over 8,000 pounds in 1864, more than many wealthy industrialists. Following this success he built his own house, Aldworth, in Sussex, in a place remote enough to keep curious visitors and tourists from his gate. For the rest of his life he divided his time between his house at Farringford and at Aldworth.

During the 1870s and early 1880s Tennyson experimented—not very successfully—with verse plays. Works such as *Queen Mary, Harold, Becket, The Falcon, The Cup, The Foresters,* and *The Promise of May* are the results of this effort. Few of them were produced during Tennyson's lifetime, none successfully. In 1883, however, the crowning achievement in Tennyson's rise to fame came: he was offered a peerage by William Gladstone, becoming Baron Tennyson of Aldworth and Freshwater, also known as Alfred, Lord Tennyson. Even in the afterglow of such public renown, Tennyson continued his literary output as if he were a young man.

One of the tragedies of Tennyson's later life was the death of his second son, Lionel, in Africa of jungle fever, in 1886. That same year, the poet published "Locksley Hall Sixty Years After, etc.," and in 1889 came his last collection, *Demeter and Other Poems.* Another product of his final years was the justly famous "Crossing the Bar," written in the matter of a few minutes as he crossed from the Isle of Wight to the mainland of England. The poem became the closing piece of all Tennyson's editions thereafter, its opening stanza recited by school children around the world: "Sunset and evening star, / And one clear call for me! / And may there be no moaning of the bar, / When I put out to sea."

Tennyson died on October 6, 1892, at Aldworth, with a copy of his beloved Shakespeare lying on his chest and his family in attendance. He was buried a week later at the Poet's Corner of Westminster Abbey. With him, as with the death of Queen Victoria not many years later, an age died. Reassessments of his work began not long after his death, and have continued to this day. Yet in the final analysis, and when looking at the best of his work, such as *In*

If you enjoy the works of Alfred Tennyson, you might want to check out the following:

Sir Thomas Malory's *Le Morte D'Arthur*, 1485.
The poetry of Lord Byron and Percy Bysshe Shelley, who were early influences on Tennyson.
The works of other Victorian poets, including Elizabeth Barrett Browning and Dante Gabriel Rossetti.

Memoriam, "Tennyson can be seen plainly as one of the half-dozen great poets in the English language," as the contributor for *Dictionary of Literary Biography* noted, "at least the equal of Wordsworth or Keats and probably far above any other Victorian." For French, the real Tennyson is "the pure sweet spirit who comes to us in the mystic beauty of 'The Lady of Shalott' and 'Sir Galahad,' the calm faith and high philosophy of *In Memoriam*, the musical harmony of many a perfect lyric, the romantic tales of the *Idylls*, or the tranquil trust of the 'Crossing the Bar.'" French further commented, "His life had little of incident, yet in his great utterances he lived more truly and exerted more potent and lasting influences than many a hero whose life has filled chapters of the world's history."

■ **Biographical and Critical Sources**

BOOKS

British Writers, Volume 4, Scribner's (New York, NY), 1981, pp. 323-339.
Buckley, Jerome H., *Tennyson: The Growth of a Poet*, Harvard University Press (Cambridge, MA), 1960.
Campbell, Nancie, *Tennyson in Lincoln: A Catalogue of the Collections in the Research Centre*, two volumes, Tennyson Research Centre (Lincoln, England) 1971-1973.
Concise Dictionary of British Literary Biography, Volume 4: *Victorian Writers, 1832-1890*, Gale (Detroit, MI), 1991.
Culler, A. Dwight, *The Poetry of Tennyson*, Yale University Press (New Haven, CT), 1977.
Dictionary of Literary Biography, Volume 32: *Victorian Poets before 1850*, Gale (Detroit, MI), 1984, pp. 262-282.

Eidson, John Oldin, *Tennyson in America: His Reputation and Influence from 1827-1858*, University of Georgia Press (Athens, GA), 1943.
Kincaid, James R., *Tennyson's Major Poems: The Comic and Ironic Patterns*, Yale University Press (New Haven, CT), 1975.
Kissane, James D., *Alfred Tennyson*, Twayne (New York, NY), 1970.
Levi, Peter, *Tennyson*, Scribner's (New York, NY), 1993.
Martin, Robert Martin, *Tennyson: The Unquiet Heart*, Oxford University Press (New York, NY), 1980, pp. 35, 37, 41.
Paden, W. D., *Tennyson in Egypt: A Study of the Imagery in His Earlier Work*, University of Kansas Press (Lawrence, KS) 1942.
Pitt, Valerie, *Tennyson Laureate*, Barrie & Rockliff (London, England), 1962.
Poetry Criticism, Volume 6, Gale (Detroit, MI), 1993.
Rader, Ralph Wilson, *Tennyson's "Maud": The Biographical Genesis*, University of California Press (Berkeley, CA), 1963.
Ricks, Christopher, *Tennyson*, Macmillan (New York, NY), 1972.
Shannon, Jr., Edgar F., *Tennyson and the Reviewers: A Study of His Literary Reputation and the Influence of the Critics upon His Poetry, 1827-1851*, Harvard University Press (Cambridge, MA), 1952.
Tennyson, Alfred, *Idylls of the King*, edited with an introduction by Charles W. French, Macmillan (New York, NY), 1917, pp. ix, xiii, xxiii.
Tennyson, Alfred, *The Poems of Tennyson*, edited by Christopher Ricks, Longmans, Green (London, England), 1969.
Tennyson, Charles, *Alfred Tennyson*, Macmillan (New York, NY), 1949.
Tennyson, Charles, and Christine Fall, *Alfred Tennyson: An Annotated Bibliography*, University of Georgia Press (Athens, GA), 1967.
Tennyson, Hallam, *Alfred Lord Tennyson: A Memoir*, two volumes, Macmillan (New York, NY), 1897.
Tennyson, Hallam, editor, *Tennyson and His Friends*, Macmillan (London, England), 1911.
Thorn, Michael, *Tennyson*, St. Martin's Press (New York, NY), 1992.
Turner, Paul, *Tennyson*, Routledge & Kegan Paul (Boston, MA), 1976.
Wheatcroft, Andrew, *The Tennyson Album: A Biography in Original Photographs*, Routledge & Kegan Paul (Boston, MA), 1980.
Wise, T. J., *A Bibliography of the Writings of Alfred, Lord Tennyson*, two volumes, privately printed (London, England), 1908.

OTHER

Alfred Lord Tennyson: An Overview, http://www. victorianweb.org/ (October 20, 2002).

Alfred Lord Tennyson Page, http://www.accd.edu/ sac/english/ (October 20, 2002).

IPL Online Literary Criticism, http://www.ipl.org/ (October 20, 2002), "Lord Alfred Tennyson (1809-1892)."

Tennyson Page, http://charon.sfsu.edu/tennyson/ (October 20, 2002).

—*Sketch by J. Sydney Jones*

David Foster Wallace

■ Personal

Born February 21, 1962, in Ithaca, NY; son of James Donald (a teacher) and Sally (a teacher; maiden name, Foster) Wallace. *Education:* Amherst College, A.B. (summa cum laude), 1985; University of Arizona, M.F.A., 1987. *Politics:* "Independent."

■ Addresses

Agent—Frederick Hill Associates, 1842 Union St., San Francisco, CA 94123.

■ Career

Writer. University of Illinois, associate professor of English, 1993—. Judge of O. Henry Awards, 1997.

■ Awards, Honors

Whiting Writers' Award, 1987; Yaddo residency, 1987, 1989; John Traine Humor Prize, *Paris Review,* 1988, for "Little Expressionless Animals"; National Endowment for the Arts fellowship, 1989; Illinois Arts Council Award for Nonfiction, 1989, for "Fictional Futures and the Conspicuously Young"; Quality Paperback Book Club's New Voices Award in Fiction, 1991, for *Girl with Curious Hair;* Pulitzer Prize nomination in nonfiction, 1991, for *Signifying Rappers;* Lannan Foundation Award for Literature, 1996; "David Lynch Keeps His Head" named National Magazine Award finalist, 1997; MacArthur Foundation fellowship, 1997.

■ Writings

The Broom of the System, Viking (New York, NY), 1987.

Girl with Curious Hair (short stories and novellas; includes "Little Expressionless Animals," "My Appearance," "Westward the Course of Empire Takes Its Way," "Lyndon," "John Billy," and "Everything Is Green"), Penguin (New York, NY), 1988.

(With Mark Costello) *Signifying Rappers: Rap and Race in the Urban Present* (nonfiction), Ecco Press (New York, NY), 1990.

Infinite Jest, Little, Brown (Boston, MA), 1996.

A Supposedly Fun Thing I'll Never Do Again: Essays and Arguments, Little, Brown (Boston, MA), 1997.

Brief Interviews with Hideous Men, Little, Brown (Boston, MA), 1999.

Up, Simba!: Seven Days on the Trail of an Anticandidate, Warner/iPublish (New York, NY), 2000.

Contributor of short fiction and nonfiction to numerous periodicals, including *Contemporary Fiction, Esquire, Rolling Stone, Paris Review, Harper's,* and *New Yorker.*

■ Sidelights

David Foster Wallace has been dubbed everything from a "hideously talented writer," according to Jonathan Levi in the *Los Angeles Times,* to the "master of voices, a writer whose sense of history and politics and morality makes itself felt in repeated, almost compulsive acts of mimicry and impersonation," as Vince Passaro noted in *Harper's.* Wallace

A classic dysfunctional family of the 1990s is the focus of Wallace's second novel, his sharp, intelligent prose capturing the trend away from human interaction into a reality formed of manufactured entertainment.

is the kind of writer whose talent leaves critics groping for the proper artistic comparison. Writers Thomas Pynchon, William Gaddis, and John Irving, filmmaker David Lynch, and even comic David Letterman have all been invoked as readers tackle the sardonic humor and complicated style that have led Wallace to be cited as Generation X's first literary hero. Wallace, according to Frank Bruni in his *New York Times Magazine* profile, "is to literature what Robin Williams or perhaps Jim Carrey is to live comedy: a creator so maniacally energetic and amused with himself that he often follows his riffs out into the stratosphere, where he orbits all alone." In two novels, *The Broom of the System* and *Infinite Jest,* and two story collections, *Girl with Curious Hair* and *Brief Interviews with Hideous Men,* as well as in his nonfiction, Wallace has charted a new, post-postmodernist course for serious American letters, beyond metafiction or minimalism: highly intelligent, endlessly self-referential, full of pithy and witty asides, unafraid to take risks—including boring and/or angering the reader—an eagerness to shotgun a plethora of facts, facts, and more facts, a playfulness and irony that edges the reader out of easy assumptions, and a distinct refusal to deal with the standard tropes of literature such as plot development and story line. "Wallace's work is ambitious and sprawling," noted a contributor for *Contemporary Novelists,* "by turns epicomical and philosophical."

Born in Ithaca, New York, Wallace is the son "of a grammarian mother and a father who studied with [Ludwig] Wittgenstein's student and biographer Irving Malcolm," as Lorin Stein reported in *Publishers Weekly.* Growing up, Wallace intended to become a philosopher like his father before him. However, reaching his junior year at Amherst College, he also reached a turning point in his life and decided to take a year off. When he went back to Amherst the following year, he followed the inspiration of a friend who had managed to be allowed to write fiction as part of his senior thesis. Thus, with most of his friends gone in his own senior year, Wallace sat down to do his own fiction-writing; what resulted was the first draft of his debut novel, *The Broom of the System.*

Graduating from Amherst in 1985, Wallace won a fellowship to the University of Arizona's writing program. Although his off-the-wall literary style and aggressive classroom behavior were not appreciated by professors, he did earn an M.F.A. in creative writing. More importantly, while still in college, he got an agent on his side, Bonnie Nadell, who sold the manuscript of *Broom* to Viking in 1986. His subsequent editor, Gerry Wallace, helped the young writer get his manuscript in shape for publication.

Literary Debut

The Broom of the System is, according to Stein, "a ribald, sophisticated novel" that deals in turns with unrequited love, a rather corrupt psychiatrist and senior citizens who have the nasty habit of disappearing. In it, Wallace blends not only Thomas Pynchon's "sense of slapstick," as Stein noted, but also "big chunks" of the language philosophy of Wittgenstein. Additionally, Wallace uses a variety of writing techniques and points of view to create a bizarre, stylized world which, despite its strangeness, resonates with contemporary American images. Set in Cleveland on the edge of the state-constructed Great Ohio Desert (also known as G.O.D.), the story follows Lenore Beadsman's search for her ninety-two-year-old great-grandmother, also named Lenore Beadsman, who has disappeared from her nursing home. In attempting to find her childhood mentor, the younger Lenore encounters a bewildering assemblage of characters with names such as Rick Vigorous, Biff Diggerence, Candy Mandible, and Sigurd Foamwhistle. It is significant that the elder Lenore was a student of language philosopher Wittgenstein, since *The Broom of the System* has been viewed as an elaborate exploration of the relationship between language and reality. Wallace orchestrates Lenore's coming of age through the use of innovative plotting and language. The character's search for her great-grandmother becomes the search for her own identity.

Critics praised the skill and creativity evident in Wallace's experimental bildungsroman. Rudy Rucker, writing in the *Washington Post Book World*, judged *The Broom of the System* to be a "wonderful book" and compared Wallace to novelist Thomas Pynchon. Despite finding the novel to be "unwieldy" and "uneven" in parts, *New York Times* reviewer Michiko Kakutani commended Wallace's "rich reserves of ambition and imagination" and was impressed by his "wealth of talents." *New York Times Book Review* critic Caryn James liked the novel's "exuberance" and maintained that it "succeeds as a manic, human, flawed extravaganza."

In an interview with Larry McCaffery for the *Review of Contemporary Fiction*, Wallace expounded on his first novel, tongue only slightly in cheek, admitting that beneath much of the intellectual and verbal pyrotechnics was most definitely a first novel. "Think of 'The Broom of the System' as the sensitive tale of a sensitive young WASP who's just had this midlife crisis that's moved him from coldly cerebral analytic math to a coldly cerebral take on fiction and Austin-Wittgenstein-Derridean literary theory. . . . This WASP's written a lot of straight humor, and loves gags, so he decides to write a coded autobio that's also a funny little post-structural gag: so you get Lenore, a character in a story who's terribly afraid that she's really nothing more than a character in a story. And, sufficiently hidden under the sex-change and the gags and theoretical allusions, I got to write my sensitive little self-obsessed bildungsroman." Wallace further noted that the "biggest cackle" he got when the book was published was when all the reviewers "praised the fact that at least here was a fist novel that wasn't yet another sensitive little bildungsroman."

In Wallace's second work, a collection of short stories titled *Girl with Curious Hair*, the author employs a mix of facts, fiction, and his own distinctive use of language to make observations about American culture. However, Wallace also told Stein that he viewed his experience with this book as his "comeuppance." Famously hard to edit, Wallace thumbs his nose not only at literary conventions, but at legal ones as well. One of the short stories in the collection is based on an actual installment of the *Letterman Show,* and Wallace neglected to tell his publisher, Viking, about this possible difficulty. *Playboy* magazine had to cancel its serial rights when the very show was re-run shortly before publication. And when the Viking legal department began looking at the manuscript, they found a veritable minefield of other difficulties involving other actual television game show hosts. As a result, Viking dropped the title from its lists, but the book was saved when Wallace's editor moved from Viking to Norton and the manuscript was subsequently cleaned up.

Published in 1989, *Girl with Curious Hair* offers readers "a whole new approach to American short fiction," according to Passaro. "Little Expressionless Animals," one of several stories that deals with American television, reveals a plan by the producers of the game show *Jeopardy!* to oust a long-time champion because of their sensitivity to her continuing lesbian love affair. The difference between appearance and reality is the subject of "My Appearance," the story of an actress's tranquilizer-induced, nervous ramblings while she is waiting to do a guest appearance on the *David Letterman Show.* In the title story, a young, Ivy League-trained corporate lawyer reveals the roots of his sadistic sexual impulses when he reflects on a Keith Jarrett concert he once attended with a group of violent punk rockers.

To reviewers, Wallace's imagination and energy have been enticing. Wallace "proves himself a dynamic writer of extraordinary talent," asserted Jennifer Levin in the *New York Times Book Review,* commenting that "he succeeds in restoring grandeur to modern fiction." Writing in Chicago's *Tribune Books,*

"ONE OF HIS GENERATION'S PRE-EMINENT TALENTS." — *NEW YORK TIMES*

"ANIMATED BY WONDERFULLY EXUBERANT PROSE...THIS VOLUME RECONFIRMS MR. WALLACE'S STATURE AS

A SUPPOSEDLY FUN THING
I'LL NEVER DO AGAIN

ESSAYS AND
ARGUMENTS

DAVID FOSTER WALLACE

AUTHOR OF *INFINITE JEST*

Wallace treats readers to seven essays that examine such cultural highlights as television, the quirky films of director David Lynch, and Midwestern country fairs through his irreverent viewpoint.

Douglas Seibold commended Wallace's "irrepressible narrative energy and invention" claiming that, "as good a writer as he is now, he is getting better." For Passaro, *Girl with Curious Hair* is a "brilliant" collection, "wildly imaginative," and one "with a strong impact on many younger writers."

Infinite Jest

Despite these early successes, Wallace had not given up on his dreams of a career in philosophy. In 1989 he enrolled in Harvard's doctoral program in that discipline, but after one semester decided to drop out. The following year he collaborated with Mark Costello on the nonfiction book *Signifying Rappers:*

Rap and Race in the Urban Present, which was nominated for a Pulitzer Prize. Little else was heard from him for six more years, though there were reports he was working on a really big book. Reports as to size, it turned out, were greatly underrated.

The buildup given to Wallace through his first books served as an appetizer to the hype surrounding his 1996 novel, *Infinite Jest*—a work that, in the words of *Chicago Tribune* writer Bruce Allen, could "confirm the hopes of those who called Wallace a genius and, to a lesser extent, the fears of those who think he's just an overeducated wiseacre with a lively prose style." The book released was massive—over 1,000 pages—and the publicity was no less so. The marketing unit of publishers Little, Brown piqued prepublication interest by sending 4,000 influential booksellers and media outlets a series of six postcards. Each card "cryptically heralded the release of an at-first-unspecified book that gives 'infinite pleasure' with 'infinite style,'" wrote Bruni. "And when blurbs to that effect became available from other authors and critics, Little, Brown put them on postcards and dispatched another series of three."

On the heels of such publicity, *Infinite Jest* became *de rigueur* as a book that literary fans bought and displayed, but would not—or could not—spend much time reading. Some of the reason lies in the volume's heft and some in Wallace's dense prose style, peppered for the occasion with numerous pharmacological references that are partly responsible for the novel's 900 footnotes.

Infinite Jest is set in the not-too-distant future, in a date unspecified except as "the Year of the Depend Adult Undergarment," corporate sponsors having taken over the calendar. The United States is now part of the Organization of North American Nations (read ONAN) and has sold off New England to Canada to be used as a toxic waste dump. Legless Quebecoise separatists have taken to terrorism in protest; what's more, President Limbaugh has just been assassinated. The book's title refers to a lethal movie—a film so entertaining that those who see it may be doomed to die of pleasure.

Into this fray steps the Incandenza brothers: tennis ace Hal, football punter Orin, and the less-gifted Mario. The boys have endured a tough childhood—their father "having committed suicide by hacking open a hole in a microwave door, sealing it around his head with duct tape and making like a bag of Orville Redenbacher," as *Nation* reviewer Rick Perlstein noted. The brothers' adventures in this bizarre society fuel the novel's thick and overlapping storylines. Readers looking for a traditional linear ending, however, are in for a surprise: Those who manage to "stay with the novel until the pages thin will come to realize that Wallace has no intention of revealing whether *les Assassins des Fauteuils Rollents* succeed or fail in their quest," Perlstein continued. "Nor whether . . . Orin will master his awful desires . . . or whether Hal Incandenza will sacrifice himself to the Oedipal grail. Readers will turn the last page, in other words, without learning anything they need to know to secure narrative succor."

For the most part, critical reaction to *Infinite Jest* mixed admiration with consternation. "There is generous intelligence and authentic passion on every page, even the overwritten ones in which the author seems to have had a fit of graphomania," commented *Time* contributor R. Z. Sheppard. Paul West, writing in the *Washington Post Book World,* was prepared for Pynchon but came away with the opinion that "there is nothing epic or infinite about [the novel], although much that's repetitious or long." As West saw it, "the slow incessant advance of Wallace's prose is winningly physical, solid and even, more personable actually than the crowd of goons, ditzes, inverts, junkies, fatheads and doodlers he populates his novel with."

Indeed, said Michiko Kakutani, "the whole novel often seems like an excuse for [the author] to simply show off his remarkable skills as a writer and empty the contents of his restless mind." Kakutani's *New York Times* review went on to laud "some frighteningly vivid accounts of what it feels like to be a drug addict, what it feels like to detox and what it feels like to suffer a panic attack." In the crowd of ideas and characters, the critic concluded, "somewhere in the mess, . . . are the outlines of a splendid novel, but as it stands the book feels like one of those unfinished Michelangelo sculptures: you can see a godly creature trying to fight its way out, but it's stuck there, half excavated, unable to break completely free."

After the Jest

Kakutani, writing in the *New York Times,* had more encouraging words for Wallace's 1997 release, *A Supposedly Fun Thing I'll Never Do Again: Essays and Arguments.* This nonfiction collection "is animated by [the author's] wonderfully exuberant prose, a zingy, elastic gift for metaphor and imaginative sleight of hand, combined with a taste for amphetaminelike stream-of-consciousness riffs." *A Supposedly Fun Thing I'll Never Do Again* covers Wallace's observations on cultural themes, such as the influ-

Wallace's 1999 short story collection includes entertaining works that first made their appearance in the pages of *Ploughshares, Esquire,* and the *New York Times Magazine,* among others.

ence television has on new fiction. It also contains recollections of the author's childhood in the Midwest, thoughts on tennis (Wallace was a highly ranked player in his youth) and even a tour of the Illinois State Fair. While finding some aspects of the collection flawed, Kakutani ultimately praised the book: it "not only reconfirms Mr. Wallace's stature as one of his generation's pre-eminent talents, but it also attests to his virtuosity, an aptitude for the essay, profile and travelogue, equal to the gifts he has already begun to demonstrate in the realm of fiction." *Esquire's* Greil Marcus, however, felt the book "wasn't as much fun as it was supposed to be."

Wallace returns to the short fiction—as opposed to short story—format with the 1999 collection *Brief*

Interviews with Hideous Men, an anthology of twenty-three question-and-answer tales stretching in length from several lines to nearly thirty pages. A *Publishers Weekly* critic called this a "bold, uneven, bitterly satirical" collection destined to garner both praise and befuddlement. In most of the interviews a man speaking to a nameless female interviewer—who most often does not bother to ask a question—reveals some aspect of his romantic life and fantasies. The reviewer for *Publishers Weekly* referred to the "pathetic creepiness" of such responses. "Sex in its more disturbing modes is the collection's underlying theme," according to *Booklist* reviewer Donna Seaman. One woman describes her rape, while another worries that her husband secretly does not enjoy their sex life together. Lawrence Rungren, writing in *Library Journal,* called this collection "dense, cerebral, and self-reflexive," and described Wallace's characters as "psychological grotesques." One story in the collection, "Think," "twists a brief adulterous tussle between a man and his sister-in-law into a moment of impotent prayer and spiritual emptiness in under two pages," noted Levi in the *Los Angeles Times,* praising the author's arts of description when staying brief. However Levi had little praise for Wallace's "obsession with information." Other tales in the collection talk about men's strategies for picking up women or making poor excuses to their girlfriends, describe family attachments by the damage they do, and generally make a "mockery of romantic love," according to Stein. For Levi, this collection "is a nasty book, a book that grinds and grinds again the thesis that men are hideous." Marcus found the book to be "made out of sex, rage, cleverness, and grammar." *Nation* reviewer Tom LeClair likened Wallace's experimentation in this collection to the work of writers such as "Borges and Beckett, Barth and Barthelme. As an undergraduate, Wallace studied philosophy and mathematics, and he seems attracted to the 'thought experiment' of fiction of [these] B-writers, the way a premise can generate its logical contradiction or create an exhausting regress." LeClair further commented, "I almost liked this book," concluding that "now that Gaddis is gone, we probably need Wallace's unlovely, unlikable hideousness."

Other critics had a more laudatory interpretation of the book. Robert Potts, reviewing *Brief Interviews with Hideous Men* in the London *Observer,* found it to be a "book of formidable creative intelligence, and real moral purpose." The reviewer for *Publishers Weekly* went on to remark that the best of the stories "show an erotic savagery and intellectual depth that will confound, fascinate and disturb," while *Time*'s Sheppard noted that *Brief Interviews with Hideous Men* is a "strikingly original collection," and one "designed to keep readers from getting too comfortable." Robert McLaughlin, writing in the *Review of Contemporary Fiction,* also found the collection praiseworthy. Noting that few of the interviews that make up the book are "stories in the conventional sense," McLaughlin concluded that "in its form, narration, language, and ideas, *Brief Interviews with Hideous Men* is a virtuoso display that builds on the achievement of *Infinite Jest* and points the way to the future of fiction."

Somewhat less successful was Wallace's 2000 experiment with electronic publishing, titled *Up, Simba!: Seven Days on the Trail of an Anticandidate.* Following the unsuccessful presidential campaign of Arizona Senator John McCain during the primaries, Wallace wrote about the event for *Rolling Stone.* In *Up, Simba!* he presents the uncut version of that article, along with his usual plethora of footnotes, this time hyperlinked for the curious lateral thinkers. More on-the-bus confessional than actual political reporting, the book was criticized by *Time* reviewer John Dickerson for "tainting" some of the "sharp insights" it offers by Wallace making up details. A contributor for *Publishers Weekly* felt that "only Wallace's most devoted fans" would agree that this longer version was superior to the magazine piece.

If you enjoy the works of David Foster Wallace, you might want to check out the following:

Don DeLillo, *White Noise,* 1985.
William Gaddis, *A Frolic of His Own,* 1994.
David Eggers, *A Heartbreaking Work of Staggering Genius,* 2000.

If Wallace sometimes fails in his work, it is because he takes risks other writers avoid. His iconoclastic prose style, full of the sort of self-consciousness most writers jettison before their first publication, is actually informed by such injection of the self into the story. For Wallace, a novel is all about involvement. "Novels are like marriages," he told Stein. "You have to get into the mood to write them—not because of what writing them is going to be like, but because it's so sad to end them. . . . Writing a novel gets very weird and invisible-friend-from-childhood-ish, then you kill that thing, which was never really alive except in your imagination, and you're supposed to go buy groceries and talk to people at parties and stuff."

■ Biographical and Critical Sources

BOOKS

Birkerts, Sven, *American Energies: Essays on Fiction,* William Morrow (New York, NY), 1992, pp. 386-392.

Contemporary Literary Criticism, Volume 50, Gale (Detroit, MI), 1988.

Contemporary Novelists, 7th edition, St. James Press (Detroit, MI), 2001.

PERIODICALS

Antioch Review, fall, 1996, p. 491.

Atlantic, February, 1996, Sven Birkerts, review of *Infinite Jest,* pp. 106-108.

Booklist, February 15, 1997, p. 996; May 1, 1999, Donna Seaman, review of *Brief Interviews with Hideous Men,* p. 1580.

Chicago Tribune, March 24, 1996, Bruce Allen, review of *Infinite Jest.*

Critique, fall, 1996, pp. 12-37.

Entertainment Weekly, March 7, 1997, p. 60; June 25, 1999, Troy Patterson, "A Brief Interview with Brainy David Foster Wallace," p. 126.

Esquire, June, 1999, Greil Marcus, "Neurotics A-Go-Go," p. 30.

Explicator, spring, 2000, Timothy Jacobs, "Wallace's *Infinite Jest,*" p. 172.

Guardian (London, England), February 19, 2000, Nicholas Lezard, review of *Brief Interviews with Hideous Men,* p. 10.

Harper's, August, 1999, Vince Passaro, review of *Brief Interviews with Hideous Men,* p. 80.

Harper's Bazaar, February, 1996, Vince Passaro, "The Last Laugh," p. 104.

Kirkus Reviews, November 15, 1986, p. 1686.

Library Journal, February 15, 1987, p. 164; August, 1989, p. 166; January, 1996, p. 146; January, 1997, p. 100; May 1, 1999, Lawrence Rungren, review of *Brief Interviews with Hideous Men,* p. 116.

Los Angeles Times, February 11, 1996; March 18, 1996, Elizabeth Weil, "A Cult of Cool," p. E1; July 18, 1999, Jonathan Levi, review of *Brief Interviews with Hideous Men,* p. 1.

Los Angeles Times Book Review, February 1, 1987; February 11, 1996, pp. 1, 9.

Nation, March 4, 1996, Rick A. Perlstein, review of *Infinite Jest,* pp. 27-29; July 27, 1999, Tom LeClair, "The Non-Silence of the Un-Lamblike," p. 31.

New Republic, June 30, 1997, Alexander Star, review of *A Supposedly Funny Thing I'll Never Do Again,* pp. 27-34.

Newsweek, February 12, 1996, pp. 80-81; February 17, 1997, p. 63.

New York, February 12, 1996, p. 54.

New York Review of Books, February 10, 2000, A. O. Scott, "The Panic of Influence," pp. 39-42.

New York Times, December 27, 1986, Michiko Kakutani, review of *The Broom of the System,* p. N13; November 5, 1989, p. 31; February 13, 1996, Michiko Kakutani, review of *Infinite Jest,* p. B2; February 4, 1997, Michiko Kakutani, review of *A Supposedly Funny Thing I'll Never Do Again,* p. B7; March 16, 1997, Laura Miller, "The Road to Babbitville," p. 71; June 1, 1999, Michiko Kakutani, "Calling Them Misogynists Would Be Too Kind," p. B8; April 22, 2000, Michiko Kakutani, "New Wave of Writers Reinvents Literature," p. A15.

New York Times Book Review, March 1, 1987, Caryn James, review of *The Broom of the System,* p. 22; November 5, 1989, Jennifer Levin, review of *Girl with Curious Hair,* p. 31; March 3, 1996, Jay McInerney, "The Year of the Whopper," p. 8.; March 16, 1997, p. 11; June 20, 1999, Adam Goodheart, "Phrase Your Answer in the Form of a Question," p. 8.

New York Times Magazine, March 24, 1996, Frank Bruni, "The Grunge American Novel," pp. 476-479.

Observer (London, England), January 23, 2000, Robert Potts, review of *Brief Interviews with Hideous Men,* p. 12.

Publishers Weekly, December 12, 1986, pp. 48-49; July 7, 1989, p. 47; July 6, 1990, p. 63; November 27, 1995, p. 50; December 30, 1997, p. 47; March 29, 1999, review of *Brief Interviews with Hideous Men,* p. 87; May 3, 1999, Lorin Stein, "David Foster Wallace: In the Company of Creeps," p. 52; September 18, 2000, review of *Up, Simba!,* p. 44.

Review of Contemporary Fiction, summer, 1989, pp. 258-259; spring, 1991, pp. 340-341; summer, 1993, Larry McCaffery, "An Interview with David Foster Wallace, pp. 127-150; spring, 1996, Steven Moore, review of *Infinite Jest,* pp. 141-142; fall, 1999, Robert McLaughlin, review of *Brief Interviews with Hideous Men,* p. 158.

Time, February 19, 1996, R. Z. Sheppard, "Mad Maximalism," pp. 70, 72; May 31, 1999, R. Z.

Sheppard, "Sex, Lies, and Semiotics," p. 97; October 30, 2000, John Dickerson, review of *Up, Simba!*, p. 94.

Times Literary Supplement, June 28, 1996, p. 22; December 26, 1997, p. 22; January 14, 2000, pp. 25-26.

Tribune Books (Chicago, IL), January 21, 1990, Douglas Seibold, "Maximalist Short Fiction from a Talented Young Writer," p. 7; March 9, 1997, Richard Stern, "Verbal Pyrotechnics," pp. 1, 11.

Washington Post Book World, January 11, 1987, Rudy Rucker, review of *The Broom of the System;* August 6, 1989; March 24, 1996. Paul West, "Reams of Acute Modernity," p. X5.

OTHER

Oregon Voice Online, http://www.uoregon.edu/ ˜ovoice/ (October 26, 2002), Chris O'Connor and Rob Elder, "Talking with David Foster Wallace."

Salon.com, http://www.salon.com/ (October 26, 2002), Laura Miller, "The Salon Interview: David Foster Wallace."*

Joss Whedon

■ Personal

Born June 23, 1964, in New York, NY; son of Tom Whedon (a television screenwriter and producer) and Lee Stearns (a high school teacher); married Kai Cole (a designer). *Nationality:* American. *Education:* Wesleyan University, degree in film studies, 1987.

■ Addresses

Agent—United Talent Agency, 9560 Wilshire Blvd., Beverly Hills, CA 90212.

■ Career

Screenwriter, producer, director, and show creator. Television work: Co-producer, *Parenthood,* NBC, 1990; creator, executive producer, and director, *Buffy the Vampire Slayer* (television series), The WB, 1997-2001, UPN, 2002; creator and director, *Angel,* The WB, 1999, and acted role of "Numfar" in episode, 2001; creator, director, and executive producer, *Firefly,* Fox, 2002.

■ Awards, Honors

Academy Award nomination (with Joel Cohen, Peter Docter, John Lasseter, Joe Ranft, Alec Sokolow, and Andrew Stanton) for best writing (screenplay written directly for the screen), and Annie Award (with Andrew Stanton, Joel Cohen, and Alec Sokolow) for best individual achievement—writing, both 1996, both for *Toy Story;* Annie Award nomination (with Scott Warrender) for outstanding individual achievement for music in an animated feature production, 1999, for the song "My Lullaby," *The Lion King II: Simba's Pride;* Bram Stoker Award nomination for best screenplay, and Emmy Award nomination for outstanding writing for a drama series, both 2000, both for episode "Hush," *Buffy the Vampire Slayer;* Emmy Award nomination for outstanding writing for a drama series, Hugo Award nomination, and Nebula Award nomination, all 2002, all for episode "Once More with Feeling," *Buffy the Vampire Slayer;* Best Show of All Time designation, SFX Millennium Awards, 2002, for *Buffy the Vampire Slayer.*

■ Writings

SCREENPLAYS

Buffy the Vampire Slayer, Twentieth Century-Fox, 1992.

(Uncredited) *Speed,* Twentieth Century-Fox, 1994.

(Uncredited) *Waterworld*, Universal, 1995.
Toy Story, Buena Vista, 1995.
(Uncredited) *Twister*, Universal, 1996.
Alien: Resurrection (also known as *Alien 4*), Twentieth Century-Fox, 1997.
Titan A.E., 2000.

TELEVISION SERIES

(And story editor) *Roseanne*, ABC, 1989-90.
Parenthood, NBC, 1990.
Buffy the Vampire Slayer, The WB, 1997-1998.
(Cowriter of several episodes) *Angel*, The WB, 1999.
Firefly, Fox, 2002.

Also creator and writer for various comic books for Dark Horse Comics, including "Buffy the Vampire Slayer," "Angel," and "Fray," as well as the graphic novel *Tales of the Slayer*, 2002.

▪ Sidelights

"The idea was, let's have a feminist role model for kids," said Joss Whedon, creator and writer of the popular television ghoul series, *Buffy the Vampire Slayer*. "What's interesting is you end up subverting that," Whedon continued in an interview with *Entertainment Weekly*. "If she's just an ironclad hero—'I am woman, hear me constantly roar'—it gets dull. Finding the weakness and the vanity and the foibles makes it fun. . . . From the beginning, I was interested in showing a woman who was [take-charge] and men who not only didn't have a problem with that but were kind of attracted to it." Subverting the model is what Whedon's "Buffy" saga is all about. Far from being the terrified female victim found in most horror flicks and terror tales, Buffy most definitely wears boots and knows how to use them, dispatching all manner of critters fair and foul who crop up from the hole leading directly to hell upon which her otherwise peaceful California town is built. "Buffy slays more than just vampires," noted T. L. Stanley in *Mediaweek*. "As the 'chosen one,' she combats everything from giant bugs and witches to her own personal demon—cheerleading." High-schooler Buffy is at the center of most episodes of this "action-thriller laced with comedy. . . . [an] amalgam of teen angst and horned monsters," as Stanley described the series.

The strange brew of Whedon's television series caught on with the public in a way that Buffy's 1992 film incarnation never had, stretching what the writer/creator thought might be a one-season pro-

Sarah Michelle Gellar stars as "Buffy" Ann Summers in Josh Whedon's blockbuster television creation *Buffy the Vampire Slayer*, which premiered on the Fox network in 1997.

gram into six seasons and beyond, and spawning the spin-off *Angel* series, based on a character who first appeared on *Buffy*. Whedon permanently switched Hollywood teams, crossing over from high-paid screenwriter and script doctor to what had been thought of as the lowlier, less creative world of television. However, he and a new generation of writers have been changing that medium into a proving ground not only for hard-hitting dramas a la *The Sopranos*, but also for off-the-wall concepts such as *Buffy the Vampire Slayer*.

His two successful series propelled Whedon into a celebrity wunderkind in Hollywood, an "acclaimed cult-pop demigod," according to Jeff Jensen in *Entertainment Weekly*, allowing him to flex his creative talents with a further series, the science fiction *Firefly*, a "*Stagecoach*-meets-*Star Wars* concept," as Jensen noted. In the usually tight-fisted world of television budgets, Whedon was given almost $9 million to play with for a two-hour pilot for the series, which premiered in 2002—not bad for a writer who never had the slightest intention of working in television.

Writing in the Blood

Whedon was born on June 23, 1964, the son of Tom Whedon, a screenwriter and producer in Hollywood who wrote for *The Dick Cavett Show, Alice, Benson,* and *The Golden Girls*. His grandfather, John Whedon, was also a successful sitcom writer in the 1950s and 1960s on shows such as *Leave It to Beaver* and *The Donna Reed Show*. Despite inheriting the writing gene, Whedon has maintained that the strongest influence came from his mother, a high school teacher who loved to write novels—none of them published—during her summer break.

Born Joseph, Whedon later changed his name to Joss, Chinese for luck. Whedon's parents divorced when he was nine and he moved from New York to live with his father and stepbrothers in Hollywood, spending summers in Manhattan and at an upstate New York artists' commune with his mother and two brothers. Whedon's interest in horror stories and superheroes developed early, as he told Robert Francis for the *BBC* online: "It was deeper, more consuming than [with] other children. While they were outside playing, I was indoors, fascinated by a large stack of comics."

Whedon attended the Riverdale School in New York as a high school freshman, but finished his secondary education in England, attending Winchester, a private boy's school. "I think it's not inaccurate to say that I had a perfectly happy childhood during which I was very unhappy," Whedon noted in an interview with Tasha Robinson for *The Onion A.V. Club*. "It was nothing worse than anybody else. I could not get a date to save my life." "For me, high school was a horror movie," Whedon further commented to A. J. Jacobs in an *Entertainment Weekly* interview. "Girls wouldn't so much as poke me with a stick." Things were somewhat better when he transferred to the all-boy's school in England, though he still felt on the fringes. "I was not popular in school," he reported to Robinson. "And I had a very painful adolescence because it was all very strange to me. It wasn't like I got beat up, but the humiliation and isolation, and the existential 'God, I exist, and nobody cares' of being a teenager were extremely pronounced for me. . . . Nobody gets out of here without some trauma."

Back in the United States, Whedon attended Wesleyan University, majoring in film studies. "I studied film as an undergraduate," Whedon told Shawna

Ervin-Gore in a 2002 interview for *Dark Horse Comics,* "but I didn't study writing, actually. We never studied writing, we just studied film. And the two are incredibly connected, of course. . . . But I had great film teachers, and they helped me understand more than just filmmaking." Graduating from Wesleyan in 1987, Whedon thought he might want to work in film, snubbing his nose at the world of television which was his father's and grandfather's. Then he discovered how much writers for television make, and he started churning out scripts that were promptly rejected. In 1989 he got a writing job with the *Roseanne* show, a "baptism by radioactive waste," as Whedon described it to Jacobs. From there he went to *Parenthood* for a season as a producer, but he was already working on the movie screenplay that would change his life.

From Silver Screen to TV Screen

By the late 1980s Whedon had hit on an idea for a film he could not let go of. "It came from watching horror movies with a funny, gregarious, somewhat dim blonde who invariably gets killed, and I always felt bad for her," Whedon explained to Ervin-Gore. "So I thought it would be funny to have that girl go into a dark alley where we knew she would get killed and actually have her trash the monster. From that came the idea for *Buffy*." In Whedon's twist on the usual vampire movie, a pert Valley Girl becomes the "chosen one" of her generation to kill roaming vampires. The film, starring Kristy Swanson as Buffy, Donald Sutherland, Paul Reubens, Rutger Hauer, and Luke Perry, was directed by Fran Rubel Kuzui. Sutherland plays the coach to vampire killers, who must train young Buffy in this case to do in Hauer as the vampire, Uno. Whedon bid television adieu once the film was in production, but his subsequent experience with movies was not what he thought it would be.

Whedon was involved in a major way with his debut film, but as he told Robinson, "I pretty much eventually threw up my hands because I could not be around Donald Sutherland any longer. It didn't turn out to be the movie that I had written. They never do, but that was my first lesson in that." According to Whedon, Sutherland changed his lines at will, not only altering the dialogue but also throwing off the action so that much of the film made no sense. By the time *Buffy the Vampire Slayer* got to the theaters, "Whedon's vision had been warped," according to Jacobs. Kuzui, wrote Jacobs, "hiked the camp factor and downplayed the terror." The result was general critical disdain and poor box office receipts. Ralph Novak, writing in *People,* felt that rather than a spoof, *Buffy* was actually a "straight-

Illustrator Tim Sale brings to life the stories of Whedon and a stable of other script writers in *Tales of the Slayers*, a 2001 graphic novel based on the television program *Buffy the Vampire Slayer*.

forward vampire movie, with lots of neck biting, blood gushing and stakes through the heart." Moreover, Novak also complained of the director's "routine bits of vampirophilia" and "unimaginative reworkings of the myth." Leonard Maltin had kinder words in his *Movie & Video Guide*, in which he dubbed the film a "cute variation on vampire sagas." Kenneth Turan, reviewing the movie in the *Los Angeles Times*, also found things to like in the movie, lauding Whedon both for his "clever job of genre-splicing," and also for providing "amusing Valley-speak dialogue for Buffy and her chums, not to mention some inspired cameos."

Despite this box office failure, Whedon progressed into a lucrative career as a script doctor and screenwriter. He worked on *Speed*, *Waterworld*, and *Twister* as an uncredited writer. "I think of *Speed* as one of the few movies I've made that I actually like," Whedon told Robinson. About his work on Kevin Costner's *Waterworld*, Whedon described himself to Robinson as "the world's highest-paid stenographer." He was brought in supposedly to help out with re-writes for about a week, but that stretched into seven, the result of which was only a few lines that made it into the movie. "I was there basically taking notes from Costner, who was very nice, fine to work with, but he was not a writer," Whedon remarked to Robinson.

More successful was his script for *Toy Story*, which won a joint Academy Award nomination. Lizzie

Francke, writing in *New Statesman,* called that movie "an incredibly knowing piece which, while working as a rollicking adventure for children, has a polished, witty script . . . that points to whom its core audience might just as likely be." Kenneth Turan of the *Los Angeles Times* also had praise for *Toy Story,* which "turns out to be smart fun on a verbal as well as visual level," supplying "enough on-screen pratfalls and visual dazzle to keep the kids occupied while luring the adults with feisty characterizations and wise-up jokes." Whedon was also elected to write the fourth installment of the "Alien" movies, *Alien Resurrection,* a 1997 production. "Whedon's script injects some of the tough, testosterone humor of 'Aliens' into a story that tries to build on the cross-species sub text of 'Alien 3,'" wrote Derek Elley in a *Variety* review of the film. *Time* reviewer Richard Schickel likewise praised Whedon's screenwriting, and called the movie "hip without being campy or condescending." Lisa Schwarzbaum, reviewing the film in *Entertainment Weekly,* found that Whedon's script tweaks the story "cleverly," and is as "late-90s wiseacreish as *Alien 3* was early-'90s portentous."

By this time, *Buffy the Vampire Slayer* had made its way to video and had established a cult following. A producer from that movie contacted Whedon about making the story into a television series, and Whedon, who had never been satisfied with what had been done to his original script, considered it. His agent thought he was crazy, for by this time Whedon was earning $100,000 per week as a film writer, but he had begun to look at his film career as "an abysmal failure," as he told Jacobs, and saw this offer as a new opportunity. Compared to the glacial speed at which movies are produced, television would offer him the opportunity to make an independent movie every week. So, he signed on as creator, writer, and producer of the television series, *Buffy the Vampire Slayer.*

The Cult of *Buffy*

Taken on by the fledgling WB network, Whedon gathered a talented group of writers and actors, including Emmy Award-winner Sarah Michelle Gellar as the eponymous heroine. The premise of the series is similar to that of the movie: in each generation someone must be chosen to battle the dark forces. Sixteen-year-old Buffy has been chosen. Up to then, her biggest kicks were shopping and cheerleading, but with the help of a Watcher, she soon is battling all the gory monsters leaking through the hole to hell over which her town—and more specifically her high school—is built. The WB network encouraged, even begged Whedon not to use the

title *Buffy the Vampire Slayer* as the series title, but he held fast, determined that if people did not get the sophomoric, retro humor of the title, they probably would not like the show, either.

From the outset Whedon saw *Buffy* as more than one more comedy-action-horror program. "I designed the show to create [a] strong reaction," Whedon told Robinson. "I designed Buffy to be an icon, to be an emotional experience, to be loved in a way that other shows can't be loved." To that end, he mined the adolescent experience in the series episodes, from first kiss to first sex. "I wanted [Buffy] to be a cultural phenomenon. . . . Barbie with kung-fu grip," he told Ervin-Gore. Still the network gurus worried about the title. But *Buffy* was an instant success, attracting over four million viewers for each of its first two episodes in 1997. The show did not last just its initial season, as Whedon predicted, but has gone on to be standard—if weird—program fare, "one of the most intelligent, and most underestimated shows on television," according to Emily Nussbaum writing in the *New York Times Magazine.* Nussbaum further noted that *Buffy* at first looked to be a "disposable toy" of various adolescent ingredients: "teen banter, karate chops, and bloodsucking monsters." However the show is, for Nussbaum, not just about a teenage girl impaling monsters with stakes; Buffy's "true demons are personal, and the show's innovative mix of fantasy elements and psychological acuity transcends easy categorization," making it the "critics' darling" and a show that "inspired a fervent fan base among teenage girls and academics alike."

Whedon commented to Lisa de Moraes in the *Washington Post* during the first season of *Buffy* that shows such as his and *Charmed* and *Sabrina, the Teenage Witch,* all of which aired the same year, were right for "the desperate spiritual searching that is taking place" with today's young people. His Vampire Slayer is simply an extreme form of the witch, empowered and connected to nature. De Moraes went on to note that of all the witch-like female protagonists on television, Buffy "is the baddest of them all, routinely cracking skulls, driving stakes into hearts and otherwise making mincemeat out of all the undead who plague her little home town of Sunnydale, Calif., which has the misfortune to sit atop a porthole where all the demons of the netherworld converge. Bummer."

"Okay, so it sounds silly," Alan Sepinwall wrote of the show's premise in a review of the series for Newark, New Jersey's *Star-Ledger,* "but 'Buffy' realizes this, and has a wry wit to go with all the ghoulies and ghosties. Whedon tries to blend comedy, horror and action, a very combustible mixture . . .

but he seems close to perfecting the formula here." In the opening season, the school librarian, Giles, plays Buffy's Watcher, while other characters include the shy Willow, sidekick Xander, the social butterfly Cordelia, and Angel. Buffy, who has recently moved to Sunnydale with her divorced mother, refuses to take Cordelia's advice to avoid the outsiders and losers such as Willow and Xander, which consigns her also to loser status. Immediately, however, she is recognized as a Slayer by Giles, who thereafter prepares her for her new superhero role. Meanwhile, Xander falls for her, which does not much please Willow, who has yearnings for young Xan; nor does it please Buffy, who has a twitch in the stomach for the darkly handsome Angel—who turns out to be a friendly vampire.

Throughout the first six seasons of the series, its reputation has continued to grow along with that of its creator and sometimes writer, Whedon. Three years were spent at the high school, exploring these relationships, but also such iconoclastic stuff as Masai stories of possession in the episode "The Pack," or dangers of Internet predators found in the episode "I Robot, You Jane." In the second season, things got a bit darker and also a bit murkier sexually with a "shift from adolescent to adulthood focuses on sexuality," according to Rhonda V. Wilcox writing in the *Journal of Popular Film & Television*. Indeed, Angel and Buffy go to bed together, a mirror of a teenager's first sexual encounter. For Wilcox, the symbolism of *Buffy* lies in the vampires representing adulthood. "Buffy," Wilcox explains, "confronts the vampires of adulthood not only with weapons, but with words of her own." Later seasons take the *Buffy* cast off to college, and introduce new characters, such as the blond-haired and sexy Spike.

Whedon and his cast have taken chances with *Buffy,* as well. There is the nearly silent episode, "Hush"; in "The Body" he deals in graphic realism to por-

Whedon authored the screenplay for *Alien: Resurrection* a 1997 film starring Brad Dourif and Sigourney Weaver and directed by Jean-Pierre Jeunet.

The screenplay of Don Bluth's animated 2000 space adventure *Titan A. E.* benefitted from the contributions of Whedon.

tray the death of Buffy's mother; Buffy herself is dispatched at the end of the fifth season, only to be meticulously resurrected for the sixth in the episode, "Bargaining." Homosexual themes have also been broached, most particularly in the character of Willow. "Over time the show's mythology has become as rich and multilayered as any work of literature," commented Nussbaum. And for Steven Vineberg, writing in the *New York Times, Buffy* "has yet to be taken seriously—to be removed from the status of cult entertainment." Vineberg felt this oversight was unfortunate, for "the show is a knockout. . . . It demonstrates what television can accomplish." Vineberg allowed that the show "has had its rocky patches," but also commented that Whedon "keeps his faith with his subjects as they approach adulthood: he honors the drama of their turbulent lives." Whedon is double fortunate: showered with critical and fan praise, he is also able to make his earnings from film writing look paltry by comparison. In 2001 Whedon signed a $20 million, four-year contract with 20th Century Fox Television for exclusive program development.

Busting TV Genres

In 1999 Whedon put a second series on the air, featuring Angel, one of the characters from *Buffy*. Aptly named *Angel,* the series moves the action to Los Angeles where Angel, played by David Boreanaz, will help those tormented by evil, aided in such endeavors by comic sidekick, Doyle, "an undead dude who serves as Angel's spiritual mentor at a low-rent detective agency," according to Dan Snierson in *Entertainment Weekly.* Cordelia also leaves suburbia to make her way in Hollywood on this series. The intention of the show is to deal with more adult themes than in *Buffy.* Reviewing that series in *Variety,* Laura Fries noted that Whedon and his other writers "have created a scenario that gives Angel's character lots of emotional and dramatic room to navigate, while still pining over his lost love [Buffy]." Ken Tucker, writing in *Entertainment Weekly* commented that in "spinning this handsome sad sack off into his own series, *Angel,* Whedon and co-creator David Greenwalt have reimagined him." According to Tucker, "these guys are serious pop artists working from their hearts and minds in the frivolous horror genre," and the results of their efforts are "riskier, more audacious" than most of what is aired on television. Tucker also noted the ups and downs of such a series: "Some weeks, the series works beautifully, moving along like the otherworldly detective show it's meant to be." Yet at other times, the show "can tip too far into jokiness."

Whedon premiered a third series in 2002, *Firefly,* a show that is "part cowboy shoot-em-up, part space opera, with a sneaky existential streak," according to Nussbaum. Starring Nathan Fillion as Mal Reynolds, captain of the starship *Serenity,* the show got off to a rocky start when its $8.7 million pilot was scrapped by executives for delivering too little action and drama and too much back story and characterization. Instead, Whedon premiered the series with "a sort of 'Great Train Robbery in space' episode," according to Jensen in *Entertainment Weekly.* Set five hundred years in the future, the show takes place much of the time on the *Serenity,* which was constructed life-size over two soundstages. Mal and his second in command, Zoe, are on the outs as rebels for some planets which wanted independence from the Alliance, basically the last of the old Earth powers, the United States and China. They now "eke out a dangerous, Han Solo-like living, running a transport business with a truly motley crew," as Jensen noted. And though—as with all modern science fiction—there are special effects, they are not the focus of the show. "I love science fiction, and making it tangible is very exciting for me, but the effects are never the point," Whedon told Sheigh Crabtree in a *Hollywood Reporter* article on *Firefly.*

The show is a risky venture for Whedon, for as Jensen noted, "*Firefly* represents a rep-making test": whether he can make it in other genres or if he should stick to his "little vampire empire." Early reviews of the new series were mixed. Caryn James, writing in the *New York Times* felt that the "wrenching together of genres [western and science fiction] is tortured." James found the season opener a "crazy quilt of 'Star Wars,' 'Mad Max,' and 'Stagecoach', just to mention the most obvious films it calls to mind." James also felt that the plot of the first episode—in which Mal and Zoe agree to rob boxes from the Alliance—to be "earnest and silly" and that it "lacks tension." Taking a much different view of *Firefly,* Tucker noted in *Entertainment Weekly* that Whedon has the power to "entrance us with elaborate narratives in which small, precise details add up to a coherent philosophy—a world view." For Tucker, the message of *Firefly,* as of *Buffy,* is self-reliance, and he called the new show Whedon's "daring attempt to go where men have gone before all too often: to the frontier." Though such a genre-splice of sci fi and Western is nothing new, Tucker further felt that *Firefly* "benefits enormously" from its creator's innate ability to give cliches a "good, hard yank." Tucker further praised the show as a "brawling saga" with a dash of "moral relativism" and "funny dialogue."

Not content to rest on the laurels of three series running simultaneously, Whedon has also branched out into comics, writing some of the spin-off volumes of *Buffy the Vampire Slayer* for Dark Horse Comics, as well as creating his own eight-episode comic, *Fray.* This story features another Slayer, a la

Buffy, who lives a couple hundred years in the future when people zip about the airways of Manhattan in flying cars and vampires are a forgotten—but not nonexistent—species. His protagonist is another strong female, Melaka Fray, who initially has no idea she is a Slayer, let alone that the weird ones called the Lurkers in her world are actually bloodsuckers. She's a professional thief before she turns fang slayer. "I always wanted to write comics," Whedon admitted to Ervin-Gore, and the budgetary constraints of television forced the conception he had for *Fray* into the world of comics. "There's no other way on God's green earth I could afford to do it any other way," he told Roger Ash in *Worlds of Westfield.* "There's a bunch of flying cars in it." Not to mention the whole of a rather desiccated Manhattan, which the future people call Haddyn. "I love comics," Whedon went on to tell Ash. "I've read them my whole life. I've always wanted to write one. I thought about this story and thought, 'instead of creating a whole new world, I can just do this and maybe it'll be self contained and it can be a little journey into comics.' I had hoped to do a couple issues of something, then it ballooned into an 8-part story because I can never shut up."

Nor do his fans want him to. Speaking up and speaking out in his own voice is what has won Whedon his fan base and critical acclaim. And for Whedon creating and writing is his life. "That's the only reason I'm alive!" he told Nussbaum. In whatever form he does it, Whedon feels he is "paying homage to the same thing: the storytelling." And for Whedon, fantasy in its many forms is the vehicle for such fiction. "I do have a fascination with fantasy," he told Ervin-Gore, "a fascination where I love being in other worlds and creating them. I think these elements have always spoken to me in everything I do." Asked by Nussbaum if he had ever considered creating a more traditional television drama, he replied, "I'm no adult!. . . . I don't want to create responsible shows with lawyers in them. I want to invade people's dreams."

■ Biographical and Critical Sources

BOOKS

Golden, Christopher, and Nancy Holder, *Buffy the Vampire Slayer: The Watcher's Guide,* Simon & Schuster (New York, NY), 1998.

Kaveny, Roze, editor, *Reading the Vampire Slayer: An Unofficial Critical Companion to Buffy and Angel,* Tauris Parke, 2002.

Maltin, Leonard, *Movie & Video Guide,* Signet (New York, NY), 1995, p. 175.

Wilcox, Rhonda V., and David Lavery, *Fighting the Forces: What's at Stake in Buffy the Vampire Slayer?,* Rowman & Littlefield (New York, NY), 2002.

PERIODICALS

Entertainment Weekly, April 25, 1997, A. J. Jacobs, "Interview with a Vampire Chronicler," pp. 23-24; December 5, 1997, Lisa Schwarzbaum, review of *Alien Resurrection* pp. 47-49; May 21, 1999, Dan Snierson, "City of Angel," p. 40; October 1, 1999, "The Boo! Crew," p. 44; December 3, 1999, Ken Tucker, "'Angel' Baby," p. 79; June 14, 2002, Jeff Jensen, "Let 'Em Eat Stake," p. 75; June 21, 2002, Lynette Rice, "On the Air," p. 64; September 13, 2002, Jeff Jensen, "Galaxy Quest," p. 96; October 4, 2002, Ken Tucker, "Flights of Fantasy," p. 135.

Hollywood Reporter, April 1, 2002, Sheigh Crabtree, "Radium Lights Fox's 'Firefly' VFX," pp. 3-4.

Journal of Popular Film and Television, summer, 1999, Rhonda V. Wilcox, "There Will Never Be a 'Very Special' Buffy," pp. 16-23.

Los Angeles Times, July 31, 1992, Kenneth Turan, "'Buffy's' Gnarly Date with Destiny," p. 1; November 22, 1995, Kenneth Turan, "The Secret Life of Toys," 1; August 10, 2002, Richard Harrington, "Will Spike Emerge from the Shadows?," p. F18.

Mediaweek, February 17, 1997, T. L. Stanley, "'Buffy' to Slay Small Screen," pp. 9-10.

Ms., August-September, 1999, Heather Olsen, "He Gives Us the Creeps," pp. 79-80.

New Statesman, March 29, 1996, Lizzie Francke, review of *Toy Story,* p. 28.

New York, December 1, 1997, David Denby, review of *Alien Resurrection,* p. 121.

New York Post, May 31, 2001, "New Buffy Spin-Off," p. 74; December 20, 2001, "'Buffy' Creator Blasts Off," p. 83; June 21, 2002, "Buff's Not Too Cool for School," p. 122.

New York Times, March 31, 1997, p. C11; October 1, 2000, Steve Vineberg, "Yes She's a Vampire Slayer. No, Her Show Isn't Kid Stuff," p. AR42; May 28, 2001, Jim Rutenberg, "Hold the Tears in Vampire Slayer's Death," p. C7; September 23, 2001, Joyce Millman, "Lessons in Being Human," p. AR21; September 20, 2002, Caryn James, "Fantasy of Future and Here and Now," p. E26.

New York Times Magazine, September 22, 2002, Emily Nussbaum, "Must-See Metaphysics," p. 56.

People, August 17, 1992, Ralph Novak, review of *Buffy the Vampire Slayer* (movie), p. 13.

Rain Taxi, summer, 2002, Steven Moore, "Layers of Slayage: Buffy as Text," pp. 24-25.

Rolling Stone, September 3, 1992, Peter Travers, review of *Buffy the Vampire Slayer* (movie), p. 75; December 11, 1997, Peter Travers, review of *Alien Resurrection,* pp. 83-84.

Star-Ledger (Newark, NJ), March 19, 1997, Alan Sepinwall, "She Slays 'Em—'Buffy' Is Boffo," p. 31.

Time, December 1, 1997, Richard Schickel, review of *Alien Resurrection,* p. 84; September 23, 2002, James Poniewozick, review of *Firefly,* p. 78.

US Weekly, November 12, 2001, Tom Conroy, review of *Buffy the Vampire Slayer* (television series), p. 59.

Variety, August 3, 1992, Todd McCarthy, review of *Buffy the Vampire Slayer* (movie), p. 40; November 18, 1997, Derek Elley, review of *Alien Resurrection,* pp. 63-64; October 4, 1999, Laura Fries, review of *Angel,* p. 52.

Washington Post, December 15, 1998, Lisa de Moraes, "Spellbound: Witches Charm Young Viewers," p. C1.

OTHER

BBC, http://www.bbc.co.uk/cult/buffy/ (September 26, 2002), Robert Francis, "*Buffy The Vampire Slayer*—Joss Whedon, Producer."

Dark Horse Comics, http://www.darkhorse.com/ (July 1, 1998), Shawna Ervin-Gore, "Interview with Joss Whedon"; (September, 2002) Shawna Ervin-Gore, "Interview with Josh Whedon."

E! Online, http://www.eonline.com/ (September 26, 2002), "Joss Whedon on Sex, Death, Gaping Holes and Horrible Things Ahead."

Entertainment Tonight Online, http://www.etonline.com/ (March 31, 2000), Vanillasky, "Joss Whedon Answers."

Joss Whedon.net (unofficial Web site), http://www.josswhedon.net/ (September 26, 2002).

The Onion A.V. Club, http://www.theonionavclub. com/ (September 5, 2001), Tasha Robinson, "Joss Whedon."

Science-Fiction Weekly, http://www.scifi.com/ (September 26, 2002), Patrick Lee, "Joss Whedon Gets Big, Bad and Grown-up with *Angel*."

Worlds of Westfield, http://westfieldcomics.com/ (September 26, 2002), Roger Ash, "Joss Whedon Interview."*

—Sketch by J. Sydney Jones

Banana Yoshimoto

■ Personal

Born July 24, 1964, in Tokyo, Japan; daughter of Takaaki "Ryumei" (a literary critic) and Kazuko Yoshimoto; married. *Education:* Nihon University, earned degree, 1987. *Avocational interests:* "To take a walk with my two dogs."

■ Addresses

Agent—Japan Foreign-Rights Centre, 27-18-804, Naka Ochiai 2-chome, Shinjuku-ku, Tokyo 161, Japan.

■ Career

Writer. Former waitress in Tokyo, Japan.

■ Member

Japan Writers' Association.

■ Awards, Honors

Izumi Kyoka Prize, Nihon University, 1986, for "Moonlight Shadow"; New Writers Prize, *Kaien* magazine, 1987, and Izumi Kyoka Literary Prize, Kanazawa City Council, 1988, both for *Kitchen;* Geijutsu Sensho, Japan Ministry of Education, 1988, for *Kitchen* and *Utakata/Sanctuary;* Shugoro Yamamoto Award, Shinchosha Publishing Company, 1989, for *Tugumi;* Scanno prize, 1993, for *NP;* Murasakishikibu prize for *Amurita;* Fendissime prize, 1996; Maschera d'argento prize, 1999; Bunkamura Duet Magot prize, 2000.

■ Writings

Kitchin (contains title novella and short story "Moonlight Shadow"), Fukutake (Tokyo, Japan), 1988, translation by Megan Backus published as *Kitchen,* Grove (New York, NY), 1993.

Shirakawa yofune, Fukutake (Tokyo, Japan), 1989.

Tsugumi/Yoshimoto Banana = Tugumi (novel), Chuo Koronsha (Tokyo, Japan), 1989.

Fruits Basket: taidanshu (literary criticism), Fukutake (Tokyo, Japan), 1990.

N. P. (novel), Kadokawa (Tokyo, Japan), 1990, translated by Ann Sherif, Grove (New York, NY), 1994.

Tokage (short stories), Shinchosa, 1993, translation by Ann Sherif published as *Lizard,* Grove (New York, NY), 1995.

Amurita (novel), Fukutake (Tokyo, Japan), 1994, translation by Russell F. Wasden published as *Amrita,* Grove (New York, NY), 1997.

Shirakawa Yofune (novellas), Kadokawa (Tokyo, Japan), 1989, translation by Michael Emmerich published as *Asleep,* Grove (New York, NY), 2000.

Goodbye Tsugumi, Grove (New York, NY), 2002.

Author of novels *Kanashii, Yokan, Honeymoon,* and *SLY;* also author of *Utakata/Sanctuary, Pineapple Pudding,* and *Song from Banana.*

■ Adaptations

Kitchin has been adapted as a Japanese television feature and as a film produced in Hong Kong, 1997; *Tugumi* was filmed in Japan in 1990.

■ Sidelights

Japanese novelist Banana Yoshimoto "favors short novels that gradually reveal thin, almost translucent layers of her characters' personalities," as a critic for *Publishers Weekly* once explained. The author has become a worldwide phenomenon, with millions of fans falling in love with her novels and waiting eagerly for the next one—a circumstance referred to on the many Web pages dedicated to her as "Banana-mania." Yoshimoto's fans tend to be fanatical in their devotion to her work, exchanging testimonials and gossip about the author on the Internet and anxiously speculating about which novel will be the next one translated into their own language.

Yoshimoto was born Mahoko Yoshimoto in Tokyo in 1964. She chose to publish under the name Banana Yoshimoto, she explained in an interview posted at her Web site, "because I love banana flowers." Her father, Takaaki Yoshimoto, was a famous literary critic, poet, and commentator; his works were extremely influential on Japan's radical youth movement in the 1960s. She majored in arts and literature at Nihon University in Tokyo, graduating in 1987. While there, she won the Izuini Kyoka prize for the novella "Moonlight Shadow," which was later published in *Kitchin.* "Her literary journey began after university, when she worked as a waitress and wrote, sometimes during slow work shifts," Nicole Gaouette recounted in the *Christian Science Monitor.* "Yoshimoto wanted to be a writer from childhood," Gaouette explained, "and is passionate

First published in Japan in 1988, Banana Yoshimoto's short story collection contains the title novella *Kitchen,* which focuses on the developing love relationship of a young Japanese college student.

about writing. 'I felt like it was my destiny,' she says." Yoshimoto explained in an interview posted on her Web site that her sister also played a role in her decision: "My elder sister was so good in drawing. Her creativity inspired me to find something of my own to do. So I started to write when I was about 5 years old."

Publishes *Kitchin*

Yoshimoto took Japan by storm in 1988 with her premier work, *Kitchin,* two short works of fiction about life and death in contemporary Japan. *Kitchin* sold over two million copies in Japan and won several literary awards. Four years later Yoshimoto's audience expanded to the United States when an English translation, *Kitchen,* made its way onto bestseller lists. Yoshimoto believes *Kitchin*'s success is a result of its appeal to a young audience, particularly women in their twenties. "I think that young people would meditate the essence of life at least once. My novel happened to have something to win the sympathy of such young people who are in deep thought about life," Yoshimoto explained to David J. Morrow of the *Detroit Free Press.*

The title novella revolves around the life of a female college student, Mikage, who struggles to cope with the death of the grandmother with whom she has lived for years. Mikage is invited to live with a friend of her grandmother, Yuichi, and Yuichi's father, who has undergone a sex change operation. When Yuichi's father/mother, in turn, is killed, the two college students console each other, a process that leads them toward a more intimate relationship. Like "Kitchen," the accompanying novella, "Moonlight Shadow," deals with the themes of love, death, and the confusion of reality. It portrays two college students, a woman and a man, both of whom lose their loves to death and cope in varying ways.

American reviewers were split over Yoshimoto's accomplishment. "'Kitchen' is light as an invisible pancake, charming and forgettable," wrote reviewer Todd Grimson in the *Los Angeles Times Book Review.* "The release of information to the reader seems unskilled, or immature, weak in narrative or plot." In the *New York Times Book Review,* Elizabeth Hanson criticized the overall effect of the book, writing that "the endearing characters and amusing scenes in Ms. Yoshimoto's work do not compensate for frequent bouts of sentimentality."

Other reviewers were more taken with Yoshimoto's debut novel. *Detroit Free Press* reviewer Georgea Kovanis found more to the book's appeal than the story elements suggest. "It's not the off-beat soap opera plot that makes Banana Yoshimoto's 'Kitchen' . . . so compelling," Kovanis wrote. "Instead, it's Yoshimoto's observation and rich detail. . . . 'Kitchen' is sad and witty and introspective and observant and dreamy. And a wonderful read." *New York Times* reviewer Michiko Kakutani called the book "oddly lyrical" and compared Yoshimoto's prose favorably to that of American authors Jane Smiley and Anne Tyler. Kakutani sounded one reservation in noting that "Yoshimoto occasionally allows her narrator to meditate at length about suffering and death, and these interludes have a way of growing maudlin. . . . Fortunately," Kakutani pointed out, "such passages are relatively rare, and they are offset by Ms. Yoshimoto's wit, her clarity of observation and her firm control of her story. She has a wonderful tactile ability to convey a mood or a sensation through her description of light and sound and touch, as well as an effortless ability to penetrate her characters' hearts."

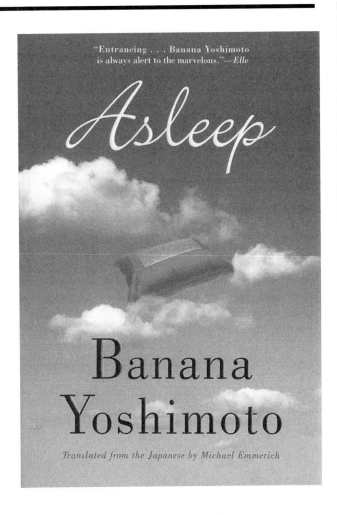

"Entrancing . . . Banana Yoshimoto is always alert to the marvelous."—*Elle*

Asleep

Banana Yoshimoto

Translated from the Japanese by Michael Emmerich

The lives of young women whose lives are overtaken by emotions which muddle the barrier between consciousness and dreamworld are the focus of each of the three stories in Yoshimoto's 1989 collection, translated in 2000.

Albert Howard Carter III, writing in *Novels for Students,* found that Yoshimoto has "an ear for young people's issues, conflicts, and yearnings. She also writes in a jazzy and often surprising style. The two stories work well as different ways of talking about love, both romantic and familial." Speaking of the novella "Kitchen," Carter believed that "The style is breezy, whimsical, lyric, maybe even a bit goofy, but it is an appropriate style for a young person dealing with disruptions of family, culture, and love. The first-person narration is reminiscent of [J. D.] Salinger's *The Catcher in the Rye,* but without the trenchant satire."

Reviewing *Kitchen* in the *New Yorker,* Deborah Garrison had difficulty in categorizing Yoshimoto as a writer: "She can't be called a Japanese counterpart of members of the American literary brat pack. She's not jaded enough—she's too adorably nerdy, and she's way too friendly. She's not a brat. In fact, she makes you wonder if bounce-and-shine is still a standard feature in the artistic youth of other nations; you just don't see too much of it around here. Yoshimoto even includes an afterword to the American edition of Kitchen in which she expresses the hope that the book will be a balm to those who have known setbacks in their lives; there's a generous, therapeutic impulse somewhere inside this fiction writer."

Yoshimoto followed *Kitchen* with the novel *N. P.,* published in the United States in 1994. The book centers around an author, Sarao Takase, who committed suicide after completing a collection of stories, and this fate is also shared by three people who attempt to translate Takase's book. Several years after the last of these suicides, the book's narrator, Kazami Kano, the ex-girlfriend of one of the unfortunate translators, becomes involved with the author's children. Their investigation of the story collection leads to startling discoveries for all involved.

Critics were mixed in their assessment of the novel. A critic for *Publishers Weekly* found the book "offbeat, intriguing, but ultimately unsatisfying." Donna Seaman in *Booklist,* on the other hand, was more positive, arguing that "Yoshimoto's fans won't be disappointed." David Galef in the *New York Times Book Review,* faulted the work for lack of depth and banal prose. Meg Cohen in *Harper's Bazaar,* however, lauded the work's "insightful prose," concluding, "*N. P.,* with its eccentric plot twists and charming superstition, proves not only that Yoshimoto has broken the language barrier but also that there's plenty more where this came from."

Lizard, dedicated by Yoshimoto to the late rock star Kurt Cobain, is a collection of six short stories concerned with young urban Japanese who reach a moment of crucial decision. Dave Edelman, reviewing the collection in the *Baltimore City Paper,* explained that the stories focus on "the inexplicable spiritual bonds that tie lovers together, or the intangible differences that drive them apart." The story "Newlywed" tells of a young man reluctantly returning home on the subway to his new and frightening role as husband. Along the way, he meets a mysterious stranger who shows him that the role he has chosen is a positive one. "The prose is as clean and smooth as a lacquered teacup," Geraldine Sherman claimed in the Toronto *Globe and Mail.* "Newlywed" was first serialized as a series of Tokyo subway posters. The title story "Lizard" tells of the romance between two people in the healing profession, a woman acupuncturist and a doctor who treats disturbed children. "It's a wonderfully sensual portrayal of an intelligent young man's love for a difficult woman," according to Sherman. Speaking of the collection as a whole, Maureen McClarnon, writing in *IO Magazine,* stated that "I'm thrilled to death at what her characters are thinking, and she lets us know, as she brings them to their epiphanies, exactly what road they're taking."

Goodbye Tsugumi
Banana Yoshimoto

TRANSLATED FROM THE JAPANESE BY MICHAEL EMMERICH

Internationally acclaimed through translations such as this 2002 novel, Yoshimoto has gained a huge American following—primarily among young urban women—since her works started appearing in U.S. bookstores in 1993.

Pens *Amrita*

Yoshimoto's *Amrita* is the story of actress Sakumi, who, after the death of her younger sister, falls down some steps and loses her memory. The novel then follows Sakumi on an emotional journey wherein she "tries to replace her lost, pre-fall self, seeking some connection between dream and reality, past and present, the dead and the living," summarized Yoji Yamaguchi in the *New York Times Book Review.*

Critical reception to the work was again mixed. Margot Mifflin in *Womenswire* argued that *Amrita* has "all the guileless zeal and intimate detail of Yoshimoto's earlier books—and none of the concision. . . . With more plot and fewer epiphanies, *Amrita* might have soared; as it is, it reads like a running commentary on a story that never quite happens." Donna Seaman, in *Booklist,* commented, "Yoshimoto 'tells' instead of dramatizes, but even so, she spins a mesmerizing and haunting tale."

Yoshimoto's 2000 work, *Asleep,* is a collection of three novellas, "each telling a somewhat mystical tale of haunted slumber," noted Kathleen Hughes in *Booklist.* The first novella is the story of a woman mourning the death of her lover; the second involves a woman who is in love with a man whose wife is in a coma; the last involves a woman who is haunted by the ghost of a woman with whom she had previously shared a lover. Each "woman sees herself as an incidental or supporting character, in refreshing contrast to Western self-involvement," wrote a critic for *Publishers Weekly.*

"The writing is introspective and, although simple, extremely thought-provoking as Yoshimoto takes her readers on a journey in search of absolution for each of her characters," remarked Shirley N. Quan in *Library Journal.* Other critics were also positive in their reviews of the work. "This collection," concluded Hughes, "is delicately tinged with sadness and lovely to read, and Yoshimoto's fervent American fan base will clamor for it."

The novel *Goodbye Tsugumi* focuses on two teenage cousins who live in a seaside Japanese village. Maria is a quiet girl whose mother is waiting for a divorce to become final so she can marry Maria's father. Tsugumi is a sickly girl whose ill-health seems to free her to be rude and shocking to other people. According to a critic for *Kirkus Reviews,* Tsugumi is "determined to take it out on everyone around her." The two girls live together at the family-owned inn run by Maria's aunt and uncle. As time goes by, Maria goes away to college, Tsugumi falls in love, and the inn must finally be torn down. A *Publishers Weekly* critic found that the story examines "the difficult but affectionate bond between the cousins." Maria ultimately learns that "loss is an inevitable part of growing up," wrote a *Kirkus Reviews* critic, who concluded that *Goodbye Tsugumi* is "lyrical, accessible, enchanting."

Several critics have noted that Yoshimoto's purpose in writing is a helpful one, her aim to bring hope to her readers and make them feel better about their lives. In *Kitchen,* Yoshimoto includes a message to her readers: "Surely we will meet someday," she

If you enjoy the works of Banana Yoshimoto, you might want to check out the following books:

Yasunari Kawabata, *House of the Sleeping Beauties and Other Stories,* 1969.
Kazuo Ishiguro, *An Artist of the Floating World,* 1986.
Haruki Murakami, *Norwegian Wood,* 1987.

states, "and until that day, I pray that you will live happily." She told Gaouette that, with all the troubles in the world, "I hope my writing will help people to forget everything."

■ Biographical and Critical Sources

BOOKS

Contemporary Literary Criticism, Volume 84, Gale (Detroit, MI), 1995.
Furuhashi, Nobuyoshi, *Yoshimoto Banana to Tawara Machi,* Chikuma Shobo (Tokyo, Japan), 1990.
Novels for Students, Volume 7, Gale (Detroit, MI), 1999.
Yoshimoto, Banana, *Banana no banana* (interviews), Metarogu (Tokyo, Japan), 1994.
Yoshimoto, Takaaki, *Yoshimoto Takaaki x Yoshimoto Banana* (interviews), Rokkingu On (Tokyo, Japan), 1997.

PERIODICALS

Baltimore City Paper, June 28, 1994, Dave Edelman, review of *Lizard.*
Booklist, February 1, 1994, Donna Seaman, review of *N. P.,* p. 996; July, 1997, Donna Seaman, review of *Amrita,* p. 1801; April 15, 2000, Kathleen Hughes, review of *Asleep,* p. 1501.
Christian Science Monitor, December 10, 1998, Nicole Gaouette, "Hip Novelist Combines Old and New," p. 13.
Detroit Free Press, April 2, 1993, pp. G1-2.
Economist, February 20, 1993.
Entertainment Weekly, July 25, 1997, A. J. Jacobs, review of *Amrita,* p. 67.
Globe and Mail (Toronto, Canada), March 8, 1995, Geraldine Sherman, "A Reflection of Japan's Cultural Confusion."

Harper's Bazaar, March, 1994, Meg Cohen, review of *N. P.,* p. 170.

Kirkus Reviews, June 1, 2002, review of *Goodbye Tsugumi,* p. 768.

Library Journal, June 15, 1997, Janet Ingraham, review of *Amrita,* p. 100; May 1, 2000, Shirley N. Quan, review of *Asleep,* p. 156.

Los Angeles Times Book Review, January 10, 1993, Todd Grimson, "The Catcher in the Rice," pp. 3, 7.

Nation, August 11, 1997, Diane Simon, review of *Amrita,* p. 30.

New Yorker, January 25, 1993, Deborah Garrison, "Day-O!," pp. 109-110.

New York Times, January 12, 1993.

New York Times Book Review, January 17, 1993, Elizabeth Hanson, "Hold the Tofu," p. 18; February 27, 1994, David Galef, review of *N. P.,* p. 23; August 17, 1997, Yoji Yamaguchi, review of *Amrita.*

Publishers Weekly, December 13, 1993, review of *N. P.,* p. 61; May 8, 2000, review of *Asleep,* p. 206; July 8, 2002, review of *Goodbye Tsugumi,* p. 29.

Time, April 14, 1997, Richard Corliss, "Love and Soup: Banana Yoshimoto's *Kitchen* Hits the Screen."

Times Literary Supplement, January 8, 1993, Nick Hornby, "Mystical Mundane," p. 18.

Washington Post Book World, January 10, 1993, Scott Shibuya Brown, "Adrift in the New Japan," p. 10.

OTHER

Banana Yoshimoto's Official Web site, http://www.yoshimotobanana.com/en (November 8, 2002).

IO Magazine, http://www.altx.com/io/ (November 8, 2002), Maureen McClarnon, review of *Lizard.*

Japan Ink, http://www.earlham.edu/~japanink/ (November 8, 2002), Rebecca D. Larson, "Yoshimoto Banana and Kawabata Yasunari" and Nathan Hopson, "From Mishima's Romanticism to Yoshimoto's Postmodernism."

Women's Wire, http://www.womenswire.com/ (July 2, 2000).*

Author/Artist Index

The following index gives the number of the volume in which an author/artist's biographical sketch appears: